JEWISH ROOTS

DESTINY IMAGE BOOKS BY DANIEL JUSTER

Israel, the Church, and the Last Days

Jewish Roots

Awakening the One New Man

JEWISH ROOTS

UNDERSTANDING YOUR JEWISH FAITH

DANIEL JUSTER

Revised Edition

DESTINY IMAGE® PUBLISHERS, INC.
P.O. Box 310, Shippensburg, PA 17257-0310
"Promoting Inspired Lives."

This book and all other Destiny Image, Revival Press, MercyPlace, Fresh Bread, Destiny Image Fiction, and Treasure House books are available at Christian bookstores and distributors worldwide.

For a U.S. bookstore nearest you, call 1-800-722-6774.
For more information on foreign distributors, call 717-532-3040.
Reach us on the Internet: www.destinyimage.com.

ISBN 13 TP: 978-0-7684-4203-8
ISBN 13 Ebook: 978-0-7684-8744-2

For Worldwide Distribution, Printed in the U.S.A.
3 4 5 6 7 8 / 17 16 15 14

DEDICATION

To the two most special women in my life: First of all, my late mother, Edith Christensen Juster, whose kindness and love toward Jewish people has been a major factor in my life; and to my wife, Patty, whose love and devotion in hard times and good times has been extraordinary; she is a remarkable wife and mother to our children and grandmother to our many grandchildren.

ENDORSEMENTS

Dan Juster's writings have been a blessing to so many of us. His book *Jewish Roots* is a balanced and solid presentation that covers many of the most important themes of biblical theology and its connection to the original Jewish context for understanding the Bible. It is both informative and inspirational. I highly recommend it.

Mike Bickle
International House of Prayer
Kansas City, MO

For over twenty-five years, *Jewish Roots* has been a valuable tool for discipleship and spiritual growth within the Messianic Jewish Movement and an excellent source of information for anyone interested in learning more about Messianic Judaism and the role of Israel and the Jewish people in the plan of God. This welcomed new addition will be a blessing to yet another generation as we face new challenges and engage new ideas.

Rabbi Howard Silverman
President, Union of Messianic Jewish Congregations

As a Gentile believer who longs to provoke the unbelieving Jew to jealousy, resulting in great harvest of souls, and leading to Messiah's return—I urge any and all to carefully digest this work. It is anointed, scholarly, and necessary. Daniel Juster is inspired and called to take us together to discover God's heart—a revelation to answer the high priestly prayer of Yeshua in John 17. Read on!

Bill McCartney
Founder, Promise Keepers

Jewish Roots is a classic, a foundational treatise in understanding Messianic theology.

John Dawson
President Emeritus, Youth with a Mission

It is worth it to gain at least an elementary grasp of this issue and its resolution. Two highly recommended books on the subject are *Jewish Roots* and *Israel, the Church, and the Last Days* by Dan Juster.

Jack Hayford
Senior Pastor, The Church on the Way

Dan Juster is one of the most astute men I know, and his exposition of theology related to the Jewish roots of Christianity is not only scholarly, but powerfully enlightening as well. I would highly recommend any work that Dan puts his pen to.

Jane Hansen Hoyt
President and CEO, Aglow International

A balanced, theological foundation for the Jewish roots of the Judeo-Christian faith is long overdue—but now has arrived! Dan is theologically sound, yet sensitive and balanced in addressing some very divisive issues (i.e., Sabbath, biblical diet, Christmas, Chanukah, Passover, and many others, that affect relationships between the Church and the Messianic Jewish community). This work is a profound contribution to destroying the reestablished dividing wall of hostility between Jewish and Gentile believers in Messiah. A must-read for all believers!

Raleigh Washington, D.D.
President and CEO, Promise Keepers

CONTENTS

PREFACE TO THE FOURTH EDITION

THE FOURTH EDITION OF *JEWISH Roots* is the first complete revision. The second edition reflected a more critical evaluation of Rabbinic Judaism, whereas the first was very positive. This edition will reflect new scholarship and more than fifteen years of further study and reflection. My essential wrestling with Rabbinic Judaism is whether or not it is a type of covenantal nomism as argued by Dr. E.P. Sanders or a works righteousness system as argued by Dr. Michael Brown. I have come to believe that the evaluation by Sanders and people who follow him show that pendulum has swung too far. Grace and law in Rabbinic Judaism in the version of Sanders almost looks like Reformed Christian Theology. God has saved us by His gracious intervention, but to walk in the covenant freely given, we have to maintain obedience expressed through His Law. With Dr. Brown, the pendulum swings the other way and sees the extensive concern with minute legalistic detail and explicit statements that teach righteous justification by works as showing that it is a false system. So to Dr. Brown, Rabbinic Judaism is a false religion, but for another friend of long standing in the Messianic Jewish movement, it is a true but incomplete religion. In the second and third editions of *Jewish Roots*, I leaned toward Dr. Brown. However, the massive scholarship on Judaism has again caused what I believe will be a final reevaluation.

Rabbinic literature reflects in numerous statements and sections, especially in the Hagaddic literature and the Siddur, that show it to be in accord with the E.P. Sanders view of Judaism. Basic Judaism is a salvation by grace where works follow, or is a covenant nomism. On the other hand, the Talmud is full of statements supporting Dr. Brown's view. It all depends on how one gives weight to texts and then sees them as more foundational in interpreting the other texts. I, therefore, conclude that it is impossible to finally and certainly decide the issue. Suffice it to say that the basic understanding of salvation as a gracious and undeserved offer of God and mercy and forgiveness as the key in our understanding of God is pervasive in Rabbinic texts. This was also important in the New Testament period, as Sanders shows. There is also a great amount of material supporting Dr. Brown. The conflict is mitigated somewhat by noting recent New Testament studies that show that covenantal nomism is the theology of the New Testament. In this regard, faith and faithfulness are one in the Hebrew language. Therefore, I need not take a position on the whole of Rabbinic Judaism except to say that the truth from a pre-New Covenant perspective is present in a very significant way, but there is enough as well to hide the truth. Religious Jews themselves show great differences in understanding this and when one asks a religious Jew, one is likely to get a works righteousness answer to the question of personal salvation. Therefore, my response to Rabbinic Judaism is a critical evaluation through the teaching of biblical theology stressing the bright light of the New Covenant revelation. We are called to endorse everything that is good and reject what does not measure up to this standard. In addition, a more positive understanding of Rabbinic Judaism does not imply that Jewish people do not need the Gospel, for the general condition of our people is that they are not responding to God in the way of the theology of Judaism reflected in the writings of E.P. Sanders and those who follow him.

The new edition of *Jewish Roots* is necessitated by the following facts. First, there have been significant gains through the number of scholars that support Messianic Jewish theological positions. While we have not yet gained the majority, we now have much greater support. The new edition of *Jewish Roots* has to take account of the most important books that have been written since the first edition. Some examples of this are the monumental book by R. Kendall Soulen, *The God of Israel and Christian Theology* (which is like a primer of Messianic Jewish theology), Markus Bochmuel's, *Jewish Law in Gentile Churches*, Peter Tomson's, *Paul and the Jewish Law*, and more. In addition, the work of Anglican Bishop N.T. Wright is crucial for Jewish backgrounds for the interpretation of the New Covenant Scriptures, though he sadly is replacement. Douglas Harink's important book, *Paul Among the Post Liberals*, receives the gains from the scholarship of Wright, while correcting his replacement theology. Jewish scholarship has also advanced. Daniel Boyarin's work, especially his *Borderlines*, is very important and adds to the view that a uni-plural understanding of God was common and accepted in the first century. So we must take all of this into account.

Second, the movement has greatly changed. The greatest growth today is in the Russian-speaking Jewish community, where the Gospel is spreading through Russia, Western Europe, and Israel. There is now an Ethiopian Messianic Jewish movement and a movement in Latin American as well. We have seen a plateau in North America, perhaps even a decline. Why? This has to be addressed. The movement needs to be evaluated—its theology, its practice, and its government. There are still assumptions that come from church streams that do not hold up to the light of biblical teaching. Then there are aberrations to be addressed, some who have fallen into the Galatian heresy and call for Gentiles to keep the whole Torah and some who strangely teach that Christians are the lost tribes. It is a wonder that movements from such teachings have gained traction, but this is the world we live in. All of this has to be addressed. So a chapter evaluating the Messianic Jewish movement worldwide and a chapter on aberrations will be added.

Jewish Roots has been in continuous publication for twenty-five years. It was, with Dr. David Stern's very compatible writings, among the first and most influential books setting out the theology of the Messianic Jewish movement. Dr. Mark Kinzer's more recent volume has added what I believe is the most significant study subsequent to our work, and most of it is compatible to my book and Stern's. I will point out some differences. I continue to recommend Stern's *Messianic Jewish New Testament Commentary* as the one most in accordance with what I teach.

It should be noted that a new version of Dr. Stern's New Testament, not replacing the first, will be published in the near future. It will feature copious notes. The revision will eliminate some of the Yiddish anachronisms that tend to be unnatural to some readers. A new revision called *A Messianic Jewish Family Bible,* to be published by Destiny Image, is also soon to be published. The New Covenant part is already published and is quite good. This will also be a very helpful text.

Messianic Judaism[1] and Messianic Jewish biblical theology are not of significance only to those who are part of Messianic Jewish congregations. Indeed because the destiny of Israel and the Church are bound together, Messianic Jewish theology has implications of great importance for all. If the Church consists of those grafted into a Jewish olive tree, the issues discussed here are of no mere parochial concern. There is still a great need for clear biblical thinking on many of the issues discussed in those pages. It is my conviction that the content of *Jewish Roots* is a trustworthy guide. I stand by the central thrust of the book on all major issues: the nature of the covenants, the call of Jewish people in the Messiah, that we are called to maintain a Jewish life, live out the proper relationship between grace and law and much, much more. I believe that the basic application of the Law in the New Covenant order of existence is as outlined in the text and as reflected in the appendix on the 613 laws. The following is an outline of some important new emphases since the first edition.

THE PROPHETIC MEANING OF THE FEASTS

Since the first edition, I have come to a greater appreciation of the eschatological meaning of the biblical feasts of Israel. All of the feasts have great future prophetic references awaiting fulfillment. Hence each feast has historic reference to God's salvation in ancient Israel, to the meaning of fulfillment in Yeshua, who brings out the deepest meaning of the feast, to agricultural significance in celebrating God as the provider, and reference to the last days and the millennial Age to Come. The book adequately covered the first three dimensions of the feasts. I now add my sense of still future prophetic significance.

Passover definitely looks forward to the last great exodus of the people of Israel from all the lands to which they have been scattered. Jeremiah 16 and Jeremiah 23 look forward to a day in which Israel will no longer say, "The Lord who brought us out of the land of Egypt," but The Lord who brought us out of all the countries in which He has scattered us and brought us back into our own land." This great return to the land of Israel is one of the most amazing prophetic happenings in our time. Much more of this re-gathering is yet to come. It is predicted throughout the prophets. This is a fulfillment of the meaning of Passover. There is more yet to come out of the meaning of Passover! I believe that Passover in its millennial context will emphasize this great exodus. Messianic Jews today do well to celebrate Passover with a great deal of reference to these prophetic events. Furthermore, the plagues of the Book of Revelation are parallel to the Exodus plagues and are part of God's working to affect this exodus.

It may also be correct to see references to the gathering of the saints out of all the nations of the earth in the Passover themes. This of course relates to the return of the Messiah Jesus to earth.

It should be noted that the feasts do not provide exclusive meanings, but overlapping themes so that some themes are emphasized more in one feast than another. This will become clear in our discussion of additional feasts.

The Feast of Shavuot, or Pentecost, has reference *not only* to the early harvest in Israel and to the giving of the Law, but also the pouring out of the Spirit upon the first disciples in Jerusalem. This feast also looks forward to a much greater outpouring of the Spirit, both in the last days revival of the people of God, what Joel calls the early and the latter rain together, and also the great outpouring that shall determine the whole character of the Age to Come. In New Testament theology, the Age to Come has broken into this age through Yeshua. Hence we note the fulfillment of Joel 2:28-30, in which the Spirit has been poured out upon all flesh and all can prophecy. So in the Age to Come, the knowledge of the LORD shall cover the earth as the water covers the beds of the seas. The Age to Come is an age of the Spirit. We partake of its realities now and are heralds of the coming age. As we are faithful to the divine mandate, we, as Peter says, hasten the day of his coming. So Messianic believers need to celebrate this feast with a real prophetic cutting edge in the Holy Spirit.

The day of the blowing of the shofar in the fall certainly looks forward to the return of Yeshua the Messiah. The preaching and teaching on this day should be full of last days meanings. If the shofar of First Thessalonians 4:16-17 and First Corinthians 15 is the same as the seventh trumpet in the Book of Revelation, and I believe it is, then our service calls upon our people to be ready for His return, for our translation into glory, for the pouring out of the bowls of God's wrath, and for the establishment of His Kingdom. In the Jewish tradition, Rosh Hashana looks toward the judgment of God. In the light of the Book of Revelation, this is likely the correct emphasis.

The fall cycle of feasts is tied together coherently in prophetic meaning. The return of the Messiah *(Yom haSho-far* or

Yom Teruah) leads to the fast of Yom Kippur. This is because His return produces the mourning and repentance in Israel predicted in Zechariah 12:10 and the mourning over the face of the whole earth predicted in Matthew 24 and Revelation 1:7. Yet this great repentance is not without fulfillment, for there is a great fountain open for the cleansing of sin (see Zech. 13), and the nations come to the knowledge of God. Hence Yom Kippur, for those who know Yeshua, is a feast of intercession for the salvation of Israel and the nations of the world. These prophetic meanings are a significant part of our celebration.

Once cleansing has taken place, we may celebrate the universal feast of God. Yom Kippur leads to the great Feast of Succot, in which the Kingdom of God is established all over the earth in the reign of the Messiah. All nations will send representatives to celebrate this feast. It is this feast, more than any other, which testifies that God is the provider and the King over all the earth. We who live in the reality of His Kingdom today look forward to the fullness of the Kingdom in the future.

Of course, the Sabbath has great future reference. The Age to Come is the Age of Shalom or peace over all the earth. It is the seventh age on earth in Jewish reckoning. It also is a foreshadowing of that bliss that belongs to those who are resurrected in the Messiah.

It is my firm belief that Messianic Jewish worship and celebration should reflect all of the multifaceted meanings of the feasts, but especially the meaning of fulfillment in Yeshua and the great work of God yet to come as predicted in these feasts. None of the feasts have been fulfilled in the sense of their meaning being already fully completed in history. There is more to come, even continuing unto the New Heavens and the New Earth.

Of course, all this implies that our practice, our liturgy, and our rituals should fully show forth the reality and power of the New Covenant.

CHAPTER ONE

THE BIBLICAL MEANING OF ISRAEL

TORAH FOUNDATIONS

I T IS NO ACCIDENT OR mistake that the Synagogue has given a special recognition to Torah, the first five Books of Moses. Some wrongly believe that the Synagogue thereby depreciates the value of the rest of the Bible. This is not the case. Rather, the early Jewish community properly sensed the *foundational* nature of Torah. The Torah records God's first and most basic covenants with Israel. Therefore, all further revelation must be in accord with these foundational revelations. Consistency to Torah teaching was a standard by which further revelation was to be judged as God-given or not (see Deut. 13).

The Torah is the pivot of Judaism, for in the Torah is recorded the Creation, the Flood, the call of Abraham, the lives of the patriarchs, the sojourn in Egypt, the rescue from Egyptian bondage, and the revelation of the priestly sacrificial system, which foreshadows the work of Messiah Himself. Any Messianic Jewish perspective, therefore, must be clear in its understanding of Torah and the early covenants God made with Israel. Our understanding is, of course, retrospective through the person of Yeshua, but it is an understanding that seeks to be fair to the original contextual meaning of the covenants as well.

THE CALL OF ABRAHAM

Jewish history began with Abraham. Although the term *Jew* was derived from the tribe of Judah, since the period before the New Covenant Scriptures (inter-testament period) to refer to all Israelites—the descendants of Jacob, or Israel, Abraham's grandson—God's covenant with Israel begins with Abraham, so in a broad sense we might say Abraham was the first Jew.

We know little of Abraham's early life. He came from Ur of the Chaldeans with his father, Terah; he settled in Haran, from whence he was called forth. Was Abraham's family completely "pagan"? Or did Abraham's family carry on a tradition of reverence for the living God, albeit distorted with certain pagan influences? These are questions we cannot now answer. We do know that there were some in the Middle East who worshipped the Creator God—or the sky God above other gods—but we do not find any monotheists at this time.[1] We are on much firmer ground in seeking to understand, instead, *the nature* of God's call to Abraham.

Abraham recognized the voice of God and obeyed when he was told, "Go from your country and your kindred and your father's house to the land that I will show you" (Gen. 12:1 RSV). God came to Abraham with a call and a command that he accepted: "So Abram went as the Lord had told him..." (Gen. 12:4 RSV). This first statement underscores tremendous promises. We read of seven: "I will make you into a great nation and I will bless you; I will make your name great, and you will be a blessing. I will bless those who bless you, and whoever curse, and all peoples on earth will be blessed through you" (Gen. 12:2-3 RSV).

A nation must have a land. We soon find that the promise of land is part of the covenant material of these chapters. In Genesis 12:7, God says that He will give this land—the land of Canaan—to Abraham's seed forever or as an everlasting possession. We consistently read that this promise is eternal (see Gen. 13:14-15; 15:18; 17:19; 26:1-4; 28:12-14). The covenant is passed down through Abraham's son, Isaac, and then to Jacob—whose name was changed to Israel—and to his twelve sons.

God's covenant is offered by His grace, not as a response to works. From the recipient, God required faith, issuing in obedience. Hence we find that Abraham "believed the Lord; and He reckoned it to him as righteousness" (Gen. 15:6 RSV). This verse becomes essential to New Testament teaching. Paul consistently shows that right standing with God is achieved by a faith response, not by works of self-righteousness, and he points to this Abrahamic Covenant as the key to this doctrine (see Rom. 4; Gal. 3). Of what did this faith consist? Firstly, it was a faith sufficient for Abraham to travel onward with God for the sake of the promise God had given. It was also manifest in the fact that Abraham believed God when told that his descendants would be as the stars of heaven when, as yet, his wife Sarah was barren.

The whole story of Abraham and the eventual birth of Isaac is miraculous and points to Messiah Yeshua. Isaac, like Yeshua, is the only son of his father, miraculously conceived, and offered up as a sacrifice to God for the sake of obedience to his father and for the benefit of others (see Gen. 22). Sarah was supernaturally enabled to bear this child just as Miriam (Mary) supernaturally conceived by God's Holy Spirit. What a joy to read these accounts and compare them, for Isaac, the ancestor of our Messiah, foreshadows Yeshua. It should be noted that the sacrifice of Isaac was a symbolic act which Judaism considers of the greatest merit. It was done in the location of the future Temple. Hence a strand of Judaism teaches that all of the sacrifices only have merit because they participate in the meaning of the sacrifice of Isaac. The sacrifice of Isaac has world redemptive implications as Abraham is the high priest of the human race.[2]

The practice of circumcision is also of note as part of the revelation of this covenant. Abraham is told that he is to circumcise all males in his household; all future male babies are to be circumcised the eighth day. Circumcision is a *sign* of the covenant of God with Abraham. As Paul argues, Abraham was justified before God gave this sign of the covenant. Circumcision is a sign of response to the covenant, not an act that makes us righteous with God. The same can be said of the New Covenant *mikvah* or baptism. Several things should be noted about circumcision that are crucial to understanding Messianic Judaism.

Circumcision is a sign of a gracious covenant that is astounding for its offer of grace and promise. Abraham's seed will be a blessing; his heirs will possess the land as an everlasting possession, etc. Hence, Paul, in Galatians, sees the Abrahamic Covenant as a statement of the good news in a way that points to God's grace in Yeshua. This Abrahamic Covenant is the primary covenant of God with Israel. It includes the promise of bringing blessing or even salvation to the nations (see Gen. 12:3). As Paul rightly argues, no later covenant (e.g., Mosaic) can annul the basic principles of this covenant; the Abrahamic Covenant includes the good news of God's salvation by grace (see Gal. 3:8). Circumcision is not only the sign of being under the Mosaic "constitutional" covenant, but rather, of being part of the Abrahamic Covenant of grace and the promise that God has given to Israel!

Circumcision clearly shows that it was God's intention for this covenant to be carried on through Abraham's physical descendants. (We will later find that one can join the community of Israel through conversion and assimilation into the national-physical people.) Circumcision emphasizes the national-physical application of this covenant to Abraham's descendants. Only the male receives the covenant sign; for, in ancient times, the father determined the religious identity of his seed. When Israel took non-Israelite wives—with God's approval—during the days of Joshua, the children were automatically considered Israelites. Later Jewish thought confuted this biblical precedent by identifying a child as Jewish through his mother, pointing both to the influence of a mother on her children and Ezra's specific injunctions to the Jews (fifth century B.C.E.) to put away their foreign wives. Ezra's decision was a response to a specific problem and does not change the essence of circumcision pointing to the father as the source of covenant identity.

Eighth-day circumcision was a unique practice. Other peoples practiced circumcision as a puberty rite signifying the entrance of the male into adult life (a rite of passage). Circumcision on the eighth day divorces the sign from the rites of passage so that it has a distinct covenant meaning. The children of Abraham exhibit the sign of the covenant of grace from the eighth day. It is amazing to note that the eighth day is the safest day for infant circumcision, for on this day the body possesses a superior blood-clotting ability.[3]

We might note that circumcision in these scriptural passages (see Gen. 17) is four times called an everlasting sign, an unconditional sign to be performed as a covenant sign forever among Jewish people who affirm God's covenant with the house of Israel. To forego this sign is to deny that we are part of Israel. Israel, in its identity, is the people descended from Abraham who are given the promise of land and blessing and the promise of bringing a blessing to the world. It is a covenant of grace. Israel is a nation constituted and preserved by God's covenant promise; this, we believe, is the central meaning of Israel's identity. We cannot forego the physical sign of these truths (circumcision) without foregoing our part in the meaning of Israel.

This, of course, leads to a question: Does Israel retain a special meaning under God's covenant promises? If so, what is that meaning? This question will occupy a major part of our attention.

No New Testament passage confutes the continuation of the Abrahamic Covenant, an unconditional and everlasting covenant. As Paul says, "The gifts and call of God are irrevocable"; Israel remains "beloved for the father's sake" (see Rom. 11:28-29). The salvation of individual Jews is not assured simply by their being part of Israel, but Israel, as a nation, still is part of this covenant, which promises to give and receive blessing, preservation, land, and purpose as a national instrument of God's purposes.

We need to emphasize that God's choice of Abraham—and Israel—was not for a narrow or limited purpose. Rather, His blessing for the whole world is the keynote. Israel might be chosen, but that choice is for service, to bring blessing to all. The covenant is universally inclusive. Traditionally, the choice of special individuals or nations was called the "scandal of particularity," for the human mind recoiled at such unfair privilege. Yet the "scandal of particularity" is the way with a truly historical faith. God works through people, accommodating Himself to people and situations in ways we cannot fully fathom. Even the Church, although universal in scope, moved out from Jerusalem and spread to others over time within the limitations of travel and communication. Those who were near to Jerusalem had an advantage. The scandal is here as well. Messianic Jews—although one with all believers—are criticized because the flesh of humanity recoils at a chosenness that is not theirs, even if it is for the purpose of service and even if it is accompanied by trial and suffering. Hence, some criticism arises because the Messianic Jew sees himself as part of the universal people of God, while yet playing a role in God's purposes through the nation Israel.

THE MOSAIC REVELATION

The patriarchs died, and the descendants of Israel found themselves in bondage to a king who did not know their ancestor, Joseph. This grievous slavery of the chosen people is the background setting for the Mosaic revelation. The revelation was an incredible demonstration of God's grace and salvation. Part of this revelation was a new national covenant from God, found in Exodus 20, Leviticus 19–26, and the whole of Deuteronomy. This covenant did not alter nor do away with the earlier Abrahamic Covenant, but it provided a constitution for the ancient nation. Hence, all of the Mosaic revelation—Exodus, Leviticus, Numbers, and Deuter-onomy—takes on the character of covenant literature, recording God's work and His will for Israel.

It is significant that God's historic revelation is manifested through a program to rescue a dispossessed slave people. The consistent picture of God revealed in the events of the Exodus—as well as by the prophets—is a God who cares for the poor, the needy, the dispossessed, the aged, the orphaned, and the widowed; that is, for all who are defenseless, God is their defender. Yeshua Himself announces His ministry in these terms, quoting Isaiah:

> *The Spirit of the Lord is upon me, because he hath anointed me to preach the gospel to the poor; he hath sent me to heal the brokenhearted, to preach deliverance to the captives, and recovering of sight to the blind, to set at liberty them that are bruised...* (Luke 4:18 KJV).

The Mosaic legislation which followed the Exodus gives special attention to strangers, for Israel was a stranger in Egypt (see Lev. 19:33; Ps. 69:32-33). Although Christians have often heard of the legal stringency of the Mosaic revelation, it is incumbent upon Messianic Jews to point out the incredible level of compassion found in the Mosaic revelation as well. It was the most advanced constitutional law system that the world had ever seen.

The Exodus events began with the call of Moses. God revealed His name to Moses, stating that He would always be known as the God of Abraham, Isaac, and Jacob (see Exod. 3). Further revelation of God's name is given in response to Moses' request so that the people might believe him. God here reveals Himself in the phrase variously translated "I Am Who I Am" or "I act as I act" or "I am He who causes to be."

Interpretations of this passage are myriad.[4] It is probable, however, that God was not speaking of His eternity (a Greek concept), but of His nature as defined by all His actions in revelation. He is the God of revelation. This phrase is caught up in meaning with the covenant name of God, spelled with the consonant *yod, hey, vav, hey,* a name that Jews do not pronounce. This is the most prevalent name of God in Scripture, *especially when Scripture speaks of God in His Covenant and revelation contexts.*

The Exodus story continues with the well-known accounts of Moses going to Pharaoh. He demands the release of his people and, under instruction from God, calls down plagues upon Egypt. Finally, when the magicians can no longer duplicate the plagues—especially the death of all firstborn males in the land of Egypt—Pharaoh lets the Israelites go.

The plagues, although grievous physical trials to the Egyptians, represent far more: The plagues undercut faith in the Egyptian gods and show the powerlessness of the Egyptian gods to protect Egypt from the God of Israel. The Nile, for example, is a "god"; it turns rancid. Hupi is the frog "god," and Egypt is given enough frogs to feast on frog legs for decades to come! The sun is a chief "god"; it is blotted out by darkness. Most alarming is the death of the firstborn—especially of Pharaoh's own firstborn—who would have been considered an incarnation of the sun god!

Egyptian religion was a very sophisticated pagan ritual of magic and superstition. Egypt was the most powerful nation of that age. Therefore, the Exodus of this enslaved people was truly a defeat of paganism, of all false gods, of all superstition and magic, a defeat authored by the one Creator—God! The defeat of Egypt and its gods by the Israelites could only lead to the conclusion that God is the Lord of all the earth. The Exodus of Israel struck terror into the hearts of the decadent, utterly corrupt Canaanite peoples whom Israel was to conquer.

The Passover in which Israel escaped the angel of death who destroyed Egypt's firstborn also teaches a great lesson, since it was the blood on the doorposts from a sacrificial lamb which caused the angel of death to pass over Israelite homes. Within these homes, the families ate lamb meat and fellowshipped with God and one another. Nothing speaks quite like the Passover in regard to sacrificial blood being the means of avoiding the penalty of death for sin.

And so Israel leaves Egypt, crosses through the sea miraculously, and the pursuing Egyptians drown as the parted waters return!

The Exodus foreshadows the greatest act of God's grace in all of history—Yeshua's death and resurrection. It is the event which foreshadows the exodus from sin and death experienced by all Yeshua's followers (see 1 Cor. 10:1-4).

Because the Exodus was an event whereby God worked through a nation to defeat the nations and paganism, it is to us a symbol and foretaste of the future world redemption spoken of by the prophets.

Well do the psalmists recount the Exodus as a totally unique event of world history (see Ps. 46:8-11; 47:8-10, verses 7-9 in some versions). Who ever heard of a rag-tag bunch of slaves defeating the mightiest nation in the world? Of all the events of Israel's history, the Exodus becomes the pivotal, formative event in Israel's concept of God: God is gracious and merciful. Israel's judgment, declared by the prophets, is not primarily a condemnation for breaking the Law; rather, Israel's breaking of the Law is symptomatic of her spurning God's love and grace.

The Exodus is at the heart of the Torah, just as God's love and grace is at the heart of the Exodus. This is the true and full nature of the Mosaic revelation and the whole of the Tenach (Old Testament).

As we continue in the Book of Exodus, we read the history of Israel's approach to the Promised Land, the tragedies of rebellion, and in Numbers, the refusal to enter and possess the land of Canaan. Forty years of wandering followed. This history, as well as legislative material, is part of the covenant documents found from Exodus through Deuteronomy. God desired the behavior and faith of future generations under His covenants to be based on the revealed lessons of history: the accounts of His grace and the disaster following the unfaithfulness of the people. In this history, we begin to discern the purpose of God for choosing Israel, both to fulfill His promise to Abraham and to be a blessing to the nations. This supersedes Israel's purpose as an instrument of judgment. Israel illustrates God's truth.

Hence we read in Exodus 19:6 that God chose Israel to be a kingdom of priests. What is the function of a priest? The priest is a mediator between God and people. Nothing could be more foolish than to say that Judaism sees no need of a mediator. The whole Torah and its system of priests interceding for the people with sacrifices refutes this gross untruth. By his mediation, the priest brought God and the people together. Therefore, if Israel's purpose was to be *a nation* of priests, then she was to be a national mediator between God and the peoples of the world. She was to bring the nations to God and God to the nations. How? By being a nation under God, under His rule or covenant, so that life would be blessed, just, and healthy. Remember, Israel was promised none of the diseases of Egypt if she followed the covenant; no, she was promised prosperity and joy!

God desired there to be a nation among the nations to demonstrate His Lordship. And He has never changed this purpose. He created nations with their variety; but nations need to come under His Lordship (see Acts 17:26). The purpose of the universal Church is different: The Church is not (strictly speaking) a nation; rather it is a people movement that transcends all nations gathered from all nations.

God, however, has never given up His purpose of preserving a nation among the nations to demonstrate His Lordship.

As Dr. Walter Kaiser stated, "He will yet have victory over the nations through Israel!"[5]

This, of course, brings us to the nature of the Mosaic revelation. We have already showed the centrality of the Exodus to the whole of this revelation. However, in recent years it has been shown by biblical scholars that there are—within the books from Exodus through Deuteronomy—specific "covenant documents." As noted before, central among these documents are Exodus 20 (the Ten Commandments), Leviticus 19–26 (the holiness code), and the whole Book of Deuteronomy. The other laws and instructions in the books are expansions and additions to these basic covenant materials and are to be understood in the light of these inspired covenants. The present writer is firmly convinced that the work of George Mendenhall and Meridith Kline in this field should revolutionize our understanding of the Torah and that we can never again see Torah as providing us with a "dispensation of Law" in the sense of a legalistic system of works-righteousness. For an updated defense of the thesis we are presenting, the recent volume by Dr. Kenneth Kitchen is very important. He also defends the Mosaic origin of the Torah.[6]

The covenant documents within Exodus through Deuteronomy provide Israel with a *national constitution* under God, a treaty between God and the nation. This treaty is the basis for Israel's morality and social-legal system as well as its system of worship, priesthood, and sacrifice. Every nation has a social-legal system. However, Israel's system is totally unique. Kline demonstrates that the structure of the covenant documents, especially Exodus 20 and Deuteronomy (which is a revised covenant treaty given before Israel entered the land), parallel the structure of Hittite treaty documents from the fifteenth century BCE. Furthermore, he showed that this structure carries with it meanings which enhance our understanding of the whole Bible. These meanings would have been apparent to the generation which received the Torah, but are sometimes hidden to modern readers. A cardinal rule of biblical interpretation is that we must interpret the Scriptures according to their historically intended meaning, as given to the people to whom they were originally addressed. This is the only objective control restricting us from interpreting the Scriptures however we like.

The true meaning of Scripture is discovered through the original languages in the context of culture in which the concepts of that language found their meaning. When Scripture is thus understood, its application to us becomes clear.

The following paragraphs are an attempt to properly understand Torah in this way. What is the structure of the fifteenth-century BCE Hittite treaties which help us define the terminology and conceptual nature of the Torah?

The first characteristic of the fifteenth-century BCE treaty form is the fact that the king of a powerful nation offered a treaty to the vassal nations under his rule or potential rule. The treaty was always couched as a gracious offer to be under the rule of the ancient king, called a *suzerain*. The king may have been a heartless tyrant. However, the form of the treaty required that he appear to be a gracious, benevolent ruler. Hence the deeds of the ruler for the people were first recounted. On the basis of the king's grace, the subject people were expected to respond in faith and obedience. This obedience included respect for and obedience to the king's governing representatives. The treaty went on to describe the great benefits of obedience, that is, the blessings that would follow. It also emphasized the great punishment that the king would bring upon his disobedient subjects, called *cursings*. We can see how such a treaty was an ideal form for God's communication, since God *truly* was the beneficent king who saved Israel by grace and called Israel as a nation to faith and obedience. Such a treaty context is an ideal setting for Israel's national legislation, which includes the heights of the call for love in human relationships, "love thy neighbor as thyself," as well as everything from the judicial system; a means for the redistribution of wealth; honesty in business; and to care for the poor, the needy, the orphan, the widow, and the stranger. The religious sacrificial system, which is integrally related to this whole constitution, also finds its meaning in this context.

It is fascinating to see the parallels in covenant form in these treaties and in the Book of Deuteronomy and the Exodus 20 passage (the Ten Commandments). The whole of the Book of Deuteronomy fits the ancient treaty form precisely. It begins with a *preamble* (see Deut. 1:1-5). The preamble is simply the introductory paragraph such as "We the people of the United States...." The second *section* is the *historical prologue* (see Deut. 1:6–4:49). The prologue is a brief summary history that, in the ancient treaties, recalled the gracious work of the ancient king *(suzerain)* for the people. In Deuteronomy's case, the acts of God's grace are recalled as well as the history of the response of the people. This prologue recounts the mighty Exodus from Egypt, God's provision of supernatural food in the wilderness (manna), the people's rebellion against God and Moses, as well as God's judgment (disciplinary measures) and mercy (forgiveness). The historical prologue of Deuteronomy contrasts with other treaties by the nature of its content. It tells what God the Creator did for Israel. This recounting of God's grace provides the ground and motivation for Israel's response of faith and obedience. Hence the *third section:* the *stipulations of the covenant.* Within this section are included the basic call to love and trust God, the Sh'ma (see Deut. 6:4 ff), the Ten Commandments (see Deut. 5), and the necessity of recalling that God's work for Israel was by grace and because of His love and faithfulness to the patriarchal promises. Israel was never to think that its inheritance came by its own power or righteousness (see Deut. 8–10). Provisions were also given for a central place of worship (see Deut. 12) to unite the nation in the worship of one God under the administration of the priests who had charge of the sacrificial system and the teaching of Torah to the nation. The rest of this section of Deuteronomy includes a basic summary of national legislation and moral guidance given through Moses. Provision is also given for testing prophets (see Deut. 13, 18), who will call the nation to Torah faithfulness, as well as declare God's leading for the nation's future.

The *fourth section* is the *blessings and cursings* section. Israel's faithfulness and obedience will be richly blessed! Her land will be fruitful, many children will be born, and disease and plagues will be kept from the land. Foreign domination will be prevented. A life with God will produce a nation without fear because of the profound security provided by God. Disobedience, however, will be followed by the very opposite of these blessings: fear, insecurity, plagues, famine, foreign domination, destruction, and the scattering of the nation. This section also includes the call for the nation to ratify this treaty—upon entering the land—with specific provisions for a ceremony of ratification that is later fulfilled in the Book of Joshua.

A most fascinating contrast to other treaties in this section is the paragraph on *witnessing to the treaty*. The ancient king called upon the gods of both nations to witness the treaty and to fulfill the blessings and cursings. The true God, however, has none higher than Himself by which to swear. Hence the treaty calls heaven and earth to witness!

We can see that Deuteronomy is a Mosaic summary given by God as an appropriate recounting of events and instruction before the departure of Moses and Israel's entrance into the land. It thus includes many provisions already given in Exodus through Numbers and is the context in which all previous national legislation is to be understood.

The last section of the treaties includes *succession arrangements*. It provides for covenant continuity by requiring the deposit of the treaty in the Temple and requiring regular public reading. It also includes the passing of leadership from Moses to Joshua.

It should also be noted that in the treaties of the other nations, the sin of rebellion is seen as seeking to be free of the lordship of the king or suzerain. This is also the case in Torah; that rebellion is not defined as following another human leader, but as all forms of idolatry—subtle or blatant—including all occult arts, witchcraft, sorcery, divination, and spiritualism, which is consulting with other gods (see Deut. 19).

The reason we belabor a summary of the structure of Deuteronomy is to provide a context for truly understanding the Torah. Since Torah is central to Judaism, a Messianic Jew must gain an accurate understanding of Torah in general if he is to know how to relate to his Jewish heritage and to Christian theology. It is essential for integrating the Tenach (Old Testament) and the New Testament into a balanced understanding in which biblical revelation can be properly seen as a whole and in which Torah is not dismissed because of debates that arose from later foreign contexts. This will become clearer as we proceed.

Scholars also point out that Exodus 20 is a covenant treaty document. Our understanding of ancient treaties has greatly improved our understanding of this chapter. To be emphasized most is the opening statement, "I am the Lord thy God, which have brought thee out of the land of Egypt, out of the house of bondage" (Exod. 20:2 KJV). The grace of God precedes the commandment and is the motivation for obedience. Blessings and curses are distributed within the document rather than coming at the end. What is of greatest note is the new understanding of the reason for two tablets and for the Sabbath command. Traditionally, it was thought that the commands were divided into two sections, the first having to do with commands in relation to God and the second concerning our relationship to humanity. This is probably not the case. Rather, our duties to God and humanity are inseparably related. All of the commands should be thought of as being on one tablet. Indeed, the tablets were probably duplicates! Why? Ancient covenant documents were always made in duplicate. One copy was placed in the temple of the subject nation and one in the temple of the ruling nation. Thus the gods of both nations would be called on to witness the covenant and to execute justice if it was violated. The two tablets in Israel were both to be deposited in the Ark in the holiest place in the Tabernacle. The Temple of God, the great

Suzerain, and of Israel, the subject people, was the same. God is the divine witness. One tablet is the copy for the people and one tablet, symbolically, is God's.

The other clarification comes in relation to the Sabbath Command. It is hoped that Messianic Judaism can bring some light to the debate on the Sabbath. It has been thought strange by some that God would place the Sabbath at the center of His lofty commands that deal with the highest dimensions of morality. How is it that there is then this intrusion of a *ritual* command? Christian responses have run the gamut from: (1) those who hold that none of these commands are obligatory for Christians since they are "no longer under law, but grace"; the Spirit produces a parallel morality in Christians called the "law of Christ"—dispensationalists—to (2) Adventists who hold that the Sabbath command is as lofty and moral as the other nine and goes back to the Creation of the world. Paul King Jewett, in a recent book, argues that although seventh-day observance is not necessary, the principle of a day of rest and worship for religious and humanitarian purposes is absolutely necessary, but that it is appropriate that it be on Sunday for Christians. Unfortunately, the whole debate has lost sight of a contextual understanding of the Sabbath command.[7]

The Sabbath reflects the pattern of God's creative work in the beginning; or, in the words of Jewish liturgy, it is a memorial of Creation. Secondly, it is the first of the feasts in memorial praise of the Exodus from Egypt and the establishment of Israel as a free nation under God. Sabbath, however, is an integral part of God's treaty between Himself and Israel. Although there may be marvelous applications from a humanitarian and religious point of view for Christians, we need first to understand the covenant context.

The Sabbath is called a sign "between me and the people of Israel." In the ancient covenants, the center of the treaty would bear a symbol or sign of the king—*suzerain*—which might have been related to his chief god. This was a stamped-in-clay image of a god or a stamp on a parchment. However, no representation of God could be made in ancient Israel. Therefore, the representation would not be a symbol, a picture, or an idol, but a unique cycle of life. Only Israel had a seven-day cycle of weeks. We do not sense today how unique Israel truly was, for the seven-day week has since become the practice of the world.

This seven-day cycle—with rest and worship on the last day—was a unique testimony to the covenant relationship between God and Israel. Hence, the whole of the commands are part of a *covenant* with Israel, and although we can discern the universal principles of this treaty, which apply to all peoples (as Paul's quoting "Honor your mother and father" in Ephesians 6:2), the treaty is an indivisible whole as given to Israel; Sabbath-keeping is just as much a part of this treaty as "Thou shalt not kill." To spurn the Sabbath as a covenant sign was to spurn the covenant and the special relationship between God and the nation Israel. Certainly, huge questions arise from this discussion. Are the Mosaic covenants still valid and in effect as a covenant? If not, are there principles that transcend the Mosaic constitution and apply today? If so, which ones? Is the Sabbath one of these principles? We shall address these questions later. Suffice it to say, at this point, that the practice of Sabbath celebrates the escape from Egypt, the establishment and the worship of God as Creator of Israel, all *of which were promised in the Abrahamic Covenant as well as found in the Mosaic economy.*

Our emphasis heretofore has been on an understanding of the Mosaic constitution as a gracious constitution offered by a God of grace. It was to provide Israel with the most exemplary and humanitarian social system that had been seen on earth. It was to enable a walk in forgiveness and fellowship with God through the Temple-sacrificial system. Israel would thus be a light to the nations, a kingdom of priests who bring the nations closer to God.

This emphasis might seem strange to Jewish and Christian readers who have hitherto seen Torah in mostly a legalistic framework, although Jewish scholars have pointed out the error of this common concept. Samuel Schultz, the late Samuel Robinson professor of Old Testament at Wheaton College, had admirably sought to present the truth to the Christian layman. In his commentary on Deuteronomy, *Deuteronomy, the Gospel of Love,* and in the *Gospel of Moses,*[8] he has argued convincingly for the gracious nature of the Torah. His thesis is that in every covenant grace is behind the "offer." Faith and love are the primary responses that lead to obedience. So Yeshua taught that our love for Him was proved by our obedience to His commandments. This is repeated in First John and throughout the New Testament. Nor is there any room, argues Schultz, for the idea of a harsh, vindictive God of justice in the Old Testament to be contrasted with a God of love and mercy in the New. Love and mercy are always offered before judgment is rendered. Yeshua's warnings concerning judgment in the New Testament are as severe as anything in the Old, even if we argue that the highest personal revelation of God's love is seen in Yeshua!

This has great implications for our understanding of the New Testament as well. For example, is Paul's argument really with the Law of Moses? Or is Paul's argument with a *system of righteousness before God by works*—a prideful approach to God—that was prevalent in some quarters in first-century Judaism? As George Ladd argues, this system developed in the intertestamental period (300 B.C.E. to 50 C.E.) and was a misunderstanding of the true nature of Torah.[9] Others argue that the system was not for personal salvation, but for priestly service to bring the final redemption and the Age to Come. Our view is that Paul's argument is with the Law as a *system of merit* and with the forcing of Jewish practice and identity upon non-Jews as well as a wrong emphasis for priestly service. This whole question will be addressed in the chapter on Paul, Israel, and the Law.

We must close this section by discussing the sacrificial system. The sacrificial system is a pervasive part of the Torah. As such, it must not be summarily dismissed by moderns. There were several different kinds of sacrifice (see Lev. 1–7). Some symbolized total dedication in which the whole animal was burned as an offering. Others emphasized expiation for sin. Here, part of the sacrifice was burned—the smoke ascending God-ward—and part was eaten by the priest as mediator. The sin was, therefore, dissolved through the sacrifice and in the priest's eating. Another sacrifice was eaten by the offerer, the peace offering symbolizing communion with God through a fellowship meal.

Sometimes combinations of sacrifices were offered, one following another. It is crucial to note the most prominent common aspects of the sacrifices. First is the substitutionary aspect. Because the offerer is willing, by faith, to identify with the animal in repentance, acknowledging his sin as well as sin's destructive nature, he is forgiven. Because God is merciful, He accepts the *identified-with-symbol* in place of the offerer's punishment *if true repentance is present.* All of this has great value for understanding the sacrifice of Yeshua, who is God's greatest love revelation and our *identification-with-symbol.* He alone ties together the central meanings of humanity, God, repentance, sin-bearing love, and forgiveness. We should also note that Judaism taught that all of the sacrifices, being rooted in the sacrifice of Isaac, have an intercessory aspect for world redemption. In addition, the idea that the Temple is that intercessory system that preserves the world in existence until the ultimate redemption of the human race is an important Rabbinic idea.[10]

Several feasts in addition to the Sabbath were instituted as part of Israel's national existence. The most prominent is Passover (Pesach); the others are Succot and Shavuot. Yom Kippur is a special day of prayer, fasting, and repentance. The offerings of the bulls for Succot were especially interpreted as intercession for the nations.

Israel as a nation, faithful to God, could rely on His protection. She was not to enter into protective alliances with other nations, for this would not only imply a lack of faith in God, but would, according to the customs of the times, require the sharing of their gods. *All of these stipulations were extraordinary.* They point to the supernatural character of Torah's revelation and would indeed make Israel a unique light to the nations. It was the breaking of the covenant by attitude and deed that brought the message of the prophets, a message of judgment, mercy, and hope.

THE FUNCTION OF THE PROPHETS

The layman assumes that the primary purpose of a prophet is to foretell the future. This is certainly not the case with biblical prophets, although we must not adopt the extreme position of some who neglect the fact that biblical prophets did, at times, foretell future events.

The biblical prophet was primarily a servant of the covenant whose main purpose was *to speak forth the Word of God.* Forthtelling is more primary than foretelling. The Word of God was addressed to the people in an immediate situation, but had relevance to all future generations. Further, the message of the prophets was generally to call the people back to covenant faithfulness—or Torah. If the people repented, God's blessing would follow, but if they did not, punishment was a likely consequence. The message of the prophets was echoed in the Torah. From Amos' lofty messages concerning social justice to Malachi's call for a right heart attitude, the prophets extended the basic principles of the love of God and one's neighbor as set forth in Torah. In the midst of national failure, the prophet looked forward to a New Covenant, enabling greater obedience and faithfulness. The days of the Messiah would bring forth a perfect social order in which love and justice would dominate, and war and poverty would cease (see Isa. 2 and 11).

Predictions abound, but within a specific context: The predictions foresaw specific judgments, as well as an ensuing Age of Peace. Some predictions were present signs while others related to the distant future beyond this age. The prophet predicted because he heard from God who is the Lord of history. His whole message must come from his gift of hearing God's Word. The work of God's anointed everlasting King, the Messiah, was also described.

A major cause of prophetic concern was Israel's idolatry. Partially the result of accommodation to the spirit of the age, and partially the result of Israel's entering into protective alliances, idolatry threatened to destroy the very reason for Israel's existence. Sharing each other's gods was an ingredient in the alliances of ancient times, which was not allowed for faithful Israelites. Hence, these alliances were not an option for Israel.

Deuteronomy 13 and 18 give the basic tests for a true prophet. The tests are not exhaustive, but central. One is that the prophet's predictions must come to pass. The other is more central; the prophet's message must be in accord with the teachings of Torah. If his predictions are true, but he incites Israel to unfaithfulness to Torah, he is stoned; he is a prophet whose powers are not from God, but from an evil source.

The Jewish tradition has venerated the Torah above all other revelation. The reason for this is clear: Torah is foundational; all other revelation is to be tested by its consistency to Torah. Therefore, although all Scriptures are inspired by God, Torah is clearly foundational. This has vast implications for our understanding of the New Testament. Any interpretation of the New Covenant Scriptures which is *inconsistent* with the revelation in the Torah cannot be true. Such interpretations lend credence to the Jewish rejection of the New Testament, for there is no revelation that can be accepted if it is inconsistent with Torah; this is the clear implication of Deuteronomy 13. Therefore, Jewish heritage venerates the Torah—Genesis through Deuteronomy—as the foundational scriptural revelation.[11]

THE PROMISE OF A NEW COVENANT

The promise of a New Covenant was anticipated by the Torah itself. Before Israel had even entered the land, Moses foresaw the nation's faithlessness toward God's covenant. Indeed, the Book of Deuteronomy called for a circumcision of the heart (see Deut. 30:4-6) from which the calloused flesh of the heart would be cut away and an attitude of yielding love and obedience toward God would ensue. But as Israel's history progressed, its continued failure prepared the prophets to receive revelation of something more to come. Israel was depleted by idolatry. First, the nation was split into north and south; then came the captivity of the Northern tribes and an end to their national existence. Finally, in 586 B.C.E., the national life in the Land of the Southern Kingdom ended as the King of Babylon conquered the last vestiges of the nation.

The prophets spoke God's Word in the context of these tragic events: Joel foresaw an age in which the power of the Spirit of God would be universally given to all (see Joel 2:28-29). Most striking, however, were the parallel promises in Jeremiah and Ezekiel of a New Covenant to be offered to Israel. Jeremiah ministered to the last remnant of people in the land of Israel before their final demise in 586 B.C.E. Meanwhile, Ezekiel ministered simultaneously in Babylon to those taken captive. Despite the seeming hopelessness due to Israel's national demise and the failure of Israel in its call of God, both prophets predicted a resurrection of Israel's national life. The dry bones vision in Ezekiel 37 and Jeremiah's prediction of a limited 70-year exile gave hope. Israel would live *(Am Yisrael Chai)*.

Both Ezekiel and Jeremiah predicted a New Covenant *(B'rit Hadashah)*. Messianic Jews believe that *B'rit Hada-shah* has been established by the life, death, and resurrection of Yeshua. However, not all the features of this New Covenant have yet been fulfilled. As regards the presence of the Kingdom, only a partial— but central—part of the New Covenant has come into being, for Jeremiah predicts that all Israelites shall personally know God through and as part of this covenant. It is not our purpose in this section to fully outline the relationship of previous covenants to the New Covenant; this will be a major theme of Chapters Two through Four of this book. It is only our purpose now to lay out the structure of this New Covenant in its original context as background material for future exposition. Our outline comes from Jeremiah 31 and Ezekiel 36.

The New Covenant is, first, with the house of Israel and Judah (see Jer. 31:31). The Messianic Age does indeed include Gentiles who have fellowship with God in an age of Israel's full restoration; but an offer of salvation to the Gentiles is not in *clear view* in these passages.

Second, the covenant will be *different* from the *Mosaic* Covenant, which God offered after the Exodus.

Third, this difference is expressed as God's Law or Torah being written on the hearts of the people of the nation (see Jer. 31:33). Ezekiel says, "a new heart I will give you... and I will take out of your flesh the heart of stone and give you a heart of flesh" (Ezek. 36:26 RSV). After adding the fourth and fifth features, he continues with the promise that God will cause them to walk in "my statutes and be careful to observe my ordinances" (Ezek. 36:27 RSV). The New Covenant is therefore not an abrogation of Torah, but an ability to walk *in* Torah! What a contrast to common teachings today! However, is it Torah in the general sense of God's ways (which is reflected in the Books of Moses), or is it the whole Mosaic system? Abraham, in Genesis 26:5, was said to have obeyed God's charge, commandments, statutes, and laws. The rabbis debated whether or not Torah would be altered in the Messianic Age. Some thought that parts of the Torah had a temporary relevance to an imperfect people, but that in the Messianic Age we would be so close to God that Torah would be altered to fit this situation. This problem will be discussed later.

Ezekiel adds a fourth promise: that we would have a new spirit. This is parallel to receiving a new heart. Fifth, God would put His Spirit within us. Sixth, the New Covenant includes the promise that Israel would dwell in its own land in safety and security (see Ezek. 24–28). *God's name will be glorified/magnified* among *the* nations through His work in Israel as *a* nation. What a contrast for those who hold that the New Covenant does away with national Israel! Seventh, the reception of the New Covenant will bring forgiveness of sin and cleansing from iniquity (see Jer. 31:34; Ezek. 36:25), whereby Israel will be God's people and God will be Israel's Lord.

Clearly the prophets, in contrasting this covenant to the Mosaic, knew the extent to which this covenant *would enable the fulfillment of God's purposes for Israel.* Was forgiveness offered under the Mosaic system? Yes. Was there an ability to love and do God's Law? Yes, if we are to believe David's meditation in Psalms 19 and 119. Yet even David had grievously sinned.

The New Covenant would come with a *power* of forgiveness previously unknown. The Spirit would be given in a direct and powerful way to all, never before known. This would enable a real knowledge of God in changed hearts to an *extent* and at a *degree* never before known. This covenant would be fully effective in producing the resulting life which the Mosaic Covenant could not. How utterly exciting is the hope of the prophets! This New Covenant is offered in Yeshua ha Mashiach, Jesus the Messiah!

ISRAEL'S CELEBRATIONS

Israel's year was to be punctuated by marvelous annual celebrations. All of them were occasions of great thanksgiving as well as times for additional sacrifices related to atonement, forgiveness, and dedication.

Leviticus 23 gives an outline of these special times. The Sabbath has already been described, a weekly feast that was considered the most prominent holy day other than Yom Kippur. Pesach (Passover) and the Feast of Unleavened Bread were also prominent. Passover was the great annual commemoration of the events connected to Israel's Exodus from Egypt. The feast recalls how the angel of death passed over the homes of the Israelites who had the Passover lamb's blood upon their doorposts. The meal of bitter herbs commemorates the bitter life of slavery from which Israel was freed. The lamb is a meal parallel to the Exodus meal, and the unleavened bread parallels the unleavened bread eaten when Israel left Egypt. The people left in such haste that the bread had no time to rise.

This is Israel's independence day. Since the Exodus was God's means of establishing the nation, Passover as well as the other holy days, were to be celebrated "forever and to all your generations" *(l'olam v'ed)* by the nation. In addition, Passover looks forward to the redemption of the whole world, the final end of exile for Israel, and the redemption of the nations.

It is possible that the "forever" referred to a people under the Mosaic sacrificial system and that once the sacrificial system was replaced, the "forevers" were of no further legal import, since the Mosaic system was no longer in force. After all, the sacrifices under the Aaronic priesthood were also commanded to be carried on forever. Some, therefore, believe that this priesthood will be restored. How, then, shall we evaluate the "forever" commands?

Although the "forevers" are all to be taken seriously, there is another dimension for understanding Israel's feasts—which is especially apparent in regard to Passover. *Although the feasts are part of the Mosaic system, they are also indissolubly tied to the Abrahamic Covenant.* The Abrahamic Covenant promised a nation to Abraham and the Exodus was a means of fulfilling the promise. Passover is the celebration of the fulfillment of the promise to Abraham! If we take the Abrahamic Covenant seriously—holding that Israel is promised the land and that Israel is still chosen of God as a nation—it is then inconsistent to do away with celebrations of the fulfillment of God's promises to Abraham.

The other feasts are celebrations of Israel's national life under God in fulfillment of God's promise to Abraham. They also all point in different ways to the end of this age and the Age of Restoration. They are a unique part of Israel's calling and identity as a nation called of God.

Assemblies of the people usually begin and end most feasts. The Feast of First Fruits, directly following Passover, includes an offering of the first products of the earth to God. By it the whole of Israel's produce is acknowledged as God's, His gift to the people.

Shavuot is the feast of the first harvest. It is a thanksgiving feast which comes fifty days after Passover. It later became associated with the time of God's giving of the Torah. It is no accident that God also gave His Spirit to Yeshua's first followers on this day, beginning a spiritual harvest through the Holy Spirit, who would enable the Torah to be written upon our hearts. Shavuot is thus a feast of the Spirit as well. It looks forward to the Age to Come as the Age of the Spirit given to all people.

Succot is the third major feast. Its significance is agricultural as well as historical, for this feast celebrates in thanksgiving the final harvest of the year. Israel is to dwell in tents or booths during a seven-day period. A great assembly follows. This practice recalls the wilderness wanderings of the nation. Israel had no material possessions; trust in God was her only recourse. Wonderfully, Israel was supernaturally given food (manna) as well as the miracle whereby her clothing did not wear out. God instituted Succot so that Israel might always remember that *"adonai yeera"*—God is the provider. In their own homes and lands, Israel's citizens are to remember that their existence depends upon God's grace, not upon their own wealth or efforts. Succot is also a time of great sacrifices of thanksgiving, a truly joyous and festive occasion. Succot is designated as the worldwide feast that will be celebrated by all nations in the Age to Come (see Zech. 14). Thus it predicts the ultimate worldwide Kingdom of God.

Israel's feasts are *all of grace:* God's grace in the Exodus miracle, God's grace in the harvest provisions, and God's grace in providing for all our needs. No taint of legalism is intended. *The feasts are also great didactic lessons for each generation so that Israel's history is given reality in successive generations.*

Other practices concerning specific days and years should also be mentioned. Trumpets is the day of blowing the shofar. This day later became associated with the new year and the Creation of the world in the Jewish heritage. As with the Christian celebration of the birth of Yeshua on December 25, we do not know for sure if this day is really the day of the Creation's beginning any more than we know if Christmas really is Yeshua's birthday. In the biblical context, blowing the trumpets (shofar) seemed to awaken us to prepare for Yom Kippur. In the New Covenant, the blowing of the shofar is connected to the return of Yeshua in both First Thessalonians 4:16-17 and First Corinthians 15.

Yom Kippur is the holiest day of the Jewish year. It is a day of fasting and repentance. On this day, the great sacrifice was offered for the sins of the nation. Another sacrifice functioned as the scapegoat, which was sent into the wilderness, symbolically carrying away the sins of the nation. It was on this day that the high priest entered the Holy of Holies in the presence of God, bringing the sacrificial blood. He sprinkled it upon the mercy seat, the top of the Ark containing the tablets of the covenant. Yom Kippur provides the major Levitical background for understanding the work of Yeshua as expressed in the Book of Hebrews. Other biblical writers connect Yeshua's sacrifice to both Yom Kippur and Passover, for He is our paschal lamb whose blood is shed and our Yom Kippur sacrifice. In John, as the Passover lambs are slain, so He is slain (see John 19). Therefore, we are to purge the old leaven of malice, replacing it with the unleavened bread of sincerity and truth (see 1 Cor. 5). It is safe to say that together with Passover, Yom Kippur is the major holy day for understanding the redemptive work of Yeshua.

Special years were also instituted in ancient Israel. First was the Sabbatical Year: Every seventh year Israel was to allow its farm lands to lie fallow; it was a year of even greater rest and sharing. It symbolized the Messianic Age as well as reflected God's creative work—seven was the number of distinct creative periods during which God made the heavens and the earth. Israel was promised a special blessing in the sixth year as well as natural produce in the seventh if it would be faithful to this statute. All Israelite slaves would be freed in the seventh year as well, for God is the Lord who releases the slaves from their bondage.

Every fiftieth year was to be a Jubilee Year. The requirements of this year were like those set for the Sabbatical Year, with the addition that all land was to be returned to its ancestral owners. Hence, land could be sold only for forty-nine years (or less); its price depended on the time remaining until the next Jubilee Year. Herein was an incredible balancing of personal initiative in economic life and the need for a measure of social equality. Wealth was based upon land, and accumulation of wealth in Israel was to have its limits. So liberty was proclaimed throughout the land (see Lev. 25); all slaves were to be freed; all debts were to be cancelled; and wealth was to be redistributed through the return of ancestral lands. Yeshua connected His ministry to the Year of Jubilee (see Luke 4) by proclaiming liberty to the captives.

Despite the limitations of the Mosaic system, we are indeed astonished at the gracious order of existence that God proclaimed for ancient Israel. Especially as we look at Israel's cycle of life through feast, fast, and jubilee—grace, love, and mercy shout out to us. We can say as the prophet of old, looking at ancient Israel, "What nation is there that has a God so great and laws so great as all this Torah which He gave to Israel?" (see Deut. 4:8).

THE SUCCESS AND FAILURE OF ANCIENT ISRAEL

The obvious failure of ancient Israel was in keeping faithful to her own covenant with God. Her fall into idolatry and paganism was the major sin of the preexilic nation. This was accompanied with laxity in regard to the feasts as well as disregard for the claims of social justice. The reestablished nation (after the Babylonian Captivity) was greatly purified of external idolatry.

The postexilic period saw a gradual movement toward externalism in religion. While Judaism without life or Spirit was never really the case, there was a definite, perceptible fall in which external legal minutiae became a prevalent misunderstanding of the Sinai revelation, especially among the Pharisees. A great number began to see Torah's instruction not as a guidance for a people who had responded to God's grace, but as a system of priestly works-righteousness by which one could earn merit to obligate God to move history toward the promised redemption. It was thought that Israel's priestly role for world redemption required a life of minute legalistic applications. A true heartfelt response to God's love and mercy, however, certainly would produce a life of obedience consistent with Torah.

These failures, in addition to a certain fixed interpretation, whereby the new revelation of Yeshua was rejected by the Jewish religious establishment—and hence the majority of the nation—demark Israel's greatest failures and have indeed undercut her role as a light to the nations as well as a kingdom of priests.

We must not simply note the failure; rather, we must understand the extent to which Israel was conditioned to perceive Messiah solely within the context of the *full revelation* of the Days of the Messiah and of a worldwide Kingdom of peace. Harsh Roman oppression caused the Israelites to yet further emphasize the political role of the Messiah on earth.

It is also important to note the successes of Israel and question whether Yeshua would have been better received in any other culture. What if He had marched to Rome? Would the Roman religious and political establishment—steeped in polytheism and crude circus entertainment—have accepted the Prince of Peace after His brief three-year ministry? Would the East, whose denial of the law of consistency (in which morality and immorality, truth and error are all part of the incomprehensible "one" in which all the contradictions of life are dissolved) have accepted Him? To the Easterners, life is but an illusion *(maya)!* Surely Israel, alone surpassed all other cultures in revelation to receive Yeshua—even to the limited extent that she did.

Scripture teaches that Yeshua's death was foreordained by God and that the sins of the whole world—including Israel's sin—placed Him on the tree. He died for the sake of Israel, that through His sacrifice we might all be redeemed (see Rom. 55:12,15).

Israel's successes are also noteworthy. Though all success is a result of God's grace, there was a sufficient response to God's grace in the nation to produce many great achievements.

Israel provided the world with its first true, monotheistic view of God. This faith, in an infinite and personal moral governor of the universe, was ultimately accepted in Israel. Because of this, Israel's history provides us with great lessons of faith—not only of failure. Examples are Joshua, the Psalms of David, the poetry of Isaiah, the hope of Jeremiah, and the amazing deliverance of Israel during the days of Hezekiah when threatened by Assyria.

After the Old Testament period (but before Yeshua), Israel still had its triumphs. The conquering Alexander the Great was so impressed by Israel's unique religion that he sought her prayers rather than her hellenization. Other rulers were not so wise as Alexander. In later times of great oppression, the faith and courage of the Maccabeus family was a light that still shines to the world. Not only did this period (166-135 B.C.E.) produce great martyrs who would not compromise their faith for a foreign-enforced idolatry, but it produced an amazing victory of deliverance from external control by God's mighty power. The "motley" Jewish forces fought with courage and gained Israel's freedom from the Syrian-Greek empire. Why? So that Israel might be true to her covenant with God!

Some years later, Pompey came to conquer Israel for Rome. He thought he would enter the Temple and find treasures of gold and silver, the secret carved images of Israel's gods. So bold was he that he would desecrate God's Temple for his own gain! He ordered the priests slain, but line after line of priests took their place to continue the ministrations of the Temple. They all died in martyrdom for God and the Torah. Pompey entered the Temple. He found no gods or treasures of great note in the Holy of Holies. He found instead, to his disgust, scrolls of the Torah. *What a crazy people,* he thought! But no, these were the people of God—unique in the world, unexplainable without God's revelation—a people without idols, but with a scroll from a God who spoke. He failed to realize that he beheld a treasure beyond the worth of gold, "More to be desired are they than gold, yea, than much fine gold: sweeter also than honey and the honeycomb" (Ps. 19:10 KJV).

It was to Israel that God's Yeshua (salvation) came. Shall we only mention the rejection, or shall we also mention those who accepted Him, the multitudes who beat their breasts and wept as he walked toward His crucifixion (see Luke 23:27)? Shall we not mention the Apostles, who spread His message beyond Israel with a zeal to spread His message to the world, *while allowing cultural freedom for non-Jewish believers in one of the most incredible decisions in the history of religion?* (See Acts 15.) And what of Paul, who spread faith in Yeshua and the God of Abraham, Isaac, and Jacob to the Gentiles? This brilliant rabbi, converted on the road to Damascus, changed the course of history. What of the myriad Jews who believed in Him and were zealous for the Law, according to Acts 21?

There are lessons to be learned from Israel's early biblical history: her faithfulness to what she perceived as God's call, her continued willingness to be martyred to "sanctify the Name" *(Kadush ha shem),* her perseverance in pogroms and persecutions—even to the reciting of the *Sh'ma* (see Deut. 6:4ff) in Hitler's death camps. The sense of community Israel built around the synagogue is a model; and the synagogue was the predecessor of the church.

We do not thereby conclude the matter of the salvation of individual Jews as if they do not need Yeshau; nor do we blunt the serious words of judgment found in the New Testament, a book written predominantly by Jews. We only say that all these faithful—Peter, Paul, James, Isaiah, Jeremiah, and Amos—were of Israel, too.

Israel maintained her identity as a nation, and God kept His promise to preserve her as a nation. Could we otherwise believe God today? Praise God for Israel! Her history—which is not yet over—continues. God shall yet demonstrate His victory over all nations through the instrument of Israel (see Zech. 12-14). Israel as a whole will accept Yeshua. Israel will be an example for the building of worldwide faith. As Paul said, her national rejection meant riches for Gentiles, who could thus accept the Gospel without the barrier of taking upon themselves Israel's calling. However, Israel's full inclusion (acceptance of Yeshua) shall yet mean life from the dead—that is the resurrection and days of the Messiah—for God's gifts and call are irrevocable (all this in Romans 11). God's intent is to preserve a unique nation, even if it is an Israel that has not yet accepted Yeshua.

Such a brief recounting of hope demands that we deal with the issue of Israel's future. What is the future that the Scriptures envision? The reader may not concur with all aspects of the following outline, but the general lines seem biblically clear.

We note that Yeshua foresaw a period during which the Good News would be preached to all nations. During this period, Israel, as a nation-state, would be scattered among the nations. The fall of Jerusalem begins this period, known as the "times of the Gentiles" or nations. In 70 C.E., Titus vividly fulfilled Yeshua's predictions—conquering Jerusalem and ending Israel's national life. Bar Kochba (the false messiah) later sought to reestablish Israel's independence, but his rebellion was an utter failure (130-135 B.C.E.). We read of this period, "They shall fall by the edge of the sword, and shall be led captive into all nations: and Jerusalem will be trodden down of the Gentiles until the times of the Gentiles be fulfilled" (Luke 21:24 KJV).

Many have understood the significance of the "times of the Gentiles" to be synonymous with the age of the Church. It is true that during this period, the Gospel "will be preached as…a testimony to the nations…then shall the end come" (see Matt. 24:14). Messianic Jews do not distinguish a Gospel of the Kingdom from the Gospel of God's grace, either; for Paul, in the Book of Acts, calls the Gospel he preaches, "the Gospel of the Kingdom." Yet it would seem that the "times of the Gentiles" has in view not the Gentile predominance in accepting the Gospel, but relates rather to the relationship of Israel as a nation among nations. Gentile means "nation" as well as non-Jew. The context is "in the times of the Gentiles," Israel ceases to exist as an independent geopolitical entity. Hence, non-Jewish nations dominate world politics.

During this period, the Gospel will indeed be offered so that a pilgrim people of faith might be established within all nations. This period is of limited duration. It is *until* the times of the Gentiles are fulfilled" (Luke 21:24). In other words, Israel again will exist as a geopolitical entity, an instrument of God's revelation and judgment that is part of her irrevocable calling and purpose (see Rom. 11:29). Many have claimed the word *fulfilled* to mean "until the full number of Gentiles accept the Gospel and come into the fold of God's people." This is very possible in Romans 11, but in Luke 21 it probably refers to relationship between Israel as a nation among the nations (Gentiles) and not of individual Gentiles and their relationship to individual Jews.

The Gentiles' time is fulfilled when evil has run its full course under the political domination of the world's principalities. This is the sense in Luke 21 of Jerusalem trodden down by the Gentiles until the times of the Gentiles are fulfilled. The parallel is God's Word concerning the Amorites (or Canaanites): Israel would be in Egyptian captivity for over 400 years. Then she would be established as a nation, a supernatural instrument for judgment upon the Canaanites. That was not to happen for some centuries: for, as God told Abraham, the iniquity of the Amorites was not yet full (see Gen. 15:16).

It is after Luke 21:24 that the apostle recounts God's wonders and judgments upon the nations. As we look down the corridors of history, we indeed see the horrors of wars and the cruelty and injustice in human governments as well as the relations between nations. Though we might be proud of our civility, it was the most "civilized" nation of the twentieth century that produced Hitler. The wrath of the nations—even to this day—has always been directed toward Israel, even though she has been scattered among all peoples. God has said of Abraham's seed, "I will bless them that bless thee: and curse them that curseth thee…" (Gen. 12:3 KJV). Surely, the nations have stored up wrath for the Day of Judgment and continue yet to do so. The recent condemnation by the United Nations of Zionism as "racism"—when Zionism is but the Jewish response to racism directed against them—is a most ironic twisting of language and understanding. The "times of the Gentiles" is most certainly close to fulfillment; they have stored up wrath for the Day of Judgment.

Where does history go from this point, now? It is in this context that we see passages of Scripture coming into play which have not yet been fulfilled. Several biblical images come together: There is the image of Israel back in the land, attacked by Gog and Magog—great and godless end-time powers of oppression. We can already see the power of Russia and Europe turned anti-Israel. Some have argued that the Gog and Magog description most clearly fits today's Middle East Islamic powers. We desire to be careful not to be overly dogmatic in seeking to linguistically prove the identity of these references.[12]

Scripture seems to foresee several great events during this time, which will usher in tribulation for the whole world. One is that 144,000 faithful Jews will be witnesses for the Good News during this period. Their witness will be a supernatural one (see Rev. 7; 14). God once again will use Israel as an instrument of His great revelation: The nations will converge upon Israel in the Battle of Armageddon. All will seem just as hopeless as when Israel stood at the edge of the sea, with Pharaoh's troops approaching. At this great moment, God Himself will fight for Israel through Yeshua. He will supernaturally defeat the nations arrayed against Israel in a victory which will make the Exodus seem pale in comparison (see Rev. 19:11-21).

This event shall issue in great repentance the whole world over. The nations are said to mourn (see Matt. 24:30), and the elect will be gathered together. Furthermore, Israel will mourn (see Zech. 12:10). The world mourns because it has rejected Yeshua. The world did not see Yeshua *as a Jew* and has rejected the chosen people or nation of Israel as well. Israel mourns as the people discover Yeshua, "whom they have pierced." The one who was thought to be the source of their persecution, thought to be an imposter, is found to be their great champion and Savior. What a day that will be! All Israel shall then be saved (see Rom. 11:26), which will bring about the resurrection of the righteous from the dead (see Rom. 11:15) and the rapture of living believers.

The Messiah with all His resurrected saints will then set up His rule over all the earth. He shall rule upon the throne of David from Jerusalem. Here is the grain of truth in the anti-Semitic lie. It is not the Jews' plot to rule the world; but Messiah Yeshua, a Jew, will rule the world from Israel. This is the underlying truth that Satan hates and fights, creating anti-Semitism to undermine this truth.

We read of many other wonderful images. One is the great brotherhood to be established between Jews and Arabs. Egypt and Assyria (Arab peoples to the northeast of Israel) will all be called God's people. All weapons will be destroyed as Isaiah said, and they shall beat their swords into plowshares. The wolf shall lie down with the lamb, and peace shall reign (see Isa. 2). The worldwide Kingdom shall recognize the Feast of Succot (see Zech. 14), sending representatives to Israel. Sabbath will also probably gain worldwide recognition, continuing into the New Heavens and the New Earth (see Isa. 63:23).

Some argue that the sacrificial system will be reestablished according to their interpretation of Ezekiel 40ff. If so, these would be memorial sacrifices to Messiah, parallel to the celebration of the Lord's—or Messiah's—Supper (communion).[13] When Messiah reigns, a whole new order will exist, certainly true to the universal principles reflected in the Mosaic constitution. But there will not be a return to the Mosaic constitution, which accommodated the needs and limitations of the people in the ancient Near East over three thousand years ago.

God indeed has a great future for Israel as a nation. But what is the role of the universal Church in all of this? Once again, our interpretation relates to Luke 21:24. Some have interpreted "until the times of the Gentiles are fulfilled" to mean that the Church Age will end and God will now work through Israel—instead of the Church. They see the Church as translated (raptured) out of the earth or removed for the seven-year period of great tribulation. We believe that this doctrine (pre-tribulation rapture) is not found in a consistent reading of the Scriptures. The "ecclesia," or congregation, of God worldwide is formed of believing Jews and non-Jews. Yeshua, in teaching His disciples throughout the Gospel accounts, relates all the signs of the endtimes to the disciples (see Mark 13; Matt. 24; Luke 21), who are obviously His followers and part of the universal people of God—as well as of Israel.

He tells His disciples "when *you* see" the various signs spoken of. When they see the fig tree come out in leaf, summer is near. The fig tree is related to Israel's destiny, but it is also a metaphor for the various signs that will take place in the end. When the disciples see these signs, their redemption draws nigh: "He is near, even at the gates." Followers of Yeshua will not suffer the wrath of God, but are warned to always be ready to endure persecution unto death. The teaching of the New Testament, then, is that the Church will continue until the end of this age in its work of saving, healing, teaching, and establishing communities of faith. The sense that the true Church will be taken out of the world, while Israel is left to suffer another great holocaust, might be a comfort to those who believe they will escape, but as Corrie ten Boom stated, it is an utterly foolish doctrine to believers all over the world who already are being tortured unto death. It is a doctrine we do not find in Scripture.

The place of the true Church in the endtimes would seem to be that of continuing its witness and supporting Israel as a nation, especially the 144,000 in God's great work of witness and revelation. God's purpose in the universal Church—and in Israel—is not at all mutually exclusive. One purpose need not work against another purpose. No. Through the universal Church, God desires a people among nations through whom He will work. Both purposes are in tandem.

The Classic Dispensational view and the view of some others on Israel and the Church is shown in the first diagram below. The second diagram below shows, as followers of Yeshua, that Jews are part of the universal people of God. Their national identity is still Israel just as a Frenchman's is France. As part of Israel, they participate in God's purposes in the nation. Hence, the relationship is not (as diagrammed) what dispensationalists describe: that one is either part of the Church, Israel, or the Gentiles.

CLASSICAL DISPENSATIONALIST VIEW:

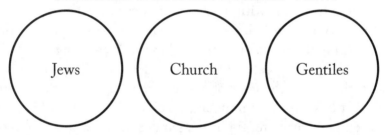

Rather, one is part of either (natural) Israel, the Gentiles, the Church, or (redeemed) Israel *and* the Church. Hence:

THE CHURCH:

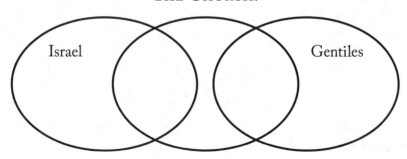

The Church is grafted into the true ancient people of God: Israel. When all Israel is saved, they will still continue as a nation, but all will be part of Yeshua's congregation too—our diagram is as follows:

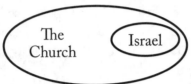

We do not accept that God's purposes for the Church ever come to an end—even temporarily—so that He might work through Israel. God has a covenant with Abraham's physical seed as well as his spiritual seed in Yeshua, and He will always work through both. God does not give the Church up for Israel or Israel for the Church. He will have mercy on all and work through both that His Kingdom might come and His will "be done in earth as it is in heaven" (Matt. 6:10 KJV). Praise His Name!

Israel's last great witness in power is crucial when we realize that most of the world has not responded to the Gospel and that that much of the world's population has not been evangelized. An intervention even greater than the Exodus is coming. No person knows the day or the hour of Yeshua's return. Although it seems to us that His return is imminent, we do not know. It could be one hundred years or more. As in the parable of the wise and foolish virgins (see Matt. 25) waiting for the bridegroom, we must be prepared for any eventuality. Our outline of the end is not at all to undercut the present responsibility of all to work for peace in the world and justice between and within nations. Neither is there any superiority to Israel's call over that of the Church. Both serve tandem, complementary purposes.

THE TORAH AND THE COVENANTS— REFLECTIONS

An outline of the relationship between the various covenants will provide an understanding of later chapters in the book.

THE ADAMIC COVENANT

The first covenant God made is often identified as the one made with Adam. Whether or not there is truly a covenant in Genesis 3, we can say that these Scriptures include God's promise to all humankind. God not only predicts the difficulties that humanity will experience after the fall, but He predicts that the seed of the woman will be bruised in the heel, but her offspring will bruise the head of the evil serpent (see Gen. 3:15). This has been taken as predictive of the Messiah Yeshua, the seed of the woman, who was indeed wounded by the evil one (the heal), but gave a crushing blow to the serpent (the head), the manifestation of Satan. We can immediately see that this promise held true: This testifies to God's faithfulness. The promise is *caught up* with the meaning of its fulfillment and its effect continues.

THE NOAHIC COVENANT

The Noahic Covenant following the flood is also a promise from God (see Gen. 9): God vows never again to destroy the earth by a flood and gives the rainbow as a sign of His covenant. He also commands humanity not to eat blood, the sacred symbol of life, as well as of sacrificial redemption. The warning against murder is also given, "whosoever sheds the blood of man, by man shall his blood be shed..." (Gen. 9:6 RSV). This covenant certainly continues in effect, for in no way does the covenant God made with humankind ever end due to God's later covenant with Israel. Nor does the New Covenant in Yeshua invalidate this earlier covenant. The rainbow still continues as a sign; God still will not destroy the earth by flood. Humanity is still expected to value life as sacred.

THE ABRAHAMIC COVENANT

We have already described the features of the Abrahamic Covenant. This Covenant is primarily one of promise. We read that "In Yeshua, all the promises of God are yea and Amen" (see 2 Cor. 1:20). God promises to make a great nation of Abraham's physical seed through whom He is going to bless the world. Furthermore, Israel, Abraham's seed, is promised the land of Israel as its everlasting possession. This covenant offered to Abraham was received by faith. Furthermore, God promised to bless those who bless Israel and to curse those who curse her. Israel, as a nation, is to be an instrument of God. Circumcision is a sign of this covenant as well as Sabbath, which was given to Israel in Exodus 20.

There is nothing to indicate that this covenant has been done away with by God. Because this covenant foresees a blessing to the nations in Yeshua, Abraham is called "the father of many nations." Hence, Paul can say of the Abrahamic Covenant, that God "preached the gospel to Abraham" (see Gal. 3:8). A careful reading of Romans 4 gives a wonderful understanding of these truths: First, the Abrahamic Covenant—so tied up with Messiah's work—was an offer of salvation to Abraham, his seed, and the world. "Abraham believed God and God accounted it to him for righteousness" (see Gen. 15:6). He (Abraham) is the father of all physical Israelites, but especially of those who are not only of the physical seed of Abraham, but who follow Abraham's faith example. This is his role as father of the nation, the *circumcised*. However, Abraham was justified (according to Gen. 15) years before he received circumcision as a sign (see Gen. 17). Hence, he is the father of those who, although uncircumcised, respond to the Good News in faith, as did Abraham (see Rom. 4; Gal. 3).

Thus, Abraham has a spiritual seed in non-Jewish believers as well. The purposes of God with the nation are never done away with because of the spiritual seed. Israel is beloved for the Father's sake in a way that is unique among the nations; she is still called elect (see Rom. 11:28-29). The Scriptures do not blur the distinction between Israel and the nations. Although there is a universal people of God—comprised of people drawn from Jewish and Gentile ranks—Scripture maintains the sense of the nation's distinct calling. (See Romans 11:29, which is crucially important.) A careful study will reveal that the terms *Jew* and *Israel* are reserved for the physical nation, also designated by circumcision.[14] Non-Jewish believers are not called spiritual Israel or spiritual Jews, but Abraham's spiritual seed or Abraham's offspring (see Rom. 4; Gal. 3:29).

Why? Because as did Abraham, they, too, have a justification from God—without circumcision. There is neither Jew nor Greek, male nor female, in the Messiah (see Gal. 3:28-29); indeed, the wall of partition precluding fellowship and mutual acceptance has been broken down. All followers of Yeshua have spiritual equality. Yet this does not do away with Israel's calling or election or her distinct purpose in God's economy as a nation among nations.

Neither do the different functions of male and female become blurred in their spiritual equality. Women will still be the child-bearers of the race; men will still perform different functions (note Ephesians 5 on marriage). The Abrahamic Covenant is one of unconditional promise. Its validity depends on—and is tied up with—the New Covenant and the sacrificial work of Yeshua. The blessing promised is only realized because of Him, but the Abrahamic Covenant in no way is done away with because of the New Covenant—which is partially envisioned in the Abrahamic Covenant.

THE MOSAIC COVENANT

The next covenant of God was given through Moses. Messianic Jews believe that there are provisions within the Mosaic Covenant that are so indissolubly tied up with the Abrahamic promises that they are practices as much tied to the Abrahamic Promise as to the Mosaic Covenant.

God promised Abraham a nation. The Exodus is the constitutive event which fulfilled that promise. Therefore, all feasts which have the Exodus in mind, as the inspiration for its celebrations, are tied to the Abrahamic Covenant; *they are celebrations of God's grace.* This is true of Passover, *Succot,* and Sabbath, all of which memorialize the distinct national history of Israel and God's fulfillment of

His promise of blessing and protection. Sabbath also recalls God's work as Creator. In Yeshua, we enter God's rest; so we celebrate Sabbath in reference to Him. The seventh-day Sabbath was not given to all nations; it was a blessing and ordinance specifically for Israel. Whenever a Jew celebrates the Sabbath, he testifies to the truth of God's Lordship over the universe (which He created in six periods, but rested in the seventh). He also testifies to God's victory over the forces of paganism in fulfilling His promise to establish Israel as a distinct nation. The Sabbath testifies to the Age to Come and the age of Sabbath rest. It is thus an eschatological proclamation.

Shavuot is a day of thanksgiving for God's agricultural blessings over the earth. It is also the festival of thanksgiving for the Word of God (in Jewish tradition) and the gift of the Holy Spirit (see Acts 2).

For a Messianic Jew, the sacrificial dimensions of each of these feasts during this age have been replaced by Yeshua's sacrifice. He is *the* center of every feast for a Messianic Jew, and we desire to show how each points to Him.

Yom Kippur is tied more to the Mosaic sacrificial system than other Levitical feasts. Yeshua is described as the high priest, the sacrifice, and the scapegoat. This day, therefore, is an especially good day of memorial, recalling His work, as well as a day of self-examination, confession, and recommitment. It is the day in which we exposit and remember how all the dimensions of the Temple system find their fulfillment in Yeshua. This holy day points forward to the cleansing of all nations. It is most appropriate, as well, to celebrate the Messiah's Supper in the bread and wine, the symbols of His body and blood, as the first meal ending the day of fasting.

A nation was promised to Abraham. A nation has a distinctive language, geographical boundaries, and a unique culture. The Jewish people's language is Hebrew; its land is Israel; and the feasts connected to the Abrahamic promises are the centers of its unique cultural inheritance of promise and blessing. All other cultural identifications other than circumcision are secondary.

The Mosaic Covenant is distinct among covenants. It was, first of all, Israel's national constitution and contains instructions for Israel's socio-judicial system as well as personal moral issues. Great prominence was also given to the religious Temple system, the most prominent features being the priesthood and the sacrifices. The New Testament period is one of transition. As such, we find Paul engaging in sacrifice to show loyalty to Israel and Torah (see Acts 21). Just how far does this loyalty go under the New Covenant? Let us note several points in this regard.

As a national constitution, the Mosaic Covenant is not now in effect. The Temple, so central to this covenant, has been destroyed. The original sacrificial dimension is, therefore, impossible to fulfill. The Aaronic identity of the priests who were essential to this constitution, similarly, can no longer be determined with certainty. As a full constitutional system—especially in the dimensions of sacrifice and priesthood—we see the truth as recorded by the writer to the Hebrews. In chapter nine he states, that in speaking of a New Covenant, the prophet Jeremiah treats the Old as near vanishing. Even then, it was growing old and passing away.

Yeshua is now our priest and sacrifice in every sense that is important. In Torah—He is the reality to which the shadows of the Temple sacrificial system points. Further, Torah applies God's principles to a people living in the Near East over three thousand years ago. They were commanded to build a fence on their roofs—because they used their flat roofs as living space—to protect human life. We must see the principle of love and protection within the command, that is the *spirit* of the Law, so we can see the applications of the Law for today.

How then shall we respond to Torah? As inspired Scripture, it is "profitable for doctrine, reproof, for correction, for instruction in righteousness" (2 Tim. 3:16 KJV). Obviously, this is a reference to the Tenach (Old Testament), because the New Testament was not yet written. Hence we must see these truths: As a constitution bound up with Temple, priesthood, and sacrifice, this (Mosaic) covenant is vanishing and becoming obsolete (see Heb. 8). Yet we should still study these aspects of Torah to enlighten us concerning the *spiritual* meaning involved in this system, as well as for a deeper understanding of Messiah's work.

The Torah presents God's universal and eternal moral standards. Once we recognize Torah's accommodations to its age (as well as keeping in mind New Testament truth), we can still be instructed by Torah as inspired Scripture. We are inspired by its commands of love toward one's neighbor, the poor, and the needy. We rejoice at its command to aid our enemy when his ox has fallen under its load: a true anticipation of Yeshua's command to love our enemies. We also recite the *Sh'ma*, that only YHWH is Lord and we are to love Him with our all. This is the greatest command of all as taught by Yeshua. The second greatest is the admonition to love our neighbor as ourselves (see Lev. 19:18). These were the foundational commands of the whole revelation in the Hebrew Scriptures. Therefore, with the psalmist we will say, "O how I love thy law! it is my meditation all the day" (Ps. 119:97 KJV).

Markus Bochmuehl of Cambridge has written an important book entitled *Jewish Law in Gentile Churches*.[15] He argues that Paul's theology reflects the distinction of the Hillel school of rabbis where Torah is seen as having two dimensions, universal ethical law for all peoples, and Jewish-specific law that is Jewish responsibility. This was later codified in the Talmud under the heading of the Noachide laws for Gentiles. His exacting study provides great confirmation for our thesis.

Nations, as well, can be instructed by the principles of business integrity, honesty, judicial wisdom, and social equality found in Torah. This is the universal dimension of Torah which shall never pass away. Yeshua taught:

> *Think not that I am come to destroy the law and the prophets: I am not come to destroy, but to fulfil.... Till heaven*

and earth pass, one jot or one tittle shall in no wise pass from the law, till all be fulfilled. Whosoever shall break one of the least of these commandments... shall be called the least in the kingdom of heaven: but whosoever shall do and teach them shall be called great in the kingdom... (Matthew 5:17-19 KJV).

We do not fulfill Torah to gain merit before God, but as those who are led by the Spirit to do God's will in response to His grace. We are to be guided by the whole counsel of the Word of God.

There is also the dimension of Torah which relates specifically to Israel's calling as a nation and its identity. As already stated, this aspect of Torah transcends the limitations of the constitution as a covenant. The feasts and other practices connected to Israel's national heritage are maintained as part of a Jewish identity and calling and connection to Abrahamic fulfillment. Some laws (such as the food lists, etc.) will be difficult to interpret as regards their present application. Are they mainly for health reasons? Are they part of the old sacrificial system (uncleanness precluded one from Temple participation)? Are they a significant part of Jewish identity today? These questions will be addressed later. People of good intentions may disagree on these points, and our freedom in Messiah on such lesser commandments should prevail. We can say, however, that rightly understood and applied by the above criteria, Jews—including followers of Yeshua—are called to maintain Torah. This is not done because of legalistic bondage; it is motivated by love and the calling to be part of Israel's national identity and is laid upon hearts by God's Spirit.

What is so exciting about the perspective we are developing is that the Scriptures are herein seen as a unified revelation; as a whole, the Scriptures are God's Word to all the people of God.

THE DAVIDIC COVENANT

The last Old Testament covenant is the Davidic Covenant, found in Second Samuel 7. This is also an unconditional covenant of promise, which remains in effect and is fulfilled in Yeshua. David is promised an everlasting throne through his descendants as well as worldwide dominion. All the Messianic prophecies concerning the everlasting rule of the Messiah are extensions of this covenant.

FOR THOSE FAMILIAR WITH DISPENSATIONAL AND COVENANT THEOLOGY

Two great theologies have predominated in the interpretation of Scripture in the Evangelical Church over the past seventy-five years. One has been called "covenant theology," the other "dispensationalism."[16] We agree with the dispensationalist view of the literal fulfillment of God's promises to Israel, including the Messiah's 1,000 year reign on earth. We find it misleading, however, to speak of the Old Testament period as the dispensation of Law and to *contrast it* with the present age as an age of grace. We agree that there is a distinction between the Mosaic covenantal government and the New Covenant government. Both, however, are covenants of grace. The Mosaic (as a national constitution) is much more concerned with judicial matters. We must not confuse the Mosaic Covenant as understood by a minority of passages in later Judaic interpretation as a system of works-righteousness. God never sought to convey, under any age, any concept other than that of salvation by grace through faith.

We might speak of the Mosaic dispensation with its system of Temple and sacrifice as a means of grace anticipating Yeshua, and contrast it with the New Covenant in Yeshua, which is our primary and sole means of entrance into God's presence. Salvation is always offered by grace in Yeshua, whether explicitly, as in the New Covenant Scriptures, or implicitly, by anticipation in the sacrificial system. We agree with the dispensationalists that each covenant should be seen as distinctive, even if intertwined with and anticipating others.

Contrary to some classical dispensationalists, Messianic Jews do not see a complete distinction between redeemed Israel and the Church; rather, we see redeemed Israel as a distinct part of the universal people of God from all ages. Furthermore, we do not perceive that Yeshua ever offered Israel the literal earthly kingdom at the time of His first coming, but then postponed it. John 6 shows that the people were only too ready to receive this literal "kingdom." Yeshua offered Israel the *spiritual* Kingdom that all might have an opportunity throughout the years to come under God's rule. Matthew 13 summarizes the nature of the Kingdom that Yeshua intended to offer. The worldwide earthly Kingdom of God will yet come as the fruition of the spiritual Kingdom when Yeshua returns. We do not find the tribulation period to be one in which the Church is removed from the earth, while Israel alone is used for God's purposes on earth. Hence, we may see a Jewish believer as both part of Israel and the universal people of God.

Covenant theologians (Reformed) also emphasize the universal dimensions of the moral law in Torah. They, too, emphasize the oneness of all God's people from all times, even seeing the saved of Israel as the "Church" in the Old Testament. Noting the graciousness of all the covenants, today's covenant theologian unifies all covenants as reflections of one universal covenant of grace. However, he sometimes goes so far in this that he misses some of the distinctions between the covenants, which are all covenants of grace. The promises to Israel are spiritualized as symbolic, and are applied to the Church. God's purpose through a nation among the nations is lost. There is no biblical reason to think that God's purpose in the Church excludes His purpose in Israel.

Most covenant theologies deny the literal reign of the Messiah on earth, which is consistently taught in Scripture (see Rev. 20; Isa. 65; 66; Amos 9; Joel 3; i.e., the Millennium). This loss of place for Israel caused the older covenant theologians of years past to think that a "Christian nation," where all citizens professed faith, could be enforced. The Church is a pilgrim people within all nations, but is not itself to directly rule the state. A state church brings oppression, for God did not call the Church to civil rule, but to be an influence as salt and light in society. Yet the Puritans of seventeenth-century America were correct to seek to base civil law and government on biblical law. The covenant theologian lost the place for Israel in God's purposes and falsely thought of the Church as a new spiritual Israel replacing ethnic Israel. We should note that the Puritans were an exception to later covenant theology and had a significant place in their theology for ethnic Israel.[17]

Replacement theology (supersessionism) is taught despite Paul's strong words concerning the gift and call of God to Israel as being irrevocable (see Rom. 11:29).

As to biblical law, the people of God should seek to influence society toward a social consensus in which biblical law has a great sway in our legal system (e.g., law based on the Judeo-Christian ethic).

We have great respect for the truths discovered by both dispensational and covenant theologians. We believe, however, that Messianic Judaism offers the opportunity of a fresh perspective, which is more comprehensive than either and maintains the best discoveries of both.

Israel's purpose remains as a test to all nations in which Jews reside.

CHAPTER TWO

ISRAEL'S CALL AND THE NEW TESTAMENT

ISRAEL'S CALL AND YESHUA

ONE OF THE MOST WONDERFUL studies that can be undertaken is that of the relationship of Yeshua to the nation of Israel. As the true representative of Israel, His life and teaching are integral to the life and heritage of the children of Jacob.

In the beginning of His ministry, Yeshua chose twelve disciples. To most observers, the twelve represent the nation of Israel with its twelve tribes. They are, therefore, representatives of Israel as well as the foundational teachers for a new universal and ingrafted people of God (see Eph. 2:20; Rom. 11:17-24).

Yeshua stated that He was sent only to the lost sheep of the house of Israel. When a Canaanite woman sought His ministry, it was only given after an amazing demonstration of tenacious faith on her part (see Matt. 10:5-8; 15:24). This was not because Yeshua lacked concern for the rest of the world, but rather because Israel was called to be a nation of priests. As a light to the world, the Israelites were to be given the opportunity to be a light in responding first to Him who was the light of the world. Indeed, as representative Israel, Yeshua is the light to the nations as predicted (see Isa.

42:1-7), but Jews who responded to Him brought that light to the Gentiles and were themselves light.

Bishop N.T. Wright is one of the finest writers on these themes and the ones that follow. He sees Yeshua bringing a Kingdom message that transcends two major tendencies in first century Judaism. The first is a trend toward violence and revolution, which he sees as including not only the Zealot parties, but some of the Shammaite Pharisees. If we revolt as part of restoring purity and faithfulness, God will put us over or reveal the Messiah to lead us to victory. The other tendency is a ghetto withdrawal as seen in some Pharisees and Essenes. In this regard, Yeshua brings a nonviolent revolution that warns against violence (he who lives by the sword will perish by the sword) and the call to turn the other cheek to the Roman oppressor. He predicts the destruction of Jerusalem as the result of the violent trends. In addition, Yeshua seeks to restore Israel as the light of the nations through His person and message. Those who follow Him become a restored Israel, living out the reality that the Kingdom has come, especially in the context of His life, death, and resurrection. However, the final end of this age still awaits His return. Wright is brilliant in his understanding of Jewish context and his writing fits what is written below. However, he lapses into replacement theology thinking that Yeshua and His band will become the ongoing meaning of Israel and replace the ethnic nation. We will respond more to this in the section on Paul.[1]

As representative Israel, Yeshua fulfills Israel's role by recapitulating its life within Himself. This is especially seen in the early chapters of Matthew's Gospel. Many have puzzled over Matthew's Old Testament quotations, i.e., "That it might be fulfilled." *Fulfillment* has meant to many that a prediction comes to pass. But this is not the meaning of *fulfill* in Matthew. When one looks up some of Matthew's quotes, there is no clear prediction. Other texts do mean that a prediction comes to pass, but with much more. If we reverse syllables of the word to—*fill-full*—we get a more adequate sense of Matthew's meaning. Matthew's sense was to bring history's redemptive meaning to its climax. To Matthew, Yeshua brought Israel's meaning to its fullest depth. He was Israel's climactic focus.

We know that fulfillment had also a broader sense than completing a clear prediction for Matthew's readers. The Qumran community that produced the Dead Sea Scrolls also sought to find a fullness of meaning in present events according to their parallels in history. Scholars call this type of interpretation "peshar."[2] Yeshua really is the climactic fullness of Israel's history as Israel's representative; the parallels of His life to Israel's illustrate the connection.

Yeshua, like Israel, is born in dangerous straits. As Pharaoh of old, Herod orders a mass annihilation of Jewish children. Like Moses, Yeshua is spared. He goes with his family to Egypt. In the words of Matthew 2:15, this was to fulfill what was spoken by the prophet: "Out of Egypt have I called my son" (KJV). The quote from Hosea 11:1, however, is not a prediction of the Messiah, but speaks of Israel's call from Egyptian bondage—Israel being God's son. The passage goes on to mention Israel's faithlessness. The more that God called, the less faithful they were. Yeshua, in contrast, is called from Egypt; He is fully faithful. He fulfills Israel's meaning as her representative. As representative Israel, Yeshua goes through the water of baptism by John. He can then bear Israel's sins and the sins of the world. Israel went through the Red Sea. In the wilderness, Yeshua is tested by Satan for forty days, a parallel to Israel's forty-year wilderness wanderings. (See Matthew 2–4 for the full accounts.) Yeshua then goes up the mountain to give the authoritative interpretation and application of the Law for the Kingdom he brought, a direct revelation, not as the *argued out* interpretations of the scribes (see Matt. 7:28). He taught with amazing authority. So also, as Moses provided manna, Yeshua provided parallel supernatural bread in the feeding of the 5,000 (see John 6). Many people expected the Messiah to be a prophet-king like Moses, who would duplicate his miracles. Hence, some sought to make Him king when they recognized the significance of His works.[3] Even beyond these great passages, Yeshua identified with Israel through its feasts and its practices and by His illustrations.

YESHUA, THE LAW, AND THE NEW COVENANT

Yeshua preached the coming of the Kingdom or New Covenant. He also taught on the Law as fitting to the New Covenant order He was establishing. Understanding Yeshua's teaching in these two areas is crucial to Messianic Judaism.

In Matthew 5–7 we have a summary of Yeshua's teaching, which centers on major aspects of the Law. It is also interesting that Matthew 5–7 has covenant features reminiscent of the Mosaic revelation.

Instead of beginning with a specific act of God's grace (e.g. the Exodus) that should cause us to respond in gratitude to the covenant teachings, Yeshua begins by promising blessing to certain people who could find a reversal of fortunes by entering into the Kingdom He was offering. Because the Kingdom has entered the earth realm, there is a great reversal. Those who are poor, mourning, or trampled upon are no longer victims. They now have the power to overcome their circumstances. Those who hunger and thirst for righteousness will find fulfillment because the Kingdom has dawned. The peacemakers will inherit the land. The pure in heart will see God. Yeshua Himself—His life, death, and resurrection—is God's act of grace that leads to a new response of faith and obedience under the New Covenant. Those who respond rightly are the truly blessed ones![4]

There then follows an exposition of Torah and a discussion of true piety and prayer. Instructions on trusting God for all our human needs are given (not laying up treasures for ourselves) as well as the example of true prayer. The section ends appropriately with *blessings and cursings* (see Matt. 7:21-27). The wise man who hears and responds obediently to Yeshua's teaching is like the man who builds his house on a rock. He will be able to withstand the storms and trials of life. The foolish man (who does not respond rightly) will be like the man who builds his life on sand. In the storms of life, he will be swept away.

These chapters are central for an understanding response to the Torah. Yeshua never confutes the intended meaning and purpose of Torah properly understood. When Yeshua, says, "It has been said...but I say unto you," His argument is with the interpretation of the Law, not the Law itself. Hence Yeshua seeks to bring out the implications of the Law in terms of its deepest intent. His emphasis is on our inner attitude or motive and not just on our external actions.

I do not find it common for Christians to embrace the utter seriousness of the background statement for Yeshua's teaching, Matthew 5:17-19, (parallel is in Luke 16:16-17):

> *Think not that I am come to destroy the law, or the prophets: I am not come to destroy but to fulfil....Till heaven and earth pass, one jot or one tittle shall in no wise pass from the law, till all be fulfilled. Whosoever therefore shall break one of these least of these commandments... shall be called the least in the kingdom of but whosoever shall do and teach them... shall be called great in the kingdom... (KJV).*

Though it seems incredible, some have actually read this passage ignoring verse 19 and have said that *fulfill* means to do away with because we now only obey the Spirit.

Others have taught that Yeshua was speaking to Jews still under the Old Testament, that Matthew 5-7 is law, not grace, but that New Covenant life is under the Spirit and not the rigidities of law.

Still others have taught that Matthew 5–7 is a Kingdom ethic for the Millennium. Yet one wonders if, in the Kingdom when Yeshua reigns, Jews will still be constrained by Roman soldiers to carry their load a mile as in the first century (see Matt. 5:41). Should they then respond by going the extra mile in the light of Yeshua's teaching! Injustice will not exist in the Millennium. Yeshua's teaching is for the present unjust age. The commandments Yeshua gave applied to His day directly.

Matthew 5–7 seeks to distill the essence of Torah insofar as it reflects God's eternal standards of love and truth. It is not the Old Testament dispensation exposited, nor the millennial ethic; it is God's Eternal Law made clear and applied to human life in this unjust world. It is clear that no one can live up to the standard Yeshua taught. Yet we only recognize our need for grace when we realize how far short we fall from God's requirement. Relaxing the Law produces the illusion of thinking we have attained righteousness by our self-effort. We would then cease to depend on God's grace in Yeshua.

Yeshua teaches that Torah is God's Word; He is not teaching the eternality of the Temple system whose demise He predicted. But *so far as the Books of Moses reflect God's Eternal Law,* they will never pass away. Until heaven and earth pass away is a way of saying until there is no human society, or never. Hence, rather than relaxing Torah, Yeshua exposits it to show the heights and depths of God's requirements in deeds, attitudes, and love so that no man will hold himself as righteous in himself.

When theologians seek to build their understanding of Biblical theology, they need to be enjoined to take every text from the whole Bible in context according to its intended meaning. There is a general consensus that Matthew was writing for Messianic Jews and perhaps even correcting some of the anti-law (antinomian) views that became rooted in the early Church through a misunderstanding of Paul. This is perhaps why Matthew emphasizes the place of the Torah in the teaching of Yeshua.[5]

Only the fruits of the Spirit can produce a likeness to the Messiah in us from "glory to glory" (2 Cor. 3) whereby we live increasingly as Matthew 5–7 teaches and as Yeshua lived. Furthermore, it is in light of the high standard here that we confess our sins and forever depend on the power of Yeshua's atonement and the Holy Spirit to produce righteousness, knowing that we are accounted righteous in Yeshua alone. Matthew 5–7 then becomes our guide under the New Covenant by the power of the Spirit.

Let us now look more closely at Yeshua's exposition, remembering that His quarrel was not with the Law, but with the misinterpretations of the Law—God's standard.

In His exposition of "You shall not kill" (see Matt. 5:21), He goes to the issue of heart attitude: The source of murder is hate in one's heart. Therefore, Yeshua teaches that anger and insult are from the same source and also bring judgment upon a person. We must not think ourselves to be pure simply because we have refrained from committing an external deed. Hence, before we bring an offering, we are to seek to be reconciled to our brother. True worship only flows from the heart that bears no bitterness and seeks reconciliation.

His exposition of the command against adultery is similar. The external act flows from a lustful heart attitude. Therefore, "... every one who looks at a woman lustfully has already committed adultery with her in his heart" (Matt. 5:28 RSV). It is that heart attitude to which we must give our attention.

Rather than allow attachment to sin to keep us from eternal life, it would be better to do away with the eye or arm, which is the organ executing the sin and hence our idolatry of the sin (see Matt. 5:29-30).

On the command to write a bill of divorce, given as an accommodation for the protection of woman and the hardness of man's heart, Yeshua reasserts God's original (Torah) standard of the lifetime commitment of marriage: "every one who divorces his wife, except on the ground of unchastety, makes her an adulteress; and whoever marries a divorced woman commits adultery" (Matt. 5:32 RSV).

In regard to the command against swearing falsely—but performing our oaths to the Lord—Yeshua goes beyond the command to the ultimate standard of God behind it. This ultimate standard is the sacredness of giving our word, the standard of honesty and truth. Hence, a man's word is to be his bond of commitment without the need to swear.

Yeshua says:

> But I say to you, Do not swear at all, either by heaven, for it is the throne of God, or by the earth for it is his footstool, or by Jerusalem for it is the city of the great King. And do not swear by your head, for you cannot make one hair white or black. Let what you say be simply "Yes" or "No"; anything more than this comes from evil (Matthew 5:34-37 RSV).

Why? Because the godly man says "yes" and his word is honest. Any need to invoke heaven or earth is extraneous to the truly righteous man.

The command of an "eye for an eye and a tooth for a tooth" was a judicial principle to guide the judges of Israel: A punishment was to fit the crime. In the ancient Near East, this limitation of vengeance respected the dignity of man. Unfortunately, some took this principle limiting revenge to be a vendetta *allowing* personal revenge. We see this in the Middle East today. One is offended or sinned against, and he can then kill the whole family of the other. To this. Yeshua responds by commanding a loving response to the enemy that reflects God's love and mercy—to turn the other cheek. Even when the hated Roman occupation troops under the law of conscription forced Jews to carry a load for one mile, their response was to take that burden an extra mile. The Torah had already taught that if your enemy's ox falls under his load, you are to go and help your enemy (see Deut. 21). This is all summed up in the command:

> You have heard that it was said, "You shall love your neighbor and hate your enemy." But I say to you, Love your

enemies and pray for those who persecute you, so that you
may be sons of your Father who is in heaven; for he makes
his sun rise on the evil and on the good and sends rain on
the just and unjust (Matthew 5:43-45 RSV).

Some have thought that this was a command against all self-defense. That is not the issue; the issue, rather, is to have love as a motive in all situations. Love may defend another or prevent evil, but the motive must be love, not selfishness. The illustrations given—turning the cheek and going the extra mile—are examples of love. Yeshua said, "You... must be perfect as your heavenly Father is perfect" (Matt. 6:48 RSV). This can only be accomplished in Him!

Yeshua also teaches on a piety that is truly godly, not an outward display for the praise of men. This involved almsgiving, fasting, and prayer, the latter exemplified by the wonderful model of prayer he taught: "Our Father who art in heaven..." The first two lines of this prayer are parallel to the Kaddish (sanctification) prayer still recited in many parts of the synagogue service. Compare the first two lines of each:

Our Father which art in heaven, Hallowed be thy name.
Thy kingdom come, thy will be done in earth, as it is in
heaven (Matthew 6:9-10 KJV).

Glorified and sanctified be God's great name in the world
which He created according to His will. May he establish
His kingdom during your days and during the life of all the
house of Israel (Kaddish).

Some scholars argue that the prayer of Yeshua was close to an abbreviated form of the great first century Jewish prayer-confession known as the *Shemoneh Esreh* or the *Amidah*.[6] This prayer is still universally in use in Synagogue worship, but with additional content.

Yeshua taught the avoidance of bondage to material things—not laying up treasures on earth—and trusting God to provide for all our needs. "Seek ye first the kingdom of God, and his righteousness; and all these things shall be added unto you" (Matt. 6:33 KJV).

Yeshua was the greatest upholder of the true nature of Torah that the world has known. He lived it! He fulfilled the Law by living it and providing a way through His sacrifice and resurrection that we might be empowered by God to live it as well!

Yeshua did have controversies with the religious leadership. Perhaps the most famous controversy was in regard to the Sabbath. Yeshua intensifies the meaning of Law by bringing out its deeper intention as opposed to the rabbinic understanding of the Law by multiplying its external requirements to protect the original command from violation (the fence around the Torah). Yeshua never invalidated the Sabbath. He taught that He was Lord of the Sabbath and that the Sabbath was made for man, not man for the Sabbath. This is clearly the implication of all the teachings in Torah about the Sabbath. Hence, Yeshua rejected the multiplication of laws defining what was and was not permitted on the Sabbath. To go through a field on Sabbath and to pick and eat the grain on the way was not harvesting to Yeshua nor work in the biblically intended sense (see Matt. 12). He invoked the example of David, who even ate the holy Temple bread in circumstances of need.

Nor was it a violation of the Sabbath to provide healing when compassion spontaneously welled up within, for this would enable another to experience Sabbath rest through the miraculous power of God's love. If circumcision was performed on the body on the Sabbath, a key covenant sign, He who had miraculous power could as well make the body whole. This was argued on the rabbinical principle, "From the minor case to the major" (see John 7).

One of the other great controversies regarded Pharisaic extensions of the Law relating to clean and unclean foods (see Lev. 11). It was held that unless one washed before meals according to ritual prescriptions, he was unclean. Galilean commoners, either uninformed or uninterested in such procedures, were considered unclean and their food unclean. Some members of the religious establishment thus despised all the *am-har-aretz,* the people of the land.

Yeshua's teaching was rejected because he was not a graduate of Pharisaic training. Yeshua taught a Torah-true spirituality which applied not only to legal scholars, but to artisans, farmers, craftsmen, and fishermen. His response was to first call into question the Pharisaic tradition as a standard of cleanliness (see Mark 7:14-23; Matt. 15). What defiles a man is not what goes into him, but what comes out. It is our corruption of heart attitude that is most serious; we must not be diverted from this main issue by questions of external cleanliness. The important issues flowing from an evil heart are "evil thoughts, fornication, theft, murder, adultery, coveting, wickedness, deceit, envy, slander, pride and foolishness. All these things come from within and they defile a man." Either Mark or an early scribe added the phrase, "Thus he declared all foods clean" (see Mark 7:21-23).

What constitutes a food? Does this mean we can now eat blood (forbidden in the Noahic Covenant) or even vermin?[7] No, because *food* is defined by the scriptural lists in Torah. To any Jew in Israel, the meaning of food was therein defined. There was no thought among any Jews of eating nonbiblical substances. Hence, in Mark 7, what God calls food is clean, whether or not rabbinical ritual and washing has been followed.

The version of Matthew 15 clarifies and interprets the meaning of Mark, "To eat with unwashed hands does not make a man unclean." The tradition of the elders was questioned, showing how sometimes this tradition contradicted Torah itself. Yeshua quoted Isaiah, who stated that they "taught as doctrines the precepts of men" (see Mark 7:6; cf. Isa. 29:13). Indeed, they rejected the intent of the command of God to maintain their tradition. The Scripture commands us to honor our fathers and our mothers, but the tradition taught that the provision that would be used to honor them could be kept back from them if it was declared "korban," dedicated to God. Thus the Word of God was voided by tradition (see Mark 7:6-13).

Yeshua's most biting criticism appears in the twenty-third chapter of Matthew, amazingly prefaced by this statement: "The scribes and the Pharisees sit on Moses' seat; so practice and observe whatever they tell you, *but not what they do...*" (Matt. 23:2-3 RSV).

They are then denounced for binding heavy burdens on men's shoulders, motivated by the desire for external show and the praise of men. The inconsistency of parts of the tradition is again demonstrated. The tradition said that if one swore by the Temple or the altar it was worthless, but to swear by the gold of the Temple or the altar, that was serious and binding.

Yeshua said,

> *You blind fools! For which is greater, the gold or the temple that has made the gold sacred?...For which is greater, the gift or the altar that makes the gift sacred? So he who swears by the altar swears by it and everything on it; and he who swears by the temple swears by it and by him who dwells in it...* (Matthew 23:17, 19-21 RSV).

This is not to cast aside the whole rabbinic tradition, but simply to question traditions or to choose between interpretations (as when He took the position of Shammai or Hillel in the debates on divorce or the resurrection, respectively). However, when tradition went against God's Word and when religious leaders missed the true essence of Torah, Yeshua was severe in His criticism. A goodly number of scholars believe that the more rigid School of Shammai dominated the first-century Pharisaic Movement. We can think that Yeshua would have been more in accord with the Hillel school, which later dominated Rabbinic Judaism after the fall of Jerusalem.[8]

Yeshua never hinted that the Torah, in its role as a reflection of God's eternal standard of righteousness, would be invalidated. He

Himself wore the fringes (of Numbers 15:37-39), and it was this religious part of the garment that the sick woman sought to touch for healing (see Matt. 9:20).

In John 5, we read of Yeshua and the Sabbath. Yeshua is the Lord of the Sabbath. He does not identify Himself as Lord of that which he seeks to abolish. In John 6, we read of Yeshua and Passover (see Lev. 23:5). The miracle of the feeding of the 5,000 recalls the Passover Feast of Unleavened Bread and the manna in the wilderness. Of course, all of the Gospels record Yeshua's last Passover Seder with His disciples. We read that Yeshua blessed the bread, possibly the *afikomen* or sacred dessert portion of the meal, and broke it as a symbol of His body broken for sin. The third cup of wine in the meal, the cup of redemption, was then made to stand for His blood, shed for the remission of sin. The Talmud enjoins that wine should be red in sacred contexts to remind us of sacrificial blood. In John's Gospel, Yeshua is the Passover lamb who takes away the sins of the world—He is slain just as the Passover lambs are slain in the Temple. And, like the Passover lamb, not one of His bones is broken (see John 19:36).

In John 7–9, the context is the Feast of *Succot* (see Lev. 23:34). On this occasion, Yeshua uses the impressive ceremonies of *Succot* recorded in the Talmud tractate *Succot* to illustrate the truths that He gives to the water of life and that He is "the light of the world." The procession carrying water from the pool of Siloam would circle the Temple and pour their libations on the altar. This was done seven times on the last day of the feast. Yeshua said,

> *If any man thirst, let him come to me, and drink. He that believeth on me, as the scripture hath said, out of his belly shall flow rivers of living water. …But this spake he of the Spirit…* (John 7:37-39 KJV).

The evening witnessed the impressive sight of the lamps being lit in the Court of the Women. Light streamed forth, illuminating the Temple with great brightness. In this context, Yeshua said, "I am the light of the world; he who follows me will not walk in darkness, but will have the light of life" (John 8:12 RSV). Yeshua is the light, which illumines our path, indicating the way to go. He is our image of what God is like and what humanity should be.[9]

John 10 mentions the Feast of Dedication (or Chanukah), a post-biblical feast which celebrated the great victory over the Syrio-Greek oppressors who desecrated the Temple in 165 BC.E. Chanukah at this time was a minor feast. In the days of the Maccabees, evil shepherds sought to compromise their religious practices with the culture of Greece in its pagan idolatry. This provided a context for Yeshua's discussion of his role as the Shepherd of His sheep.

Yeshua established the New Covenant. This is clear in Matthew 3–7, where He recapitulates the life of Moses and gives the stipulations of a new covenant.[10] Wright also points out that Yeshua recapitulates the life of David as David's greater Son. As David, he is outside of the establishment and falsely persecuted, then is finally vindicated as King.[11] The nature of this covenant only becomes clear in His death, resurrection, and ascension and the interpretation of these events by the rest of the New Testament writings. However, we see aspects of this New Covenant in other Gospel teachings. Key chapters are Matthew 13 and 16 and John 17.

Matthew 16 records the great confession of Peter that Yeshua is the Messiah, the Son of the living God. We recall that "son of God" was a title *for Israel* (see Hos. 11:1), Israel's *king representative,* and hence especially of the Messiah. At this point, Yeshua makes His great statement concerning a new worldwide movement of faith, although its extent outside of Israel may not at that time have been clear to the disciples. He says, "...Upon this rock I will build my congregation [Kahillah—original language of speech] and the gates of hell shall not prevail against it" (see Matt. 16:18).

This new movement of God worldwide must have a covenantal basis. That covenant is the New Covenant; entrance into it is through the confession of the Messiahship (Lordship) of Yeshua

though immersion in water. Its foundation is the death and resurrection of Yeshua. As seen from the rest of Matthew 16, His
Messiahship entails not only the kingly crown, but His suffering
death as a prelude to the reign of resurrection power. The New
Covenant includes the way of entrance into the presence of God
through Yeshua's atonement, the reception of the Holy Spirit and a
newly recreated human spirit (see Ezek. 36:26-27), and incorporation to the universal body of Messiah.

John 17 makes it clear that Yeshua seeks the salvation of the
world. He prays for His disciples to love one another—to be one
as He and the Father are one—and that those who believe in His
name through their witness might be one in love in the same
way. Then *shall the world* know that He was in the Father and the
Father in Him. Jochaim Jeremias brings out the universal scope
of the ministry of Yeshua in his fine little book, *Jesus' Promise to
the Nations.*[12]

Yeshua's goal is not to do away with Israel's purpose as a nation,
but to establish a worldwide spiritual Kingdom. In Matthew 13,
we find that Yeshua's intention was not to set up the worldwide
(earthly) Messianic Kingdom at that point in history, but a spiritual Kingdom under the rule of God that would spread among
all peoples. It would be a grain of mustard seed, starting from
the tiniest beginnings, but growing into a large bush. It would
be as wheat among tares or weeds. Both grow together until harvest. Any attempt to root out all the weeds before harvest would
also destroy the wheat. So, *too*, Yeshua's Kingdom would grow in
the midst of an evil society. It would itself be contaminated by it.
This Kingdom would be manifest in congregational communities
and in all spheres of life where His followers would have influence. However, at the harvest, the Messiah's return, the Kingdom
would be fully separated from evil.

Yeshua's words after His resurrection were to:

> *Go therefore and make disciples of all nations, baptizing
> them in the name of the Father, of the Son and of the Holy*

Spirit, teaching them to observe all that I have commanded you; and lo, I am with you always, to the close of the age (Matthew 28:19-20 RSV).

We note that obedience to a command is not contrary to the spirit of the Gospel!

The covenantal nature of Yeshua's work is brought out especially in the accounts of His crucifixion. When He died, the curtain of the Temple was torn in two, from top to bottom (see Matt. 27:51). The curtain separated the Holy of Holies from the rest of the Temple. Only the High Priest entered this holiest place annually, with the blood of atonement for Israel on Yom Kippur. The separation was an ever present reminder of our transgressions separating us from God's presence. The torn curtain indicated that through Yeshua's atonement, we now had entrance into God's presence. As we were in Him, the separation from God was removed.

The Temple system was central to the Mosaic Covenant. The torn Temple curtain demonstrated the reality of a new covenant and a new sacrifice superior to the old system (see Heb. 7–9). So, too, Yeshua's promise of the coming of the Spirit (in all of the Gospels as well as in Acts 1:8) is clear reference to a fulfillment of the promise of the New Covenant, which includes the promise of the Spirit in Ezekiel 36. In the midst of all this, the crucial place of the call on the nation of Israel is not lost. Luke 22:28-30 promises the disciples a place in the Kingdom, judging the twelve tribes of Israel. Judges are rulers. However, the passage in Acts 1:6-7 is even more significant. At the end of his forty-day period of post-resurrection teaching, before His ascension, the disciples ask: "Lord will you at this time restore the kingdom to Israel?" (Acts 1:6 RSV).

Yeshua replied, "It is not for you to know times or seasons which the Father has fixed by his own authority" (Acts 1:7 RSV). The disciples were clearly concerned about the literal establishment of the Kingdom of the Messiah on earth during which Yeshua would reign on the throne of David over the nation of Israel, and from Israel, over the whole world. The disciples saw themselves as part of this restoration even though they were followers of Yeshua during the *age of the universal body of the Messiah.* Hence, Jewish believers do not lose their calling to maintain their part in the call of the nation Israel. It is amazing that some read the passage as if the disciples' expectation was not valid.

It would have been so easy for Yeshua to correct His disciples' misconception, *if it was a misconception.* For forty days after His resurrection—and especially at that moment—He could have conveyed to them that this hope was a mistake of their too literal understanding of the Scriptures and that the kingdom would never be restored to Israel. But no, He indicated that this hope would come to fruition some day, but only the Father knows the *times and the seasons* during when these things would take place. Yes, the gift and call of God remain for Israel, as well as the fact that Yeshua truly established a New Covenant that would include Gentiles who responded in faith.

THE NATURE OF MESSIANIC PROPHECY

Before leaving the topic under discussion—Yeshua and the call of Israel—it would be wise to state our viewpoints concerning the nature of Messianic prophecy or those passages from the Old Testament which are usually used to "prove" that Yeshua is the Messiah.

At times, followers of Yeshua have been zealous to quote passage after passage as predicting the details of His life. Unfortunately, thoughtful people who have checked out these references claim that some do not speak of the Messiah at all, but of Israel or King David or Solomon. If what we have written heretofore is correct, the problem is not that Yeshua doesn't fulfill many predictions, but that the word *fulfill* does not always mean to resolve a prediction. It oftentimes means to fill up the meaning of Israel's history and to bring it to its epitome of meaning.[13]

We believe in Yeshua because of the reality of our faith-walk with God wherein we experience answered prayer, supernatural healing, and peace. It is the total scope of living within a worldview based on our faith in Yeshua. We not only believe in Yeshua because He fulfills the predictions, but because of the evidence that He is the representative of Israel and Israel's meaning as focused in one individual. Further, we believe because of the nature of the Gospel record of His wonderful teaching, His amazing healing ministry, and the excellent testimony to His resurrection.

We have already looked at those passages which speak of His solidarity with Israel. They are not predictions, strictly speaking, but tell of events that fill up the meaning of Israel's history in the Messiah-representative. We have looked as well at His marvelous teaching, incisive and with authority, not as the scribes. His resurrection is the best attested fact of ancient history.[14] There are several sources: the Gospels and the writings of Paul, James, Peter, John, and Jude. They all assert a real resurrection and an empty tomb. The disciples of the disciples—the early fathers of the Church from 90 c.e. through 150 c.e.—verify the testimony of the disciples as well as the fact that most of them died for this testimony of truth. These are not the stories of liars or deluded men. The disciples testified that Yeshua appeared publicly and taught, ate, and fellowshipped with them over a period of forty days before His ascension.

Those who opposed the movement only had to produce His body to end the movement. Yet, as the late great Wheaton College scholar Merril Tenney said, "Only the reality of the resurrection can explain the establishment of this movement among thousands of Jews in Jerusalem and its spread to the uttermost part of the earth."[15] No other theory does justice to all of the facts. After years of personal skepticism and searching out every angle, I can testify that this evidence now speaks more strongly than ever. Read the Gospels in an unbiased way. Who but Yeshua died as a sacrifice in love and even as He hung on the cross said, "Father forgive them for they know not what they do"? Here the depths of the love of God touched the human race.

Since my earlier days of skepticism, I have witnessed miracles of healed lives through the mighty name of Yeshua, bodies healed, the healing of inner hurts, families restored, addicts healed without withdrawal, and schizophrenia healed—all through the ministry of prayer in Yeshua's name. In the light of the whole context of Israel's purpose to be light, in the light of the fact that through Yeshua the Scriptures have spread to the non-Jewish world, in the light of all the foregoing, I can only ask, how can you not believe in Yeshua?

In addition, there are those real predictions. Only Yeshua ties together the meaning of the Scriptures and human history in a coherent way: His birth in Bethlehem was predicted (see Mic. 5:2). It was predicted (see Dan. 9:25ff) that the Messiah would be cut off before the destruction of the second Temple and then confirm a covenant to the nation. It was predicted that the New Covenant would be established and the Holy Spirit would be poured out on all flesh. This occurred as recounted in Acts 2 (see Joel 2; Ezek. 36). People from all over the Mediterranean world—Jews who spoke different languages of the countries of their habitation—came to Jerusalem for the Feast of *Shavout*. All heard the Good News of Yeshua preached in their own tongues by people who didn't even know these languages.

Isaiah 53 refers to Yeshua, His sacrifice and resurrection for us. I remember a brilliant biology professor in Chicago who came to our congregation. He had become interested in the Bible and began to teach the Tenach, after he first studied it, to Jewish people from all over the city. He had five evening classes with several rabbis in attendance. When he came to the Messianic prophecies that have been taken to refer to Yeshua, he avoided the conclusion that Yeshua was the Messiah and convinced himself of other interpretations. However, when he came to Isaiah 53, no other interpretation fit but that this passage referred to Yeshua.

In turmoil, he cancelled all his classes. Later, he became a follower of Yeshua. What was so convincing to the professor? It was a description that fit Yeshua perfectly and no one else. We do not deny the fact that Israel, also, has played a role as the suffering servant. However, as the servant songs of Isaiah progress (there are four major songs from Isaiah 40–53), the image becomes more and more focused on an individual who works as a representative of Israel. A simple reading of the chapter shows us that these texts cannot be fully applied to Israel!

> *He is despised and rejected of men; a man of sorrows, and acquainted with grief… and we* [Israel] *esteemed Him not…He was wounded for our transgressions, he was bruised for our iniquities…* (Isaiah 53:3,5 KJV).

Could it be said of Israel that "He made his grave with the wicked and with a rich man in his death"? Yet Yeshua died between the wicked and the rich man, Joseph of Arimathea, was with Him in death and buried His body. Yeshua returned from the dead, fitting the sense of this chapter also.

The Scriptures teach that Yeshua died as an atonement for our sins. This teaching grates upon modern sensibilities and pride, but is a perfectly consistent doctrine, though of great depth. How is this so? Scripture teaches the truth of our own individual responsibility for our own acts. However, it does *not* teach that we can adequately atone for our own sins. In fact, Scripture does not see men and women as separate individuals, but sees them rather in terms of their identity within the family, the nation, and the human race.

In Scripture, we are *a fallen race*. Adam died because of his sin; the whole human race dies because it is also under the power of sin through its connection to Adam. Our connection with a fallen race is part of our identity. We are considered dead to God. The Bible teaches that we are to be perfect, just as God is perfect. God is perfectly holy and cannot look upon sin without judgment. What then is the solution?

We can accept Yeshua's death for us and His resurrection and be accounted as having died in Him and been raised to new life in Him. In other words, we may change our spiritual racial descent from the fallen race of Adam by identifying with the perfect man: Yeshua. We are accepted by God in Him. We are considered as having paid the price, in Him. Biblical scholars have long known of this truth about the idea of peoples' connection to the human race and to its representatives. They have called this the concept of "corporate solidarity." When we identify with God's work in Yeshua for us and receive Him as Savior, we are recreated in the depths of the inner person. We are not fully perfect, but are given a recreated spirit (see 2 Cor. 5:17). His life is in our lives, and we are bound up with Him.

Let us note that the biblical idea of atonement is not just a concept of another person dying for our sins so we go free no matter what we do or no matter what kind of people we are. This is a common misperception. Yeshua, rather, is representative-God and representative-man. As representative-God, He demonstrates the love of God and the suffering that God Himself experiences for the human race. God suffers our every sin and pain and yet desires to forgive. This is manifested most fully at the cross. As representative-man, Yeshua, in His loving identity with us, suffers what we would not suffer. He shows fully the destructive nature of sin, which seeks to destroy Him, the perfect man. When we believe in Him, we repent of our sins and identify with Him in such a way that He lifts our burden. To be under His atonement we must be part of Him.

Yeshua is not just a separate being from us who dies in our stead. God expects us to respond to this great act of mercy, and if we do, we are under His representative cover, racially and spiritually in him. Just as Adam's sin corrupted the whole race, so the righteousness of Yeshua is now in us. In the resurrection, He will bring us to perfection. Therefore, both because He paid the price representatively and we are judged as part of Him by God (as some have said, when God looks to us, He sees the righteousness of Yeshua) and because we are now children of God headed toward perfection, God can fully accept and forgive us while yet maintaining the absolute holiness and inviolability of His Law. The Bible teaches that we have an experience of co-death and resurrection with him (see Gal. 2:20; Rom. 6:11ff).

Certainly this presentation does not begin to plumb the depths of the atonement. Yet it fits the nature of life itself. We find that children do participate in the life of their parents, but are not totally bound by their inherited tendencies. We find that people who love us suffer terribly when we sin, yet they are willing to bear the cost of our sin and forgive us when we repent. We find that when another cries and suffers with us, the burden of shame and grief is lifted.

In Yeshua, God brought these realities to bear upon the whole human race that we might have our burden lifted, that we might be forgiven and be made new creatures in Him. It is to this that the Mosaic sacrificial system of substitution points. Praise God for these wonderful truths and the power of goodness that comes into our lives by faith when we truly believe.

THE COVENANT STRUCTURE OF THE OLD AND NEW TESTAMENTS

Meridith Kline, from his studies of the covenant documents of the Torah, perceived that the whole Bible takes on the character of covenant documents.[16] The parallel structure and coherence between the Tenach (Old) and the New Covenant Scriptures is amazing! The present arrangement of the Scriptures is not accidental; it reflects that covenant structure. Even if placed in somewhat different order in the Jewish and Christian versions, the general structure of the Bible shows a very coherent character, which yields a deep sense of inspiration by the same covenant-making God.

The Tenach (or the Old Testament) begins with the Torah, the five Books of Moses. These books are the covenant foundations for all of Scripture. They record the Creation, the Fall, the Noahic Covenant, the Abrahamic Covenant, the lives of the patriarchs (who were the recipients of the Abrahamic Covenant), and the Mosaic Covenant.

Actually, four of these books are devoted to the history of the Exodus period and to the covenants and legislation, which became the foundation of life in ancient Israel. We have called this covenant material the Mosaic Covenant. Israel is the recipient of the Abrahamic and Mosaic Covenants. These documents are foundational for all future revelation, for God's character and Law are revealed in them. Furthermore, prophets are to be judged by their consistency to these Covenant documents (see Deut. 13 and 18).

Prophetic-historical books follow the Torah: Joshua, Judges, Ruth, First and Second Samuel, First and Second Kings, Ezra, Nehemiah, Esther, etc. These books are not mere history, but inspired accounts that interpret the meaning of Israel's history in the light of her responses to the Torah. As such, the books are based squarely upon Torah, as well as serving to inspire fidelity to the Torah as the covenant foundation of Israel's life.

Even the Book of Ruth shows us life among the covenant people in a personal vein. And the Book of Esther shows us the preservation of God's covenant people, as promised to Abraham. All is built squarely upon Torah.

The poetical books then follow in the Christian Bibles, but the prophets follow in the Jewish Bible. The poetic books describe the expressions of faith by a covenant people in literature, worship, and proverb. After poetry, the prophetic books follow in the Christian Bible and precede the poetry in the Jewish Bible. The role of the prophets was consistently to call Israel back to Torah. Their predictions of judgment and blessing followed from the promises and curses laid down by God in Torah (see Lev. 26). At times, their predictions were amazing, such as in the detailed fulfillments of judgment.

It was in the light of Israel's national failure that the prophets looked forward to the coming of the New Covenant. This hope was also based upon Torah truth, for the prophets looked for a way that people could both be accounted as righteous before God and empowered to perform His Law by the power of the Spirit (see Ezek. 36). The Messianic prophecies as well are coherent with the Torah. This includes the promise of worldwide blessing given through Abraham, to be fulfilled finally and most fully in the Messianic Days or the Millennial Kingdom. It also includes the need of Messiah to suffer, die, and rise again, for the whole Temple sacrificial system pointed to Him. Yeshua could well say that Moses wrote of Him and His ministry.

The New Covenant Scriptures, built upon God's revelation in the Tanach, exhibit an amazing similarity of structure. The four Gospels, parallel to Torah, are the primary covenant documents. They record the history of the One who made the covenant, as well as the foundation event of the covenant in His life, death, and resurrection. They record His words instituting the people of the New Covenant (see Matt. 16, etc.) as well as the promise of the Spirit, which is central to the New Covenant. Dr. Thomas McComiskey, in his very fine book, *Covenants of Promise*,[17] presents the relationship of the covenants. He argues that the Abrahamic Covenant is permanent, while the Mosaic Covenant is a temporary administration of the Abrahamic. It centers in Temple and sacrifice. The New Covenant is made with the Jewish people and fulfills the promise of the blessing to the nations given to Abraham. It is the permanent administration of the Abrahamic Covenant. It preserves the Jewish nation as God's elect people.

Yeshua Himself, in a sense, is our New Covenant with God, and the Gospels are the portraits of Yeshua. The Book of Acts is also a prophetic-historical book, telling us what happened among the people who accepted the New Covenant. It also interprets the implications of this New Covenant.[18] The twenty-one letters to the various New Covenant congregations parallel the writings of the prophets. They call the people to fidelity to the New Covenant in the midst of their straying and in the context of other difficulties. They apply the New Covenant and its implications to the specific situations that arise. They also have predictive sections and look forward to the return of Messiah and His reign through Israel over all the earth.

At the end of all this material is one great book of prophecy which ties together all the material of Scripture concerning the dangers of the last days, as well as the coming of the Messiah to rule and reign upon earth. This book strengthens believers in the midst of persecution by showing the ultimate Lordship of Yeshua over all the forces of evil.

The Bible is a marvelous, unified, and coherent revelation. Truly "men "spake as they were moved by the Holy Ghost" (2 Pet. 1:21 KJV). Their personalities were not violated, but they conveyed the very words God intended to communicate—whether through the dictation to Jeremiah of a "Thus saith the Lord" and, "Write these words," to the letters of Paul to his spiritual son Timothy. The Scriptures are uniquely the inspired Word of God, revealing a God who acts in history and speaks in history. God is one who seeks to redeem history as it progresses to the Age of Messiah. Indeed, the Bible is "His-story," which has no parallel in any of the religious literature of the world.

THE BOOK OF ACTS AND MESSIANIC JUDAISM

It is only in recent years that the Book of Acts has been given its due as a most significant book for our understanding of New Testament teaching. In years past, the Book of Acts was read as an exciting history of what happened during the forty or so years after Yeshua's ascension. However, when issues of doctrine were at stake, the Book of Acts was passed over and people turned instead to the epistles for answers. This was unfortunate, for the Book of Acts provides the *context* for understanding the epistles.

Furthermore, a deeper reading of the Book of Acts—the sequel to the Gospel of Luke—exhibits a selection of material and an organization that is clearly intended to bring out a more complete understanding of the movements of the followers of Yeshua. *Central to this purpose is the clarification of the relationship between Jews and Gentiles in the "kahee-lah," or Church of the Messiah.* It is now commonly recognized among biblical scholars that Luke is a writer who seeks to convey theological understanding.[19] Luke, the travel companion of Paul, researched his material well and wrote his work after most of Paul's epistles. The epistles of Paul are written for very specific situations, and a lack of understanding of those situations can cause us to generalize from the epistles in ways that illustrate poor interpretation. However, Luke's perspective is general: a summary made after the epistles were written. The perspective of his work on the issues that involve Messianic Jews will therefore be less misleading.

The Book of Acts begins with the record of Yeshua's ascension. As previously noted, the disciples are concerned about the establishment of the Kingdom on earth through Israel. Yeshua, however, reminds them to be patient and to do God's work; the times and seasons are in the hands of the Father (see Acts 1). As we concluded earlier, this passage foresees a continued purpose for the nation of Israel, as well as an eventual coming to the world of the earthly reign of the Messiah, as presaged by the prophets. However, the disciples are told to wait for the outpouring of the *"Ruach Ha-Kodesh,"* the Holy Spirit, after which they will be mighty witnesses of all that God has done through Yeshua (see Acts 1:8). Their ministry is to have worldwide dimensions, according to this passage. Yet the disciples believed that this worldwide dimension was to come by witnessing to Jews scattered all over the world. They believed that Gentiles would also respond, but they thought they would do so by turning to God at the return of the Messiah after Israel had accepted His Good News.

The account of the coming of the Spirit on the day of Shavuot (Pentecost) is one of the most amazing in all of Scripture. Remember that the 120 who were gathered in the upper room in prayer on this day were all Jews. The actual miracle probably took place at the Temple, enabling thousands to gather to them. We read that there appeared tongues of fire on each one of them, and they began to speak other languages as the Spirit gave them utterance.

We should recall that the Feast of *Shavuot* is one of the three major feasts of Israel, for which men were to travel to Jerusalem. Hence we read that devout men from every nation under heaven were dwelling in Jerusalem for the feast. This fact is incredibly overlooked: The men at the feast from all these nations were Jews, Jews who spoke the languages of the countries from which they resided. This miracle of languages points to the truth that the Good News was for every nation and tongue. Yet at that time, it was the Jews from those nations who were hearing the Good News. We read of the crowd who gathered that "they were bewildered, because each one heard them speaking in his own language." They were amazed and asked,

> *Are not all these who are speaking Galileans? And how is it that we hear, each of us in his own native language? Par'thians and Medes and E'lamites and residents of Mesopota'mia, Judea, Cappado'cia,, Pontus and Asia, Phryg'ia and Pamphyl'ia, Egypt and the parts of Libya… and visitors from Rome…we hear them telling in our own tongues the mighty works of God* (Acts 2:7-11).

It is probably true that proselytes were present on this occasion, but proselytes were converts to Judaism or would-be converts. It was Peter who stood up and gave the great interpretation of the event. His message is a ringing affirmation of the truths of the Messiah's life, death, resurrection, ascension, and return. He calls upon the people gathered to repent: The miracles during His ministry were undeniable; now Yeshua had been resurrected. Many signs and wonders were done, and those who were added to this young congregation of Yeshua-believers numbered about 3,000. A significant congregation of Jewish believers in Yeshua thus was established at Jerusalem. Their lives were changed, and there was a demonstration of love and an unparalleled sharing. They sold their possessions to meet each other's needs, broke bread in one another's homes, and enjoyed a deep fellowship and praise toward God.

The disciples—most prominently Peter and John—continued their miracle works and teaching under the power of God. Although the Jewish religious establishment sought to prohibit them and whipped them for doing so, they continued the work under obedience to the Spirit. This they considered a privilege—to suffer for Yeshua and righteousness' sake.

There are a few things to note in these chapters for our discussion: First, the number of followers swelled to over 5,000 (see Acts 4:4). Second, we note that Peter still addressed the people as "sons of the prophets and of the covenant which God gave to your fathers...to Abraham..." (Acts 3:25 RSV). The covenant with Abraham is still perfectly valid and is fulfilled and will be fulfilled in Yeshua's ministry according to Acts 3:26 and Acts 4. The story of Acts continues with the death of Ananias and Sapphira for lying to the Spirit of God about their contribution, the arrest and beating of disciples, great miracles of healing, the famous speech of Gamaliel to let the movement be, "for if it is not of God it will come to naught..." (see Acts 5:37-39).

In Acts 6, we read of the appointment of deacons to serve the congregation, thus freeing the apostles for teaching and prayer. This was occasioned by the fact that Hellenistic Jews (Greek-speaking) complained of unfair treatment toward their widows and needy in the distribution of community funds. One of the deacons appointed was Stephen.

Stephen had a powerful preaching and teaching ministry. Others hated his teaching and conspired to have Stephen arrested on trumped-up charges of blasphemy. Acts 7 records Stephen's great defense in a sermon that recounts the whole of Israel's history. At the end of his speech, Stephen made a strong accusation against his accusers, calling them stiff-necked, uncircumcised in heart and ears, resisting the Holy Spirit, and following in the tradition of those who killed the prophets. They were enraged and stoned Stephen (illegally) on the spot, but Stephen saw a vision of Yeshua and prayed for Him to receive his spirit. Saul of Tarsus, the disciple of the great Rabbi Gamaliel I, was present, consenting to his death.

In all of this, the Good News still had not spread beyond geographic Israel. The struggle was between Jews who followed Yeshua and a Jewish religious establishment dominated by the Sadducees that sought to destroy the movement. It was the persecution which followed (in Acts 8) which finally became the means of forcing the Good News out of its confinement.

As already stated, there was no sense yet that the Gospel was to be offered freely to Gentiles; the Good News was for Jews only! Chapter 8 begins the story of God's preparation for a change of understanding by spreading the Gospel to the Samaritans, the amazing conversion of Saul to the movement, and the surprising story of Peter and the conversion of the Gentile-proselyte Cornelius. This prepared the Apostles to accept a ministry to the Gentiles. The most prominent ministry was the work of Saul, the former leading persecutor of the "followers of the Way," the earliest name for believers in Yeshua (see Acts 7:58; 8:1).

Chapter 8 records Philip's preaching to the Samaritans. The response was tremendous. Many believed and were cleansed from unclean spirits; many were healed. Philip baptized them in water in the name of Yeshua, but strangely, the Holy Spirit did not come upon them. The story of Acts 8 is not an example of the way the Spirit must come to indwell a person, but is rather exceptional because these people were Samaritans. In general, people could receive the Spirit without the Apostles' laying on of hands. Unless the Apostles became the source of their receiving the Spirit, however, the conversion of the Samaritans would be suspect, for the

Samaritans were not accepted as Jews. They were considered "half-breeds" who no longer followed the truth.

Over 700 years earlier, when the Assyrians took the northern tribes captive and scattered most of them to various parts of the empire, non-Jews were settled in the region of Samaria and intermarried with the few remaining clans. Some hundred years later, when the Jews returned from the Babylonian captivity to reestablish the nation and Temple, the Samaritans, fearing the loss of their own political position, opposed them. Great hatred grew between the Jews and Samaritans. The latter worshipped at Mount Gerizim, not Jerusalem. They accepted the Torah (namely, the Books of Moses), but not the prophets, and they were accommodated to some pagan elements. Many Jewish "followers of the Way" would certainly have held that Samaritans could not accept Yeshua unless they renounced their Samaritan religion and converted to full-fledged Judaism. Peter and John laid hands upon the Samaritans, and they received the Holy Spirit with supernatural manifestations. We are not told what these manifestations were. It might have been prophecy, tongues, etc. However, it was a clear manifestation of the Spirit, and there would be no dispute from the Jerusalem Congregation as to its veracity. Yet to accept the Samaritans, who, despite their errors, had a Jewish ancestry and accepted the Torah, was quite different than accepting Gentiles (non-Jews) who were foreign and pagan.

How providential was the conversion of Saul (Acts 9)! He was a student of Gamaliel, the greatest rabbi of his day; he was a Roman citizen from Tarsus; he was a Pharisee of the Pharisees (see Phil. 3:5-6). He journeyed to Damascus with letters of authority from the Jerusalem establishment to bring the followers of "the Way" to Jerusalem to be beaten and imprisoned. It was while on the road to Damascus that he saw his great vision of Yeshua and was blinded and told to enter Damascus.

This event was truly one of the great events of history. The liberal theologians, who seek natural explanations of this event by such theories as "Paul's malaria" or "epilepsy" or "propensity to visions," are to be pitied. They ignore the rest of the story. For a disciple at Damascus named Ananias also had a vision and was told to go to the house of Judas in Damascus to find the blinded Saul. God also gave Paul another vision: to expect Ananias to come and lay hands on him to receive back his sight. Ananias was not acting out any "wish fulfillment." He didn't even know that Paul was there, but when told of his coming, he argued with God, for he had heard of Saul's great record of persecution. Then we read of the great revelation that salvation is to be offered also to the Gentiles, for God says to Ananias, "Go, for he is a chosen instrument of mine to carry my name before the Gentiles and kings and the sons of Israel, for I will show him how much he must suffer for the sake of my name" (Acts 9:15-16 RSV).

And so Ananias obeys and Saul receives his sight and is baptized, accepting his commission.

Saul now preaches the Good News in the synagogues; he escapes an attempt to kill him and seeks to join the disciples at Jerusalem, who cannot believe that he, too, is a disciple. Through the intervention of Barnabas, who recounts the story of Paul's conversion, they accept him. In danger again, Saul is sent to Tarsus. As yet, we still have only a Jewish movement for Yeshua! Acts chapter 10 is the great turning point. It is crucial for us to realize at this point that we are still reading Jewish history. Against all the prejudice of the ages, we must shout that Yeshua is the Messiah and Savior of Jewish people.

Once again, it was the supernatural work of the Spirit of God that brought the progress of the next chapters. No human intention was behind it, but the Spirit worked against the intentions and proclivities of the Apostles to bring the Gospel to the Gentiles without the restrictions of having first to become part of the call of Israel! Who was to be chosen for this work of the Spirit? None other than the burly Peter.

Once again, God's method of communication was by supernatural visions: A vision was given to Cornelius, a man who feared the God of Israel. He was told to send for Peter in Joppa. While his messengers journeyed, Peter had a vision of a sheet descending from heaven containing all kinds of non-kosher or unclean food. Yet Peter was told to kill and eat. Peter refused, protesting that he had never eaten anything unclean. God's response was, "What God has cleansed, you must not call common (Acts 10:15 RSV)."

To make a deep impression, this vision occurred three times. Some hold that God hereby signified an end of the applicability of the food lists in Torah for Jewish people. Yet we never read that Peter ate the food or thought that the vision implied anything about food laws. Instead, we read, "Peter was inwardly perplexed as to what the vision he had seen might mean..." (Acts 10:17 RSV). As Peter reflected, the messengers arrived from Cornelius in the perfect timing of God. Peter was told by the Spirit to accompany them. *The significance of the vision was that Gentiles who turn to the God of Israel in Yeshua are not to be considered unclean.*

This then is the issue of Acts: are Gentiles fully accepted by God in Yeshua without adopting the call of the nation of Israel? *It is never an issue that Jews might be called to give up their calling as part of the nation of Israel along with their practice of the Jewish-biblical-national heritage. It is assumed that they will maintain their heritage in a biblically consistent way as Jews.*

So Peter preaches the Good News to Cornelius and makes the marvelous statement, "Truly, I perceive that God shows no partiality, but in every nation anyone who fears him and does what is right is acceptable to him" (Acts 10:34-35 RSV). While Peter preached, the Spirit fell upon the listeners. The believers from among the circumcised were amazed because the Gentiles were given the gift of the Spirit! They spoke in tongues and extolled God, yet they had not become Jews! Further, the usual order of Acts 2 (repent, believe, be baptized, and receive the gift of the Holy Spirit) is reversed: Here they believe and receive the Spirit *before* baptism. Peter says, "Can anyone forbid water for baptizing these people who have received the Holy Spirit just as we have?" (Acts 10:47 RSV).

We also note the supernatural manifestation of the Spirit in this case as in Acts 8. It is completely unprompted. Again, this manifestation and the apostolic presence would be used to enable the Jerusalem disciples to accept these events. Many people in the Book of Acts believed the Gospel, but it was only in three incidents after Pentecost that the supernatural accompaniments were emphasized. In each case, it was for the purpose of enabling the disciples to overcome barriers to the acceptance of others as one in faith with them. In Acts 8, it was the Samaritans; in Acts 10, it was the Gentiles, a designation covering everyone else. Late in Acts 19, it was the exceptional group known as disciples of John the Baptist, who still existed years after the beginnings of the movement for Yeshua.

In Acts 11, Peter was questioned concerning his actions by the Jerusalem community. They asked, "Why did you go in to uncircumcised men to eat with them?" All Peter had to do was recall the supernatural work of God's Spirit, which he could not resist. Their response is recorded in verse 18.

> *When they heard this they were silenced. And they glorified God saying, "Then to the Gentiles also God has granted repentance unto life"* (RSV).

The work of God's Spirit prepared the Jerusalem leadership for a new situation which arose in Antioch: there the Good News was preached to Greeks. Previously, even those who were scattered spoke "the word to none except Jews." Hence, Barnabas was sent to Antioch, a mixed congregation of Jews and non-Jews. Barnabas then went to Tarsus and, upon finding Saul, brought him to Antioch. For one year, they taught this congregation. They also sought to exhibit unity with the Jerusalem leadership by sending aid to them (see Acts 11:29-30).

All of this led to the endeavor to spread the Good News among Gentiles. It was the ministry of Saul of Tarsus. Saul and Barnabas were called out by prophecy from the Antioch congregation in which they faithfully ministered. They embarked under the guidance of the Holy Spirit.

The ministry of Saul will be the primary focus of the Book of Acts. Who was this man, vilified by some as the adulterator of the simple truths of Yeshua's teaching, criticized as a renegade Jew, and hailed as the founder of Christianity?[20]

In Saul we find a zealous Jew, educated in the best tradition of Pharisaical (later Rabbinic) Judaism (see Phil. 3). We find a man who used the Jewish methods of reasoning in which he was so steeped. Yet we also find one who was a Roman citizen who could quote the philosophical views of his day (see Acts 17). Here was a man who could tell the Corinthians that he did not come with words of human wisdom in great oratorical power, for it was necessary that his message gain adherence by the power of the Spirit and not by human ingenuity. Perhaps the problem in seeking to understand Saul is ours, not his: a man too great for our limited understanding, with a perspective so vast that we distort it by our ability to only see certain facets of it.

Barnabas and Saul believed in a big God, big enough to reach out to the Gentiles with the Good News of Yeshua. Yet they never forgot God's chosen people of whom they were. In every town, a pattern was repeated. As they traveled from country to country, they went first to the synagogue. The synagogue had the "Torah and the Prophets," which were the source for conveying the truth of the Gospel. The response varied from town to town. Many Jews believed; many did not. However, perhaps in ways unexpected, Gentiles responded in droves:

> *The next Sabbath almost the whole city gathered together to hear the word of God. But when the Jews saw the multitudes they were filled with jealously and contradicted*

what was spoken by Paul and reviled him (Acts 13:44-45 RSV).

We must note that in those days, some schools of Judaism made it a proselytizing religion. Many Gentiles sensed the bankruptcy of pagan religion and attached themselves to the synagogue and its high view of one great God and the ethics of the Bible. Some converted, but many could not take the final step. The barrier was circumcision. Greeks looked upon this sign as barbaric, even a scandal, especially for adults. So there were the so-called "proselytes of the gate," who remained close to the synagogue, but did not become Jews.

The preaching of Paul enabled the Gentiles to be blessed by a life and fellowship with God on a high spiritual and moral plane without requiring their conversion to Judaism. This incited the Jewish synagogal leadership to jealousy, for they lost many of the "proselytes of the gate," for whom they had labored long and hard. The movement of the Gospel among the Gentiles thus dampened the prospects of adding converts to Judaism. Although the disciples in Jerusalem had rejoiced at Peter's explanation of Cornelius' conversion, the influx of Gentiles would soon require a clear and definitive decision regarding the relationship between Jewish and Gentile "followers of the Way," as well as the requirements *vis-a-vis* Judaism for the Gentiles.

Acts 15 presents the controversy that was the catalyst for a discussion on these issues. We read:

> *But some men came down from Judea and were teaching the brethren, "Unless you are circumcised according to the custom of Moses, you cannot be saved." And when Paul and Barnabas had no small dissension and debate with them, Paul and Barnabas and some of the others were appointed to go up to Jerusalem to the apostles and elders about this question...But some believers who belonged to the party of the Pharisees rose up, and said, "it is necessary to circumcise*

them and to charge them to keep the law of Moses" (Acts 15:1-2,5 RSV).

This is the story of what became known as the "Judaiz-ing" controversy. The term *Judaizing* is easily bandied about today by many who do not truly understand what the controversy. This is a sad example of human carelessness in handling the holy Word of God. What is Judaizing? Let us begin with a negative and then a positive. Negatively, according to Scripture, it should not be a term to be applied to believing Jews who maintain their practice and heritage in their call to be part of the nation of Israel. Neither does *Judaizing* refer to non-Jews who have a love and appreciation for Jewish things. As the Scriptures define it, the issue is the view that unless you are circumcised according to the custom of Moses, you cannot be saved, i.e., "It is necessary to...charge them to keep the law of Moses " (Acts 15:5).

Judaizing is any position that holds that circumcision and following the whole Law is necessary to salvation. It can also apply to the idea that the call to be a Jew places an individual on a "higher plane of spirituality" with God that is otherwise unobtainable.

The Books of Acts and Galatians are the primary sources for understanding this controversy. The former provides the broader context, the latter, a specific situation. It is the writer's view that the Book of Galatians not only was written before the Book of Acts (this being universally acknowledged), but that the book was written before the events described in Acts 15. The bases of this view are beyond the scope of this book, but can be found in several books on the date, authorship, and purpose of Galatians.[21] If this is so, the Book of Galatians reflects the situation when the apostolic authorities did as yet not settle the Judaizing controversy in the congregations. Acts 15 would then be the definitive statement of authority in regard to that controversy.

The problem in Galatians is essentially the same as the problem in Acts 14 and 15: Congregations had been terribly troubled by the teaching that circumcision was necessary for salvation. The response of Saul of Tarsus to this controversy was multifaceted.

First, there was his verbal chastisement of those who would fall away from the Gospel. The Gospel is a message of salvation by grace through faith. No human work can be a prerequisite for that salvation. Paul then went on to assert his apostleship as of equal authority to the Jerusalem Apostles, and dependent upon a direct call of God. This apostleship and the validity of the Gospel he preached were clearly recognized by the Jerusalem Apostles (see Gal. 1:11; 2:10).

If the Acts 15 decision had already transpired, it would have been strange indeed that Paul did not quote the decision, which had the backing of all the Apostles in Jerusalem, to silence the Judaizers. He did not quote it because the decision had not yet been reached. Paul then recounted history to show the truth of his position that Gentiles are saved by grace through faith, without adopting the call and life of Israel. The example from history related to Peter: For "James and Cephas and John, who were reputed to be pillars, gave to me and Barnabas the right hand of fellowship, that we should go to the Gentiles and they to the circumcised" (Gal. 2:9 RSV). (Some argue Apostles and elders affirming the Gospel he preached was the Acts 15 decision, but I do not interpret the text this way.)

The great *but* comes in verse 11, for Peter came to visit the Antioch congregation. In an incident unrecorded in the rest of Scriptures, Paul discusses a controversy he had with Peter. Peter had been willing to eat with Gentile believers but, in fear of the Judaizers, he drew back and separated himself. Paul publicly rebuked Cephas (Peter) "before them all" (Gal. 2:14 RSV). The issue is that Peter was not sincere about the Gospel. The chapter continues with Paul's rebuke:

> *"If you, though a Jew, live like a Gentile and not like a Jew, how can you compel the Gentiles to live like Jews?" We ourselves, who are Jews by birth and not Gentile*

*sinners, yet who know that a man is not justified by works
of the law, but through faith in* [Yeshua ha Masiach],
even we have believed in [Messiah Yeshua] *in order to
be justified by faith in* [Messiah], *and not by works of the
law, because by works of the law shall no one be justified*
(Galatians 2:14-16 RSV).

Some credible scholars think that works of the Law here are
not the ethical standards that are intended for all, but the markers of Jewish covenant membership, such as circumcision, Sabbath
days, and purity laws (especially food).[22]

A full exposition of Paul's view on the relationship of law,
grace, and the covenants awaits the next chapter. Here it is clear
that Paul was saying that the Judaizer's position implied that people were righteous and had status as the people of God by works
according to the Law, rather than by faith in the atonement and
resurrection of Yeshua. This was heresy.

Peter was called insincere about the Gospel because he *refused
to eat with Gentile* believers. It is crucial to understand the implications of this: To the practicing Orthodox Jew, the Gentile was
unclean. In Acts 11, Peter was first questioned as to why he would
stoop to eat with unclean Gentiles.

The uncleanness stemmed from the fact that they engaged
in all sorts of practices forbidden in the (clean-unclean) lists of
Leviticus and Deuteronomy. To touch a dead body, to eat blood,
to eat pork or shellfish, to not be purified from bodily emissions,
all made a person ritually unclean and not privileged to engage in
Temple worship or service. To maintain cleanliness, Jews would
distance themselves from Gentiles.

However, if a Gentile had accepted Yeshua, he was spiritually
clean in Him. This was the import of Peter's vision in Acts 10,
accompanied by the words, that "What God has cleansed, do not
call it unclean." If Gentiles were clean in Yeshua, then the truth
was to be reflected by eating with them. In the culture of the Near
East, table fellowship was *the* symbol of mutual acceptance and

spiritual unity. Peter's withdrawal under the pressure of the fear of man undercut the whole sense of the truth of salvation by grace and the spiritual unity of Jews and Gentiles in Yeshua.[23] Table fellowship was, therefore, a key issue in Galatians.

Paul's words to Peter were biting. He called Peter a Jew who lived like a Gentile, but who, by his actions, was hypocritically requiring Gentiles to live like Jews. The only explanation for Paul saying that Peter lived like a Gentile is by comparison to his very strict Pharisee standards. To a trained Pharisee, a Galilean fisherman would be living like a Gentile. All of the evidence of early Church history justifies the view that Peter continued his Jewish practice. Paul then goes on to say, "We who are Jews by birth and not Gentile sinners" (see Gal. 2:15). That is, we are people under God's covenant with the opportunity to live accordingly. We *are* Jews; we still have the covenant call as Jews; but we also understand justification by faith and *must not do anything to undercut it.*

There is great humor and irony in the well-trained Pharisee taking a Galilean fisherman to task for trying to appear so Jewishly kosher, when he, the trained Pharisee, undercuts Peter's whole attitude of withdrawal as contrary to the very Gospel he seeks to profess.

Paul's whole point in retelling this event is that Peter accepted the rebuke. The story provides an incident whereby all would know the Judaizing teaching was wrong, as proved by Paul's correction of Peter. If Paul had the decision of Acts 15 to go by—which he later enthusiastically communicated as an emissary of the Apostles (see Acts 15:27,30-31)—he would have simply quoted it at this time.

Therefore, it is of utmost importance to understand the implications of Acts 15 and all later passages in the Book of Acts connected with it. In Luke's account of the Acts 15 council on Judaizing, Peter is first to speak. He recalls the supernatural work of the Spirit leading to his preaching to the Gentiles in Acts 10. They were given the Spirit even though they were not Jews (see

Acts 15:8). God did not distinguish the Jew and non-Jew in regard to the gift of His Spirit. Hence, Peter speaks against any Jewish yoke for Gentile believers. Barnabas and Paul speak next. They point to God's great work among the Gentiles through their ministry. However, it is ultimately James who gives the viewpoint that becomes the definitive view of the council.

Who was this James? He was none other than the brother of Yeshua, the author of the epistle bearing his name. His name is actually Yakov, or Jacob. The testimony of history is that Jacob became a firm believer after the resurrection of Yeshua and was soon accepted into the apostolic circle. Eventually, he became leader of the Jerusalem community of Yeshua. According to Josephus and Eusebius (quoting Hegissipus), James' piety and loyalty to the Jewish biblical heritage were absolutely steadfast.[24] So much was this case that when James was murdered by the plot of the wicked high priest (a Sadducee), the Pharisees were incensed. They proceeded to agitate the people against the priest, and through their efforts, he was deposed.

Jacob's speech first recalls those Scriptures that point to the salvation of the Gentiles by the Messiah's work. He clearly has great leadership sway over the whole council, for his judgment becomes the position of the gathered council.

He says,

> *Therefore my judgment is that we should not trouble those of the Gentiles who turn to God, but should write to them to abstain from the pollutions of idols and from unchastity and from what is strangled and from blood. For from early generations Moses has had in every city those who preach him, for he is read every sabbath in the synagogues* (Acts 15:19-21 RSV).

The gathered elders then sent Paul and Barnabas, along with Judas and Silas, as witnesses from their own community with a letter recording the decision for all the congregations. The letter indicates that those who troubled them were not sent by the Jerusalem eldership. Next, the letter conveys that the decision is from the gathered assembly of elders and Apostles (see Acts 15:25). The decision is said to be the decision of the Holy Spirit (see Acts 15:28).

What exactly is the meaning of this decision? Of great note is that not a word of the decision or the discussion leading up to it questioned the propriety of Jews maintaining their call and heritage. This was never at issue in the New Testament period, but was assumed to be the natural stance of Jews.[25]

The only reason we do not find much New Testament material specifically teaching this is that it was so obviously assumed. The New Testament books were written to settle problems and controversies as they arose. Early Church history testifies that Jewish believers maintained their heritage.[26] This was so obviously accepted by all the Apostles that it was never addressed as an issue until after their death! Scholars today are beginning to perceive that the apostolic position was that Jews *should* maintain their biblical calling and heritage.

In his First Letter to the Corinthians, Paul makes his position clear.

> *Only let every one lead the life which the Lord has assigned to him, and in which God has called him. This is my rule in all the churches. Was any one at the time of his call circumcised? Let him not seek to remove the marks of circumcision...* (1 Corinthians 7:17-18 RSV).[27]

We note the same distinction in Galatians 5. Those who are circumcised are responsible for the whole Law. Therefore, Paul warns them not to be circumcised because they will have a responsibility not intended for them. In addition, their reason for doing so, to be acceptable to God, makes the salvation of Yeshua of no effect. We do think that the Torah has to be applied in a way that is fitting to the New Covenant order.

Acts 21 is Luke's key chapter for applying the decision to Jews. As for Gentile believers, they are given the direction to "abstain from the pollutions of idols and from unchastity and from what is strangled and from blood" (see Acts 15:29). We recognize here one of the historic Jewish positions: A Gentile who is to be accepted as righteous must follow the Noahic Covenant. That covenant (in Genesis 9), universal for all humankind, was interpreted as forbidding idolatry, immorality, and the eating of blood. Hence, James is affirming the fact that Gentiles can be in Messiah without becoming Jews and are spiritually one with the community of faith. Yet those basic stipulations would be certainly followed by anyone in the Messiah. These fit what later became known in Rabbinic Judaism as part of the Noahic commandments for all peoples. Acts 15 affirmed the basic moral dimensions of the Law as universally applicable as well as the sanctity of blood. It is not saying that people can murder, steal, or dishonor their parents. This was understood and assumed.

It is also of note that this is the minimum standard for Jews and Gentiles to achieve table fellowship, that great symbol of spiritual unity. Table fellowship in the early communities of Yeshua was celebrated with the Messiah's Supper *(Shulhan Adonai)*, thus making mutual acceptance through a common meal crucially significant.

Jews, by implication, would have to lower their standards of rigorous Pharasaic ritual cleanliness to maintain such fellowship, whereas Gentiles would avoid grossly offensive practices in regard to eating things forbidden in Leviticus 11. (See Romans 14 on the principle of mutual love in non-biblically binding standards.) The interesting statement of Acts 15:21 is also significant: "For from early generations Moses has had in every city those who preach him, for he is read every sabbath in the synagogues" (RSV). Jacob here is saying that the testimony to what Gentiles must do to be in relationship to the Jews is taught in the synagogues of the Diaspora. Gentiles may also learn more about Jewish roots for their understanding. However, this does not imply that they are called to grow into living a more Jewish life. The job of the Apostles is to spread the Good News of Yeshua without any barriers of culture or national calling standing in the way of its acceptance.

Acts 21 is commentary on this decision. It is a most crucially important passage in the New Testament for gaining an understanding of the Apostolic position on the practice of Jewish believers. *It reflects what was the assumed stance of the Apostles and makes what was only implicit in the New Testament explicit.*

In Acts 21, Paul travels to Jerusalem. He goes with prophetic warnings of danger to his life, but is constrained in spirit to go.

When Paul arrives in Jerusalem, we read that the brethren "received him gladly" (Acts 21:17). The next day, Paul meets with Jacob (James), who formulated the Acts 15 statement regarding Judaizing, and all the elders. After Paul testified of God's mighty work among the Gentiles, those gathered "glorified God." However, a problem had arisen:

> *...And they said to him, "You see brother how many thousands there are among the Jews of those who have believed; they are all zealous for the law, and they have been told about you that you teach all the Jews who are among the Gentiles to forsake Moses, telling them not to circumcise their children or observe the customs"* (Acts 21:20-21 RSV).

The Good News had greatly spread in the Jerusalem area. The Greek word is that there were myriads that believed. They were all zealous for the Law.

Paul, at this point, had an opportunity to admit that he did teach Jews to forsake Moses and to not circumcise. Luke's purpose in this passage is clearly to show that Paul was loyal to his heritage and that his later arrest was unfair in the light of this loyalty. The advice Paul is given is to purify himself with four men under a Nazarite vow. This was a special vow taken for service to God during which the person neither drank wine nor cut his hair.

Paul was to take the men, purify himself with them, and pay their expenses for offerings. In the words of the chapter, the purpose is, "Thus all will know that there is nothing in what they have been told about you, but that you yourself live in observance of the law" (Acts 21:24 RSV).

Clearly, the facts as the elders knew them testified that Paul lived in observance of the Law. That he taught Jews to forsake their observance was considered a vicious rumor: "there is *nothing* in what has been told about you..." (Acts 21:24 RSV).

There is no argument; Paul does exactly as advised. However, he is later arrested due to the force of the rumor anyway.[28]

It has been argued that Paul compromised under pressure. Did Jacob also compromise? He gave us the Book of James (Jacob) and maintained his observance until his death. If Paul compromised, why is there no hint of it in the text? Why is Luke so misleading? Did the same Paul who was stoned and whipped for the Gospel—who went up to Jerusalem knowing that he would be arrested—compromise at this point? It is so out of character that it is an unacceptable conclusion. Further, Luke, in the same passage, notes that the elders recalled their decision in regard to Gentile freedom.

> *But as for the Gentiles who have believed, we have sent a letter with our judgment that they should abstain from what has been sacrificed to idols, and from blood, and from what is strangled, and from unchastity* (Acts 21:25 RSV).

Why is this passage included? It is so we will understand that Paul's maintaining his heritage was not a compromise of the principal freedom in the Gospel laid down in Acts 15. No! Paul did not compromise! Luke is clearly revealing the difference of calling in one universal body of faith: Jews are part of the call and identity of the nation Israel, whereas Gentiles are free from this call. The view that Paul compromised at this point in his life is given its death sentence in Acts 18:18 where we read, "At Cenchreae he cut his hair, for he had a vow" RSV. The vow related to cutting the hair was a Nazarite vow based on the Torah (see Num. 6). It was the same vow that was taken by the four men in Acts 21!

Here, Paul observes the Law with no external pressure. Furthermore, we find indications of such observance throughout Paul's whole life. Clearly his epistles must be interpreted in this context:

- ❖ In Acts 15:22, Paul agrees to carry out the decision of the apostles, which allows full Torah identity for Jews.

- ❖ In Acts 16:3, we find Paul in the synagogue on the Sabbath *as was his practice.*

- ❖ In Acts 20:16, we see Paul hastening to be at Jerusalem for *Shavuot* (Pentecost). This was one of three major feasts wherein Jewish people were commanded to appear before God in Jerusalem.

- ❖ In Acts 22:3,12, Paul defends himself as having done nothing against the Law.

- ❖ In Acts 23:1-5, he quotes the Law in response to his own necessity of respecting rulers—even the high priest.

- ❖ In Acts 24:11-17, Paul argues that his accusers are angry with him due to his belief in the resurrection. He recounts his Acts 21 action as part of maintaining a clear conscience of witness before men (see Acts 24:17).

- ❖ In Acts 25:8, he says, "Neither against the law of the Jews, nor against the temple...have I offended at all" (RSV).

- ❖ In Acts 26:5-8, Paul testifies that he has lived as a strict Pharisee with no qualification stated in regard to recent practice or change of commitment. In Acts 26:19-20, Paul said he called for deeds worthy of repentance. This is strictly Jewish phrasing.

❖ Acts 28:17 is a real clincher. Paul says to the Jews in Rome, "Brethren, though I had done *nothing against the people or the customs of our fathers,* yet I was delivered prisoner..." (RSV).

The conclusion becomes inescapable: the evaluation of the elders concerning Paul was absolutely correct; there was nothing to the rumor that had been spread about him.[29]

There are many biblical scholars who have recognized this truth. H.L. Ellison states that to be part of his nation, Paul would have worn the fringes of Judaism,[30] which were memory aids to recall our responsibility to live according to Torah. So also J.H. Yoder, who states that Paul's concern *was not* with Jewish loyalty to the Law for he himself conformed to the Law.[31] The most stirring statement comes in the classic work of W.D. Davies, *Paul and Rabbinic Judaism.*

> We begin with the significant fact that throughout his life Paul was a practicing Jew who never ceased to insist that his Gospel was first to the Jews, who also expected Jewish Christians to persist in their loyalty to the Torah of Judaism, and who assigned to the Jews in the Christian no less than in the pre-Christian dispensation a place of peculiar importance.[32]

The conclusion of this chapter on the Book of Acts is clearly to support the thesis of this book as a whole, namely that Jews under the New Covenant are still called to maintain their historic national identity as part of Israel. Being part of the universal body does not remove the specific expression of that salvation in a way that befits the call to be a part of the nation of Israel in its distinctive task of witness. Many believers have diverse calls to different nations and cultures. The call to Israel is valid.

In addition, we must express our belief that the Apostles are our authorities in doctrine by their teaching *and example.* We cannot, as Karl Barth said, look over their shoulders and correct their notebooks. If they, including Paul, maintained their Jewish practice and identity, that settles the issue for us. They did! Even Paul, the Apostle to the Gentiles, maintained his Jewish practice and identity as did the disciples of the disciples, the Nazarenes or Followers of the Way. Praise God for the revelation of His truth. We should note the distortion in scholarship in calling these Messianic Jews Christians. We have no evidence that this was their term for themselves. Messianic Jews would be a much more fitting designation.

We then continue our practice, knowing that Yeshua is the One to whom all things point. All is done with an eye to its fulfillment in Him. And ours is a rich heritage of the acts of God, rooted in history, exemplified by the Apostles, and full of God's grace, a witness to the world of God's faithfulness to Israel and all the children of God.

CHAPTER THREE

PAUL, ISRAEL, AND THE LAW

I N ALL OF SCRIPTURE, THERE is no greater theological depth than in Paul's teaching on Yeshua, Israel, and the Law. This teaching is central to the meaning of the Good News itself. Yet, how tragically this teaching is misunderstood, both by Yeshua's followers and those who do not follow Him. The error is usually one of carelessness. A verse is taken out of context and false conclusions are drawn, when the true meaning of the verse can be seen only in the light of Paul's *whole* connected presentation. Further, various meanings of the word *law* or *nomos* are not distinguished; all are lumped together. Yet, in everyday speech, we know one word may carry several meanings according to the context of usage. In addition, there are plays on words, so loved by Jewish thinkers, but totally missed by the modern reader. We believe that Paul's teaching is thoroughly in line with his profession and example in the Book of Acts and fully in accord with Messianic Judaism.

Any teaching on Paul and the Law must take note of his key foundational statements in relation to Torah as God's revelation, as well as a reflection of His eternal standard of right and wrong. So far as the Law reflects this eternal standard of God, it is irrevocable. As such, we should note these verses:

❖ Romans 3:31—faith establishes the Law. "Do we then overthrow the law by this faith? By no means! On the contrary, we uphold the law" (RSV).

❖ Romans 3:2 states that the Law is a gift of God.

❖ Romans 3:7 teaches that the Law defines what sin is, while Romans 6:1-2 says we are not to continue to sin.

❖ Romans 7:12 states that the Law is holy. "The commandment is holy and just and good" (RSV).

❖ Romans 7:14 states that the Law is spiritual; Romans 7:16 says that the Law is good.

In the Law, the great wisdom of God's standards is revealed. Only the Bible reveals an infinite, personal, *ethical* God!

Paul certainly had the Law in mind when he said,

> ***All Scripture*** *is given by inspiration of God and is profitable for teaching, for reproof, for correction, and for training in righteousness that the man of God may be complete, equipped for every good work* (2 Timothy 3:16-17 RSV).

This verse was written before the New Testament came into being. The Torah is to be a source of our correction and training. As Paul said, the Law is good if one uses it rightly (see 1 Tim. 1:8-11).

Paul also quoted the Law to give ethical direction to congregations under the Spirit. In Ephesians 6:1-3, he writes:

> *Children, obey your parents in the Lord, for this is right. Honor your father and mother (this is the first commandment with a promise), that it may be well with you and that you may live long on the earth* (RSV).

Paul takes it that the promises of Torah will apply to them who obey.

Paul also maintained the validity of the Law as uniquely related to Israel's continuing religious national identity and special witness as a people as noted in our exposition of Acts.

Then what is the problem? Is it that there are passages in Paul addressed to the misuse of the Law, which are interpreted to invalidate the Law itself? Is it that there are uses of the word *law* that do not refer to the revelation in Torah, but are, instead, false applications of it?

The major concern of Paul's writings is in regard to the wrong use of the Law is as part of a system of works-righteousness. According to this system, man stores up merits before God by keeping the Law, i.e., earning God's acceptance and salvation. Such a view produces hypocrisy, since the person with such a view does not see how much he breaks the Law, though professing to keep it. It also produces self-righteous pride. The exposure of the wrongness of this view is critical. We must first see that God's standard is absolute holiness and perfection. Falling short of this, we stand condemned by the Law before a holy God. Paul quotes a medley of passages from the Psalms and Prophets to show God's view of *our self-righteousness*—from Psalm 53:3, "There is none that doeth good, no, not one" (KJV). "They have all fallen away...all alike depraved" (RSV). Paul's conclusion is, "All have sinned and fall short of the glory of God" (Rom. 3:23), and "The wages of sin is death," spiritual separation from God (Rom. 6:23).

A recent book by Professor Stanley Stowers of Brown University gives a very profound exposition.[1] Paul's central concern is how people can find transformation and can overcome sin. In Greek thought, the study of ethics and philosophy was thought to provide deliverance. The Jewish response to such Greek Stoic views was to assert that the study of Torah would provide deliverance. While the Law still has an important place in Paul, the center of his theology is identification with the death and resurrection of Yeshua that begins with water immersion. Transformation is a supernatural transaction. We could call Paul's theology the *theology of supernatural transformation through identification with Messiah*.

Some think we can earn God's righteousness because we tend to compare our achievements with others, not God's absolute holy perfection and standard of total love and selflessness (see Deut.

6:4; Lev. 19:18). We may seem miles ahead of others, but are still light-years away from real perfection when we examine our heart attitudes and motives. Our self-righteousness further calls into question whether we are really ahead of others at all. Before God's Law, we all stand condemned, not justified.

There is within us a nature that desires to break the Law, to sin; it is called a sin nature. The rabbis perceived this in their doctrine of the *"Yetzer ha ra,"* the evil impulse. This sin nature is such that the Law may even inspire us to desire to sin more since sin finds the forbidden fruits sweeter. This is a principle that Paul also calls a law, making a "play on words" with *nomos* or *law*. It is a law within me (*law* used in a different sense than Torah) that when I want to do right, evil lies close at hand. To eliminate misunderstanding, Paul, in this same chapter, calls *the Law* (Torah) "holy, just, good" and "spiritual," which of course is not the case with the law (principle) "that evil lies close at hand."

These facts evoke two other principles also called law in a play on words; *again, they are not the Torah*. They are the laws of sin and death. The law of sin is the principle that God's holy righteous Law is more a source of temptation to fallen man than a source of righteous motivation. This is not because of any fault in the Law, but because of sin's nature.

"But sin, finding opportunity in the commandment, wrought in me all kinds of covetousness" (Rom. 7:8 RSV). The weakness of the Law is not its high standard, but that it is powerless to cause the sinful man to fulfill it. "For we know that the law is spiritual: but I am carnal, sold under sin" (Rom. 7:14 KJV). The law is "weakened by the flesh" (Rom. 8:3 RSV). So Paul says, "I see in my members another law at war with the law of my mind and making me captive to the law of sin which dwells in my members" (Rom. 7:23 RSV).

Breaking the Law leads to greater bondage, to more law-breaking and sin. The pervert, for example, holds that one more indulgence of curiosity will assuage his desires. This is so, but only temporarily. Later temptations are stronger and even grosser. The liar, the drunkard, the thief, and the glutton all find a similar operation of sin in their lives!

This law of sin leads to death, in all its ramifications. The law of death is the law of the wages of law-breaking, separation from fellowship with God, physical death and, finally, eternal death.

What an incredible tragedy that some think the law of "sin and death" is the Torah! How unfortunate this false interpretation!

As John said, "Sin is the transgression of Law" (see 1 John 3:4 KJV); in Paul's words, "Where there is no law there is no transgression" (Rom 4:15). All, therefore, stand "guilty."

Paul's central question is: How then shall we stand as righteous, not guilty, or justified before God? He finds his solution in Abraham: According to Genesis 15:6, Abraham believed God and God accounted it to him for righteousness. Abraham was justified by faith! Only years later did he receive the sign of circumcision as the sign of his covenant relationship with God (see Rom. 4:12). We do have to add the fact that it is not faith in faith, but a faith response that connects us to the death and resurrection of Yeshua. We die in Him and are raised with Him. It is a real experience (see Rom. 6:11).

In Galatians, Paul argues that any interpretation of the Mosaic revelation must be based on the foundational revelation of the Abrahamic Covenant. The Mosaic Law, which came 430 years later, "does not annul a covenant previously ratified by God, so as to make the promise void" (Gal. 3:17 RSV). Paul is not, as some think, pitting the Mosaic revelation against the Abrahamic. They have different but complementary purposes. "Is the law then against the promises of God? Certainly *not...*" (Gal. 3:21 RSV).

Paul next asserts that we can be accepted as righteous before God by faith, by believing in Yeshua's life, death, and resurrection. Combining the truths of the old sacrificial images and of the teaching on Abraham, Paul argues as follows: As Adam (and all humanity) fell and became *a fallen, sinful race,* so there is a new humanity in Yeshua. We, by faith, must recognize that He died for our sin. He is the representative of the race, and the race is tied together into one human family. Our reality is not only our separate, individual selfhood, but the reality of the whole inter-connectedness of the race.[2] In identity with us, the sinless One pays our penalty. He also exhibits the suffering love and mercy of God and reveals the destructive nature of sin that seeks to annihi-late the one righteous and perfect man. His sacrifice was accepted, and He arose from the dead. By faith, we accept these truths. By faith, we are accounted as "in Messiah." These words, *in Messiah*, are perhaps the two most significant words in the New Testament. We are part of His reality now. By faith we are given a new nature of righteousness (see 2 Cor. 5:17) and are given the Spirit of God to dwell within as promised in Jeremiah 31 and Ezekiel 36. We are not guilty, but are justified in Him by faith. Galatians 2:20, the central verse that is parallel to Romans 6:11, says that we have been crucified with the Messiah but "never the less we live."

So Paul can quote David, who was not justified by the Law, but by God's mercy and grace: "Blessed is the man to whom the Lord reckons no sin" (see Ps. 32:2). "Wash me thoroughly from my iniquity and cleanse me from my sin!" (Ps. 51:2 RSV).

The believer now has supernatural power in identifying with His atonement, which puts sin to death as he prayerfully applies its power, and in the new nature or spirit he is given, and lastly by the power of the Spirit, which motivates him and enables him to do God's will. His eternal fate is sealed; he is righteous *in Messiah* and has eternal life. Progressively, this life works itself out into daily growth so he becomes more like the Messiah.

Now, what is the relationship of the Law to all of this? First, we no longer turn to the Law, seeking to find intrinsic righteous-ness by keeping it. To the whole legalistic preoccupation with the Law, we have died in the Messiah. Paul gives the example of a woman whose spouse's death has freed her from the legal bondage of the marriage. We have died to the Law (see Rom. 7:4) in the sense that there is no longer a penalty to be paid or legal bondage. Our primary focus now is on the power of the Spirit and His love working in a life lived according to the law of love. Paul may also be indicating here that we now relate to the Torah by applying it as fitting to the New Covenant Order and are not under the Mosaic Covenant with its sacrifices as our primary covenant of relationship to God. This fits the idea of New Covenant Judaism and Jeremiah 31:31ff.

A new perspective on the Book of Galatians may also be helpful. Writers such as N.T. Wright and James Dunn have argued that "works of the law" did not refer to the Law in its dimensions of universal moral standard, which as Wright says, is the implication of Galatians 5. Rather, the "works of the law" were those specific markers that distinguished the Jewish people as an ethnic group. The new evaluation of Judaism in the first century since E.P. Sanders argues that Judaism did not teach that one must earn salvation by good works. Rather, one was in the covenant by God's grace. Then one was expected to live an obedient life to maintain one's place in the covenant. The Jewish markers part of the Law, however, were interpreted as important for people to be declared righteous in the sense that they are part of the people of God. The understanding is based both on the law court and the covenant with God. What is required for God to declare one as righteous and part of the people of God? The circumcision party argued that circumcision to enter the covenant and then intending to keep the whole law was required. Jews were already the people of God in this orientation. With the coming of the New Covenant, the primary mark of the people of God is faith in the death and resurrection of Yeshua, and I might add, His transformation of the person. Jewish markers may still determine that one is ethnically Jewish, but no longer mark those who are God's people from those who are not. The argument that this was the issue of Galatians and not works-righteousness in its traditional sense is convincing.[3] We should note that Wright does not value the markers as continuing points of ethnic identity in Jewish calling. We disagree. However, there now is to be full table fellowship between Jew and Gentile. On the other hand, the exposition of sin and righteousness in Romans fits the idea of the danger of earning righteous status so I do not think this idea can be dismissed. Perhaps both ideas are involved in Paul's thinking.

If love is real and not mere sentiment, then the Law makes its reappearance as a guide and teacher under the power of the Spirit. Without Law, love has no structure and slips into humanistic sentiment. Love must be guided by law. Without the power of the Spirit and the power of the atonement of Yeshua as our focus of dependence, our old nature shall reassert itself. This is also the case with the mistaken focus on the over 1,000 commands in the New Testament, which can also become a focus of works-righteousness.[4]

The Law will now be kept progressively in Spirit and truth in response to God's mercy and grace. The whole Bible, including the Mosaic Law rightly applied, will be our guide, "profitable for doctrine, reproof and training in righteousness" (see 2 Tim. 3:16). The reformers rightly perceived the important use of the Law as a guide, as well as a standard by which we are convicted by the Spirit "to continually confess our sins and find forgiveness." They call this the third use of the Law.[5] The Law is a mirror for seeing the blemishes of your life; Yeshua is the living Torah. Hence, the Reformed Christians found no conflict parallel to the conflict of today's misinformed Christians in reciting, "Oh, how I love thy law!" (Ps. 119:97 RSV).

This view of Law and grace may seem paradoxical, but when understood, it is certainly consistent and full of depth and truth. Even psychologists have learned that on a human level, acceptance and forgiveness must precede obedience. Forgiveness and acceptance by grace thereby become the motive for obedience.[6] This is our focus; this is the emphasis of all Scripture; "I am the Lord thy God which brought you out of the land of Egypt [by grace]" (see Exod. 20:2). Therefore, "You shall have no other gods before me"

(Exod. 20:3). To think we can earn God's love and salvation is an affront to His holiness.

The confusion comes also from those who say that salvation by grace through faith will lead to a moral laxity. This shows a superficial understanding of grace, indeed. For the acceptance of God's grace is the acceptance of a new nature that wants to obey God, and the acceptance of God's own Spirit, who Ezekiel said would dwell in our new spirit, causing us "to walk in" God's "statutes" (Ezek. 36:27 KJV). Paul also had to answer the foolish arguments of those who did not understand, of those who said we could "continue to sin that grace might abound." If we have living faith and love for God, we can respond as Paul did: "How can we who died to sin still live in it?" (Rom. 6:2 RSV). There are a few phrases that tend to cause confusion, but with a little prayerful thought they become clear. One we cover here: "For sin will have no dominion over you, since you are not under the law but under grace. What then? Are we to sin because we are not under law but under grace? By no means" (Rom. 6:14-15 RSV).

Again, some take the phrase "not under law but under grace" to imply that we have no relationship to Law or Torah. This cannot be in the light of Second Timothy 3:16-17 and all the other verses we have previously recorded. The context gives the solution. The key word is *under*. The Law is no longer a tyrant of condemnation to us. We are not *under* the *condemnation* of the Law. We are not in bondage and fear, seeking to obey the Law through our own power as a way to please God, which is impossible. This becomes clear if we substitute Paul's own definition of sin, since the Law defines sin—"Therefore by the deeds of the law there shall no flesh be justified in his sight: for by the law is the knowledge of sin" (Rom. 3:20 KJV)—or, as John and James say, "sin is the transgression of law," or law-breaking (see 1 John 3:4 KJV; James 2:8-10). If Law is a euphemism for the Mosaic Covenant, Paul could also be saying that we are under the New Covenant order of Yeshua where all must be reapplied.

125

Let us then paraphrase: For law-breaking will no longer have dominion over you since you are not under the condemnation of the law or a system of works righteousness, but under grace. What then? Are we to "break the Law" because we are not *under* law but under grace? By no means (see Rom. 6:14-15).

It is the same teaching as in Ephesians 2:8-10.

> *For by grace you have been saved through faith, and that not of yourselves; it is the gift of God, not of works lest anyone should boast. For we are his workmanship, created in* [Messiah Yeshua], *for good works, which God prepared beforehand that we should walk in them* (NKJV).

And in Titus 3:5, "Not by works of righteousness which we have done, but *according to his mercy he saved us,* by the washing of regeneration and renewing of the Holy Ghost..." (KJV).

Often we hear Romans 10:4 quoted out of context as well. "For Messiah is the end of the law..." The word here is *telos,* which is *end* in the sense of goal or purpose. Many have pointed out that the word *telos* does not in this context mean the end in the sense of the finish or abolition of something. What does it mean to say that Yeshua is the *telos* of the Law?

In Romans 9:31, Paul says the problem is not that Israel pursued the Law, but that "they did not pursue it through faith, but as if it were based on works..." (RSV). Israel's problem was not that they pursued the Law, but *the way* they pursued the Law. In context, Messiah is *telos* in these senses. Again, some of the new perspective on Paul writers here believe that the issue was not works-righteousness, but that Israel pursued their distinctive ethnicity to have status as God's people in a way that thwarted the fulfillment of their calling as a witness to the nations.

Yeshua is the personal embodiment of a human life lived in spirit and truth according to Torah standards. He is the living Torah. He is the goal of Torah, the perfect life to which holy standard and sacrificial system had pointed. He is the finisher of the misuse of Torah as a system of works-righteousness, whether as the superior status of a people or of a personal earning righteousness. When we believe in His sacrifice, we understand the true purpose of the Law was never to be a system of merits by works. The *telos* of the Law leads us to embrace transformation by identification with Messiah.

The *telos* of the Law, however, does not mean doing away with the Law as a moral standard since the cardinal rule for interpreting Scripture is that the true meaning of a passage must always be understood both in the original intent of the passage and in the light of the whole of the Bible! *Scripture is a consistent revelation* from the infinite personal God of the universe.

I believe that we shall find Scripture to bear out this exposition. Salvation is "by grace through faith" indeed! Yet God is a God of law, of principles upon which basis the universe rests. God Himself could save us and yet be righteous according to His own standard of justice only by the righteousness of the Messiah and His death for our sins. We are counted as righteous in Him (see Rom. 3:26).

So we also hope with the prophet, "For out of Zion shall go forth the law, and the word of the Lord from Jerusalem" (Isa. 2:3 RSV).

PAUL AND ISRAEL

The preoccupation of much religious preaching today is personal peace and happiness. The desire for God is really that He might make us happy. Fellowship with God is the greatest joy and treasure to be enjoyed by human beings. However, God desires us to lose our self-preoccupation and be enveloped in prayerful intercession for the salvation of the world. Every person won by the Good News or by the coming of God's Kingdom to earth through the reign of the Messiah Yeshua in us is a fulfillment of God's real goal and burden on our hearts. Therefore, God seeks to have us fulfill this burden in our own witness and prayer for our immediate contacts—neighborhood and city. If our hearts are knit with Him we shall also *hear* the Word, "God so loved the world" (John 3:16).

Great saints have at times understood that the full coming of God's Kingdom and the hope of every creature hearing the Good News are tied up with God's purpose of manifesting Himself through Israel. Thus, Rees Howells interceded and prevailed after years of prayer for the state of Israel to be formed.[7] So Messianic Judaism believes in a crucial future for Israel. Furthermore, Messianic Judaism itself may somehow be significantly related to that future. One of the keys to understanding all of this is Paul's teaching on Israel.

Romans 9–11 are the central chapters in the Pauline writings on a theology of Israel. The ninth chapter begins with Paul's statement of his great burden of sorrow and anguish for Israel. Surely this was a prayer burden. He even says that he could wish himself cut off for their sakes. Furthermore, Paul fully recognizes Israel's national calling and in the *present continuous tense* says that they *have* "the sonship, the glory, the covenants, the giving of the law, the worship, and the promises; to them belong the patriarchs, and of their race, according to the flesh, is the [Messiah]" (Rom. 9:4-5 RSV).

Paul then goes on to state, however, that not all who are descended from Israel are spiritually considered to be Israel. This is the doctrine of the remnant, an important concept that we must unpack. Next, he responds to those who would accuse God of injustice in the matter of Israel's failure as a nation to embrace Yeshua as Messiah.

Romans 9 seems like a very "harsh" chapter; it concerns itself with Israel as a nation. It is not speaking of the opportunity for individual salvation. In the affairs of nations, God's wisdom goes far beyond our intellectual capacity. We cannot accuse God, for "who are you, a man, to answer back to God?" (Rom. 9:20 RSV). Then Paul gives a lesson in pottery, a lesson greatly misunderstood.

He names several vessels: wrath, mercy, honor, and dishonor. Honor was a beautiful vessel, chosen to be displayed in table service, for pouring water to drink, etc. Dishonor was a vessel that did not come up to such a high standard of beauty; it was used to wash feet or for other menial uses, perhaps in the kitchen. The potter makes the choice as to which vessel he will make, but both are needed. A vessel of mercy is a vessel which breaks in baking, but is repaired and rebaked. If it stays together, it will be used, a vessel of mercy. If it does not, it is a vessel of wrath or destruction. Note that Romans says that God "endured with much patience the vessels of wrath made for destruction" (Rom. 9:22 RSV).

Any judgment by God took place after much long suffering, seeking to repair the vessels in mercy.

The mercy of God to Jews and Gentiles is even more pronounced in the light of this; and despite our sin, we are vessels of mercy made for His glory. The decision, however, must be left up to God's sovereignty. Now that Paul has boldly asserted this sovereignty, he can delineate some considerations through the Spirit that reveal God's continued purposes in Israel.

First are prophetic intimations. In Hosea, we see that God's relationship to different groups changes: "Those who were not my people I will call my people" (see Hos. 2:23). Isaiah in his day (see Isa. 10:22-23) says that only a remnant would be saved from war's destruction.

There are other reasons, too. One is that Israel pursued the Law in the wrong way, as a system of works-righteousness in the classic interpretation or in the newer views as primarily to mark themselves off from other people. Israel did not succeed because they did not "pursue it through faith, but as if it were based on works" (Rom. 9:32 RSV). This produced an attitude of self-righteousness whereby Israel, "being ignorant of the righteousness that comes from God, sought to establish their own" and did not "submit to God's righteousness" in Yeshua (Rom. 10:3 RSV). Hence the Gentile, who did not have the pride of the Law, was more capable of seeing his need and submitting to God's righteousness than was Israel that in a self-righteous pursuit of the Law did not see their need! God declares us righteous when we have faith in Yeshua.

In addition, the Gospels clearly show that Israel expected the Messianic king to defeat their enemies and set up His worldwide reign of righteousness from Jerusalem. This is certainly one of His roles. However, so preoccupied were the Israelites with this image of the exalted King Messiah, that there was little room for another Messianic visitation in which the Messiah's role would be a suffering servant who bears the sin, grief, and sickness of the world as a first stage step toward His reign. The Messiah King would die a shameful death on a cross of wood: "Cursed is he that dies on a tree" (see Deut. 21:23; Gal. 3:13), which was more than many Israelites could accept. This strikes at the honor-shame systems of most cultures of the world by which people find their sense of worth. First-century Judaism also included an honor-shame way of approaching life. Yes, that curse and that shame was in identity with us, for us, and in our place. Yet only God's Spirit could open up hearts to this truth, for this message was a "stumbling block" to Jews, a scandal! How could they accept that their Messiah, the one who is their glory as a nation, would be shamed in death on a cross? (See First Corinthians 1:23.) To the reasons for the Jewish nonacceptance of Yeshua, we can add the importation of pagan elements that came into later institutional Christianity—even if such elements were rebaptized and changed (worship of saints, prayer to Mary, and statues as aids to worship). In addition, there is the periodic persecution by the institutional Church for over 1,900 years, despite the fact that non-Jewish followers of Yeshua were counseled in Romans 11 to make Israel jealous for their own Messiah by great acts of love and mercy (see Rom. 11:13,30-31).

The capstone to Paul's argument is found in Romans 11:1. Has God rejected His people? By no means! Paul points to himself as proof that God has not rejected Israel. What meaning this must have in the light of Paul's own recollection of his past as a persecutor of "the Way"! Indeed, there were 7,000 more than Elijah realized who were true to God in his day (see 1 Kings 19:18)! "So, too, at the present time there is a remnant chosen by grace" (Rom. 11:5 RSV). This remnant should not be thought of as excluding the rest of the nation as God's elect, but as a first fruit pointing to the eventual salvation of the nation as a whole. Verse 16 is very important for the first fruits make the whole lump of dough holy. So the saved remnant sanctifies the whole nation and is still part of the nation.

Paul quotes the prophets and David to show that the lack of response on Israel's part was foreordained. The whole situation of Israel and its pursuit of righteousness by works (in chapter 10) now brought God's judgment. For now, Paul states that Israel's unbelief is an act of God as well. "...Have they stumbled so as to fall? By no means!" (Rom. 11:11 RSV). The Greek here implies, "Is their stumbling fatal, an irretrievable fall?" Paul's answer is an emphatic "No!" Israel shall yet have its day! However, their trespass in not recognizing the righteous way of God in the Messiah is the means by which "salvation had come to the Gentiles" and "riches for the world" (Rom. 11:11-12 RSV).

What could Paul mean by this? Why would Israel's unbelief have anything to do with the Gentiles' salvation? The historical context of the Book of Acts makes this clear. Whenever possible, in each town to which Paul traveled, he went first to the local synagogue. Some Jewish people accepted the Good News of Messiah, but the majority usually rejected the Gospel. However, Gentiles came in large numbers *when they were given the opportunity to know the God of Israel without the barriers of circumcision and the Jewish national lifestyle* being required of them.

Let us note Paul's controversy with the Judaizers, whom I prefer to call Jewish legalists. These Jewish followers of Yeshua taught that Gentiles could not be saved, or considered part of the people of God, unless they were circumcised and kept the Law of

Moses. With great difficulty, the Apostles prevailed (see Acts 15) and refuted this view. Many Jews did accept the Gospel—myriads according to Acts 21—as well as numerous Gentiles; yet these believers were still a minority in Israel. Part of this minority doggedly hounded Paul and the Gentile converts. Marcus Bockmuel, formerly of Cambridge, identifies them with the Shammai school of Judaism, as we noted before. This school of Pharisees influenced some of the Messianic Jews. The Hillel school did not hold to this position, but they were not dominant in Israel in the first century.[8] The problems they brought are addressed in Paul's epistles.

What if, instead of a minority, the majority of Jews had accepted Yeshua? The percentage of Judaizers was not small. In every major city, there was a large Jewish presence, not to mention powerful Jews of the land of Israel. One to two million it is estimated were in the land, four to five million in the Diaspora. Imagine the pressure for the Judaizing viewpoint from three to five million Jews "all zealous for the law" (Acts 21). This would have been a huge barrier to the Gospel among the Gentiles, who were not called to be part of the nation Israel. Now we see the sense of Paul's words, but once the purpose of hardening has been accomplished, "how much more will their full inclusion mean!" Jewish rejection also caused an intensified effort in preaching to non-Jews.

Paul would see Israel made jealous for their own Messiah through the riches Gentiles had received by the grace of God Therefore, he "magnifies" his ministry. That is, he points to the manifest signs of the presence and power of God in his work. This is our task as well. Then comes a semi-climax in the argument:

> For if their rejection means the reconciliation of the world, what will their acceptance mean but life from the dead? If the dough offered as first fruits is holy, so is the whole lump; and if the root is holy, so are the branches (Romans 11:15-16).

As the first fruits sanctify the whole harvest, so Israel as a whole is sanctified and will someday be accepted, as evidenced by Jewish believers who are first fruits.

In other words, Paul foresees the acceptance of Israel by God, and this event will mean the resurrection of the dead and the establishment of the Kingdom of God over all the earth. This is why Paul can say that the Gospel has come to the Gentiles for this purpose (see Romans 11:11-12). Paul breaks off his argument for a moment and now anticipates the possible response of Gentile converts.

He likens the community of salvation to an olive tree. Some natural branches were broken off, but not all (see Rom. 11:17), and wild branches were grafted in, that is, non-Jews who had no "cultivation" as a covenant people. Paul warns them not to boast, but to stand in awe, for the root of salvation history in Israel supports them, not they, the root. They are to stand in awe, for if God did not spare natural branches, He will not spare them unless they stand in humble faith. Now Paul begins an argument again in relation to Israel. In verses 23 and 24, we read that, "God has the power to graft them in again...how much more will these natural branches be grafted back into their own olive tree" (RSV). And this is exactly what will happen:

> *Lest you be wise in your own conceits, I want you to understand this mystery, brethren: a hardening has come upon **part of Israel, until** the full number of the Gentiles come in, and so **all Israel will be saved**...* (Romans 11:25-26 RSV).

Again we are amazed to learn that some take "all *Israel* to be saved" as meaning the Church! How would this destroy non-Jewish conceit? Indeed, such an interpretation makes the whole argument of the chapter superfluous. Certainly the salvation of the Church is not at issue here, but the nation of Israel. Could Paul quickly change the meaning of the terms here and, after speaking of Israel, all of a sudden be speaking of "spiritual" Israel, the equivalent of the Church? Incredible! The rest of the chapter looks toward matters that totally refute this false view. Paul quotes Isaiah 59:20-21, that "the Deliverer will come to Zion; he will banish ungodliness from Jacob; and this will be my covenant with them when I take away their sins" (Rom. 11:26-27 RSV).

To Paul, this will still yet happen, for the New Covenant we are under shall be confirmed to all of Israel.

> *As regards the gospel they are enemies of God, for your sake; but as regards election they are beloved for the sake of their forefathers. For the gifts and call of God are irrevocable* (Romans 11:28-29 RSV).

This verse is the absolute proof that ethnic Israel is still elect and the promises to them in the Hebrew Prophets will yet be fulfilled, for even as enemies they are still chosen.

If Israel is still elect of God, we can ask *elect for what?* To witness that God is creator and the One who established them as a nation. Sabbath and Passover proclaim the call of Israel. In Israel's preservation, the world sees the faithfulness of God. As a nation, Israel shall yet be God's instrument in gaining His rule over all nations. There will yet be a large minority in Israel that will witness to the truth of the Good News. In addition, Israel's practices are prophetic and point to the events of the end of the Age and the glory of the Age to Come. Their practice has an intercessory element and calls for the fulfillment.

Mention should be made here of the phrase "fullness of the Gentiles" (Rom. 11:25 NKJV). It could mean until all of the Gentiles are saved who will be saved. Or it could parallel the phrase "fullness of Amorites" in Genesis 15:16 and in Luke 21:24 (times of the Gentiles fulfilled). This implies the fullness of the stored up iniquity as parallel to the Amorites, whereby it would be the right time for Israel to be used as God's instrument of judgment in history.

The iniquity would consist of all godless wars, killing, murder, and rebellion against God. Even more, God said, "I will bless them that bless thee, and curse him that curseth thee" (Gen. 12:3 KJV).

Surely, the period of Auschwitz when six million of our people were slaughtered while nations watched in apathy has brought God's judgment. Israel's history in the Diaspora, although a severe discipline, has also been a test for the nations, and we can discern in the historical maltreatment of Israel a corresponding correlation in the decline of the nations and people who acted unjustly. Israel's prophetic purpose thus continues even in the age of Diaspora; but now that Israel is in her own land, as predicted in Scripture, one can even now hear the steps of Messiah approaching.

I do think these ideas are rightly based on Luke 21, but think that Romans 11:25-26 can be credibly interpreted in the more common way as the full number of Gentiles that will come in. They respond rightly to the invitation during this time of opportunity to join in the priesthood of the Bride of the Messiah.

Paul concludes his chapter by reviewing the course of history. First, Israel is obedient; then she is disobedient while Gentiles are obedient; then Israel is again obedient. The reason for all this? That God may have mercy on all! Only words of praise can now leave the apostle's lips. "O the depth of the riches both of the wisdom and knowledge of God!" (Rom. 11:33 KJV).

Nothing in Paul's teaching here blunts the truth of Messianic Judaism—or that Jewish followers of Yeshua may still maintain a glorious call as part of their people in their witness to the world and in a personal witness to Israel of salvation in Yeshua.

It should be noted that Romans 11 gives us a progressive view of history as eschatological. First there is a saved remnant of Israel. Then this leads to a saved remnant from all the nations. Then the saved remnants of Israel and the nations lead to all Israel being saved. This then leads to the nations coming to the knowledge of God and God having mercy on all.

One other issue must be briefly discussed: Does Paul use the term *Israel* to refer to the Church, including non-Jews who are in Yeshua? Is the Church "the new, true spiritual Israel," as one person put it?

Many who hold that Paul might have used the term *Israel* of the Church argue that the Scriptures retain a definite place for national Israel.

It is this author's view that the terms *spiritual Jew* and *spiritual Israel* are never used by Scripture to refer to non-Jewish believers in Yeshua. This has been thoroughly argued in many articles.[9]

We have already concluded that Romans 11 does not use these terms in this sense. Romans contains an often quoted verse, though, which is thought by some to refer to non-Jewish believers as spiritual Jews.[10]

> *For he is not a real Jew who is one outwardly, nor is true circumcision something external and physical. He is a Jew who is one inwardly, and real circumcision is a matter of the heart, spiritual not literal. Its praise is not from men but from God* (Romans 2:28-29 RSV).

There is no reason to think that the real Jew within the verses is a Gentile who has a circumcised heart toward God. The word *Jew* is related etymologically to the word *praise*. Paul is saying that if a Jew is to be a praise to God and is to truly fulfill his destiny, he must not only have external circumcision, but the circumcision of the heart. This is what Moses told the people in Deuteronomy 10:16-17: "Circumcise therefore, the foreskin of your heart and be no longer stubborn" (RSV).

Indeed, the uncircumcised externally (the non-Jew) who keeps the Law will condemn the circumcised who do not. The true Jew, however, is one who has *both* circumcisions.

Romans 4 is a key to making the proper distinction. Here, Gentiles who accept the Gospel are called the children of Abraham by faith. They are not called the children of Jacob or Israel. There is a reason for this. The Gentile has a glorious place in God's eyes when he turns to God. Like Abraham, he is not descended physically from a people under God's primary covenant. He is justified by faith without being first circumcised. His life parallels Abraham's more than Jewish people, who are simply physically descended from Jacob. The promise of blessing through Abraham rests on *faith*—both for the adherents of the Jewish Laws (Israel) and for those whose lives parallel Abraham's (see Rom. 4:16). As we study further, we find that non-Jewish believers are the seed of Abraham or children of Abraham by faith! Spiritually, the Gentile convert is no longer a Gentile, at least in any sense of the word *pagan,* but neither is he a Jew, although *his spiritual* status before God is equal to the Jewish follower of the Gospel. He is a Gentile in the sense of still having his ethnic identity.

It is important to note that this is a radical change from first-century Jewish perception because now, not only Israel, but all those who embrace the Gospel through water immersion become part of the elect people of God, a holy priesthood.

Galatians 6:16 states, "Peace and mercy be upon all who walk by this rule, upon the Israel of God" (RSV). However, it could as well be translated *"and* upon the Israel of God," distinguishing those Jews who did not follow the false teachings of the Judaizers.[6] Enough has been said to establish our view that calling the Church "spiritual Israel" is not biblical terminology. "Commonwealth Israel" would be a more accurate term (see Eph. 2:12 RSV). It reflects that Gentiles have been grafted in, but do not replace Israel proper. Yet they have become part of the commonwealth under the Messiah's rule. Besides these few passages, the whole of the New Testament is silent on any such use for the term *Israel.* This silence should cause us to forego the use of the term *Israel* to refer to the Church.

OTHER PASSAGES SUPPORTING OUR CONCLUSION

First Corinthians 7:17-20 provides an important window into the idea of distinctive callings. It states that Paul's rule in the congregations is that if one is called to Yeshua as a Jew, one is not to seek to remove the marks of that calling. If one is called as a Gentile, then one is not to seek to become a Jew. Each is to remain in the calling that was theirs when they embraced the Gospel. This important passage is a major focus in the PhD dissertation of Dr. David Rudolph. It is also a subject of an important paper recently published in an important journal of Jewish and Christian dialogue.

Even Galatians, so often misinterpreted as being against the Messianic Jewish position, provides us with an amazing distinction in apostolic mission. "They saw that the gospel for the uncircumcised had been committed to me, as the gospel for the circumcised was to Peter" (Gal. 2:7 NKJV). This looks very much like what Messianic Jews argue, that there are difference streams in the one Body of the Messiah, and the Messianic Jewish community is one of the key ones.

Romans 15 provides a picture that confirms the continued call of the Jewish people. Paul is zealous to bring an offering to the Jerusalem Messianic Jewish community to express love and foster the unity of the Jerusalem community with the congregations he had planted. He then quotes texts with the implication of the salvation of the Gentiles, but also with the continued election of the Jewish nation. Here is the full quote from verses Romans 15:8-12:

> *Now I say that* [Yeshua the Messiah] *has become a servant to the circumcision for the truth of God, to confirm the promises made to the fathers, and that the Gentiles might glorify God for His mercy, as it is written:*
>
> *For this reason I will confess to You among the Gentiles,*
>
> *And sing to Your name.*
>
> *And again He says:*
>
> *"Rejoice, O Gentiles, with His people!"*
>
> *And again:*

"Praise the Lord, all you Gentiles!

Laud Him, all you peoples!"

And again, Isaiah says:

"There shall be a root of Jesse;

And He who shall rise to reign over the Gentiles,

In Him the Gentiles shall hope" (Romans 15:8-12 NKJV).

The passage confirms the idea that Israel and the nations continue to be a true distinction for our understanding. His people, the Jewish people, will join with the Gentiles in this great unity of praise to God.

Revelation 7 is not a Pauline passage. I mention it because it comes at the end of the first century. In Revelation 7, we find two very distinct groups. One is the 144,000 from all the tribes of Israel. The passage is amazingly specific and describes 12,000 from each tribe. Following this is a description that no one can number from all nations, tribes, and peoples. That scholars think the two descriptions are different descriptions of the same group is amazing to me. The writer seems obviously to be distinguishing two groups, one that is numbered and is described as ethnic Israel. The other cannot be numbered and is from the nations. Here within the Body of the Messiah, we see unity with distinction.

RECENT REPLACEMENT THEOLOGIANS

This is a good place to discuss the return of replacement theology (supercessionisim) in the Church. Actually, replacement theology was never dead, but after the Holocaust most major denominations of the West repudiated it. The Roman Catholics are quite explicit on this and have made the election of the Jewish people an explicit requirement of Catholic doctrinal belief.[11]

I have already referred to N.T. Wright recently of Oxford. Dr. Wright is a thoroughgoing replacement theologian (supercessionism). Wright's work is magisterial. His understanding of first century Judaism and some of the implications for New Testament interpretation are profound.

Yet, Wright sees replacement theology as beginning with Yeshua. Parallel to the Essenes, the community of Yeshua's followers see themselves as the ongoing meaning of Israel, the community of fulfillment. One can only remain part of the election by choosing to embrace Yeshua. The fullness of Israel is in the person of Yeshua Himself. There really is no reason but assumption to hold that the Yeshua movement was a fulfillment-replacement movement rather than a fuflllment-renewal movement. The idea of a righteous remnant can be interpreted as that group which will eventually lead to the renewal of the whole nation (not every last person, however). In Wright, Yeshua anticipates and Paul affects the understanding that Israel now is made up of all those who embrace Yeshua, first the Jewish responders and then the Gentiles who respond. "All Israel saved" simply means that all true Christians are saved. Other writers who follow the same line are Colin Chapman, Thomas Sizer, and the early writings of Gary Burge, who writes in more strident tones. It is quite amazing that such writers also have taken a very hard line against Israel and see no fulfillment in the return of the Jewish people to the Land.[12]

There are several criticisms that are devastating to this presentation. Three of the best are Douglas Harink, David Wright, R. Kendall Soulen, and Barry Horner.[13]

I recommend Harink's book as a shorter but very powerful summary. Harink presents three, what to me are, irrefutable arguments. The first is that text after text in context in the Hebrew Scriptures promises a great deliverance of ethnic Israel, a national turning to the Lord, and a full end of exile. Yes, to get there will be difficult and some will not be part of the joy of the Age to Come, but the promise of the prophets is clear. Language is not radically flexible such that one can now reinterpret these texts to mean Yeshua and those who follow Him. At the end of this chapter,

I will reprint a selection of these texts. Such a claim of radical reinterpretation is so without warrant in dealing with the Hebrew texts that, were it true, any Jew would be duty-bound to reject the New Testament, for *later revelation has to cohere with the earlier.* Again, texts are not fungible without limit! The inaugurated fulfillment in Yeshua does not bring us yet to the place of ultimate hope wherein of ethnic Israel, we read, "All Israel will be saved." Wright's reinterpretation and that of the other writers mentioned, according to Harink, would be a most cruel joke on Israel. The text then would not really mean what it says. The promises mean something else. For Wright, the worldview of Christianity overlaps that of the worldview of Israel. It is a Jewish worldview, but radically reconstituted such that Yeshua, Paul, and Hebrews subvert the ordinary reading of the text. Harink, Horner, and David Wright quote several of these texts.

Second, Wright and the others have a woefully inadequate interpretation of Romans 9–11. Indeed, to make their case, there is sometimes no quote of the most important verse, Romans 11:29, which declares that the Jewish enemies of the Gospel are still elect and beloved for the sake of the fathers. This implies a special obligation for the Gentiles who have been saved. The absence of Romans 11:29 in replacement interpretation is stunning and only can be explained by prejudices that simply do not see the text. In addition, Romans 11 makes it clear that the remnant that is saved by grace (see Rom. 11:5) is not a group taken out of ethnic Israel and no longer connected to ethnic Israel. This was well pointed out by Harry Ellison in *The Mystery of Israel*. The first fruits and the lump of dough that is offered sanctify the whole. So the remnant is the anticipation that the ethnic nation will eventually turn and embrace Yeshua. Hardness has happened in part *until* according to the text. The *until* means it is a temporary situation. There are many, many exegetes that see this from John Murray in his commentary on Romans to C.E.B. Cranfield.[14]

Harink also faults Wright with an individualistic view of salvation in regard to Israel and the Church. Yes, the invitation of the Gospel brings one into the Church, but God also works with nations and ethnic groups and seeks to deal not just with the offer to individuals, but to the corporate. For Walter Kaiser, Israel is an instrument of God gaining sovereignty over the nations, for she is a literal nation among the nations. Jewish history is so stunning, the regathering is so unique that no one can legitimately think that this all means nothing. For Soulen, the thrust of the Bible is that the nations come into the Kingdom of God, and like Wright, the whole cosmos will be renewed and restored. However, this includes the category of nations in mutual blessing based on the distinction of Jew and Gentile. Life from the dead in Romans 11:15 means more than just the new life that Jews would have in being born again. It means that the full acceptance of the corporate nation as a key to the transformation of the cosmos, which Wright so appreciates. Furthermore, Romans 11 indicates that the salvation of Israel is the capstone victory of the Church. She will succeed in making Israel jealous.

I would add that the problem with Wright and his fellows is that they do not handle paradox well, at least not on this subject. This is a key point of W.D. Davies in *Paul and Rabbinic Judaism*. Davies even used the term *contradiction* for Paul's theology, between his assertion of the continued importance of ethnic Israel and the importance of the new people of God from all nations, including his Jewish followers. Yet when we unpack these assertions, there is no contradiction in the apparent paradox. Instead, the Church is corporately rooted in the Jewish people and their destinies are tied together. Concepts and analogues using terms referring to Israel such as priesthood, chosen generation, etc. are in addition or enlargement to Israel, not in replacement. It is a wonderful surprise.

Lastly, it should be noted that the theology of the rejection of ethnic Israel, now asserted in Wright and others, has been a key root of anti-Semitism. We see how this devolves in statements by Colin Chapman that I think are anti-Semitic, but defended as only anti-Zionism. Mark Kinzer in his important book, *Post Missionary Messianic Judaism*, calls for a hermeneutic of love. If there are two equally persuasive interpretations (and with regard to replacement theology, the two are not equally persuasive), we should choose the one that increases love in the world. Replacement theology has been a source of hate. Is hate logically entailed? Probably not. However, the correlation is very strong.

CHAPTER ADDENDUM: TEXTS THAT CANNOT BE REINTERPRETED TO THE EXCLUSION OF FULFILLMENT IN ETHNIC ISRAEL.

KEY PASSAGES AND A FEW COMMENTS

There are so many passages concerning Israel's restoration in their own land and entrance into a glory that will not fade that we can only quote a few that are noteworthy.

AMOS 9:15

"I will plant Israel in their own land, never again to be uprooted from the land I have given them," says the Lord your God.

Does this verse speak to the ethnic-national people or a metaphorical future people from all nations who will inherit the eternal Kingdom that is metaphorically the Land? Would this be a comfort to faithful ancient Israelites?

JOEL 3:20

"Judah will be inhabited forever and Jerusalem through all generations. Their bloodguilt, which I have not pardoned, I will pardon." The Lord dwells in Zion.

This passage comes after the description of a severe world judgment of the nations that are described as invading Israel. It is hard to see how this is the Church. This has not yet happened.

Isaiah 49:6

It is too small a thing for you to be my servant to restore the tribes of Jacob and bring back those of Israel I have kept. I will also make you a light for the Gentiles, that you may bring my salvation to the ends of the earth.

There is no legitimate way to confuse the meaning here. The promise is to Israel and includes the salvation of the nations. A new Israel of Jew and Gentile replacing Israel cannot be the interpretation.

Isaiah 49:15-20; 22-23

Can a mother forget the baby at her breast and have no compassion on the child she has borne? Though she may forget, I will not forget you! See, I have engraved you on the palms of my hands; your walls are ever before me. Your sons hasten back and those who laid you waste depart from you. Lift up your eyes and look around; all your sons gather and come to you…Though you were ruined and made desolate, now you will be too small for your people, and those who devoured you will be far away. The children born during your bereavement will yet say in your hearing, "This place is too small for us; give us more space to live in"…

See I will beckon to the Gentiles, I will lift up my banner to the peoples; they will bring your sons in their arms and carry your daughters on their shoulders. Kings will be your foster fathers, and their queens your nursing mothers…

Can this be the situation after the first return after Babylonian captivity? No, for this glorious turning of the nations to favor Israel to this extent has not yet happened. Indeed, first return was a small minority. The Jews of the first century were a minority, less than one third of Jewry. Israel remained under foreign domination except for one brief and corrupt period.

Isaiah 60 Selections

Arise, shine, for your light has come, and the glory of the Lord rises upon you. See, darkness covers the earth and thick darkness is over the peoples, but the Lord rises upon you and his glory appears over you. Nations will come to your light, and kings to the brightness of your dawn. Lift up your eyes and look about you: All assemble and come to you; your sons come from afar, and your daughters are carried on the arm. Then you will look and be radiant, your heart will throb and swell with joy; the wealth of the seas will be brought to you, to you the riches of the nations will come...Surely the islands look to me; in the lead are the ships of Tarshish, bringing your sons from afar, with their silver and gold, to the honor of the Lord your God, the Holy One of Israel, for he has endowed you with splendor. Foreigners will rebuild your walls, and their kings will serve you. Though in anger I struck you, in favor I will show you compassion. Your gates will always stand open, they will never be shut, day or night, so that men may bring you the wealth of the nations—their kings led in triumphal procession. For the nation ...that will not serve you will perish; it will be utterly ruined... The sons of your oppressors will come bowing before you; all who despise you will bow down at your feet and will call you the City of the Lord, Zion of the Holy One of Israel...You will drink the milk of nations and be nursed at royal breasts, Then you will know that I, the Lord, am your Savior, your Redeemer, the Mighty One of Jacob. Instead of bronze I will bring you gold, and silver in place of iron... and iron in place of stones...No longer will violence be heard in your land, nor ruin or destruction within your borders, but you will call your walls Salvation, and your gates Praise...the Lord will be your everlasting light, and your days of sorrow will end. Then will all your people be righteous, and they will possess the land forever. They are the shoot I have planted, the work of my hands, for the display of my splendor.

Of course, we would not deny that there is application to all the people of God, but is this the primary meaning? It cannot be, for this is a comfort to the nation going into exile. It is a comfort to know the future glory of Jerusalem that has been destroyed. The glory predicted here has never been fulfilled. The sons of the oppressors who come are those nations who oppressed the ethnic Israel-Jewish nation. It is not about the persecution of Christians, though God may certainly speak from these verses to their hearts. Context makes it abundantly clear that this is about the ancient nation.

Isaiah 62 Selections

For Zion's sake I will not keep silent, for Jerusalem's sake I will not remain quiet, till her righteousness shines out like the dawn, her salvation like a blazing torch. The nations will see your righteousness and all kings your glory...for the Lord will take delight in you and your land will be married.

Here the Jews of exile are comforted by the promise of the restoration of Jerusalem, not comforted, by a spiritual metaphorical Jerusalem from heaven. This would not have been such a comfort.

Jeremiah 23:7-8

"So then, the days are coming," declares the Lord, "when people will no longer say, 'As surely as the Lord lives, who brought the Israelites up out of Egypt,' but they will say, 'As surely as the Lord lives, who brought the descendants

of Israel up out of the land of the north and out of all the countries where he had banished them.' Then they will live in their own land."

Can this be the Church? No, the Church was not banished. Can this be the return from Babylon? No, this was a small remnant that returned and 500 years later was still a minority of the Jewish people, perhaps less than a third. There was never such a mighty and great return such that this language was used, that is until today. There is still more to come from this verse. This return is to yet make the Exodus pale by comparison. This has to be a prophetic word about the literal national ethnic people.

JEREMIAH 31:31-37

"The time is coming," declares the Lord, "when I will make a new covenant with the house of Israel and with the house of Judah...I will put my law on their minds and write it on their hearts. I will be their God and they will be my people...They will all know me, from the least of them to the greatest," declares the Lord. For I will forgive their wickedness and will remember their sins no more."

This is what the Lord says, he who appoints the sun to shine by day, who decrees the moon and stars to shine by night, who stirs up the sea so that its waves roar—the Lord Almighty is his name: "Only if these decrees vanish from my sight," declares the Lord, "will the descendants of Israel ever cease to be a nation before me." This is what the Lord says: "Only if the heavens above can be measured and the foundations of the earth below be searched out, will I reject the descendants of Israel because of all they have done declares the Lord.

Here is food for thought. The New Covenant is made with national/ethnic Israel. It includes the promise of the forgiveness of their sins and that they will all know God. It includes the promise of their ethnic-national preservation. When Christians hear the words *New Covenant,* this context of meaning is hardly in their minds. So how is it that Christians are part of the New Covenant? It is by the fact that the salvation of the Gentiles is part of the Abrahamic Covenant, and the New Covenant enables its implementation. However, this covenant has only been partially fulfilled. It includes, as part of it, the restoration of the Jewish people. The affirmation to the physical seed in this passage could not be clearer. There is no way that the Church can be read as the intended subject of the last part of the quote above.

Ezekiel 36:24-29

For I will take you out of the nations; I will gather you from all the countries and bring you back into your own land. I will sprinkle clean water on you, and you will be clean; I will cleanse you from all your impurities, and from all your idols. I will give you a new heart, and put a new spirit in you; I will remove from you your heart of stone and give you a heart of flesh. And I will put my Spirit in you and move you to follow my decrees, and be careful to keep my laws. You will live in the land I give your forefathers; you will be my people, and I will be your God. I will save you from all your uncleanness....

In this passage on the New Covenant, parallel to Jeremiah 31, we have an amazing promise to the ethnic/national people that has not yet been fulfilled. The meaning is plain. The promise of being born again is connected to the return to the Land, and there is a national conversion. Certainly Paul had many passages in mind when he wrote looking forward to this national conversion in Romans 11.

Ezekiel 37

I will not quote it. The famous dry bones passage repeats the promise of Ezekiel 36 of the people coming back to the Land and receiving the Spirit. They will be one nation under one King. This is happening and will continue to happen.

ZECHARIAH 12–14 SELECTIONS

I will make Jerusalem an immovable rock for all the nations. All who try to move it will injure themselves.... A day of the Lord is coming when your plunder will be divided among you. I will gather all the nations to Jerusalem to fight against it; the city will be captured, the houses ransacked, and the women raped. Half of the city will go into exile, but the rest of the people will not be taken from the city.

Then the Lord will go and fight against those nations as he fights in the day of battle. On that day his feet will stand on the Mount of Olives, east of Jerusalem and the Mount of Olives will be split in two from east to west, forming a great valley...then the Lord my God will come, and all the holy ones with him.

Then the survivors from all the nations that have attacked Jerusalem will go up year after year to worship the King, the Lord Almighty, and to celebrate the Feast of Tabernacles.

When I have shared this passage with replacement proponents, they often simply say that they do not know how to fit this in. This is because the passage is so blatantly about one real place that is actually on the earth. It describes Jerusalem surrounded by armies and then delivered. Zechariah writes after Jerusalem was resettled after the first exile in Babylon. It cannot be the first century war because Jerusalem was then destroyed. It can only be an event connected to the Jewish people at the end of days when the city is again inhabited as a Jewish city.

There are so many more passages that could have been chosen. However, the ones we have chosen give us the thrust of the prophets concerning the restoration of ethnic/national Israel and the glory that will be hers. Paul's strong words on the irrevocable election and calling of Israel are in the very context of these passages. He expected, with absolute confidence, a fulfillment of God's promises to the ethnic/national nation. That fulfillment would bring "life from the dead" to the whole world (Rom. 11:15). That the ingrafted Christian people share in like promises by analogy is indubitable, but that the ethnic/national people will come into their promised inheritance is indubitable.

CHAPTER FOUR

MESSIANIC JUDAISM— DIFFICULT PASSAGES

MESSIANIC JEWS ESTABLISH CONGREGATIONS OF Jewish and non-Jewish followers of Yeshua whose worship style is Jewish and Hebraic. In addition, we teach that the Jewish follower of Yeshua is still a part of Israel as well as the universal people of God. Therefore, Jewish members of these congregations are encouraged to maintain appropriate biblically-grounded Jewish practices and identity that are fitting to the New Covenant order.

Jewish life is a glorious calling that witnesses to great truths about God. By being loyal to his heritage, a Jew maximizes the opportunity to share his faith with other loyal Jews who would otherwise dismiss it out of hand. As First Corinthians 9 states, "To the Jews I become as a Jew, in order to win Jews; to those under the law I became as one under the law...that I might win those under the law" (1 Cor. 9:20 RSV).

However there are several passages that are used by some to refute this position. It is to these passages that we turn.

FIRST CORINTHIANS 9:20-21

At first glance, these verses would seem to support Messianic Jewish conclusions. However, there are interpreters who find in two phrases a source of anti-Messianic Jewish viewpoints. We quote the passage in its entirety.[1]

> *To the Jews I become as a Jew, in order to win the Jews; to those under the law I become as one under the law— though not being myself under the law—that I might win those under the law. To those outside the law I became as one outside the law—not being without law toward God, but under the law of Christ—that I might win those outside the law* (RSV).

We should first note that Paul here establishes a valid principle for sharing the Good News, specifically that we are to have a loving identification with those that we seek to win. The clear statement that one may practice the law heartens the Messianic Jew, "I become as one under the law." One reason for the practice of the heritage, but certainly not the sole reason, is loving identification with those we seek to win. Two other phrases bring various interpretations. "Though not being myself under the law" is taken to mean that the Mosaic revelation with its standards and practices no longer has any meaning for the New Covenant believer. Rather, the believer is now under the "law of Christ." The "law of Christ" is variously explained as loving God and our neighbor or as all of the New Testament commands.

However, there are problems with this view. First, the command to love God and our neighbor (quoted in Mark 12 and the other Gospels) is a quotation from Torah. Some say that when the New Testament quotes Torah, it becomes part of the "law of Christ," but otherwise has no force over us. This view is certainly "forced." When the New Testament quotes Torah, it does so because it is Scripture. This settles the issue (see Eph. 6:1ff.). First Corinthians 9:8 says, "Do I say this on human authority? Does not the law say the same?"

It is clear that Paul, by example and teaching, taught the valid inspiration and authority of the Torah (see 2 Tim. 3:16). The laws against incest are not found in the New Testament. Someone could say that since incest laws are not quoted in the New Testament, they are not part of the "law of Christ." Therefore, incest is permissible? My response to this argument is, "No! Of course not!" The same is the case with just weights and measures.

The author believes that the phrase *law of Christ* is a synonym for "Law of the Spirit" found in Romans 8:2. When we are in the Spirit, we are no longer under the *Law as a fearful taskmaster,* or under the Mosaic order *per se*. Our essential and central content of faith is the love of God, the atonement in Yeshua, and the power of the Spirit. This produces a new approach to Scripture whereby the Spirit places God's desires upon our hearts as well as empowers us to perform God's will. The reading of Scripture is a primary means for the Spirit to give us a depth of conviction and power. This all occurs on the basis of an intimate fellowship with God rather than the maintenance of a code that seems external to us. Yet it is the very Torah that the Spirit will use to "instruct" in God's ways and to "train in righteousness" (see 2 Tim. 3:16; Ezek. 36; Jer. 31). The "Law of Christ" might as well mean the application of Law as fitting to the New Covenant order.

However, none of God's eternal standards are invalidated; all are made part of the covenant relationship of walking in the Spirit.

Furthermore, Paul seeks to present himself and the Gospel in such a way that there will be no stumbling blocks to his listeners' acceptance of the Good News. Gentiles were not required to take on the call of national Israel. This does not mean that Paul ceased to be a Jew in Gentile settings, but he certainly did not make his Jewish markers so prominent that it would compromise the spread of the Gospel. When Paul says in verse 22, "To the weak I became weak," he does not mean that he literally gave up his courage, faith, and strength. It means he identified with the weak in such a way that his presentation of the Gospel would meet them where they were.

The law of Christ does not replace Torah, but is a principle of approach to all of Scripture in the power of the atonement and the Spirit. This passage is perfectly exemplified by Paul's life and practice in the Book of Acts.

Of special significance is the fact that the Apostle to the Gentiles, because of his Jewish identity, never ceased to care for his people and his heritage. Though called to Gentile ministry, he lived as a Jew. If this be the case, how can Jewish followers of Yeshua, who believe themselves called to Israel, live in ways that befit non-Jews? We do not seek to bring anyone into bondage; all must be done in the Spirit. However, the example of all the Apostles, even Paul the Apostle to the Gentiles, properly causes us to believe that those who are negative to the Jewish biblical heritage have not heard the Spirit in regard to these questions.

PASSAGES IN GALATIANS

We will not repeat the basic discussion of passages in Galatians already covered in the section on the Judaizers in the chapters on the "Israel's Call and the New Testament" and "Paul, Israel, and the Law." The reader should turn to these chapters for more information on Law and grace and the Judaizing controversy. We do recall for the reader that: (1) In my view, Galatians was written before the Acts 15 decision on Gentile freedom in the Gospel; and (2) the Judaizers were a group which taught that a person who is uncircumcised must follow the law of Moses or embrace the marks of being Jewish to be saved or to be included in the people of God. Their view thoroughly invalidated the Gospel of salvation by grace through faith, that we are declared righteous by faith in Yeshua. (3) Furthermore, to the Judaizer, the Gentile was unclean and not qualified for table fellowship. Table fellowship is the proof of the spiritual equality of Jew and Gentile in the Messiah.

We should note that the Book of Galatians does *not* address the issue of Jewish followers of Yeshua maintaining their Jewish practice and identity. This is not even in view; Alan Cole states that Galatians does not at all preclude such Jewish practice and identity, but that its principle of freedom in Messiah fully allows for the possibility.[2] *The question of Jewish practice in Yeshua must be settled by those passages which speak to it*—the Book of Acts, the testimony of history concerning Apostolic practice and identity, and the whole drift of scriptural teaching on Israel.

Galatians 5 warns Gentiles to not be circumcised. If they are circumcised, they are responsible for the whole Law. Here is an artless assertion that implies that Jewish people are still responsible for the Jewish life based in the Torah!

Once again, in all of the discussion on the Law in Galatians, we must remember that Paul does not demean the Law as a standard of God. Rather, with the advent of the Messiah, all is done in His power and under the inspiration of His Spirit. We approach the Law as "adults," not as children who have rules set over them due to their immaturity, hence, the analogy of the schoolmaster and the Law before Messiah. In Messiah, we are sons of God's Kingdom and not under the Law as a custodian, but under the power of the Spirit as sons who follow by inspiration and reason, not rote. The New Covenant order does supersede the Mosaic Covenant with its sacrificial system. We are not under Moses especially in that sense. However, the New Covenant promises Jewish preservation and the application of the Torah in that covenant. Having given these general comments, we turn to these specifics:

GALATIANS 3:28

There is neither Jew nor Greek...for you are all one in Christ Jesus" (RSV; Col. 3:11 is a parallel).

It is sad that we even have to respond to the use of this verse as a proof-text against Messianic Judaism. Incredibly, the answer would be obvious if the *whole* verse was quoted. The left out portion is "there is neither slave nor free, there is neither male nor female." Paul is not saying that all distinctions between men and women have been obliterated! This would lead to the end of marriages and families. In what sense is there neither male nor female, then? It is defined in verses 26 and 29—"In the Messiah, Yeshua, you are all children of God, through faith...And if you are Messiah's, then you are Abraham's offspring, heirs according to promise." Men and women are exactly one in this, that they are equally children of God and spiritually of equal significance. In no way does God envision men bearing children or an end to all the wonderful joys that the male-female distinction brings to life as a result of His creation-order. Men and women have different callings in life, though they are one in Messiah.

It is precisely the same with Jew and non-Jew in the Messiah. Both may be called to different styles of life and witness, to different fields of service, yet they are spiritually one in the Messiah. The oneness spoken of does not lead to a dullness of all peoples, nations, and races becoming the same in speech, manner, dress, mission, and style. What a horribly boring world that would be! It would be like a symphony orchestra composed of all violins! God's unity is a symphonic unity, blending all together under the head conductor, the Messiah. Oneness in the Messiah leaves ample room for varieties of life and calling, especially in regards to Jew and non-Jew. Note as well, non-Jews are called (in verse 29), not spiritual Israel, but the offspring of Abraham by faith.[3]

EPHESIANS 2:14

For he himself is our peace, who has made the two one and has destroyed the barrier, the dividing wall of hostility.

Messianic Jews, on the basis of this passage, are often accused of re-erecting the "wall of partition" between Jew and Gentile. It is charged that because Jews maintain their Jewish-biblical heritage, they become distinct from other believers, hence re-erecting the wall.

The wall of partition does not refer to a difference of practice and lifestyle by which Jews and non-Jews may be distinguished. It rather refers to practices that precluded table-fellowship between Jews and Gentiles and produced hostility.[4] Gentiles were pagans, idolators. According to biblical Law, contact with unclean meats precluded on the food lists of Leviticus and Deuteronomy, contact with blood and with death, made a person unclean. Uncleanness precluded visiting the Temple for a specified period of time, one to seven days. Since it was impossible to know if a Gentile had such contact, the oral tradition of Judaism concluded that contact with Gentiles made one unclean. The solution for the religious was to avoid all contact with Gentiles.

In Yeshua, however, the Gentile is no longer a pagan or unclean (see Acts 10). Both Jew and the non-Jew are spiritually one in Yeshua. The non-Jewish believers are given a charge to avoid those things that would be especially abhorrent to Jewish believers (see Acts 15). Now in Yeshua, Jew and Gentile accept one another and have table fellowship, prayer, and praise together! This does not imply, however, that they are to have *identical calling and lifestyles.* As J.H. Yoder argues, the wall has to do with acceptance and table fellowship that was such a crucial demonstration of acceptance.[4] The rejection of fellowship implied that the other person was not spiritually acceptable. The wall of partition is not a wall of distinctions, but a *wall of hostility,* as Ephesians 2:14 clearly states. Now in the light of this, let's quote the whole of the passage from Ephesians 2:13-16:

> *But now in* [Messiah Yeshua] *you who were once far off have been brought near in the blood of* [Messiah]. *For he is our peace, who has made us both one, and has broken down the dividing wall of hostility, by abolishing in his flesh the law of commandments and ordinances, that he might create in himself one new man in place of the two, so making peace, and might reconcile us both to God in one body through the cross, thereby bringing the hostility to an end* (RSV).

I note that uncircumcised Gentiles could not partake of the Passover sacrifice. Yet in Yeshua, we partake together in the Passover Lamb, Yeshua, as we partake of the bread and wine representing His body and shed blood.

The commands and ordinances are not necessarily and intrinsically referring to the Torah, but the oral extensions of these laws that made Gentiles unclean and contact with Gentiles something to avoid. As well, it would abolish commands precluding a Jew worshiping in the most intimate way with a Gentile since the Gentile, in Yeshua, is no longer an idolatrous sinner, but has been cleansed by the blood of Yeshua. In the Messiah, a universal body of believers of Jew and Gentile is formed. This does not preclude a Jew's special calling—for he is both part of the universal body and the nation of Israel. It does not preclude the instruction of Torah (see 2 Tim. 3:16-17).

It is possible that the wall of partition refers to the separation wall in the Temple between the court of the Gentiles and the court of the women. Gentiles were not to pass beyond this wall. They could enter in only so far. But in Yeshua, we together come into the deepest level of entering even to the very throne of God. The wall has been broken down.

It is crucial here to note that a Messianic Jewish congregation is a *New Covenant congregation* in which Jews and non-Jews fellowship together in oneness. Each has equal privilege in Yeshua. However, the style of worship is Jewish, and Jewish members are encouraged in their identity and calling. Because there is mutual acceptance rather than seeking to press one another into preconceived molds, true love can flourish. The greatest proof of an end to the wall of hostility is the Messianic congregation where Jews and non-Jews—in significant proportions—worship together. In a non-Jewish congregational setting, where a lone Jew has lost his practice and identity, there is little testimony of this truth. However, there is a place for Jewish segments (groupings) in predominantly non-Jewish congregations that maintain their Jewish involvement in the present and future through *their children*. A Messianic Jewish congregation is just one kind of expression of the universal body of the Messiah!

GALATIANS 4:8-10

Verses 9-10, in particular, speak of this—"You observe days, and months and seasons and years! I am afraid I have labored over you in vain."

The obvious conclusion drawn by the foe of Messianic Judaism is that Paul here is against anyone observing Jewish holidays. However, what were the *special months* and *years referred to in Judaism?* They are not found in Scripture, except for the seventh Sabbatical Year when slaves were freed and the land was given beneficial rest. Once again, the context of preceding verses is essential. According to what we know of the region of Galatia historically, Paul is writing to predominantly non-Jewish people.

He says:

> *Formerly, when you did not know God, you were in bondage to beings that by nature are no gods; but now that you have come to know God, or rather to be known by God, how can you turn back again to the weak and beggarly elemental spirits, whose slaves you want to be once more. You observe days, and months and seasons and years! I am afraid I have labored over you in vain* (Galatians 4:8-11 RSV).

The full context has prompted many commentators to hold that Paul here is not speaking of Jewish biblical celebrations *per se.* There must have been another problem in Galatia, it is thought. This problem, it is said, is connected to astrology. It is also known that heretical groups existed which *connected some of the Jewish holidays to astrology* and superstition.[5] Paul could not be speaking of celebrations given by God as putting people under the bondage of evil spirits! Nor could he be speaking of Jewish holidays in saying that they, a non-Jewish group, are *turning back* to weak and beggarly elemental spirits.

Apparently, what Paul refers to is a drift into superstition connected to special years, days and seasons—akin to astrology. This is bondage, for during such days, some actions are safe and others are unsafe, some endeavors are to be undertaken and will be especially fruitful, while others are especially dangerous. This actually brings bondage to evil spirits. There may have been a perverted Jewish content added to some of this. Certainly, in the light of this background, this passage has nothing to say against Jewish people celebrating God's grace in their history through feasts of Israel. There is no superstition connected to this and no bondage to evil spirits! I should note that the Christian feasts do have observances of days, months, and seasons. The Christian celebration of the death and resurrection takes place during the time of the Jewish feast. This is the same with Pentecost that is a Jewish feast. The exact day is different, but close in time and based on the Torah feasts. Again, Paul's example in life shows the critics of Messianic Judaism to be misinterpreting this passage, ignoring not only the historical context, but the very words of the whole passage itself. We might also note that the famous charismatic Christian teacher, the late Derek Prince, in a taped message, quotes this passage in regard to astrology. He notes that the wording recalls Deuteronomy 18:10-14 in speaking against astrology as "observing seasons." Second Kings also says, in a context of astrology, that Manasseh "observed times" or seasons (see 2 Kings 21:6).

SARAH AND HAGAR—GALATIANS 4:21-31

There is a very unusual allegory given whereby Paul states that Hagar and her son, Ishmael, parallel the covenant from Mount Sinai, representing children who are slaves. This, says Paul, stands for the present city of Jerusalem. However, there is a Jerusalem above that is free. It is this Jerusalem who is our mother. We are like Isaac, children of the promise, and like Isaac—who was born by the Spirit—we are persecuted by the son born of the flesh.

Sarah's words are then quoted: "Get rid of the slave woman and her son, for the slave woman's son will never share in the inheritance with the free woman's son" (Gal. 4:30). The conclusion is that we, as followers of Yeshua, are not children of the slave woman, but of the free woman. The whole allegory is given to enlighten those who desire to be under the law of works-righteousness—that is, those who have accepted the *theology of the circumcision party*. This is a very difficult passage of Scripture to interpret. We do not know the exact nature of the situation in which Paul would respond with such an unparalled offensive analogy. This passage should definitely be understood in the light of the clearer, straightforward passages, such as those in the Books of Romans and Acts.

A quick reading of this passage has caused some to conclude that Jews who follow their calling are under bondage and are slaves; they should, therefore, give up all Jewish practice and identity. This, however, *cannot* be the meaning of this text, for several reasons. It was not the example of Paul in the Book of Acts nor the import of his teaching in the Book of Romans on the value of being a Jew. Next, *Isaac is the son of promise* according to the analogy. He was the one given the promise of blessing, land, and nationhood from his father Abraham. Because Isaac is the son of promise and the product of miraculous birth, Jews exist today. Paul, therefore, cannot be saying that being a Jew is a slave-type bondage.

The contrast is not at all about being called to Jewish life or not, but is rather a contrast between flesh and spirit. Paul is contrasting the spirit, promise, and faith to the flesh and *a fleshly understanding* of the Law.

Abraham was given the promise of many descendants, a great nation through which all the world would be blessed. He believed God, but Sarah was barren. Hence he sought to bring about God's promise by human fleshly (ordinary) means. In the ancient Near East, if a man's wife was barren, she could give him her maidservant. The children born to the servant would count as their own.[6] Hence, Abraham would have descendants; human means would be used to secure the promise of God. However, this was contrary to God's way of working. Abraham was to have the son of promise miraculously—by his own wife—by the power of the Spirit.

The circumcision party also sought to use human means to fulfill God's divine purposes. Keeping the Law, by human effort according to some interpreters, they would bring salvation or the great final redemption. Indeed, they taught that Gentiles must accept circumcision (become Jews) and keep the Law of Moses to be saved or be included in the people of God. Human works would produce the salvation of God. How similar to Abraham's use of human work in producing Ishmael by Hagar.

The approach of the circumcision party to the Sinai covenant is tantamount to slavery and parallel to the slave woman and her child. Those who seek justification before God by their own good works will find only greater condemnation, and even bondage to sin (see Rom. 7:8). Only dependence on the grace and promise of God will bring true freedom and deliverance. Hence, although the circumcision party members in the flesh are sons of Isaac, they act more like sons of the slave woman, Hagar. They are acting in the flesh and do not give a true testimony to the meaning of God's promises to Abraham's descendants. In fact, they are like the then-present state of Jerusalem—in bondage to Roman occupation—rather than the future Jerusalem of promise *to* be brought about by the power of God's Spirit. The slave does not inherit the promises of God, but remains in bondage to the way of human works.

There is nothing in this passage to suggest that fulfilling the God-given call to be part of the nation of Israel is, itself, bondage. Both Jew and Gentile are children of promise—like Isaac—when they approach God by faith unto salvation. However, in the leading of the Spirit, both may indeed have a difference of calling and lifestyle. The Jew who follows the way of the Spirit may sense a love for his nation and a call to witness to God's purposes in it. The non-Jew may take a different path. Paul had no argument with a Jew expressing his faith by identity with the calling of Israel, and he expected both Jew and Gentile to reflect the moral dimensions of the Law in the life of faith. His quarrel was with legalists who sought to bring non-Jews forcibly into the role of Israel by their teaching that no salvation was otherwise possible. They showed themselves to have completely misunderstood the Good News.

Why would Paul use such a difficult analogy to make this point? We cannot know for sure, but we are comfortable in that the above exposition is acceptable to the evidence of Scripture. Perhaps the best suggestion was given by R.N. Longnecker, who held that Paul was probably responding to an analogy that the circumcision party used.[7] They would have been teaching that non-Jews must become Jews and adopt the whole of the Sinai revelation and Jewish practice in order to be children of the promise. Otherwise, they would be castoffs, like Hagar and her child, Ishmael. Paul thus uses this argument to turn the tables on his opponents, holding that they show themselves to be akin to the slave status of Hagar and Ishmael by their legalistic *bondage-producing* teaching.

THE BOOK OF HEBREWS—CENTRAL CHAPTERS

For Messianic Jews, the Book of Hebrews is a wonderful book. It presents the greatness of God's revelation in Yeshua in an unparalleled way, revealing Him as Prophet, King, and—most of all—High Priest. The assertion of His deity is especially strong in chapter 1. The middle chapters of the book bring out the dimensions of the work of Yeshua as priest and sacrifice, primarily by contrasting His work with the priesthood and sacrificial system that foreshadowed and pointed toward His redeeming work. Yom Kippur, the Day of Atonement, in which the High Priest entered the holiest part of the Tabernacle and sprinkled blood upon the Ark for the nation's sin, is the central Holy Day emphasized. In its sacrificial dimensions, Yom Kippur is the great pointer to Yeshua's work.

Why then is Hebrews listed among difficult passages? It is because there exists an interpretation of the book that is anti-Messianic Jewish. This interpretation is not in accord with the biblical context or history, yet it has gained popularity. The view teaches that Hebrews precludes following the calendar of Judaism and any identity with Israel's feasts and festivals, because all of these things have been replaced by a New Covenant that does away with the Law. Chapter 8 is the central chapter for this discussion. For we read:

> *The ministry* [Yeshua] *has received is as superior to theirs as the covenant of which he is a mediator is superior to the old one, and it is founded on better promises. For if there had been nothing wrong with the first covenant, no place would have been sought for another* (Hebrews 8:6-7).

The writer then goes on to quote Jeremiah 31:31-34, which gives the promise of the new Covenant and says, "By calling this covenant 'new,' he has made the first one obsolete and what is obsolete and aging will soon disappear" (Heb. 8:13).

A critic of Messianic Judaism thus draws the conclusion that all dimensions of Jewish identity and practice are part of what is obsolete and should be forsaken. Furthermore, we are even accused of making the blood of Messiah of no effect and spurning His sacrifice when we remember our national origins in the Exodus by celebrating Passover!

> *It is impossible for those who have been once enlightened, who have tasted the heavenly gift, who have shared in the Holy Spirit, who have tasted the goodness of the word of God and the powers of this coming age, if they fall away, to be brought back to repentance, because to their loss they are crucifying the Son of God all over again and subjecting him to public disgrace* (Hebrews 6:4-6).

How this interpretation can be *fairly* gleaned from these passages without great violence to the context is paradoxical. Let us respond as follows. If this is the true interpretation of Hebrews, all first-century Jewish believers (including Paul and the other Apostles) would have been guilty of these horrible sins. Yet these Apostles are our examples. The problem of Hebrews for Messianic

Judaism dissolves when we take the time to carefully read just what is being said to whom!

Recent studies have shown—by language parallels and emphases—that the Book of Hebrews was probably written to a group of *Essene* Jewish followers of Yeshua.[8] At least, the language is very parallel to the language of the Essense. The book emphasizes the Tabernacle in the wilderness instead of the fixed Temple that was built later. All its imagery and teaching on sacrifices is related to the Tabernacle. The Qumran community (an Essene-like community) held the Temple and the contemporary priesthood to be very corrupt. They, therefore, expounded the sacrificial system dimension of Scripture in relation to the Tabernacle, even though the Temple was then the scene of these rituals and the Tabernacle did not exist.

Qumran also emphasized the Melchizedekian Priesthood in their teachings. Moreover, Qumran rejected the then present high priesthood as illegitimate since they were not descended from Zadok. It is now a common view that the Book of Hebrews was addressed to a group of Essene-like Jewish followers of Yeshua, of which there were probably many in the first century.[9]

They were in danger of giving up their faith in the work of Yeshua and returning to the hopes of the Essenes who did not follow Him. They would hence be depending upon Essene ritual for salvation and the hope of the reestablishment of a true Zadokite priesthood that paralleled the purity of the period when Israel worshipped and sacrificed at the ancient Tabernacle that anteceded the Temple. Their emphasis was then on the Mosaic sacrificial system purified,[10] as the way of bringing the power of God to Israel and deliverance from the hands of oppressors. It is thought that in this time of national crisis—perhaps during the Roman invasion of Israel to quell the rebellion of 66-70 c.e.—that the Jewish believers in Yeshua here addressed were forsaking their faith and in danger of returning completely to Essenean-type beliefs. By doing this, they would spurn the Gospel and crucify the Son of

God afresh. It was not by remaining Jewish that they did this. This is why there is such exhortation in the face of grievous trial (see Heb. 12:7-13).

The essence of the argument of the book is to not place our hopes in ritual or in a purified human priesthood because in Yeshua we have *a better sacrifice, a better priesthood,* and *a better Covenant. There is no statement to the effect that we have a better Law,* for as we have seen, *the New Covenant promise is to write God's Law, statutes, and ordinances upon our hearts* (see Ezek. 36:27). Further attention to the Book of Hebrews shows that what is referred to as being "obsolete" is the whole Temple-priestly sacrificial system. Indeed the word *obsolete* is interpreted as in "process of vanishing" in the original. Paragraph after paragraph emphasizes the limitations of the blood of bulls and goats and the repeated ministrations of the priesthood. Our hope is not the reestablishment of that system in purity.

The writer to the Hebrews emphasizes that the Mosaic Covenant, as a covenant, is essentially connected to this system—which is vanishing. The New Covenant replaces this Covenant because of the weaknesses inherent in that old system, which was given only for a time to point to the sacrificial-priestly work of Yeshua.

We have stated clearly that we believe the Abrahamic Covenant with Israel is still in effect (see Rom. 11:29). We have also argued that the Mosaic Covenant, as a covenant, is no longer in full effect and that God has sovereignly removed the possibility of following this covenant by allowing the Temple to be destroyed. Hence, *as a covenant by which we gain entrance into the presence of God, this covenant is superseded.* Note that the writer of Hebrews is clearly referring to the Mosaic Covenant and *emphasizing its priestly-sacrificial dimensions when he states that it, as a covenant, is vanishing* (see Heb. 8).

The suspension of the sacrificial system is thought by many to have reference only to this age of the Temple's suspension and that a reestablishment of the Temple system will occur in the

Millennium, under the Messiah. However, as the Temple system in ancient times pointed forward in anticipation of Messiah's work, so it will point back in the future. The sacrifices also exemplified dedication and thanksgiving.[11] However, this would not be the *same* Temple system as before (see Ezek. 40–48). Others interpret Ezekiel as symbolic and do not anticipate a future literal Temple.

This does not mean that the Mosaic writings are not Scripture, profitable for doctrine, reproof, correction, and training in righteousness (see 2 Tim. 3:16). Nor does it mean that these documents (Torah) cannot give guidance to a Jewish calling and identity. This transcends the sacrificial-priestly system. The feasts, for example, are the national celebrations of Israel and exist because of God's promise to make of Abraham a great nation. They celebrate God's acts of grace to Israel. Although recorded in the Mosaic writings, they are essentially connected to the Abrahamic Covenant, a covenant of faith and promise still in effect. Nowhere does Hebrews even hint that the writer is opposed to the celebration of God's faithfulness in Jewish history when Yeshua—not the sacrifices—is the center of every feast.

The Book of Hebrews is one of the most "Jewish" books from the first century! By its specific emphasis, it shows the meaning of Yeshua in a most Jewish way. Because it only emphasizes the obsolescence of the Temple-sacrificial system and not of Israel and its national life, and because it appeals to the great heroes of Jewish history as the major example and spur to faith, it is a book which certainly supports a Messianic Jewish calling.

SECOND CORINTHIANS 3:7-18

Now if the dispensation of death, carved in letters on stone, came with such splendor that the Israelites could not look at Moses' face because of its brightness, fading as this was, will not the dispensation of the Spirit be attended with greater splendor? For if there was splendor in the dispensation of condemnation, the dispensation of righteousness must far exceed it in splendor. Indeed, in this case, what once had splendor has come to have no splendor at all, because of the splendor that surpasses it. For if what faded away came with splendor, what is permanent must have much more splendor.

Since we have such a hope, we are very bold, not like Moses, who put a veil over his face so that the Israelites might not see the end of the fading splendor. But their minds were hardened; for to this day, when they read the old covenant, that same veil remains unlifted, because only through [Messiah] *is it taken away. Yes, to this day whenever Moses is read a veil lies over their minds; but when a man turns to the Lord the veil is removed. Now the Lord is the Spirit, and where the Spirit of the Lord is, there is freedom. And we all, with unveiled face, beholding the glory of the Lord, are being changed into his likeness from one degree of glory to another; for this comes from the Lord who is the Spirit* (RSV).

This chapter provides us with several unusual statements. Here a contrast is made between the New and Old Covenant ministries. We should note that the references contrasting the New Covenant relate not to the Tenach or the Old Covenant Scriptures as a whole, nor even the Torah (Genesis–Deuteronomy), but only the covenant ministry Moses received from God. There is no contrast with the Abrahamic Covenant recorded in Genesis 12–22. Of this Mosaic Covenant received from Sinai, we read these descriptive words: "The written code kills," "the dispensation of death," and "dispensation of condemnation." In contrast, the New Covenant is called the "dispensation of the Spirit" and the "dispensation of righteousness." Indeed, the New Covenant is compared to the Old as one that has greater splendor and permanence, while the Old is fading away.

A superficial reading of this passage causes some to reach very popular, untenable conclusions. A reading in the light of the whole context of Pauline theology, however, gives an understanding that is both rich and consistent. Among the untenable conclusions reached by some are that: (1) We should have nothing to do with the content of Torah, since its content produces spiritual death; (2) A Jew who accepts Yeshua, but practices his heritage of feast and nationhood, seeks to remain under a dispensation of death rather than fully embracing the new dispensation of life in the Spirit.

The first conclusion is utterly false. Need we again quote Second Timothy 3:16-17: *"All Scripture* is inspired by God and is profitable for doctrine, reproof, correction...." The psalmist says, "The law of the Lord is perfect, giving life to the soul" (see Ps. 19:7). Is Scripture contradictory? Does what brings life in Psalm 19 bring death in Second Corinthians 3? Obviously not! Paul clearly says of the Law that God gave it as part of His revelation:

> *So the law is holy, and the commandment is holy and just and good. Did that which is good, then, bring death to me? By no means! It was sin, working death in me through what is good, in order that sin might be shown to be sin and through the commandment might become sinful beyond measure. We know that the law is spiritual; but I am carnal, sold under sin* (Romans 7:12-14 RSV).

This passage gives the solution to false interpretations that despise Torah. When Paul called the Mosaic Covenant ministry the dispensation of death, it was not because of its inherent nature. It was rather because of what people made of the Torah by their approach to it. Because humans are sinful, they approached Torah as a system of works-righteousness and falsely sought to earn God's favor by their own merits or to bring the Age of Restoration by human means. Although the Law is a guide under the leading of the Spirit of God, when used as a written code to be followed in our own fleshly power, it condemns. For by the Law's high standard, we all stand condemned (see Rom. 3:23). So as to not face this condemnation, a person rationalizes his faults and becomes self-righteous. Yet Scripture says God dwells with those who are of a contrite and humble heart (see Isa. 57:15). Hence, an approach to the Law with this self-righteous attitude served to separate people from God, producing a dispensation of death.

The Mosaic revelation itself was not a dispensation of death; but humanity's approach to it produced this legalistic orientation. Even the foremost sixteenth-century Christian theologian, John Calvin, said of this passage, "There are some rash teachers who hold we should throw out the tablets of the law calling the law a dispensation of death." He responded, "Perish this wicked thought from our minds."[12]

The issue is not whether the Torah is used for guidance, teaching, and correction (see 2 Tim. 3:16-17) but rather, the attitude of approach. Approached with dependence upon God's mercy, the Law, as Psalm 19 says, gives life to the soul.

What of the contrast between the Mosaic Covenant and the New Covenant in terms of glory? The Mosaic Covenant of Exodus 20 and Deuteronomy was glorious. However, the New Covenant—which outstrips it in power—has much greater glory! It is by the light of the New Covenant that we see, once and for all, the end of all self-righteousness. As humanity gazes at Yeshua hanging on the tree, all pretensions to merit-by-works are utterly stripped away. All self-based honor is destroyed.

The New Covenant replaces the Mosaic as the way of entrance into the presence of God. It provides a new way of approach to God by the sacrifice of Yeshua, which replaces the sacrifices of the Mosaic revelation that were so central to it. The splendor of Yeshua's personal revelation and the ministry that follows from it makes the other revelation fade in comparison. It is as a floodlight compared to a candle. It does not provide a new Law, but rather the power to do the Law in Him. In that covenant, we are accepted as righteous before God and are privileged to enter boldly unto the throne of Grace. Hence, the Mosaic mediation system of priest and sacrifice is superseded. Nothing in this passage, however, removes the gift and call of God to Jewish followers of Yeshua, which Paul calls (in Romans 11:29) "irrevocable." The Apostles' example in maintaining their heritage is clear. Some years *after this passage was written,*[13] Paul testified that he lived in observance of the Laws and customs (see Acts 27). He was not contradicting his own writing. The call of a Jew to the purposes of Israel is a result of God's everlasting covenant with Abraham. Jewish national practices rooted in Torah primarily celebrate the fulfillment by God of those promises. In every practice, we see Yeshua's meaning and light. The message of this passage is parallel to that of Hebrews, as delineated above. For it is now by the Spirit and His conviction that we are guided to do God's will and follow His call with the Scriptures as our resource. This is freedom indeed. In this walk, we are transformed step-by-step into the likeness of the Messiah (see 2 Cor. 3:18).

There is one more very amazing verse, part of the context, that fully dispels the misunderstanding. It is that the New Covenant proclamation itself that should give life can as well become a means of death if not rightly received. Second Corinthians 2:16 states that, "We are the aroma of death leading to death." This is said in regard to those whose choice causes them to be described as those who are perishing, for whom his emissaries are the aroma of death to death.

Of course, I recognize that Yeshua's teaching applies Moses in the New Covenant in a much more exacting way. The Torah is intensified. There are new commandments in the New Covenant Scriptures as well.

ALL FOODS DECLARED CLEAN (MARK 7:19; ACTS 10)

This passage is usually quoted to imply the end of any relevance for the food laws of Leviticus 11 and to give evidence that all practices rooted in Torah (Genesis–Deuteronomy) are also to be eliminated.

Messianic Jews have various interpretations of the food lists contained in Leviticus 11. Their approaches seek an understanding of the purposes of the lists. Some hold that these laws are related to the symbolic meaning of animals as not fitting a concept of wholeness or because they feed on carrion and are thus too tied to the death and decay (symbols) resulting from sin for proper usage.[14] Others hold that these laws have definite health value and are still valid today. Some teach that the "clean-unclean laws" only precluded a person from Temple worship for a day or a week, etc. They were ritual laws. Hence, without a Temple system, these laws lose direct relevance for those who are in Yeshua. Others hold that these laws have continuing validity in keeping Jews a distinct people through being unique in what they do not eat.[15] Chapter Seven will give my perspective on these laws. However, the issue of food laws must be settled in the light of their purpose. We must also take into consideration the elimination of the Temple system by the work of Yeshua. The phrase in Mark has little bearing on the issue.

A careful reading of the passage in context proves that the passage does not eliminate the distinctions of Leviticus. In Mark chapter seven, Yeshua was criticized because His disciples ate without following the prescribed hand-washing ritual by the tradition of the Pharisees. According to tradition, this made the food unclean. Yeshua's response was first a criticism of the tradition which set aside the commands of God by interpreting them in such a way that the actual command in its intent is disobeyed!

Yeshua taught that the more important issue of clean and unclean is not foods or rituals of washing, but the nature of one's heart and the behavior that flows from it. This is ethical or moral and not just a matter of ritual purity. Real spiritual defilement does not depend upon what goes into a person and passes out, but relates to the spiritual heart of the person, which, when corrupt, is the source of sin (evil) thoughts, sexual immorality, theft, murder, adultery, greed, malice, deceit, etc.[16]

Yeshua did not directly teach that the food laws or the biblical heritage of Jews was then at an end. Indeed the statement, "Jesus declared all foods clean" may be a scribal addition, as noted in English versions by brackets. We cannot be sure that it comes from Mark himself. Let us assume that it does. If so, it does not say, as often misquoted, that "all things are clean," but that all *foods* are clean. A *food* could be defined as that which was listed as acceptable in Leviticus 11 and Deuteronomy. Hence, the passage may only mean that foods not ritually treated according to the extra-biblical Pharisaic tradition are yet acceptable for eating. When we turn to the parallel of Matthew 15:20, this becomes almost certain—for Yeshua there concludes that, "eating with unwashed hands does not make [him] 'unclean.'"

The issue clearly is the clean and unclean nature of foods in regard to ceremonial washing and handling. Pork would not be considered a food. Certainly, poisonous plants are not options for our eating. "You shall not test the Lord your God" would apply to the foolishness of eating poisonous foods knowingly and expecting God's protection. Some hold that the unclean foods of Leviticus 11 possess such dangers in more limited degrees.

However we may interpret the above Scripture, the application of the biblical kosher laws cannot be determined on the basis of this passage alone. The passage gives little weight to a generalized conclusion that all celebrations of the Jewish biblical heritage are now to be eliminated.

MATTHEW 6:7

And in praying do not heap up empty phrases (vain repetitions) *as the Gentiles do; for they think that they will be heard for their many words* (RSV).

Jewish worship, even in the time of Yeshua, was partly liturgical. The word *liturgy* does not connote a dangerous practice to avoid. Liturgy simply is an order of prayers and readings that are written or orally memorized and repeated as part of worship. It

carries the meaning of that which is *authorized* by legitimate leaders. The Psalms, for example, are part of Jewish liturgy. Jewish
prayers—some of which go back to the time of Yeshua—primarily
weave Biblical verses, promises, and teachings together and put
them into prayer form so that Scripture will be prayed into one's
life and the life of the community. Spontaneous prayer, memorized prayers, and biblical passages are all integral to worship that
is pleasing to our Father in Spirit and truth (see John 4:24). Many
see some passages in the New Testament part of the liturgies
of the early Messianic Jewish community. This includes Colossians 1:15ff., Hebrews 1:1ff., and Philippians 2:5ff. Of course, to
Christians that are part of liturgical churches, this objection has
no weight. The objection comes from Christians who are in non-
liturgical churches.

The problem, as indicated, is simply this: Messianic Jews have
adopted some of the great prayers of Judaism that are biblical in
content. Despite the fact that such material *is* biblical in theology
and content, Messianic Jews are accused of engaging in vain repetition that is contrary to the Spirit. To some accusers, only worship
that is made up "on the spot," spontaneously is of the Spirit. These
folks do not recognize that such a view would actually *eliminate*
their choruses and hymns as well. But since music makes these
forms more enjoyable to them, they are accepted.

A hymn is a prayer sung to God; and there is no reason why
a spoken prayer may not be as spiritual as a hymn that is sung.
The accusation of *vain repetition* comes because the prayer may be
repeated daily or weekly, as well as from the allegation that such
prayers are not as *emotionally* moving to some people as musically-
sung choruses and hymns. The interpretation of this passage in
some quarters arises from a contemporary cultural prejudice
against form, and is, itself, fraught with difficulties.

What is Yeshua saying in Matthew 6? He was first teaching
His disciples not to pray like *Gentiles or pagans*. The characteristic of
pagan religion He probably had in mind was its magical-legalistic

character. Pagans envisioned that if they said a phrase over and over it would produce certain definite results. The prayer could be babbled over and over without *any meaning* or thought, but as a magical way of manipulating the gods or nature.

Yeshua's point is that when we pray, we are coming before our personal heavenly Father. Hence our prayer must be given consciously as a *heart-intended* offering to Him of praise or a *heart-intended* request of intercession. If the prayer is written or memorized, it should be said with thought so that we will mean it! We must make it *our own* through our heart attitude. If the prayer is spontaneous, the same holds true. How vain are the repetitions of those so-called spontaneous prayers that are babbled out without thought or heart-intention! Imagine coming before a person and saying *Hallelujah* over and over again as fast as you can, without putting your heart and mind behind it! Yet some who criticize us for praying a psalm do just this and are themselves guilty of vain repetition. They do not direct their hearts to God, but are emotionally "psyching themselves up" through fast repetition.

To cap the argument, Yeshua goes on to teach the Apostles a simple memorized prayer that can be said *with* meaning and used with other prayers. This prayer is in mnemonic form, as can be seen in modern translations that put it into poetical form. Furthermore, the prayer is parallel in its content to the ancient Jewish prayer known as the *Kaddish*, which Yeshua probably prayed in the synagogue:

Yeshua's Prayer   Kaddish

Our Father in heaven,   Glorified and sanctified be God's

hallowed be your name.   great name in the world which he created according to his will.

Thy kingdom come.   May he establish his kingdom

Thy will be done in earth   during the days of your life

as it is in heaven.   and all the house of Israel.

The importance of heart-intention is crucial to infusing repeated prayers and psalms with meaning. It is also crucial in keeping spontaneous prayer from degenerating into stereotypical phrases and clichés that have no meaning. The rabbis called such heart-intention *kavanah* and taught that without it, prayers are vain!

The best teachers of worship have always taught that both spontaneous prayer *and* repeated content are important to balanced worship. Repeated content teaches us how to pray scripturally by making scriptural content the center of our prayer so our heart's desire is God's own desire. Spontaneous prayer then is enriched by biblical content and brings freshness to the worship. All worship should be offered to our God who is present, a real person before whom we bring offerings of praise and intercession.

The issue should not be primarily our boredom, but God's (see Mal. 2:1). We know from God's directives for worship in Torah that He enjoined acts of worship that were precisely repeated daily, weekly, and annually. He also delighted Himself in spontaneous acts of praise and prayer. Problems in worship are not only matters of style, but issues of whether or not our spirit is open to the inspiration of the Spirit in all acts of worship so our love and imagination soar toward God! "God is spirit and those who worship Him must worship in spirit and truth" (John 4:24 RSV).

Colossians 2:16-23

Therefore do not let anyone judge you by what you eat or drink, or with regard to a religious festival, a New Moon celebration or a Sabbath day. These are a shadow of the things that were to come; the reality, however, is found in [Messiah]. *Do not let anyone who delights in false humility and the worship of angels disqualify you for the prize. Such a person goes into great detail about what he has seen, and his unspiritual mind puffs him up with idle notions. He has lost connection with the Head, from whom the whole body, supported and held together by its ligaments and sinews, grows as God causes it to grow. Since you died with* [Messiah] *to the basic principles of this world, why, as though you still belonged to it, do you submit to its rules: "Do not handle! Do not taste! Do not touch!"? These are all destined to perish with use, because they are based on* **human commands and teachings**. *Such regulations indeed have an appearance of wisdom, with their self-imposed worship, their false humility, and their harsh treatment of the body, but they lack any value in restraining sensual indulgence.*

This passage is somewhat obscured by the fact that we do not know the circumstances to which it was addressed. Some quote the passage as proof against celebrating Jewish festivals. Yet the passage is far more complex, for the situation evidently reflected not only those who were judgmental in regard to Jewish observances, but who also worshipped angels (see Col. 2:18), "practiced asceticism" in a harsh treatment of the body (see Col. 2:23), and were involved in superstitions of not touching or tasting. These superstitions involved participation in the "elemental spirits" of the universe—which are demons. All of this is called "philosophy and empty deceit according to the elemental spirits of the universe." But it is clearly *not* speaking about biblical Judaism; that could not be described as connecting Israel to demons!

This has prompted *many scholars* who are students of the passage to hold that Paul was not addressing a group of Jews who were in the mainstream of Judaism, but one of those heretical Jewish groups (or even superstitious Judaized non-Jews) who were *influenced by pagan superstition* and seeking to teach their doctrine at Colosse. Hence, Paul could enjoin the Colossians not to be brought under judgment by those who would enforce Jewish observance on them. The very ones who are doing such mischief are engaged in superstition.

Jewish observances point to Yeshua, the substance of the faith which they already have. Therefore, it is not incumbent on them to be forced into these practices. At the same time, Paul enjoins them to avoid clearly pagan practices connected to the disarmed "principalities and powers," a phrase which is usually taken to refer to the most powerful of demonic rulers. Paul would *never* call the content of Torah human commands and teachings connected to the powers of darkness.

Clearly, what is in mind *is not* the call of a Jew to maintain his celebration of God's gracious work in the history of Israel and the world. Rather, it is the imposition of such practices on non-Jews that is forbidden, as well as the whole *quasi-magical superstition present at Colosse.*

Paul does not contradict his own practice, as recorded in Acts. The passage says nothing negative to a Jew who, in light of the whole of biblical history, senses a call of God's Spirit to remain part of his people and to celebrate God's faithfulness to Israel through the festivals that are now used to extol salvation in Yeshua as well. God has faithfully preserved the Jewish people according to His covenant, and the Messianic Jew is a unique witness to the covenant-keeping God, that gives confidence to *all* people of God's faithfulness. As a witness to his own people as well, his involvement in the concerns of the Jewish community—as well as in the biblical heritage—is necessary if the love of the Messiah is to be demonstrated. Only then is the truth heralded that, "God has not forsaken his people" (see Rom. 11). Israel is a unique people with a unique biblical-cultural life. So far as it is consistent with Scripture, the Messianic Jew will be involved in identification with Israel—on many possible levels. He or she should not shirk the work involved, for the Spirit can strengthen him to every good work. God did not spend 2,000 years creating a context for understanding the Gospel only to destroy the context of understanding.

TITUS 3:9

But avoid foolish controversies and genealogies and arguments and quarrels about the law, because these are unprofitable and useless.

Paul here speaks of divisive people who will not submit themselves to spiritual authority. They are contentious, always looking for arguments, and therefore, dangerous.

The phrase sometimes cited against Messianic Judaism is to avoid "quarrels about the law." This is taken to mean that we are to avoid the Law or any discussion of its meaning or purpose since the Law no longer has relevance for us. How false is this view in the light of Second Timothy 3:16-17, which calls "all Scripture profitable" and Second Timothy 2:15, which calls us to diligence in studying, to correctly handle "the Word of truth." To have a sincere concern to understand the meaning and purpose of the Law in the light of all Scripture is clearly a God-given mandate. This is indeed a major theme of Romans 2–8. Paul is not contradicting his own concern to understand "God's holy, just, good and spiritual law" (see Rom. 7) in the light of God's purpose for it. Quarrels and controversies we *are* to avoid, but those who are anti-Law also engender such quarrels and are similarly to be avoided as "lawless men."

SUMMARY

We have sought to explain many of the passages that are used by the critics of Messianic Judaism. Our summary of these passages—in light of all the evidence of Scripture—supports rather than detracts from Messianic Jewish conclusions.

Often the naive follower of Yeshua will find an erstwhile opponent stringing these passages together *out of context*. He is then shaken by the seeming weight these passages carry in contradiction of Messianic Judaism. However, we could just as easily string together pro-Messianic Jewish passages.

The problem is that prejudice and *preconceived* conceptions have caused the very picking and choosing of these passages. Bias illicitly uses Scripture for its own purposes. When all of the passages are seen in the light of the *whole* teaching of Scripture and in the *context* of the situation to which each passage was addressed, the problems dissolve. The Messianic Jewish understanding can then be seen to be that which is in accord with Scripture. May this chapter strengthen faith in the marvelous consistency and wisdom in the revelation of God.

It is principle that when Scripture seems to speak against the Law, it is generally speaking of the *misuse* of the Law as a means of gaining merit for salvation by works-righteousness or depending upon the Law for our relationship with God. Our obedience is rather the response of love produced by God's Spirit in us.

Chapter Five

SURVEY OF THE HISTORY OF JUDAISM AND CHRISTIANITY

A T THE CLOSE OF THE New Testament period, we find the following picture: Jewish followers of Yeshua maintained their identity through the practice of their biblical heritage as part of their continued call from God. They were thus both witnesses to the *world* of God's historical revelation and God's eschatological plan and witnesses of Yeshua to their *own people*.

Extra-biblical records also prove the continued Jewish way of life among first and early second century Messianic Jews.[1] The very disciples of those who *knew* Yeshua maintained this lifestyle. The practice of New Covenant Jewish groups in the early second century, however, was not uniform. Several groups can be distinguished.

The Ebionites are discussed by Jerome and Eusebius. Apparently they carried on the anti-Paul stance of the circumcision party mentioned in the New Testament. They rejected most of the New Testament except for Matthew, which they produced in a unique version of their own. They also rejected the divinity of Yeshua. The name *Ebionite*—which means "poor one"—could be a reference to a weak or poor view of Yeshua or to the fact that they lived with little material wealth.[2]

The second group was the Nazarenes. This group was probably closest in viewpoint to the disciples and those closest personally to them. The work of recent scholars has capably distinguished them from the Ebionites. They were biblically-oriented in a very full sense and accepted the central doctrines of the New Covenant Scriptures. They practiced their Jewish heritage as part of their life in Yeshua. Messianic Jews today identify most often with this group.[3]

The third group was the Assimilationists. These were Jews in Greek-speaking lands that were distant from their Jewish heritage. In accepting the Gospel while acculturated in a predominantly non-Jewish setting, their Jewish identity was eventually lost.

We are indeed thankful that God has provided us with records by which we can understand the perspectives of these communities.[4]

The writings of early Church fathers preserved by Eusebius and the work of Josephus, the Jewish historian, provide important information on these groups.

After the death of the disciples, leadership among the Jewish believers in Yeshua passed to James' (Jacob's) cousins. By the middle of the second century, however, the situation had vastly changed. Great change first occurred between 68 and 100 C.E.. Unfortunately, the exact nature of the process is hidden by a lack of sources from this period. However, by the end of this period we see a church and synagogue at war with each other while Messianic Jews were rejected by both groups.

The progress of this split can be mapped in basic terms. First, the New Testament was written in Greek to convey the message of God to a more universal audience. Although the background of the New Covenant was Hebraic, Greeks often applied its content to a Greek context, leading them to adopt teachings and ways of expression that were Greek-oriented. Hence, the Church became more foreign to Jewish people.

After the death of the Apostles, the leadership of most of the Church passed to non-Jewish leaders. Unfortunately, many of these leaders did not appreciate Jewish people or their Jewish biblical heritage. The fall of Jerusalem was evidence to them of God's *ultimate rejection* of Israel in spite of Paul's teaching in Romans 11. That "all Israel would be saved," was interpreted to mean that all Jews and Gentiles who accepted Jesus—and were thus spiritual Israel—would be saved. Judaism, to them, was dead. Passages in the New Testament which condemned the hypocrisy of the Jewish religious establishment were interpreted as condemning all things Jewish.

Hence we find in Justin Martyr's *Dialogue with Trypho the Jew* (130-150 c.e.) that a condescending attitude was often projected. Although aware of the Jewish Nazarenes, he could not understand their continued practice of their Torah heritage. He could accept that they were "saved," but found it inconsistent that they practiced what Yeshua fulfilled—which he took to mean eliminated.[5]

The Epistle of Barnabas (100 c.e.), according to H.L. Ellison, used such language about Jews, Judaism, and the Law as to make any effective contact with the Synagogue impossible.[6]

Ignatius of Antioch (early second century) spoke as well of the uselessness of all things Jewish.[7]

Yet in the midst of all this, it is crucial to remember that the Nazarene Jews were the very relatives of Yeshua and disciples of the disciples who carried on their practices!

The continued development of official Church doctrine concerning Jews in the centuries following brought a wider gap between the Church and Synagogue. The Church was not only "New Israel," but the only "true" Israel. Old Israel was reprehensible before God. Bishop Ambrose (fourth century) therefore allowed the burning of synagogues and stated that this was not a sin. Augustine argued that Old Israel served only one purpose: to exhibit the wretched plight of those who reject God.

These viewpoints led to the spiritualization (allegorization) of the prophecies and promises in Scripture that referred to the physical descendents of Abraham. All reference to Israel's promise of land forever was taken to mean the Church's inheritance of the Kingdom. That God would gain His ultimate triumph over the nations through Israel and then bless the world through Israel was taken to mean the triumph of and blessings for the Church. As one writer succinctly put it, the Church took all the blessings and left Israel with all the cursings.[8]

The Synagogue, on the other hand, rejected the Nazarene Jews and developed its viewpoint in parallel opposition to Church views.

Before the fall of Jerusalem to the Roman General Titus in the year 70 c.e., there were several divisions within Judaism. The Pharisees, the Saducees, and the Essenes represented the three most prominent sects. The Nazarene Jews constituted an additional perspective within Israel. We do not know all of the reasons for the rejection of the Nazarenes by the Jewish community, but some prominent reasons stand out.

When the Roman armies approached Jerusalem to quell Israel's rebellion, the Nazarenes fled the city, taking up residence in Pella. They thereby avoided the terrible destruction and slaughter by the Roman army. The rest of the Jewish community branded the Nazarenes traitors, no longer to be accepted. Why did the Nazarenes flee? The major reason was the prophecy and command of Yeshua! In Luke 21 and Matthew 24, Yeshua predicted that armies would surround Jerusalem. His followers were told that when they saw this beginning to occur, they were to "flee to the mountains." They were not traitors; they were simply following Yeshua's teaching.

Another reason for their rejection, no doubt, was their theology. It was abhorrent to many Jews to think of their great King Messiah dying on a cross as a common criminal. The idea so went against the common idea of the Messiah's role and majesty that any explanation of how the suffering role was a prelude to the kingly role was not allowed. So severe was the rejection of this view in some circles that there was no acceptance of the people who held it. The Messiah being so shamed was considered a great affront to the honor of the Messiah and the Jewish people.

In addition, prominent Synagogue leaders were angered because the preaching of the New Covenant blunted their efforts to gain converts from Gentile ranks. A Gentile could accept Yeshua, worship the God of Israel, and claim salvation and priestly status without the stigma of circumcision or the necessity of adopting all the practices of the Jewish tradition. Many potential converts left the Synagogue for the new movement.

After the Temple fell, only one party within Judaism— the Pharisees—had the strength to assert leadership. The Sadducees were too connected to the Temple system and the Essenes' losses were too severe. Pharisaic Judaism was the precursor to today's Orthodox Rabbinic Judaism. The rabbis moved to preserve and unify the Jewish community under their teachings and sought to exclude all other forms of Judaism. Orthodox Rabbinic Judaism soon became normative Judaism. The Nazarenes received special condemnation by the rabbis. The Sanhedrin of Jamnia (90 c.e.) not only defined Judaism, but it also condemned heretics.

Some believe that at this time the *"Berkat ha Minim"* was added to the Twelfth Benediction (some argue it was added before this time). It prayed a prayer of condemnation for heretics. Although this prayer was later altered by force under Christian rulers, it probably originally singled out the Nazarenes and prayed for their destruction.[9] A Nazarene Jew in the synagogue would not be able to pray this and would thus be excluded. Thus, the Nazarenes were cast out of rabbinical synagogues.

Further reflection of this rejection is found in the Talmudic story where a Rabbi Jacob was sick. Upon questioning, it was learned that his sickness was caused by once being pleased by a saying of Yeshua that a follower of His quoted.[10]

We recognize that the rabbis of this age preserved much of the great heritage of Jewish history. However, this was overlaid with material contrary to Scripture, including the interpretations that rejected the Messiahship and work of Yeshua. Rabbinic Judaism as a system was in some ways a new thrust away from the things most important to the heart of God.

The Bar-Kochba Revolt further intensified the separation of the Nazarenes from the rest of the Jewish community.

Bar Kochba, a ruthless military leader, spearheaded a second revolt against Rome in the 130s c.e.. He recruited the Jewish population still in the land for his revolt. At first, it seemed that the Messianic Jews followed Bar Kochba and sought by this means to demonstrate their loyalty to Israel. However, during the war, the venerable Rabbi Akiba proclaimed Bar Kochba the Messiah.[11] Other rabbis rejected this proclamation, but the damage was done: Messianic Jews could not follow a false Messiah. Only Yeshua was the Messiah. Bar Kochba massacred those who would not give him total allegiance. The Romans quelled this revolt. A great loss of Jewish lives resulted; Rabbi Akiba and Bar Kochba were slain. Despite the tragic ruthlessness of Bar Kochba and the error of Akiba, the Nazarenes were again branded as traitors for not fighting in the revolt. Over the next few centuries, the Nazarene communities dwindled and ultimately vanished.[12]

I did not yet mention the issue of the deity of Yeshua, which was very clear after the writings of the New Covenant Scriptures. The Jewish reaction to this was very intense. Orthodox Jewish scholar Daniel Boyarin argues that the idea of a plurality in God that is similar to the later understanding of the Son was common in Judaism, even the majority consensus. However, Judaism sought to cleanse this idea out of its tradition. Boyarin presents massive evidence for this thesis.[13]

The result of this history was the loss of the testimony of loyal Jews who believed in Yeshua. Without such a community within the Jewish community, the bridge of understanding between Jewry and the Church was lost as well. Messianic Jews could have kept alive the picture of a Jewish Jesus. This would have done much to stem the tide of future anti-Semitism. With the loss of this bridge of understanding, Church-Synagogue hostility increased. Both the Church and Synagogue fought for proselytes among the Gentiles.[14] In competition, they formed their theologies in opposition to each other. Christian theological positions were adopted because they freed the Church from Jewish roots and were contrary to Jewish teaching. To the theologians of the day, there was no longer a covenant with Israel as a nation; there was no longer a purpose for Jewish identity. The Church was seen as all in all in God's purposes. Some positions that were adopted were *anti-Semitic* as the next section will recount.

The Synagogue also honed *its* theology in opposition. God's unity was thus a singular numerical unity that allowed for no sense of plurality at all, this concept being contrary to the Trinity.[15] All the passages of Scripture which pointed to a suffering Messiah as well as any concept of substitutionary atonement for sin were played down.

Church ritual, statues as aids to worship, and Greek theological concepts intensified the Jewish view that the Church was a semi-pagan institution. When the Roman Empire adopted Christianity as its official religion in the fourth century and institutional Christianity became a persecuting Church, hope for understanding and reconciliation diminished.

I think it is important to note that this separation was not total. The intense opposition of Church Fathers to Judaism was sometimes in a context of Christians being attracted to Synagogues and attending so as to gain a better understanding of the Bible. There were philosemites, as Oscar Skarsaune, the Norwegian biblical scholar, points out in an article in Norwegian, but not available to us in English.

A History of Anti-Semitism

So, I ask, have they stumbled so as to fall? By no means! But through their trespass salvation has come to the Gentiles, so as to make Israel jealous. Now if their trespass means riches for the world, and if their failure means riches for the Gentiles, how much more will their full inclusion mean! Now I am speaking to you Gentiles. Inasmuch then as I am an apostle to the Gentiles, I magnify my ministry in order to make my fellow Jews jealous, and thus save some of them (Romans 11:11-14).

Here we read the directive of God through Paul—that Jewish people are to see the riches of the Gospel in the lives of Gentiles (those from the nations) and be moved to jealousy because of the reality which such a life and love manifest. By this jealousy, they would turn to the Messiah and receive Him. Sadly, the history of the Church hardly fulfilled this mission.

Soon after the Jewish Apostles died, the leadership of the Church was transferred to people who had no great respect for Jews or Judaism. Rather than seeing the Jewish people as erring brethren to whom they were indebted for the gifts of Scripture, the Messiah, and biblical saints, the Jewish people were looked upon as reprobates hated by God. The views expressed against some Jewish leaders by Jewish followers of Yeshua was used by later non-Jewish leaders as an indictment of all Jewish people.[16]

The Epistle of Barnabas, from the end of the first century, reflects this negative attitude and applies it to Jewish practices as well. As H.L. Ellison put it:

Already the so-called Epistle of Barnabas, which may go back to the last decade of the first century, uses such language about Jews, Judaism and the Law, as to make any effective contact between the two sides virtually impossible. As soon as it had the power, the Church did its utmost to defeat God's purpose. It persecuted and bullied, thereby automatically putting itself in the wrong. It spread the vilest calumnies about the Jews.[17]

Many writers did not display an accurate understanding of the very things they criticized, including the nature of the revelation in the Hebrew Scriptures. Ignatius of Antioch, in the same period, was clear in indicating the uselessness of all Jewish things.[18]

Justin Martyr, one of the famed leaders of the early second century, spoke of Jewish people and practice in condescending terms. In his *Dialogue with Trypho the Jew,* he expressed dismay over the fact that Jewish followers of Yeshua still maintained their cultural identity and practice.[19] He accepted the possibility of their salvation, but could not understand Jewish practice as a way of expressing their faith. Justin believed that fulfillment by Yeshua eliminated Jewish practice.

As the decades passed, the Christian polemic against Jews and Jewish practice continued. Bishop Ambrose, in the fourth century, even went so far as to suggest that burning a synagogue was no sin. Why? Because the Jews rejected Yeshua; therefore, what could be considered a crime against others would not be a crime against Jews. This interpretation overlooked the fact that it was the Jews who first followed Yeshua and who originally spread the Good News throughout the Roman Empire; it overlooked the great number of Jews who did follow Yeshua; and it overlooked Judaism as the original context of Christian faith.

John Chrysostom, however, is the author of the greatest viru-lence. Chrysostom was threatened because Christians in Antioch visited synagogues to gain a better understanding of the Jewish roots of their faith. Chrysostom held that the coming of Chris-tianity eliminated the value of Jewish practice and identity. To destroy any Christian interest in Judaism, Chrysostom wrote eight sermons against the Jews. The poisonous hate of these sermons has not been surpassed. Nor was Chrysostom just an isolated individual. He was a renowned Church leader. His viewpoint, therefore, became part of the attitude of institutional Christianity.

Augustine himself, the great theological giant revered by both Catholics and Protestants, added his own fuel to the fire. He explained the purpose of the continued existence of the Jewish community in strictly negative terms. The reprobate state of the Jews, who were under God's judgment, would provide a witness to the truth of Christianity, he said, as well as an example of what happens to people who turn against God. Some have pointed out that there is a more positive side to Augustine, and his hope of the eventual salvation of the Jews, especially in his later writings. However, his statements on their present state were grounds for hatred and rejection.

Perhaps we could point to many parallels of religious and social prejudice. The venom released in intense religious dispute is great. Institutional Christianity became the favored religion when Emperor Constantine converted to Christianity in the fourth century. Religious bigotry thus became part of state policy; severe economic and social sanctions were progressively applied to the Jews.[20] The church-state collaboration in discrimination was maintained for fifteen centuries.

When we come to our own age, we find that Nazi leaders defended their actions by claiming to follow the history of Church tradition. Luther's sermons against the Jews were widely disseminated. The historical image of the "insidious Jew" prepared the way for Auschwitz. The Church found it difficult to recognize its own complicity; for although it had demeaned the value of Jewish people, it did not draw the implication that they had no right to exist. The Nazis drew this implication.

It is often asked, why did so many of the people of "Christian Europe" stand by during the Holocaust? Human weakness, ignorance, fear of taking risks for others, self-protection, and a crowd mentality are often mentioned. Some point to the very work of the devil himself in blinding the minds of people. However, to all of these reasons, we must add another key reason: The historic tradition of the Church in its teaching on Jews and Judaism served to undercut concern for the Jewish people.

In all fairness, we must mention that there were individual Christians who stood with Jewish people against this tradition. Some through their close walk with Yeshua gained a deep love for Jewish people, in many cases sacrificing their lives for their Jewish friends.

We should note that some have traced the origins of anti-Semitism to early Jewish persecutions of Christians. Although there was fierce persecution of Jewish followers of Yeshua, this was an intra-Jewish battle. The most competent scholars who deal with this early period now consider Jewish persecution of non-Jewish Christians an unwarranted assumption.[21]

The greatest irony can be seen in the fact that Yeshua's disciples opened the door to anti-Jewishness by adopting a liberal policy toward Gentiles and their admission into the universal Body of Believers. They were permitted entrance without the cultural restrictions of Jewish identity. This freedom was a great spur to the spread of the Gospel among the Gentiles. However, although the original identity and way of life among Yeshua's followers was Jewish, when the later non-Jewish majority was in control, they restricted freedom and would not allow for Jewish identity within the Body of Believers. Regional Church councils like Alvira and Antioch condemned Jewish practice among Jewish Yeshua/Disciples. Nicea II in 787 c.e., a universal Church Council, condemned such continued practice as well.

The most glaring example of this is the Inquisition in sixteenth-century Spain. Those of Jewish origin who claimed to follow Yeshua, but yet celebrated Passover, were burned at the stake. We must also mention the Crusades to free the Holy Land from Arab-Islamic control in the twelfth century. The cross was used as a symbol on the implements of war. The Crusaders were offered freedom from hell and purgatory by participating in a Crusade. The cry went out that it was inconsistent to seek to rid the Holy Land of infidel Muslims when infidel Jews lived within the midst of the lands of Europe. Hence the Crusaders held their crosses high as they pillaged and destroyed Jewish lives and property throughout Europe on their way to the Holy Land. Many were burned alive and tortured. In his book, *The Anguish of the Jews*, Fr. Edward Flannery made the perceptive statement that the cross—which was an intended symbol of giving up one's life for another, a symbol of pacifistic (in relation to violence) but active love—was thoroughly adulterated. It was now a cross sharpened into a sword to torture, kill, and plunder.[22]

Who can evaluate the extent of suffering during the numerous expulsions from many nations, from Spain in the eighth century, 1492, and throughout Jewish history? Who can evaluate the damage from forced conversions at the point of the sword from Charlemagne in the ninth century and throughout later centuries? Or how can we sum up the economic and social deprivation? Even the Reformation brought little relief to Jewry. The early Luther was sympathetic to the Jewish plight, but the later Luther attacked the Jews when they did not convert to Lutheranism. He called for making them into a caste of menial laborers for the rest of the nation.

The widespread nineteenth-century pogroms in Russia were devastating to Jewish life once more. Eastern European governments made Jews the scapegoat during difficult times.

The saddest chapter of all might be the Jewish turncoats. These supposed converts to Christianity led the pogroms and Torah burnings. Their purpose was self-serving. Joseph Pfeferkorn in sixteenth-century Hungary was responsible for many Jewish deaths. When some Jews think of Jewish Christians, it's his image that comes to mind. How tragic! Yet could there be many who honestly converted to Christianity when the Church required the convert to renounce all things Jewish, to change one's Jewish name to a "Christian name," and to give up contact with Jewish people? Each "convert" had to sign a document swearing an oath to all of these requirements!

The major ground for this anti-Semitism was often said to be the New Testament. A closer examination of the New Covenant Scriptures shows that its passages are not anti-Jewish, but can be classified instead as follows:

(1) *Statements which are negative to the established leadership* at Jerusalem consisting of Sadducees (a party which did not accept the resurrection of the dead or the prophets) and Pharisees. These were criticized severely either for a self-serving compromising life (the Sadducees) or a narrow legalism that was oftentimes self-serving and contradicted the spiritual intent of Scripture. (2) *Scriptural statements which were critical of "the Jews" in the Gospel of John,* but which were actually referring to the *Judean* leadership establishment from the perspective of Galileans.[23] For example, Americans are known as Yankees in other countries, but in the South, *Yankee* is used as a sectional term to refer to the North. In the same way, Galilean Jews referred to the *Judean Jewish establishment* as "the Jews." The word in Greek for the Judeans is the same as the word translated "Jews." (3) *Statements concerning the judgment that would fall on the nation due to the blindness of the leadership at the time.* Nations as a whole suffer under the blindness of their leaders. This was fulfilled in the wars against Rome. Thus, though nations are judged corporately, there is no right to judge all the individuals in the nation.

These statements were made by Jews but were never intended to condemn all Jewish people. Most of the statements referred to only a particular group within the nation and are not meant as universal statements. These are statements of criticism between family members and are totally invalid when repeated by non-Jews as applying to all Jews. Anti-Semites never quote John 4:22—"salvation is of the Jews" (KJV)—and admit that Jesus, the Savior of the world, was, is, and forever will be a Jew descended from Jacob!

Nor do they quote Romans 11:28-29—"...As regards election they are beloved for the sake of their forefathers. For the gifts and the call of God are irrevocable" (RSV). Neither do they quote the Gospel statements that testify, "The common people heard Him gladly," that many wept at Yeshua's death and beat their breasts, and that the priestly establishment feared all of Jerusalem following Him (see Luke 20:19,22; 23:7; 24:20). Nor is it mentioned that myriads of Jews followed Yeshua (see Acts 21) or that it was the Jewish blood of the Apostles and many other witnesses which was spilled by non-Jews.

The Jewish Apostles spread the Good News of Yeshua throughout the world. The debt of the Church is to Israel as Paul states, and the proper scriptural response is gratitude and love. As Paul says, "It is not you that support the root, but the root that supports you" (Rom. 11:18 RSV). The whole of the biblical testimony refutes the principles of anti-Semitism.

Let us note that the reason the leadership of Jerusalem handed Yeshua over to the Romans was that His popular following threatened the leadership. Let us also note that it was a Gentile Roman *instrument* of capital punishment, the cross, which was the type of execution.

Theologically, it was God's plan that Yeshua would die on the cross for the sins of the whole world (see 1 Pet. 2:24). It was our collective and universal sin that placed Him on the cross. He died not only for our punishment, but that through Him we might be freed from condemnation.

Too few gave their lives in love for Israel. How few were those like the ten Boom family who fearlessly gave themselves with courage![24] This remarkable family lost a brother, father, and sister in the Holocaust. Brother Willem ten Boom was a writer against anti-Semitism and argued against the assimilation of Jews into Western Christian forms of Christianity. He adopted Messianic Jewish conclusions back in the 1930s. The story of Corrie ten Boom is available. It is a marvelous story of God's grace in service to Israel. She received her understanding from her parents and her parents from grandparents who supported Zionism.[25]

The history of Christians and the Jewish people is a cause for much sadness. The bridge between the Church and the Synagogue, the Messianic Jews, for the most part ceased to exist. The Church and the Synagogue were light years apart in understanding each other. Yeshua was seen as a false god of the Gentiles by Jews and as a Gentile Savior by establishment Christianity. Gone was the great vision of Acts 15 of two great wings of one universal people of God: a Jewish wing and a non-Jewish wing, each part of one Body, but each, in freedom, following their distinctive callings. Neither side would seek to dissolve the other, but there could be Hebraic congregations in Jewish areas, non-Hebraic in non-Jewish areas and mixed congregations where this was most feasible—all under the Lordship of Yeshua. Jews would be believers in Yeshua, but still loyal citizens of the Jewish people. How Messianic Jews could have given the truth to the lie to anti-Semitism! How they could have reflected the Jewishness of Yeshua as a witness to the Jewish community and the Church! What a gain there would have been toward a deeper biblical understanding of Israel and the Church in the purposes of God, thereby thwarting anti-Jewish theologies.

THE RESPONSE OF HEBRAIC CONGREGATIONS

Messianic Jewish congregations are forming in response to Scripture and the impact of history. Messianic Judaism is not a *completely* new movement, but rather the resurrection of a very old movement.

We have sought to show that the identity described under the term *Messianic Judaism* was the identity of the Apostles and the community of Jewish "followers of the Way" in the first and second centuries. Since that time, many Jewish believers in Yeshua have enriched the Church as pastors, theologians, and laymen. It is true, however, that a Messianic Jewish style of existence has been lacking subsequent to the early centuries. Indeed, the Church sought to have its converts literally change their names and give up all identity as Jews.

The Synagogue, as well, sought to have followers of Yeshua ostracized from the mainstream community. A Jew who accepted Yeshua was considered no longer Jewish.

The early history of Jewish missions was often a sordid affair, with self-serving missionaries seeking to enrich themselves at the expense of gullible church members.[26] However, there were always some who understood the place and calling of Israel and whose lives were exemplary.[27]

Count Ludwig Von Zinzendorf, the founder of Hernhutt, the famous Hernhutt community in Germany, founded an underground Messianic Jewish-type community in the 1740s, as documented by Lutheran Pastor Heirbert Binder of Austria. He provides pictures of archives with illustrations of gatherings![28]

In 1825, theologian J. Toland argued that a careful reading of Scripture would lead us to believe that Israel is still called by God as a nation and that Jewish followers of Yeshua should maintain their identity and heritage as Jews.[29]

In the mid-nineteenth century, the Hebrew-Christian Alliance of Great Britain was formed. It sought to bring Jewish Christians together in periodic fellowship so as to maintain their Jewish identity. In 1915, the Hebrew-Christian Alliance of America also began to foster a purpose of Jewish identity and witness within Israel. In 1925, the International Hebrew Christian Alliance was formed. In the original founders of the Alliances one finds a deeper appreciation of Jewish identity and practice than was some-times to be found in later followers. Of note in those years was Mark John Levy, the General Secretary of the American Alliance. Levy argued indefatigably that Jewish Christians were called to maintain their heritage of feast, festival, and Hebraic worship. He traveled worldwide and in 1914 convinced the Episcopal Church to adopt, as its official position, that congregations of Jewish believers should be formed for the preservation of Jewish identity and as the best means of witness to the Jewish community. Levy was himself a gentleman, scholar, and saintly man. Even Rabbi Eichorn, who has researched the seediest aspects of Jewish missions, conceded his high character.[30]

Others of note during these years included Rabbi J. Litchenstein of Hungary, who was a district head rabbi. He became a follower of Yeshua by reading the New Testament when the light of God's grace, love, and power in Yeshua dawned on him.[31] This rabbi saw Yeshua as a Jew. He taught the New Testament from his pulpit and refused assimilation into any Christian denomination so as to remain with his people. He was so respected that for a time he could not be dismissed from his congregation—despite his unwillingness to recant his beliefs before higher authorities. He may be said to have had the first visible Messianic Jewish congregation in 1400 years. There was also Joseph Rabinowitz, who held similar views to Litchenstein and traveled in Eastern Europe and Russia. He founded a Messianic Jewish Congregation in Kishnef, Moldova.

Of special note is Theodore Luckey, who edited *The Messianic Jew* at the turn of the century. This Eastern European was a man of such kindness and piety that Dr. Henry Eimspruch called him a *"lamed vavnik,"* or one of the thirty-six righteous men of each generation who, by their saintliness, stave off God's judgment on the earth.[32] Dr. Luckey lived a life of Jewish practice and called Jesus "the bone of our bones and flesh of our flesh." Luckey argued our basic positions eighty years ago.

Strong currents were afoot in America, however, which would impede new progress toward an authentic Messianic Judaism. Fundamentalist dispensationalism, a turn-of-the-century movement, discovered the truth of God's promises to Israel—to be regathered to their land, to recognize their Messiah, and to be in the land of Israel as the geographical center of God's Kingdom. However, they held to a rigid distinction between Christians and Jews. To many, a "Christian" was a former Jew or Gentile who became part of the Bride of Christ—the Church. The converted Jew thus was to find his total spiritual identity within the Church and not in the nation of Israel. The nation had a separate identity and future salvation, but was not to be confused with those "saved" during the present age. Hence, a converted Jew, being part of the Church, could remember his origins intellectually, but was no longer to practice Jewish holidays and festivals, for these were said to be part of the "old" dispensation, while the believer was in the new dispensation of the Church. Although early Fundamentalists were fine scholars,[33] many later dispensational Fundamentalists became narrow, legalistic, and even obscurantist. This is why many contemporary evangelical Christians do not accept the Fundamentalist label.[34]

These narrow attitudes and rigid distinctions became common in the American Alliance and progress toward a more authentic Jewish movement for Yeshua was precluded. One of the casualties during these years was the enigmatic figure of Hugh Schonfeld, who is notorious for his book, *The Passover Plot*. This book seeks to discredit the resurrection of Yeshua. Schonfeld was also the author of *A History of Jewish Christianity*, which is a fine historical account and *defense* of the tenets of what we today call Messianic Judaism, though it was deficient on the deity of Yeshua. Schonfeld was a member of the British Hebrew Christain Alliance and sought to foster a more authentic Jewish expression.

When I learned of this, I was mystified as to how he had changed so radically. However, I had a sense that this sensitive young man was probably badly mistreated for his viewpoint, left the Alliance, and harbored bitterness toward Jewish Christians. This bitterness could partly explain his later skeptical writings. I corresponded with him to see if my sense was correct. It was! Furthermore, he also indicated another central problem that explained his writings. Schonfeld had occult abilities that he took to be natural abilities, but which many Christians and Messianic Jews know to usually have their source in Satan (the demonic realm) and from which a person needs deliverance. The later Schonfeld received visions of historical events and wrote the footnotes afterward to prove the truth of the visions. What a tragedy! This is documented in his book the *Politics of God*. What if Schonfeld had been treated discreetly and supportively? What if he had been delivered from occult bondage? Perhaps he could have been a great Messianic Jewish scholar. However, since that time, for several years, the Alliance made little progress toward Messianic Judaism.

This does not mean that progress was not made anywhere. Progress occurred mostly in the United States. Many European thinkers and leaders who were tending toward an authentic Jewish identity among Jewish followers of Yeshua died in the Holocaust.[35] In America, the Presbyterian Church established several important works, some of which still continue as of this writing (2012). Hebrew Christian churches were established in Los Angeles, Philadelphia, Baltimore, and Chicago. The latter two still exist, but are not longer part of the denomination.

The most influential work was the Peniel Center (est. 1921) and the First Hebrew Christian Church (est. 1934), which became Adat Hatikvah (1975). Rev. David Bronstein was the founder of both these works. Although by my theology they did not achieve an authentic Jewish expression of faith, progress toward this ideal was made. Accusations of re-erecting the "wall of partition" were made against Bronstein then, as today against Messianic Judaism. Although Christian hymns and Sunday worship provided a church atmosphere, Bronstein's own teaching, the symbolism and design of the worship hall, and the remembrance of feasts by preaching and demonstration were closer to a Messianic Jewish style than anything else in America. Rev. Bronstein's brother-in-law, Rev. Morris Kaminsky, an ordained Anglican, was called as his successor. He previously had led a Jewish Christian Congregation in Toronto.

The bridge to contemporary Messianic Judaism can be seen as we look at the ministries of Edward Brotskey, Manny Brotman, Martin Chernoff, and Ray Gannon. As a student at Moody, Brotman fostered a vision for producing materials that would speak the Good News in a thoroughly Jewish way.

This was an influence on Marty and Johanna Chernoff, who founded a Messianic Jewish Congregation in 1970 in Cincinatti. Ray Gannon and Phil Gobel, Assembly of God ministers, without knowledge of the others, founded a Messianic Jewish Congregation in 1972 in Los Angeles. These two congregations are still in operation. The First Hebrew Christian Church in Chicago, under my leadership, transitioned to a Messianic Jewish expression from 1972-1974. Ed Brotsky's congregation was a Messianic Jewish expression in Toronto, perhaps before these efforts. Space and time do not permit us to credit all who had a significant role in Messianic Judaism. We should mention the spur given to Jews who are believers in the Messiah by the Jews for Jesus under the leadership of Moishe Rosen. There was also the theological help that was given by Dr. Louis Goldberg of Moody Bible Institute, who sought to provide balance to the Messianic Jewish movement theologically from 1975 until his death some thirty years later.

Beth Messiah of Washington, D.C., which I pastored from 1978-2000, is typical of the progress of Messianic congregations. Beth Messiah was founded by a handful of Jewish believers, including Paul Liberman, Sid Roth of Messianic Vision, Sandra Sheshkin, and Marc Sircus. It was spurred on by the outreach ministry of Manny Brotman, who was called as the first leader. Since 1973, this congregation has brought scores of Jewish people to know Yeshua. It was the first independent Messianic congregation to own its own facility. It was also the planting agency for another ten congregations.

Ed Brotsky headed the first Messianic Jewish congregation in Philadelphia. Rev. Brotsky came to the faith through the ministry of Rev. Kaminsky while he was still in Toronto. A significant work under Daniel Feinstone in Philadelphia also developed into a congregation. It became Messianic Jewish in orientation under the leadership of Rev. Herb Links. It was also a Presbyterian-affiliated congregation.

The late Rev. Martin Chernoff planted an important Messianic Jewish congregation in Cincinnati in 1970. He was won to Yeshua by Rev. Morris Kaminsky and had continued contact with Chicago. Marty Chernoff next led a congregation in Philadelphia planted by Joe Finklestein after he left the work of Rev. Herb Links. His son Joel was known for pioneering Messianic Jewish music. Several Jewish missions also established small congregations of varying success and Jewishness.

In 1975, the Hebrew Christian Alliance of America changed its name to the Messianic Jewish Alliance, reflecting the growing Jewish identity of Jewish followers of Yeshua. It is at this point that a major question comes into focus: What is the distinction between Messianic Judaism and Hebrew Christianity, which was the traditional designation for Jewish believers in Yeshua?

Hebrew Christians, traditionally, have not *emphasized* the planting of Jewish congregations, but Messianic Jews have. Hebrew Christianity, at times, saw Jewishness as merely an ethnic identity, whereas Messianic Judaism saw its Jewish life and identity as a continued call of God. Of course, there are many exceptions for those who use either label. An airtight distinction cannot be made. In general, however, Messianic Judaism has emphasized the planting of Messianic Jewish congregations and fidelity to the Jewish biblical calling. The exact nature of this is still being defined. Furthermore, Messianic Jews have avoided using the term "Christian" due to its cultural sense—not being Jewish (which is a Jewish understanding of the word)—rather than its linguistic meaning, "One of the Messiah's."

An interesting aside is the story of Willem ten Boom, who we mentioned earlier. He was the brother of the famous Corrie ten

Boom. Willem ten Boom became a student of the history of the relationship between Jews and Christians. Through his studies, he came to the conclusion that it was God's desire to not have Jews assimilate, but that Jews under the Abrahamic Covenant were still chosen as a distinct nation. He came to believe that a Jew who comes to Yeshua should do so within a context of maintaining his own heritage.[36] This leads us to a practical question—How is this to be done?

The issue of Messianic congregations is a pragmatic answer to several such questions: How shall an ongoing Jewish lay witness to Israel be established? How shall a Jew be enabled to maintain his heritage of Shabbat and feast while holding to the capstone of revelation in Yeshua? How shall a Jew enable his children to grow up with a sense of heritage, to be Bar Mitzvah and maintain an ongoing involvement in the Jewish community? The Synagogue will not usually open its door to train his children, and the majority of local churches will not provide for this. The answer is clearly congregational, for achieving this individually or through a monthly fellowship is inadequate or too difficult to sustain for the average person. Many who are brought up without a Jewish congregational context have little understanding of their heritage or felicity in its practice. Without such a strong context of a Jewish fellowship of believers, an effective outreach is also blunted. Furthermore, a congregation is the most effective center of discipleship for new Jewish followers of Yeshua.

Without a visible community of Jewish and non-Jewish followers of Yeshua in a clear Hebraic fellowship, how shall the truth of Israel's call be reflected for the Jewish community and the Church? And how shall the Jewish people see Yeshua *as her* own anointed King? Such a visible community, capable of fulfilling all these goals and drawing the full resources of God's power, is only to be found in the local body (see Matt. 16).

A Messianic Jewish congregation provides the social and spiritual context to reflect the whole of biblical truth. A congregation of Messianic Jews is as well a New Covenant congregation, whose membership is open to Jew and non-Jew who are called to it and who affirm its purpose and mission. Such a congregation is a local expression of the universal Body of Believers. It fully expresses Jewish heritage in the context of New Covenant fulfillment and truth. Yeshua only established one type of organization to be empowered to carry out his work: the *Kehilah* or Congregation. There need to be such congregations within Israel to carry out His commission of witness and discipleship, rather than only "professionals" doing the work of God. Lay people in a congregational base multiply witness.[37]

Furthermore, we have to ask what institution—outside of life in Israel—is able to adequately help Jewish believers in Yeshua be established in their Jewish identity. In the light of God's supernatural preservation of Israel, in the light of untold Jewish suffering throughout the centuries, culminating in the Holocaust, and in the light of Romans 11:29—"the gifts and call of God are irrevocable"—we assert that the assimilation (loss of identity) of Jews is *not* God's will. It was the devil's desire to destroy the Jewish people as a distinct people. Can we, in the light of all history, diminish the Jewish nation by our own assimilation?

A Messianic Jewish congregation provides the social and spiritual context of discipleship in the Messiah without assimilation. Other examples of non-assimilation without congregational life usually manifest some marks of a congregation by having worship services, fellowship times, witness training, and activities to foster Jewish observance. They have simply not taken the step to be congregations or have not yet been *named congregations*. One example worth exploring is a dual expression congregation. In such a congregation, the Jewish members are encouraged to have a weekly Jewish service (which is open to the other members as well) or to have *chavurah* groups that provide the motivation for Jewish life and outreach.

Since I first wrote this argument for Messianic Jewish congregations, Dr. Mark Kinzer, in his parallel defense, has called this orientation, bilateral ecclesiology. As he argues, there is one Body of Believers, but with two types of primary distinction in expression, a Jewish expression and those expressions of the churches of the nations. The Messianic Jewish congregation is called to maintain unity with the larger Body of Believers in its locality and beyond.[38]

In 1976, the board of the Messianic Jewish Alliance called for the formation of a union of Messianic Jewish congregations as an independent organization, but in fraternal relationship to the Alliance. At the invitation of Adat Hatikvah and B'nai Macadeem, in the spring of 1978, a successful preliminary meeting of congregational leaders from nineteen congregations was held in Chicago. They agreed that they would form a union of congregations. The official incorporation meeting was set for June. Finally, in June 1979, nineteen congregations joined together in Mechanicsburg, Pennsylvania, and formed the Union of Messianic Jewish Congregations to help one another foster the goals of Messianic Judaism. This union, as of this writing, has membership of over eighty congregations. The author was elected its first president.

The Messianic congregation is a practical answer to the two-thousand-year tug-of-war between the Church and the Synagogue. In the very teeth of controversy and anti-Semitism, it can adequately testify that Yeshua is the Messiah and Savior of Israel to the Jewish community and to the Church that Yeshua is a Jew, a son of Israel and that anti-Semitism is anti-Jesus. It can be a living bridge of understanding between the Church and the Synagogue. It can be, at once, part of the Jewish community and an expression of the single universal Body of Believers.

There is another model of dual expression noted that could also bear much fruit. It is the model of a non-Jewish congregation that understands and encourages the Jewish identity of its Jewish members to the enhancement of the whole congregation.

This option hardly seemed possible twenty years ago; but today, we have examples of it. Messianic Jews must stand for—and with—the whole Body of Believers.

CHAPTER SIX

THE FAITH AND LIFE OF MESSIANIC JEWS

MESSIANIC JEWS LIVE IN THE period between the "already" and the "not yet." *Already*, they know that the Kingdom of God has come spiritually in Messiah Yeshua. As communities, they seek to demonstrate this reality of the present Kingdom by lives of love, power, reconciliation, and healing. The Kingdom has not yet come in its fullness to all the earth. Only when Messiah Yeshua returns will the Kingdom be a reality in fullness over all the earth.[1] Hence Messianic Jews live in expectation of that Day of the Lord, when "His will shall be done on earth as it is in heaven" (see Matt. 6:10). The life of Messianic Jews, however, is a life with definite concepts of authority, the way of salvation, the work of God's Spirit, the Messiahship of Yeshua, what it means to be Jewish, and how all this is manifest in one's lifestyle and practice.

THE AUTHORITY OF THE BIBLE

Messianic Jews accept the full authority and truth of the Bible. Whatever Scripture teaches is to be believed and obeyed. It is crucial, however, that there is an accurate understanding of the meaning of the authority of the Bible. The Bible is certainly true, *but how do we* ascertain its truth? What do we mean when we say the Bible is inspired?

Basically, the inspiration of the Bible means that God super-intended the biblical writers in such a way that what they wrote conveyed what God desired to convey. That which was taught was all truth and not error. God did not usurp the personalities of the writers by placing them in "trance-like" states. Rather, He used their unique styles and personalities to convey His truth. Paul can ask Timothy in a very human way to bring his cloak, and we gain a glimpse into the intimate life of the Apostle. This was God's desire. However, Paul also can write that his teaching is the commandment of God (see 1 Cor. 14:37). Scripture therefore says, "All Scripture is given by inspiration of God" (2 Tim. 3:16 KJV). The Greek sense of inspiration is "God-breathed." And in Second Peter 1:20-21, we read, "No prophecy of the scripture is of any private interpretation. For the prophecy came not in old time by the will of man: but holy men of God spake as they were moved by the Holy Ghost" (KJV).

It is crucial to understand that the highest authority and court of appeal for all teaching in Messianic Judaism is the Bible. However, what a person understands the Bible to teach varies from reader to reader. Each perceives within his own limitations of knowledge and ability as illuminated by the Spirit and influenced by the community in which he lives his life. What we seek to understand is the intended teaching of the Biblical author.

The only *objective* means of sorting varying interpretations is to understand Scripture in *context*.[2] By *context*, we mean several things. First, the verse is to be understood in the *context* of the whole book and then of the whole Bible. As one writer aptly stated, "A text without a context is a pretext." Second, part of the context for better understanding is the original language of revelation (Hebrew or Greek). Third, the original language, words, sentences, and literary styles must also be understood according to the *usage* of the time of writing. To whom did the author write? Why did he write? And *how would his audience* have understood his writing in their circumstances and their language usage? When we understand these things, we can make more accurate applications of the Scriptures. It is crucial to respect biblical scholarship and to avoid narrow, *subjective* interpretations. These are the laws for understanding any piece of literature.

Every Bible translator depends upon the above type of interpretive pursuit and seeks to ascertain all of the above information in making his translations. However, a translation is an abbreviation of the fullness of meaning. The translator uses cultural-historical studies, commentaries and linguistic-grammatical studies to produce an English translation. Messianic Jews must, therefore, eschew the rejection of scholarship. The Bible teaches only truth, but our understanding of the Bible depends upon a proper interpretation (see Acts 8, Philip and the Ethiopian eunuch).

Does not this place the Bible beyond the average layman and overlook the teaching ministry of the Spirit? Not at all! The Spirit does not teach us to parse Hebrew and Greek verbs, but He indeed illumines the Scripture to every sincere reader. Every sincere reader of a good translation receives much understanding of the basic teaching of the Bible on salvation, love, and service. The Spirit reveals this to our hearts, empowers us, and helps us to apply the Word. However, our perceptions of the Spirit are fallible: We see now through a glass darkly (see 1 Cor. 13:12), and controversial biblical issues require more information for solution.

Furthermore, it is crucial that we understand the Spirit's work, what He does and does not do. The Spirit illumines the Word, but He will not give us Hebrew lessons! He will give us insight, but insight is a subjective perception unless it is tested by the objective tools of biblical study. The Bible enjoins us to "test the spirits" and to not believe another gospel (see 1 John 4:1-3; cf. Gal. 1:8-9). The only objective test for interpretation is the tools to accurately understand Scripture in context. The Word is the test of the Spirit, but without the Spirit, the Word is dead and unapplied to our lives. The Spirit and Word go together, but we must never elevate the Spirit and His illumination above the objective Word. We have seen groups give themselves to wholesale heresy and deception by having no objective test for their understanding in the Word. The Bible is for all to read and grow by. The Spirit is likewise given to all believers; but let us not be foolish in rejecting the tools for a more accurate understanding, and all should read the Word in dependence on the Spirit.

Why do we believe the Bible? There are many reasons, of which we summarize only a few. There is first, the claim within the Bible, a unique claim in comparison with other religious literature. The Mosaic writings regularly testify to having been written according to the *instruction of the Lord*. This is also the case with the prophetic books, in which the words, "Thus says the Lord," are regularly found prefixing the message. The same is true in the New Testament, where we read in Second Timothy 3:16 that "All Scripture is given by inspiration of God and is profitable for doctrine, for reproof, for correction and instruction in righteousness." Paul, the Apostle, writes in First Corinthians 14:37, "What I am writing to you is the Lord's command." These claims are so unique that they give import to the unique inspiration of the Scriptures.

We also find great evidence from the teaching of Yeshua. He who rose from the dead as proven by the best of historical evidence,[3] is our authority and teacher. He taught the inspiration and authority of all Scripture, stating that "until heaven and earth pass away, not a jot or tittle shall pass from the law until all be fulfilled" (see Matt. 5:18). Further, He stated, "The Scripture cannot be broken…" (John 10:35). His whole teaching demeanor demonstrated His attitude toward Scripture. He used several words—"It says," "Scripture says," "It is written," and "God says"—as interchangeable. A quotation from the Tanakh (Old Testament) settled the matter.[4] For Yeshua, then, the Hebrew Bible was inspired and true in all its teaching. He also made provision for the New Testament by giving His Apostles full teaching authority as witnesses and interpreters of His truth (see John 16:12-14; 14:26). This is reflected in the apostolic writings as well, for Ephesians 2:20 says that Yeshua's congregation is "built upon the foundation of the apostles and prophets." Peter says, "We did not follow cleverly devised myths…but we were eyewitnesses of his majesty" (2 Pet. 1:16 RSV).

Furthermore, the Bible through and through gives evidence of being the supernatural Book of God. For example, the nation of Israel began with a miraculous deliverance from Egypt, the reception of the Law at Sinai, and the conquering of the land of Canaan. Archaeology bears out the conquest of the very cities described in Scripture.[5] Only the account of the Torah adequately explains the existence of this singular nation, Israel, which alone believed in one personal God, characterized by His justice and love. The archaeological record reveals the idolatry of Canaan and an amazing freedom from idolatry in the periods of Israel's righteousness, just as the Bible recounts.

The Bible amazingly predicts the future history of nations. For example, the Bible predicted the utter destruction of Tyre and even mentions the causeway that would be built to finally destroy the ancient city some 300 years later (see Ezek. 26). Yet the sister city, Sidon would have a sad, bloody history, but not be destroyed (see Ezek. 28). The Bible sketches history with amazing accuracy, predicting the progress of world empires—down to our own day! Daniel 2 and 7 predict and describe the successive empires of Babylon, Medo-Persia, Greece, and Rome, and a last-day confederation of nations which will oppose God.

The Bible also predicts the dispersion of Israel (see Lev. 26) and her last-day regathering from all over the earth (see Isa. 11). Bernard Ramm tabulates the amazing accuracy of the biblical predictions of God's future judgments on nations and cities. All the references are given in his account.[6] The Bible predicts the following of nations:

❖ Egypt will remain, but decline as a world power.

❖ Israel (Northern tribes) will cease as a nation.

❖ The Jews will remain.

❖ Philistines will cease.

❖ Moab and Ammon will continue after the Babylonian exile.

❖ Edom will cease completely.

Of cities:

❖ Tyre will be fully destroyed.

❖ Sidon will remain.

❖ Thebes will be destroyed.

❖ Nineveh will be destroyed.

❖ Babylon will be destroyed.

❖ Jerusalem will remain.

Need we mention the incredible prophecies concerning today's regathering of Israel that we witness—the second regathering (see Isa. 11), during which the desert would bloom (see Isa. 35; Ezek. 36)?

Even more supernatural are the Bible's predictions of the Messiah. He was predicted to be born in Bethlehem (see Mic. 5:2), to be born of a virgin (see Isa. 7:14), to be rejected, to die as a sacrifice, and to rise from the dead (see Isa. 53; Ps. 22), to be cut off before the destruction of the Second Temple in 70 c.e. (see Dan. 9:25-26), and many, many more.

Surely this is an amazing Book, inspired and unlike any in history! As to why we accept all the books of the Bible, we mention the following. We know Yeshua accepted the Jewish Bible of His day. From Jewish tradition and Josephus, we know this Jewish Bible consisted of just those books today designated as the Hebrew Bible or Tanakh by the Jewish community or the same books called the Old Testament by the Protestant communities.

The Hebrew Bible consists of the covenants of God with Israel and the records of prophets who called Israel back to Torah and instructed the nation on the basis of the Mosaic revelation (see Deut. 13; 18).

Provision for the writing prophets was made in Torah itself. The Hebrew Bible is the covenantal record of the relationship between God and Israel.[7] As we said, the New Testament is the product of the Apostles chosen by Yeshua. His resurrection, testified to by apostolic and other martyrs who died for the truth of their witness to His resurrection, authenticates His teaching. The early communities preserved and testified to those books, which had true apostolic origins, and these became part of the New Testament, our foundation for doctrine and teaching.[8] The Bible thus stands alone among all ancient books, its historical accuracy tested by archaeology and its supernatural origin attested to by fulfilled prophecy and the resurrection of Yeshua.

Even more important, however, is the moral character of the Bible and the spiritual nature of its message. No other book reads with the quality, majesty, and depth of the Bible. It has the ring of truth. Only the Bible reveals a God who acts and speaks in history and reveals Himself through Yeshua. Only the Bible has brought God's life-giving message to millions, turning them from despair to hope and purpose.

As Messianic Jews, we may gain wisdom and insight from our Jewish tradition. The tradition, however, is to be tested by the Bible, which alone is accepted as totally true. Tradition does not have this authority. That which is consistent and coheres with the Scriptures can be accepted; that which does not must be rejected. The Bible is the final rule of faith and practice. It is our authority.

SALVATION BY GRACE

The popular use of the words *salvation* and *saved* is a distortion of the rich biblical meaning of the terms. In Scripture, *salvation* includes the fullness of deliverance from a meaningless life of transgression, emptiness, alienation, and darkness, to a life of fellowship with our Creator, as well as hope, healing, community with others, and the assurance of everlasting life with God. Unfortunately, the word *grace* is a misperceived concept as well in much popular thinking. Many, for example, believe that *grace* means that God has suspended the moral standards of His Law to accept us. Because He has accepted us, we need only believe—it does not matter what we do after. This is totally contrary to the biblical view of grace. We should understand that the Gospel is the Good News of the Kingdom. With the coming of Yeshua, people are invited into the Kingdom, to live in and from the reality of this realm. We enter in only by an offer of His grace, by undergoing a co-death and resurrection in Him. Our sins are forgiven, and under His Lordship, we are straightened out. We are part of a new community that is submitted to Him under elder servant leaders.

In Scripture, grace is God's offer of unmerited forgiveness to us, despite the fact that we are sinners or lawbreakers. Yet God upholds His character and Law in His offer because Yeshua paid the penalty of the Law. In Him, we can be counted as fulfilling the Law. It is crucial to understand that God judges us as a people *in Him.*

We are "in Him" (Gal. 2:20) and are *in Him* accounted righteous. He is perfect according to God's Holy Law. Hence, David can say in Psalm 32:2, "Blessed is the man to whom the Lord imputes no iniquity" (RSV). It is also clear in Psalm 51 that David cast himself totally on the mercy of God for forgiveness and did not depend on his own merits. He said, "Be merciful to me, O God, according to thine abundant mercy, blot out my transgression...Purge me with hyssop and I shall be clean, wash me, and I shall be whiter than snow" (see Ps. 51:1,7). Eternal life is God's gift (see Rom. 6:23), and no one can earn it, for none are righteous (see Ps. 53:3). Hence, God can say of Israel that He did not choose them because of any righteousness or might of their own (see Deut. 8–10).

However, the reception of God's gift in Yeshua requires a response of faith. We can only be righteous before God because *we are in Him, and He alone is perfectly righteous* according to God's Law. Faith grasps the gift of God, and by faith we are born again and given a new Spirit (see Ezek. 36:26; 2 Cor. 5:17). The Hebrew word *faith (emunah)* cannot be divorced from the word *faithfulness (emunah)*. A true response to God issues in a heart or spirit whose desire is to obey and please God. The true teaching on salvation by faith never leads to moral looseness when rightly understood. Paul can thus say in Romans 3:31 as he recounts God's Law as upheld in Yeshua and our new heart to obey, "Do we then overthrow the Law by this faith? By no means! On the contrary, we uphold [or establish] the Law" (RSV). Jeremiah well reflected the relationship between faith and faithfulness when he stated that the Spirit would write God's Law upon our hearts (see Jer. 31:33).

God's grace is effective. It is God's power within us, enabling us to do His will. God in Yeshua has delivered us from the penalty of the Law, but we do not cast away the Law or its value for teaching and guiding (see 2 Tim. 3:16-17). First John 3:4 says that "Sin is the transgression of law" (RSV). Romans 6 says that we are "not to yield ourselves to sin" or "continue in sin that grace might abound." We are said to have died to sin and risen with Yeshua. Obviously, if our hearts have responded to God, we will not desire to break His Law. Sin is the transgression of Law (see 1 John 3:4). Because we are free from the bondage of the penalties of the Law and our fleshly efforts to keep the Law, which end in failure (see Rom. 7), we can now do the Law *by God's power* (see Rom. 8:1-4). We can say with the psalmist, "O how I love thy law! it is my meditation all the day...sweeter than honey to my mouth!" (Ps. 119:97,103). Scripture's message never divides grace from obedience, but teaches that the heart must be changed first.

"For by grace are ye saved through faith… is the gift of God: not of works, lest any man should boast" (Eph. 2:8-9 KJV); "For God is at work in you to will and to do of his good pleasure" (see Phil. 2:13). James says, "Faith without works is dead" (see James 2:20). Titus teaches we are "justified by grace" (Titus 3:7) *and* then exhorts us to be careful to "apply ourselves to good deeds" (*mitzvot*) for "these are excellent and profitable to men" (see Titus 3:8).

The Tenach also records this relationship between faith and works and the Law, for we read of Abraham, "Abraham believed God and God accounted it to him for righteousness" (see Gen. 15:6), but Genesis 26:4-5 says, "…In thy seed shall all the nations of the earth be blessed; because that Abraham obeyed my voice and kept my charge, my commandments, my statutes, and my laws" (KJV). We are justified (accepted as righteous) by faith, but the justified one has a heart for God's will and Law or Instruction. (See James 2, which comments on Genesis 26.) We desire to be obedient and to do His commands.[9]

SPIRIT AND LAW

Another subject of great contemporary misunderstanding is the relationship between the Spirit of God (within each disciple of Yeshua) and the Law. Some put Spirit and law in total opposition, which is a biblical impossibility. The central chapters of the Bible for understanding the correct teaching are Romans 6–8. These chapters must be read with great care or false conclusions may be drawn.

Again, let us note that sin is the transgression of Law: "Whosoever committeth sin transgresseth also the law: for sin is the transgression of the law" (1 John 3:4 KJV). Paul clearly shows that the relationship of the Spirit to the Law is not antithetical. The Spirit revealed the Law; He will write God's Law on our hearts (see Jer. 31:33; Ezek. 36:26). So He can say,

> *Are we to sin* [transgress the Law] *because we are not under Law, but under grace? By no means! Do you not know that if you yield yourselves to anyone as obedient slaves, you are the slaves of the one whom you obey, either of sin* [the transgressing of the Law] *...or of obedience, which leads to righteousness?* (Romans 6:15-16).

What Paul has in mind is that the *Author* of the Law would dwell within, giving us an intuitive sense of right as well as a love which obeys the Law in its true spirit and intent. We would then serve not a set of external articles with dos and don'ts (a written code), but in newness of the Spirit. In other words, the Spirit will make obedience a personal response of love, not mere self-effort.

Romans 7 and 8 are the great chapters that summarize that the way of obedience is through the power of the Spirit. This is because, from our own power in our fallen nature (called the flesh), it is impossible for us to obey the Law or to overcome those passions and desires that enslave human beings.[10] The problem is not the Law. It reflects God's eternal character and standard. Yeshua said that not a jot or tittle of the Law would pass away until *all* is fulfilled. Heaven and earth would pass away before God's Law (see Matt. 5:17-18). Thus Paul can say,

> *If it had not been for the Law, I should not have known sin...the Law is holy, and the commandment holy and just and good. Did that which is good, then, bring death to me? By no means!...We know that the law is spiritual...Now if I do not do what I want, I agree that the law is good* (Romans 7:7,12,13,14,16 RSV).

This should be enough to convince anyone of Paul's positive regard for the Law. The problem is not the Law, but our sinful nature that is bent toward transgressing the Law. So fallen is man that he even uses the commandment as an occasion to imagine the forbidden action and is drawn, falling, into the act.

I should not have know what it is to covet if the Law had not said, You shall not covet." But sin, finding opportunity in the commandment, wrought in me all kinds of covetousness... (Romans 7:7-8 RSV).

So Paul describes the man who seeks to obey the Law by his own power as not able to do the very things he desires. This is the law "principle" of the sin nature, and it perpetuates a state of spiritual and physical death (the law or principle of sin and death).

The cry thus goes forth, "O wretched man that I am! who shall deliver me from the body of this death?" (Rom. 7:24 KJV). The solution is, "Thanks be to God through *Yeshua ha Meshi-ach*" (see Rom. 7:24). For through Him, we are given a reborn spirit, and in recognizing that we died to our old self in Him and rose to new life, we are empowered by the Spirit to no longer be in bondage to sin. We may still fall, but we now have the power to obey. From our position in Yeshua, we can grow in progressive obedience in love. Hence, the Spirit enables us to fulfill the Law (see Rom. 3:31). Thus,

There is therefore now no condemnation for those who are in [Messiah Yeshua]. *For the law of the Spirit of life in* [Messiah Yeshua] *has set me free from the law of sin and death. For God has done what the law,* **weakened by the flesh,** *could not do: sending his own Son in the likeness of sinful flesh...he condemned sin in the flesh, in order* ***that the just requirement of the law might be fulfilled in us,*** *who walk not according to the flesh but according to the Spirit* (Romans 8:1-4 RSV).

The issue is not a conflict between Law and Spirit, but between flesh and spirit. Do we seek to please God by our own fleshly efforts to keep the Law, or do we depend on the resurrection power of His Spirit within? We are to set our minds on depending on the Spirit. By His power, we can please God.

With this understanding, the Messianic Jew has no ambivalence in approaching the *whole* Bible as "profitable for doctrine, for reproof, for correction and instruction in righteousness" (see 2 Tim. 3:16-17). Truly, he can say with the psalmist, "O how I love thy law" (Ps. 119:97 KJV). Yet, even more does he love the demonstration of the meaning of the Law in Spirit and in truth in *Yeshua ha Mashiach.*

Salvation and Jews Who Do Not Know Yeshua

In recent times, it has become popular to believe that Jewish people have a covenant with God and may have eternal life with Him by this covenant—even if they do not *explicitly* accept salvation by faith in Yeshua.

We must make a distinction between two groups who hold this viewpoint, the liberal theologians and followers and the evangelicals and Messianic Jews. To the liberal, this is often a reflection of a tolerance or embrace that is maintained for all peoples and cultures. For the liberal of today, it is questionable whether religious truth can be discovered with any degree of objectivity. If pressed, he would give equal credibility to Hindus and Buddhists, claiming that he only favors the biblical tradition because it is his tradition. Because we believe the Bible to be the Word of the living God, we must judge all matters by its revelation. Our concern is with those who truly affirm the Scriptures and teach what has been called a wider hope. Do they have something to teach us on this issue?

Many hold that unless one consciously and explicitly makes a decision for Yeshua—who is understood as the One who lived, died, and rose again in the first century—there is no salvation. Although Scripture is not teeming with verses to support this position, there are Scriptures that seem to support this view.[11]

Acts 4:12 states, "Neither is there salvation in any other: for there is none other name given under heaven among men, whereby we must be saved" (KJV). So also, "He that hath the Son hath life; and he that hath not the Son... hath not life" (1 John 5:12 KJV) and "Whoever believes the Son has eternal life, but whoever rejects the Son will not see life, for God's wrath remains on him" (John 3:36). We should point out that the text from Acts 4:12 is traditionally interpreted in a too individualistic way for salvation for the individual. In the first-century Jewish context, Simon (Peter) is announcing that the salvation Israel seeks, deliverance from foreign pagan domination, the hope of all the prophets, and one's personal participation in it will be found only in the name of Yeshua.

Our two-covenant theorist points to other passages to support his claims and gives a different slant to these verses. Elmer Josephson would be the most extreme of two-covenant theorists among evangelicals, believing that every circumcised Jew who does not repudiate the covenant with Abraham through explicit renunciation—or implicitly through gross immorality and assimilation—is saved under the Abrahamic Covenant.[12] We, of course, cannot elaborate all of the reasons given by two-covenant theorists. Basically, however, they would argue as follows.

Because of God's covenant with Abraham, Jews are a covenant people under God's grace and salvation, just as Christians are saved under the New Covenant. Of course, the reason the Jew has salvation in the Abrahamic Covenant is because of the atonement provided by Yeshua. A Jew, however, may be connected to this atonement through the Abrahamic Covenant without explicitly accepting Yeshua. Josephson seems extreme in applying this to almost all Jews unless they repudiate Judiasm. Others would hold that unless there is a faith-response to God's offer of grace in the Abrahamic Covenant, there is no salvation. A Jew may talk as though his good deeds save him, but in his heart of hearts, he may really be depending on God's grace and mercy.

The two-covenant theorist would especially point to these biblical facts *to* support his view. Jews were saved in the pre-Yeshuic period by faith, without *explicitly* accepting Yeshua. Implicitly, however, by accepting the Scriptures and God's mercy in the sacrificial system, they were joined to Him. Doesn't it seem, they would argue, that this is the case with Jews also today? Jewish prayer enshrines these principles. For example, the *Al Het* Yom Kippur prayer asks for God's forgiveness and mercy. The *Avinu Malkainu* prayer states that we have no deeds that can save us. The petitioner admits that he has *no* merit of his own by which to claim salvation, but is a sinner who has broken God's Law in countless ways. Furthermore, he requests to be forgiven on the basis of past sacrificial offerings since there is presently no Temple. He even invokes the sacrifice of Isaac (which points to Yeshua's sacrifice) for forgiveness.

Further, the proponent would argue that God has hardened Israel's heart to the message of Yeshua for the purposes of His work among Gentiles (see Rom. 11:7). He can point to a multitude of verses that seem to support his position that God has not rejected His people (see Rom. 11:1,11). Israel is still God's people. So, also, Paul in Romans 11:16 seems to be saying that those of Israel who have accepted Yeshua are as first fruits, which make Israel, as a whole, still a chosen people and beloved. "If the dough offered as first fruits is holy, so is the whole lump; and if the root is holy, so are the branches" (RSV).

Yes, Paul recognizes that some branches were broken off through *explicit* unbelief and rejection, but Israel in general is still God's people. As the first fruits offered to God from the crop made the whole harvest holy and profitable in Israel, so also are the believers in Yeshua from Israel related to the whole nation.

Clearly, Israel will someday accept Yeshua, and this will herald the general resurrection from the dead (see Rom. 11:15), and so "All Israel will be saved...[for] they are beloved for the sake of their forefathers [and *elect*]. For the gifts and the call of God are irrevocable" (see Rom. 11:26,28-29 RSV). Thus, in conclusion, the proponents of this view would say that Jews can readily be saved under the Abrahamic Covenant as much as Christians are under the New Covenant.

How are we to respond to this mode of argument? It must first be acknowledged that preaching the Good News of Yeshua affords human beings everywhere the greatest opportunity to respond and be saved, that is to enter the Kingdom of God now and eventually to participate in the fullness of the Age to Come. It is God's clearest supreme revelation. The two-covenant theorist sometimes forgets this, for the Abrahamic Covenant is only really fulfilled because of the New Covenant in Yeshua. It is only through the truth that salvation is in Yeshua that grace was offered in the Abrahamic and Mosaic Covenant periods. We must not forget the words of Paul, that the "Gospel is the power unto salvation to everyone who believes, *to the Jew first* and also to the Greek" (see Rom. 1:16).

The two-covenant theorist is in danger of acting as though Jewish people do not need the Gospel, that what they have is adequate. Yet Jeremiah 31 and Ezekiel 36 make it clear that the New Covenant is offered to Israel and that Israel needs the New Covenant so that God's Spirit might be in them and the Law written upon their hearts. Indeed, aspects of New Covenant promises to Israel include their planting in the land and walk of faith with God, as well as these aspects of the New Covenant that followers of Yeshua have received (see Jer. 31; Ezek. 36). We still await the *totality* of the New Covenant's manifestation in the return of Yeshua. Clearly, however, the New Covenant is for Israel! Paul preached first in the synagogues! In the light of Western anti-Semitism and the desire to befriend the Jewish community, we can understand how our two-covenant theorist would desire to be inoffensive. However, we cannot blunt scriptural emphases because of this desire. The Gospel provides the fullest opportunity for salvation to the Jew first (see Rom. 1:16).

However, I think we must reexamine the older evangelical certainty of being able to determine just who is and who is not hell-bound. Jews were saved under the period of the Abrahamic and Mosaic covenant through their response to the covenants. Scripture makes it clear, however, that a personal faith response was necessary, as well as the outward sign of Jewishness:

> *For he is not a real Jew who is one outwardly, nor is true circumcision something external and physical. He is a Jew who is one inwardly, and real circumcision is a matter of the heart, spiritual and not literal. His praise is not from men but from God* (Romans 2:28-29 RSV).

If Jewish people were granted fellowship with God and everlasting life in the Older Covenant period, why should it be precluded now? Let's say that a righteous Jew died an hour after the resurrection (or the gift of the Spirit at Shavuot or Pentecost, if you wish this to be the time of responsibility); would he be hell-bound then, but heaven-bound if only he had died an hour earlier? This is unthinkable, and indeed, unscriptural. Scripture clearly teaches that "lostness" is a condition that results from rejecting the revelation of God that can be known. Romans 1 judges the heathen *not* for rejecting the Gospel, which they had not been given, but for rejecting the revelation of God in the created order which they have been given (see Rom. 1:19-21). Romans 2:1 points to the revelation to conscience as another means of rendering men to be without excuse.

To whom much is given, much is required. Jewry clearly was given a fuller revelation in the Hebrew Scriptures (Tenach) than heathens (see Rom. 2). For this revelation, they were responsible. When the preaching of Yeshua was understood, they were responsible for this. However, at no time can we biblically draw a line and say, "From this time forward, if a Jew hasn't accepted Yeshua, he is lost." The time when people and individuals are responsible is when revelation is given, and this time is different for everyone. It is only when the Spirit-revealer is spurned that "lostness" ensues. The decisions of Jewish leadership in the first century, followed by the persecution of centuries, has rendered the Hebrew Scriptures the main source of revelation and response for most Jews.

Does this not destroy the motive of giving the Gospel? Not at all! For although we recognize a possibility of responding to natural revelation and to the Abrahamic Covenant, *Scripture and experience show that most have not responded to the revelation they have.* The pagan has eschewed true revelation for idolatry. Despite the clarity of the Tenach, the great majority of Jews today have not responded in faith to the Abrahamic Covenant. The religions of the world have taught salvation by systems of works-righteousness. Judaism itself sometimes falls into works righteousness "because they did not pursue it through faith, but as if it were based on works"[13] (Rom. 9:32 RSV). Thus the biblical message is not truly understood. The general condition of world Jewry today, in fact, is one of unbelief. *Thus, the only way that they will respond to God at all is by the preaching of the Gospel with power.* The preaching of the Good News maximizes the opportunity of salvation. However, we cannot preclude the possibility of Jews responding in faith to God's revelation in the Tenach. This view does not blunt our zeal to spread the Good News, but blunts our judgmentalism as applied to individuals, which Scripture forbids (see 1 Cor. 4:5). *Jewish people need the Gospel;* Jewish people do have the Tenach, if they would pursue its message, *but most do not.* For most, the Tenach is encrusted with false interpretations; only the New Testament revelation can break through.

I should add that when Peter says there is no other name, and salvation is only found in Yeshua, we tend to read into the text the evangelical preoccupation with what happens after we die or in the Age to Come. This is important, but Peter may well have been using the term as his contemporaries and thinking of the corporate salvation of Israel, deliverance from oppression and more. This will only take place when Israel embraces Yeshua (see Rom. 11:15,25-29).

Some might object to this presentation because Jews under the Old Testament period had the means of atonement in animal sacrifices, but today's Jews do not. However, the animal sacrifices were only symbols of spiritual reality that pointed to Yeshua's atonement. As Hebrews says, "It is impossible that the blood of bulls and goats should take away sins" (Heb. 10:4 RSV). Rather, it was faith in God's mercy that connected the offerer to the Messiah! So, even though a Jewish person today does not have the sacrificial system, he can still respond in faith to the *meaning of* the sacrificial system as enshrined in the prayers of the synagogue.

What of the exclusionary verses that were quoted? First, let us note that one can't reject something he or she has not been clearly offered. John 3:36 says the wrath of God abides on the one who *rejects* the Son. So also, First John 5:12 says, "He that hath the Son hath life; he that hath not the Son of God hath not life" (KJV). Did the believing Jews of the Tenach in a spiritual sense *have* the Son even though he had not yet come? Most would say yes. Why not then Jews one hour after the resurrection, or one year, or one hundred years later? Let us also remember that John teaches a spiritual reality to the Son that is not limited to His sojourn on earth. He says of the Word, Messiah, "That was the true light which lighteth every man that cometh into the world" (John 1:9 KJV). The same meaning of a universal light from the Messiah can be given for Acts 4:12.

In a day when our ancestors looked for delieverers from Roman oppression, Peter was able to say, "There is salvation in no one else." In other words, all saved people—from Adam until the present—are saved only in Yeshua. "He is the only name given under heaven among men by which we must be saved."

Yeshua is the only *name* of the Reality by which all must be saved. Indeed, when the Gospel is heard and understood, there must be an explicit response to the Name. Otherwise, as with the pre-New Covenant saints, there must be an implicit response to the Reality that the Name reveals. In the Semitic understanding,

"The Name" stood for the inner essence of the spoken-of Reality. God was simply called "the Name." Peter was not only calling for an explicit response to Yeshua in Acts 4:12, but was teaching *that all* salvation has always been in Him. The same Peter could also say in Acts 10:34, "Truly I perceive that God shows no partiality, but in every nation anyone who fears Him [faith] and does what is right is acceptable to him" (RSV).

If a person still believes that a conscious, explicit response must be made for Yeshua before death, we would point to the possibility of further revelation even at the moment just before death for those who have responded in faith to the revelation they have been given. John Wesley divided humanity into the saved, the lost, and those in a prevenient (before full salvation) grace state who were responding to the truth as they could perceive it. This third group would somehow be led on to faith in the Messiah.

Considerations such as these as well as an examination of the meaning of *remnant* in Romans 9–11 have prompted H.L. Ellison, a venerable Messianic Jewish scholar, to come to similar conclusions. He exposits the remnant to be that minority within Jewry who have responded in faith and, therefore, sanctify the existence of Israel (see Rom. 11:5). So also, he argues that the "Christian" Church is full of unbelievers, but it is the believers within the Church who sanctify the existence of the visible Church.[14]

It is crucial to see that Judaism is a religion with the Tenach as a prime source. We grant that Judaism sometimes diverges from the truth and quenches the light of the revelation. However, most of the prayers and many of the teachings are derived from the Bible.

Some of the old time Hebrew Christians through ignorance approached the Jewish tradition with total disdain. For them, it was only a creation of hell-bound sinners, a tradition with no value. Such an attitude bordered on anti-Semitism. However, if the tradition (some of which is first century or earlier) was partially derived from the Bible, God's truth could be seen therein.

How is it that some clearly saw that the Messiah suffered for our sins in Isaiah 53?[15] How is it that prayer enshrines the knowledge of salvation only by grace through no merit of our own, even to the extent of appealing to the sacrificial system and the sufferings of the Messiah?[16] So also the Talmud teaches that Habakkuk reduced all the commands to one: "As it is said, the righteous shall live by his faith" (see Hab. 2:4). Some of the traditions are so old that it would seem that Paul drew from them to illustrate his teaching on faith.[17]

In conclusion, we have argued that the Gospel is for all and "to the Jew first" (Rom. 1:16). We have also argued that it is possible for a Jew to respond in faith to the Abrahamic Covenant and be connected to Yeshua. Yet in our view, most of Jewry is characterized by secularism and unbelief. Many religious Jews seem to be following a system of works-righteousness for salvation. (Therefore, the Gospel is a tremendous necessity and maximizes the opportunity for salvation).

THE MESSIAHSHIP OF YESHUA

Our purpose in defending a distinctive Messianic Jewish stance does not require a comprehensive summary of the reasons for our belief in the Messiahship of Yeshua. We only briefly recount here a summary of the Messianic hope and our reasons for affirming that, "He is the One of Whom the prophets spoke."

The Messianic hope begins in Genesis 3:15, where God promises to the human race a seed of woman who will crush the head of the Serpent (Satan, the representative of evil), even though this seed will be bruised in the heel. The story fits the religious symbolic literature of the ancient Near East in recounting deep spiritual truths through natural phenomena. Although it is not of absolute proof value, there is evidential value in the fact that the verse teaches that a seed of a woman, not a man, bruises the head of the Serpent though Satan bruises *its heel*. Satan receives the fatal blow; the seed, a serious, but limited blow. This fits Messiah

Yeshua, born of a virgin. Jewish writings also reflect this Messianic identification…as in Targum Onkelos, which speaks of the seed as her son. The great expositor David Kimchi clearly identifies the seed as "the Meshiach, the son of David, who shall wound his heel."[18] The Targums are ancient Jewish Aramaic translations and paraphrases of the Hebrew Bible. They are crucial for understanding Jewish thinking from the first to the fifth centuries.

We shall see that there are several promises in relation to *seed* which, when traced, have great Messianic significance, although not limited to the Messiah in meaning. The next passage, which talks about seed is Genesis 12. Abraham, who is called to a new land, is told, "By your seed all the families of the earth shall blessed." Blessing is to flow to the world through the nation Israel. However, there are hints that the seed-promise given to Abraham looks forward to an individual. Sarah, Abraham's wife, is childless. The seed-promise is to be applied to *her* offspring, not to any other. Sarah herself gives birth to only one son, Isaac. Isaac is thus the recipient of the seed-promise. The Messianic Jew cannot help but see the parallels. Isaac, the only son of his mother, is a child of a miraculous birth, for Sarah was beyond childbearing age (see Gen. 18:12-13). Isaac is called the only son of Abraham in Genesis 22 despite the fact that Abraham was the father of Ishmael. Most amazingly, Abraham is commanded to offer his son Isaac on Mount Moriah as a sacrifice. This is a test of his faith and obedience. Isaac is not killed, but the symbolism of his being offered as a sacrifice is carried out in Genesis 22. Moriah is the future site of the Temple; traditionally, among Jews, it is the exact bedrock where the altar later stood. That the image of Abraham's only seed is a sacrificial image should cause us to note the parallel to Yeshua, who is also a child of miraculous birth, the only son of his Father, who is offered as a sacrifice.

The *seed-promise* is next passed on to Isaac's son, Jacob, and then to the twelve children of Israel. However, there is a promise to Judah that indicates that the Messianic ruler will stem from

Judah. "The scepter shall not depart from Judah, nor the ruler's staff from between his feet, until he comes to whom it belongs; and to him shall be the obedience of the peoples" (Gen. 49:10 RSV). Either Shiloh in this passage is a title of the Messiah or is "he to whom it [rulership] belongs." All of the Targums identify this promise with the Messiah.

Many centuries passed before the seed-promise became more explicit. The figure of Moses, a prophet, priest, and ruler of his people, was considered to prefigure the Messiah by many Jewish people before Yeshua came.[19]

In Second Samuel 7, we find the next great seed-promise. Its subject is the future ruler and representative of Israel. David is promised in an *everlasting throne* through his descendants. Isaiah later makes it clear that this will be fulfilled by one child. In Isaiah 7:14, a promise is given of a Messianic king who shall be named Immanuel, God with us. The contrast is drawn between this child and the wicked king Ahaz, who would not ask for a sign to prove God's will as requested by the prophet Isaiah. That Isaiah 7:14 has in mind the Messiah is clear since no other child of the time was given the name Immanuel. Hezekiah, the ancestor of the Messiah, might have also been born at this time as a sign of the greater birth to come. Lest there be doubt, however, in the Messianic character of Isaiah 7:14, we point out these two facts. First, the translations of the Septuagint recognized the passage to be predicting a virgin birth. *Almah,* meaning young woman, is used of a young woman of marriageable age who is *presumed to be a virgin.* The Septuagint translated it *parthenos,* "virgin," before there was any debate. This translation was the authoritative Jewish translation into Greek in the first century. Second, the title of the king, Immanuel, is a parallel title to those given King Messiah in Isaiah 9:6-7 (Isa. 9:5 in the Hebrew Bible). Other promises concerning King Messiah as the stem of Jesse are found in Isaiah 11:1-10.

In Isaiah 9:6-7, we read:

> *For to us a child is born, to us a son is given; and the government will be upon his shoulder, and his name will be*

called "Wonderful Counselor, Mighty God, Everlasting Father, Prince of Peace." Of the increase of his government and of peace there will be no end, upon the throne of David, and over his kingdom, to establish it, and to uphold it with justice and righteousness, from this time forth and for evermore... (RSV).

Here we note that the Messiah is given uniquely divine titles. Our translation is very close to the literal Hebrew; other translations seek to blunt these titles by adding interpretive material. There is no traditional Jewish disagreement that these verses are Messianic. We now see that blessing flows to the world through Israel and through Israel's Messiah. Of the Messiah, we read that the Gentiles, non-Jewish peoples, shall seek after Him. He shall be a sign to the peoples and "to it shall the Gentiles seek" (see Isa. 11:10ff).

Of the Servant of the Lord in Isaiah 40–66, we read that He will bring forth justice, and He will be *a light to the nations* (see Isa. 42:3-4,7). Though Israel is God's servant in some of the servant passages, so is the Messianic King. For the promise of the servant of the Lord includes the same content of being embraced by the Gentiles as we find in the promise of King Messiah in Isaiah 11.

There is a special connection of the Messiah to Bethlehem, not only because this was David's city, which was obviously known. Micah 5:2 connects the Messiah to Bethlehem to show that His birth there shall parallel David's. It is a sign. Hence, the scribes of Matthew 2 could easily answer Herod's question as to where the Messiah would be born—"in Bethlehem." They then quoted Micah 5:2, which states that the ruler of Israel shall come forth from Bethlehem. Micah also says of the Messiah that His "goings have been from of old, from everlasting." Messiah in some way has a reality before His actual birth. Some traditional Jews see that pre-birth reality of the Messiah as in the being of God; He is, in some special sense, part of God and preexists the Creation.[20]

However, more astonishing than all these passages is the scriptural indication that the Messianic figure must suffer and die before He rules and reigns. This gave rise to the Talmudic idea that a suffering Messiah, son of Joseph, would precede the triumphant Messiah.[21] We have already noted that the Servant of the Lord of Isaiah 40–66 has both references to Israel and Israel's king. Of this "servant of the Lord," we read that He suffers as a sacrifice for sin (see Isa. 53) and experiences many other sufferings.

Isaiah says:

> *He is despised and rejected of men; a man of sorrows and acquainted with grief: and we hid as it were our faces from Him…All we like sheep have gone astray; we have turned every one to his own way; and the Lord has laid on him the iniquity of us all* (Isaiah 53:3,6).

Of this One, we also read that He is with both criminals and a rich man in His death. In the Gospels, we read that Yeshua was crucified between criminals. Joseph of Arimathea, a rich man, buried Him in his own tomb.

Because of his sacrifice, we read:

> *He shall see his offspring, he shall prolong his days…he shall see the fruit of the travail of his soul and be satisfied; by his knowledge shall the righteous one, my servant, make many to be accounted righteous, and he shall bear their iniquities* (Isaiah 53:10-11 RSV).

The One who dies as a sin offering lives again. How well this fits Yeshua! Jewish voices are not lacking who refer this passage to the Messiah, even though they do not accept Yeshua as the Messiah. The Talmud, in Sanhedrin 98b, gives a title to the Messiah, "the leprous one," because Isaiah in chapter 53 said He bore our diseases. The famous kabbalist R. Elijah de Vidas from Safed in Upper Galilee is most emphatic that this referred to the Messiah, saying, "It follows that whosoever will not admit that Messiah thus suffers for our iniquities, must endure and suffer for them himself."[22] So also the Targum Jonathan, a very ancient source, sees the Servant as King Messiah.[23]

In Zechariah 12:10, we find one who is pierced. We read:

And they shall look upon me whom they have pierced, and they shall mourn for him as one mourneth for his only son, and shall be in bitterness for him as one who is in bitterness for his firstborn (KJV).

That this refers to a suffering Messiah is clear in most ancient Jewish interpretations. The Talmud (Succah 52:1) interprets this as the Messiah, the son of Joseph (not son of David), as does R. Alschech and Kimchi.[24] However, what is the warrant for holding to two Messiahs instead of one Messiah who must first suffer before reigning?

Daniel 9:25-26 gives an astonishing reference to the Messiah. In this prophecy, the Messiah is predicted to be cut off before the destruction of the second Temple. Seventy weeks of years were decreed from the time of Artaxerxes that brings us to the time of the Messiah Yeshua (490 years). Even beyond this, "the Messiah the Prince" is cut off in the sixty-ninth week (483 years) and the Temple and city are destroyed soon after. Many Rabbinic references show that this is the Messiah.[25]

When we observe all of these passages together, it is amazing how precisely Yeshua fulfills the passages on the Messianic hope as it is developed in the Tenach. He is the seed of the woman who gives Satan his fatal blow (see Gen. 3:15); He is the only child of Abraham, a child who, like Isaac, is the only son of His Father and is offered as a sacrifice by His Father (see Gen. 12:1-3; 22); He is the prophet like Moses (see Deut. 18); He is a descendant of David (see 2 Sam. 7), the one born of a virgin and given supernatural titles (see Isa. 7:14; 9:6-7), born in Bethlehem but from Ancient Days (see Mic. 5:2); He is the light to the nations, for it is only by turning to Yeshua that non-Jews received God's scriptural revelation (see Isa. 42:11); He is the One who is pierced and dies in the image of a sacrifice, but yet sees His offspring (see Zech. 12:10; Isa. 53); and He is the One who comes before the destruction of the second temple, which occurred in 70 C.E. (see Dan. 9:25-26).

Yeshua alone fits the biblical hope. Furthermore, His life, miracles, death, and resurrection multiply the strength of the evidence. Only the Spirit of God can open the eyes of those who are blinded, but the evidence is extraordinary. No man ever taught like Yeshua. Read His summary of the heart meaning of the Law, in Matthew 5–7, or His parables in Matthew 13. No one ever performed miracles of compassion like Yeshua. No other man ever was raised from the dead like Yeshua. The evidence for His resurrection is not just good evidence—it is the best evidence we have for any ancient event. We have only positive evidence for the resurrection, no negative evidence.[26] The sources are all early; the four Gospels, the letters of Paul, Peter, James (Jacob), Hebrews, and Revelation were *independently* written and all testify to the resurrection. The early fathers of the Church maintain this testimony. Most of the disciples died for their faith in Yeshua's resurrection, never recanting under pressure. The Apostle Paul could testify that 500 brethren were witnesses to the resurrected Messiah at one time, most of whom were still alive (see 1 Cor. 15). The implication is that his readers could go and ask the witnesses about the truth.

There is no sufficient explanation of the resurrection by the early critics of the Yeshua movement. One explanation was given, that His disciples stole His body, the same disciples who died for the truth of their testimony! The dead body could not be produced because Yeshua was alive again.

Yeshua alone fits our hope and the scriptural expectations of the Messiah. He identified with Israel and personally paralleled Israel's life; His family fled to Egypt and was called out of Egypt (see Matt. 2:15); He went through the waters of baptism, paralleling Israel going through the sea; He was tempted in the wilderness for forty days, paralleling Israel's forty years (see Matt. 4); He exposited the Law on the mountain (see Matt. 5). His life was integrated into all the Jewish feasts (see John 5–10). He is certainly the One of whom the prophets spoke. He shall yet return to rule on the throne of David, fulfilling each of the prophecies that are part of Israel's Messianic hope.

IS THE MESSIAH DIVINE?

To raise the question of Yeshua's divinity is to revisit one of the greatest debates between Jews and Christians.[27] This question leads to the whole debate about the Trinity, since the Messiah is said to be divine as one part of the One Triune God.

Christians have locked themselves in Greek philosophical definitions of the Trinity. Jews ask, "Do Christians believe in one God or three?" In reaction to what they perceived as tri-theism (belief in three gods), Jews have also defined their God in opposing Greek categories of oneness. Maimonides, who is quoted and referred to for the Jewish doctrine of God, explained God's oneness as singularity, formlessness, and simplicity after the teaching of Aristotle. The term *trinity* or *tri-unity* is not in the Bible. We, therefore, are not so concerned to argue for the term as for those aspects of the biblical revelation that the term reflects. We have to begin with the salient fact that Jewish literature itself reflects something of the mystery of God. This is evident in speech about the Shekeenah, or Holy Spirit. He is spoken of as God and yet as separate from God. When the Temple was destroyed, the Shekeenah is said to have gone into exile with Israel. The Shekeenah is also said to have moved from the Temple mount to the Western Wall. It is this author's contention that the literature of Judaism and the Bible always reflected this mystery of God, wherein God is spoken of as one, but manifestations of God are spoken of as to some degree distinct from God. Jews spoke functionally and did not draw a firm theological conclusion concerning oneness or threeness during all of the ages of history before Yeshua. Christians, however, who were Greek-oriented, drew clear specific theological (ontological) conclusions from this functional language. The Jewish reaction to the Christian doctrine was to finally draw an opposite and contrary conclusion. God was defined as *"yachid,"* completely and totally singular.

In Genesis 1:26, God said, "Let *us* create man in our own image." *Eloheem* (God) itself is a unique uni-plural form that takes a singular verb, but could be translated "gods." It is possible that the "Let us" structure could be a regal plural of majesty, such as found in Queen Victoria's speech, though we have no evidence of this usage. However, God says, "God created man in his own image...male and female *created he them*" (Gen. 1:27 KJV). The fact that male and female *together* are in God's image probably bears some significance. Further, God says of marriage, "For this reason a man will leave his father and mother and be united to his wife, and they will become *one* flesh" (Gen. 2:24). The word for *one* here is *echad*, the same used in the *Sh'ma*, "Hear O Israel, the Lord is our God, the Lord *alone (echad)*" (see Deut. 6:4). One Jewish authority personally admitted in a class at a prominent Jewish college that the *Sh'ma* was not a statement at all about God's mathematical singularity, but that this invisible God of revelation was to be worshipped apart from all other idols. Furthermore, if the *Sh'ma* is an assertion of God's singular ontological oneness, it would be a statement counter to the obvious indications of plurality in the Tenach (see Ezra 2:64; Ezek. 37:17). *Echad,* however, does not connote singular oneness in many usages.

The examples of plurality in the Tenach are arresting to say the least. In Genesis 18, one of three angels is designated the LORD, the Holy name of God. Here is a manifestation of God, yet He is *not all of God Himself.* Is it God or an angel of God? It is both.

In Genesis 32, Jacob wrestles with the Angel of God, called a man in verse 24. Jewish literature explains this as only an angel. Yet how then do we explain Jacob's words in verse 30? "So Jacob called the place Peniel, saying, 'It is because I saw God face to face and yet my life was spared.'" Jacob was amazed because it was believed that no man could see God and live. Jacob did not see God *fully;* no one ever has. However, this was a manifestation of

God in human form that cannot be put aside by calling it a powerful angel which, being from a divine level of reality, would cause the fear. This explanation completely ignores Jacob's own words.

In Exodus, the Angel of the Lord is distinguished from God Himself and yet is continually called by the holy name of God Himself, written The LORD (all caps) in English and YHWH in Hebrew:

❖ Exodus 14:19—the Angel of God travels before the people in a pillar of cloud.

❖ Exodus 13:17 ff.—God Himself leads the people.

❖ Exodus 13:21—God is called The LORD who went ahead.

❖ Exodus 33:14—God says, "My *Presence* will go with you."

Moses prays for God's presence to precede Israel, in verse 16. However, in verse 9, the presence is identified with the Lord, as Moses prays for the presence of the LORD to go with Israel. Clearly, the LORD goes with Israel in leaving the Tabernacle, in Exodus 40:36-38.

There are several other examples where the Angel of God is distinguished from God and then called God or the LORD. In Genesis 22:11, we have the Angel of the Lord, but in Genesis 22:12, He is God (cf. Gen. 16:7,13).

In Exodus 23:20-23, God's Name is said to be in the Angel in such a way that he can pardon sin.

> *Behold, I send an angel before you, to guard you on the way and to bring you to the place which I have prepared. Give heed to him and hearken to his voice, do not rebel against him, for he will not pardon your transgression; for my name is in him.*

But if you hearken attentively to his voice and do all that I say, then I will be an enemy to your enemies and an adversary to your adversaries.

When my angel goes before you, and brings you in to the Amorites and the Hittites, and the Perizzites, and the Canaanites, the Hivites, and the Jebusites, and I blot them out, you shall not bow down to their gods, nor serve them, nor do according to their works, but you shall utterly overthrow them and break their pillars in pieces. You shall serve the Lord your God, and I will bless your bread and your water; and I will take sickness away from the midst of you. None shall cast her young or be barren in your land; I will fulfill the number of your days. I will send my terror before you, and will throw into confusion all the people against whom you shall come, and I will make all your enemies turn their backs to you. And I will send hornets before you, which shall drive out Hivite, Canaanite, and Hittite from before you. I will not drive them out from before you in one year, lest the land become desolate and the wild beasts multiply against you. Little by little I will drive them out from before you, until you are increased and possess the land. And I will set your bounds from the Red Sea to the sea of the Philistines, and from the wilderness to the Euphrates; for I will deliver the inhabitants of the land into your hand, and you shall drive them out before you. You shall make no covenant with them or with their gods. They shall not dwell in your land, lest they make you sin against me; for if you serve their gods, it will surely be a snare to you (Exodus 23:20-33 RSV).

Judges 13 brings out the phenomenon clearly. Beginning with verse 9, we read, "The angel of God came again to the woman while she was out in the field...Menoah got up and followed his wife. When he came to the man he said... [and] the Angel of the Lord replied...." Menoah inquired of the name of the Angel of the

LORD (see Judg. 13:17). Then Menoah said to his wife, "We are doomed to die! We have seen God!" (see Judg. 13:22). However, his wife assured him that *if* they were to die, the LORD would not have accepted the offering. Just as in the story of Jacob wrestling with God, we have the Angel of God both distinguished from God *and* identified with God.

Most astonishing of all the examples is Exodus 3, where the "Angel of the LORD" appeared to Moses in flames of fire from within a bush. What did He say? "I am the God of your father, the God of Abraham, Isaac, and Jacob." As Menoah, Moses asked His name, and God gave the inscrutable name which He did not give to Menoah in Judges 13 saying, "I am who I am" (a variant of YHWH).

So the Angel is God and yet distinct from God.

Other references show forth similar mysteries. Is God's Spirit of Shekeenah somehow God and yet distinct from God? What of all those passages where it is spoken of in this way? We note especially Isaiah 48:12-16:

> *Hearken to me, O Jacob, and Israel, whom I called! I am He, I am the first, and I am the last. My hand laid the foundation of the earth, and my right hand spread out the heavens; when I call to them, they stand forth together.*
>
> *Assemble, all of you, and hear! Who among them has declared these things? The Lord loves him; he shall perform his purpose on Babylon, and his arm shall be against the Chaldeans. I, even I, have spoken and called him, I have brought him, and he will prosper in his way. Draw near to me, hear this: "from the beginning I have not spoken in secret, from the time it came to be I have been there." **And now the Lord God has sent me and his Spirit.***

In this passage, God is the speaker, but then at the end of the passage, says that He is distinguished from the LORD and the Spirit. And, as is commonly known, rabbinic literature regularly speaks of the Shekeena, the Spirit's presence, as a distinct person with intelligence, will, purpose, emotions, etc.[28]

Furthermore, there are hints of the Messiah being more than just human. In Isaiah 9:6-7, the Messiah is given the names of God—literally in Hebrew, "Wonderful Counselor, Almighty God—Everlasting Father, Prince of Peace."

This child who is born will rule and reign over all the earth. The Messianic king is addressed, "The Lord said to my Lord" (Ps. 110:1). Who is this that David calls Lord? How this question puzzled Yeshua's listeners!

> *"What do you think about the* [Messiah]*? Whose son is he?"*
>
> *"The son of David," they replied.*
>
> *He said to them, "How is it then that David, speaking by the Spirit, calls him 'Lord'? For he says, 'The Lord said to my Lord, sit at my right hand until I put your enemies under your feet.'"*
>
> *"If then David calls him Lord, how can he be his son?"*
>
> *No one could say a word in reply...* (Matthew 22:42-46; see also Mic. 5:2; The Messiah is from Ancient of Days).

Some rabbinical responses to the literature of the Tenach are quite unconvincing. Jacob's wrestling with the Angel is overlooked or glossed over.[29] The reason the Angel of God is called God is not because he is God, but because God's Name is in Him. What is this supposed to prove? If we can call an Angel by the holy Name of God (YHWH) because God's Name is in Him, so also could we not call Yeshua divine because God's Name is in Him? The evidence of Tenach leaves us with a belief in one God with a plural dimension seen in manifestations of God. This revelation provides for an understanding of the New Testament revelation and its teaching on God and Yeshua. In the Tenach, we find the Angel of God, God the Father, and the Shekeenah distinguished.

In the New Covenant Scriptures, God's plurality is clearly manifest in a sense of threeness. The Spirit is spoken of as distinct from God and yet God. The Spirit will be given when Yeshua leaves (see John 14:15-31). He will be given by the Father. (Note the personal pronoun *He* for the Spirit.)

Yeshua is not only a man, but uniquely carries the name, nature, or stamp of divinity in a way that is not true of other men. He is born of a virgin as predicted in Isaiah 7:14 (which was translated *parthenos* [Greek for virgin] before Yeshua's time by the Jewish translators of the Septuagint version, 100 B.C.E.). As being born of a virgin, His origin is part human and part special creation by God to carry the nature of God. In the very Jewish virgin birth account in Luke, which continually talks of the hope of Israel and Israel's deliverance from oppression, the virgin birth is spoken of as the act whereby Yeshua will be called the Son of God. Let us note that Israel was called God's son (see Hos. 11:1) and that David was promised that Solomon would be God's son (see 2 Sam. 7). However, this is not in the same unique sense of Yeshua. Although the New Testament does not emphasize Yeshua's divinity in an out-of-balance way without also emphasizing His humanity, it clearly brings out this truth. In John 8:58, Yeshua claims to be one with the "I Am" saying, "...before Abraham was I am" (cf. Exod. 3:15).

In John 5:17-18, Yeshua claims oneness with the Father, who, according to rabbinic teaching, did not rest on Shabbat because He had to maintain the world's order. He also called God His Father in a special sense. We have already quoted Matthew 22:41-46, where Yeshua asked how David could call the Messiah, his son, his Lord. The writings of the rest of the New Testament also bring out this truth.

Matthew 28:19 commands the *Mikvah* (baptism) to be performed in the name of the Father, Son, and Holy Spirit. So also the Messiah is called the One in whom "all the fullness of the

Deity lives in bodily form" (Col. 2:9). He was in the form of God (see Phil. 2:6), but emptied Himself, becoming a servant. As a result of this, every knee shall bow and every tongue shall confess that Yeshua the Messiah is Lord (see Phil. 2:10). This applies Isaiah 45 to Yeshua, which speaks of all bowing the knee to the LORD (YHWH).

Yeshua, however, is not all of God's totality. He is one person or one aspect of that plural manifestation of God (from the Tenach), who became a human being. He, therefore, is a man who depends on the Spirit, prays to the Father, gets weary, and dies. His divine nature and His person never ceases to be, but He is human as well as divine. As such, prayer in the New Testament is not primarily addressed to Yeshua, but to "Our Father" in the name of Yeshua. For Yeshua is the human revelation of the Father.

This should not be thought so incredible. Man alone is created in the image of God. He alone, therefore, can be the perfect revelation of God. A perfect man who carries God's Name or nature, but is not all of God, fits into the whole character of biblical revelation. Yeshua, the man, did *not* exist before the first century; but His divine nature and person did! Yeshua is not all of God, but is a man embodying God's nature. He gives preeminence to His Father (see John 5:19; 17:1-5; 16:25-27). So Yeshua is described in Scripture as without sin (see Heb. 4:15; 1 Pet. 2:22; John 8:46). If God is a uni-plural being, this is perfectly sensible, although beyond our complete understanding. Jews shunned this doctrine, but it is not at all impossible. They have rejected Christian prayer, which seems to limit God to Yeshua—as if Jesus was in Himself, the complete Christian God.

Sometimes Christians speak as if they have lost sight of God the Father, what G.E. Wright called a "Christo monism."[30] Yet the New Testament, although recognizing Yeshua's divinity, recognizes that God is more than Yeshua. It *only rarely* addresses prayer to Yeshua, while recognizing that by His life, teaching, death, and resurrection, He is the fullest revelation of God to man.

Jewish ways of expression are needed, ways more consistent to the New Testament, if Jews are to penetrate Christian rhetoric and cultural expressions to see the truth of Yeshua's divine nature.

Jewish literature is not totally silent on the mystery of God's plurality. It should be mentioned that this literature sometimes reflects the reality of God's plurality. The Zohar, the text of Jewish mysticism, mentions that the Ancient One is revealed in three heads "which are united into one," "described as being three," "But how can three names be one?" "[This] can only be known by revelation of the Holy Spirit."[31]

Once we accept the divine nature of Yeshua—a teaching both consistent with Tenach on the uni-plurality of God, as well as the New Testament teaching on Yeshua—we might ask other reasons why God would reveal Himself in this way. There are several.

In terms of revelation, since man is created in the image of God, only a man would be able to bring the fullest revelation of God. A perfect man, however, would need to bear the nature of God to maintain perfection when born of our race. God reveals Himself in a man to benefit our understanding, a level of revelation we indeed can comprehend.

As a demonstration of God's unity with and love for the race of man, a revelation of God in a human being is the greatest possible way God could personally and intimately show His great love (see John 3:16).

Such a revelation also has a unique redemptive significance. The sufferings of the Messiah are not only the substitutionary sufferings of a separate agent being punished for sin instead of the guilty party. Rather, the Messiah's suffering is the suffering love of God revealed, which forgives in the midst of devastating hurt—if man will only turn in repentance. "Father forgive," said Yeshua when He was crucified (Luke 23:34). Such love awakens us to our sin and wins us back in repentance. Yeshua, as representative man—also in love—carries the hurt and destruction of the race for them or in their stead, as a parent would suffer in love to free his wayward children and turn them to the right. As the divine Messiah, His sacrifice has infinite value. If we are spiritually one with Him, God *accepts us in Him.* He thus is our mediator and high priest, not in the sense that we pray to Him *instead of* the Father, but, *because we are "in the Messiah"* (see Gal. 2:20), *we can go directly to God.*

The divinity of the Messiah is not idolatry, but reflects the fullest revelation of God. It is like the revelations of God in human form in the Tenach, which also were not of an idolatrous nature. In the Messiah, the revelation is conveyed in a human being that remains forever a human being.

The Scriptures thus communicate to us the impression of one great divine reality of three inseparable manifestations of God. The relationship of love and accord blends the three into eternal oneness beyond human comprehension. Yeshua prays to the Father, thanks Him for His love, and asks that He would be glorified with the love He had with the Father *before the foundation of the world* (see John 17:5). The love relationship then is the highest eternal reality. This love overflows in Creation. God gives Himself in love to the Creation, and the creation gives itself back to God in love.

When we say that God is love, God was not before the Creation loving Himself narcissistically. Rather, a reciprocal *giving relationship* of love is eternally existent within the plural unity God. This love then expands to human beings and forms them into the communities of the Spirit in Him that manifest the same sacrificial love to one another and sacrificial love for humanity.

Chapter Seven

MESSIANIC JEWISH PRACTICE

T HERE IS MUCH CONFUSION BECAUSE two questions are not distinguished: "Who is a Jew?" and "What does it mean to live as a Jew?" According to Halakah (traditional Jewish legal interpretation), a person is Jewish if born of a Jewish mother, circumcised if a male, and is not a convert to another religion (Maimonidies). Talmudic rabbinic authorities considered the Jewish convert to another religion to still be Jewish, but would not consider his children Jewish if they were raised in the new religion. This definition is also expanded to include those who convert to Judaism through instruction, decision, the ritual mik-vah (Jewish water immersion), and circumcision for men.

The major problem with this position is its contradiction to the scriptural indications that Jewish identity was carried through the father. The covenant was originally made with Abraham. The father clearly determined the religious identity of his family. The covenant sign of circumcision indicates that this was a covenant applying to physical descendants through the father.

Many Israelites of prominence took non-Jewish wives as well. They were an accepted part of the Jewish family—with no for-mal conversion. The wife of Moses, who was a Cushite, is one example. It is true of Ruth the wife of Boaz, the ancestors of King David. It is also true of the wives of Jacob. That Jewish identity can be passed on through the father becomes notably clear in the case of Athaliah, the wicked pagan queen descended from Jezebel. Ahaziah, the king, the son of Athaliah, was an ancestor of the Messiah! Though Athaliah sought to destroy the royal Messianic line, her grandson, Joash, survived and became king. Certainly, no one would claim that Jezebel and Athaliah were legitimate converts to Judaism; yet Athaliah's son and grandson were Jews! Therefore, to the traditional definition of who is a Jew, we must add the element of descent from the father.[1]

The definition of a Jew must be more inclusive than just physical descent and circumcision if we are to preserve Jewish identity. Whole tribes have converted to Judaism and were then part of the nation.[2] Many times, over the years through marriage, the children of these converts also became partakers of the bloodline from Abraham. What is important to note, however, is that others could also become part of the nation of Israel. Recent genetic studies now show that the Jewish people have a genetic continuity beyond what most would have expected.

David Ben Gurion, when asked who is a Jew, was so loose in his definition that he simply stated that it was anyone who desired to identify himself as a Jew. This seems to overlook the seriousness of taking on a Jewish identity with real conviction.

We conclude from this that a person is a *Jew* who (1) is descended from a Jewish father or mother and (2) who is circumcised as a Jew if a male and (3) maintains that he or she is a Jew. One can also become a Jew by conversion, including mikvah and circumcision.

Why, then, did the Halakic definition define Jewish descent through the mother alone? Some think that the reason goes back to Ezra. At that time, the Jewish remnant that returned to the land was disposed toward an adulteration of its religious purity through the influence of spouses. Ezra commanded the men at the time to divorce and send away their non-Jewish wives. The conclusion of the later rabbis was that their children would then not be considered Jewish. It is also thought that the mother's early upbringing of the child as well as the certainty of the child's descent from the mother—but uncertainty in the case of the father—lent weight toward adopting this viewpoint. Others argue that this definition change did not take place until after the Rabbinic period in the second century. Suffice it to say that the role of the father and descent from the father is also crucial.

WHAT DOES IT MEAN TO BE JEWISH?

The question of who is a Jew is important when considering what it means to be Jewish or to live as a Jew. We are not saying that someone who does not live a "Jewish" life is not Jewish any more than an American who is not patriotic is not an American. We do maintain that a Jew who does not live a Jewish life weakens the link of Jewish identity within his family and undercuts the perpetuation of a unique and identifiable Jewish people.

Many responses are given to what it means to live as a Jew. Some see support of Israel and Jewish community causes as central; others point to synagogue attendance or the celebration of the feasts. All of these aspects contain nuggets of truth, but the full truth can only be seen in the light of Scripture's own teaching. The fullest sense of what it foundationally means to be a Jew is biblically defined.

As stated throughout this book, God has called Israel to be a unique nation among the nations, a witness to His truth and faithfulness. As a nation, they were given unique practices, such as the practice of the Sabbath and the feasts, so that the people would be unified by the memory of what God had done in graciously establishing the nation. The nation would also then be unified in recognizing its unique purpose in showing forth the truth of the Scriptures and the faithfulness of God. The biblical heritage of feast and festival and identity with the nation is crucial.

If we ask what makes up a nation from a sociological perspective, we gain further insight. In light of the fact that God has committed Himself to preserve the nation of Israel and that we desire to be in accord with this purpose, these insights are important. In its strongest sense, a nation usually requires three major elements: a land (today defined as borders), a common language, and a common culture and heritage. Weakening of any of these factors that constitute a nation weakens the survival of the entity constituting a nation.

Presently, for example, we could note the weakness of Canada due to the cultural and linguistic differences between French and English-speaking Canadians. Historically, nations have disappeared when uprooted from their land. Israel is unique because she maintained her nationhood though uprooted and living in the Diaspora. Jews were not in Israel, but the land of Israel was within the Jews! Hence, the importance of national location and borders became lessened in Israel's case because the land of Israel became part of Israel's religious-cultural future hope.

Israel in the Diaspora was preserved by God through a common language and heritage. Although Hebrew was not Israel's spoken language, it was preserved as the language of the synagogue. A Jew could worship in Russia, Poland, France, or England with no language barrier. In addition, the biblical practices of feast and fast, as well as the rabbinic tradition, provided for an amazing cultural continuity. This was the case even where the fullness of the biblical meaning of Israel's call as a nation was lost. This common heritage gave rise to a universal sense of Jewish brotherhood that continues to this day. This includes Jewish community concerns for those in need, support for Israel, and maintaining of other Jewish cultural ties in music, dance, and literature.

The full scope of being a loyal Jew thus includes involvement in the Jewish community and support for Israel. However, *even more,* it means the preservation of the very historic biblical roots of the Jewish heritage that makes these involvements possible today. It includes Sabbath, the feasts, Hebrew language, unique tunes and sounds in worship, as well as Bible-based discerning appreciation of Jewish history, literature, and wisdom. Not all will be able to give themselves to the whole of the Jewish heritage, but as loyal Jews, we should do so to the extent that we can within the ultimate rule of the leading of the Spirit of God. God has preserved Israel; He has done so through the Jewish heritage.

Being a Jew is not just a physical thing. Messianic Jews should be on guard against tailoring their identity to a life pattern that is weak in heritage identification because of the influence of Jews who become believers and are themselves weak in their heritage identification. This weakness is to be countered if there is to be a dynamic Messianic Judaism. No amount of ignorant comments concerning the "dead nature of Jewish tradition," "coming under bondage to the Law," and all other such misapplications of Scripture should shake us from recognizing the essentially biblical and spiritual calling which we have from God to love and be part of the heritage of our people. Israel's calendar is from God; her preservation through her heritage is also from God. She is, therefore, a unique witness to God's faithfulness and His Lordship over all of history. The "gifts and the call of God to Israel *are* irrevocable" (Rom. 11:29 RSV). In addition, parts of the Rabbinic Jewish heritage cohere well with the New Covenant order.

We should also note that central to the Jewish heritage is the prophetic call to social righteousness, concern for justice, compassion, and mercy. Biblical Law is a foundation of social law for many Western nations. Messianic Jews should be in the forefront of witnessing to these prophetic truths.

However, Messianic Jews should seek a creative appropriation of our heritage as we are led by the Spirit. It must come from within rather than being artificially and rotely imposed from without, because there is a feeling of bondage to do it exactly as some other group does it.

SHABBAT

The Sabbath is a central pivot of Jewish life. As taught by Yeshua, "The sabbath was made for man, and not man for the sabbath" (Mark 2:27 KJV). It was never meant to be a day of legalistic conformity and concern for minute detail. Sabbath is a day of crucial significance to Jewish identity. The principle of weekly rest, worship, and renewal is one with universal significance. In this sense, the Sabbath principle is a spiritual and humanitarian guide for all peoples. Christians are free to incorporate this principle on Sunday or other days. The seventh day Sabbath for Israel is a special *central sign of the covenant* between Israel and God. Hence, to abrogate the sign of the covenant as a Jew is to cast doubt on whether we uphold the continuing covenant of God with Israel. Sabbath itself antedates Israel's existence and is a reflection of the Creation order. However, Israel is given Sabbath as a memorial of God's gracious rescue from slavery as well as a memorial of Creation and God's resting on the seventh day (period).

Messianic Judaism looks to Yeshua, who proclaimed Himself "Lord of the Sabbath" (see Mark 2:28), to gain a sense of direction for observance. The day is meant to be a break from the routine of work, whereby we may be renewed through worship, fellowship, and rest. By this rest and renewal, Messianic Jews testify that God is Lord of creation and that man need not be subject to work as though the economic sphere of life has a tyrannical control over our lives. The person of faith knows the "rest of faith" in Yeshua and testifies to the world that God is gracious and kind and will provide for us by faith even if one-seventh of our lives is spent in freedom from providing for our own material needs. Of course, with the rest of the feasts as days of rest, this is much more than one-seventh.

In Exodus 20:8-11, the nature of Sabbath is described as a testimony to God's own Lordship over the Creation. The Messianic Jew testifies against all theories of atheism, agnosticism, evolutionary naturalism, and pantheism by upholding the truth that, "In the beginning God created the heavens and the earth" (Gen. 1:1).

In Deuteronomy, both the Sabbath as a memorial of the Exodus as well as the Sabbath as a humanitarian law are stressed. On this day, rich and poor, free and slave achieved a measure of equality in freedom from the domination of work. The Sabbath is an essential faith principle. We believe God's Word sufficiently to let go of our anxiety for food, clothes, and shelter, believing that He is our loving Father and provider; we need not fear!

When we turn to the Prophets, we find the basic importance of Sabbath reaffirmed. Isaiah says, "Blessed is the man...who keeps the Sabbath without desecrating it, and keeps his hand from doing any evil" (Isa. 56:2). The passage goes on to delineate the blessings that shall be received by those who love God's covenant and express it in a heartfelt recognition of Sabbath.

We also read in Isaiah 58:13-14 these words:

> *"If you keep your feet from breaking the Sabbath and from doing as you please on my holy day, if you call the Sabbath a delight, and the Lord's holy day honorable, and if you honor it by not going your own way and not doing as you please or speaking idle words, then you will find your joy in the Lord, and I will cause you to ride on the heights of the land and to feast on the inheritance of your father Jacob."*
> *The mouth of the Lord has spoken.*

The prophets knew that desecration of the Sabbath struck at the heart of Israel's faith as to whether or not He was Lord, as to whether Israel was God's Covenant people!

The pages of the New Testament do not at all contradict the sense of Sabbath given in the Tenach. Nor did Yeshua break the Sabbath in its true sense. He calls Himself "Lord of the Sabbath" in Mark 2:27, decrying the legalists who would make Sabbath a burden instead of a delight by multiplying legalistic restrictions beyond the standards of the Torah! The Pharisees criticized His disciples for eating grain as they walked through the fields. Their action was a natural response, unconnected with work. However, in the legalism of the day in some quarters, this constituted harvesting! Yeshua perceived that such legalism would cause people to be concerned with scores of restrictions, thereby missing the sense of the day—its joy, its refreshment, its renewal. As Lord of the Sabbath, He set the record straight. Legalism is not the standard of God, but human regulations that do not properly apply the intention of the Torah of God.

Outside of a Jewish context, the Apostle Paul allowed for freedom in regards to worship days. But he nowhere speaks against Jews who follow the Sabbath. He would not, however, allow an imposition of the Sabbath on non-Jews. Our historical documents show that the Jewish believers of the first several centuries continued to practice Shabbat as part of their heritage and witness.

The Jewish influence was significant in the first century. Amazingly the seven-day week became universal in the Roman Empire at the end of the first century. The Christian Church adopted the Sabbath principle, though its day of worship and rest was Sunday. We should note that Sunday in Christian practice is one day in seven for worship, renewal, and rest!

How is it that Christendom adopted the "first" day as its day of worship? Some have held that the early believers gathered on Sunday morning to celebrate the resurrection and celebrated both the Sabbath and Sunday. It is also taught by some that the Church perceived that, under the New Covenant, the seventh day Sabbath had been abrogated and that Sunday was a proper replacement of the Sabbath.

The most recent scholarship suggests that this explanation for the switch from Saturday to Sunday is mistaken. Adventist Dr. Samuele Bacchiocchi has probably written the definitive work on all of the evidence involved. A summary of his work appears in the *Biblical Archaeology Review* (Sept/Oct 1978) and a fascinating debate ensued as recorded in future editions.[3] The basic evidence seems to be that Sunday worship was not introduced as an authoritative apostolic practice. Part of the evidence is that "Paul refused to take a stand on the question of observance of days, advising rather to follow one's convictions and to respect differences of viewpoint"[4] (see Rom. 14:3,5-6;10-13;19-21; 2:16-17). Sabbath was not imposed on Gentiles, but it seems that Sunday-keeping did originate in Gentile communities. However, if Paul *had* introduced such practices, this innovation would have caused great controversy, which, historically, is not the case.

Bacchiocchi traces the exclusive observance of Sunday to the time of Emperor Hadrian (117-135 c.e.), when Roman anti-Jewish repression influenced a policy of deliberate differentiation from Jewish customs.

The only examples in the New Testament of a first-day meeting were probably Saturday evening rather than Sunday morning! In Jewish reckoning, the next day begins at sundown! Hence, in Acts 20:7, Paul preached all night and left on Sunday morning! He was not taking a day of rest and worship on Sunday.

The early believers did gather in the evening to celebrate the Messiah's memorial supper as is indicated by Paul's description of the rite as "supper-deipnon" (see 1 Cor. 11:20). This could have occurred on Saturday night as a counterpart to the Jewish Saidah Shlishi (the third Sabbath meal), preceding the ceremony ending Sabbath (Havdalah). Non-Jews could have mistaken this celebration as a first-day Sunday morning institution, which it clearly was not. As part of the nation of Israel, Jewish believers in Yeshua would have worked on Sunday, but not on Saturday. Jewish believers were part of other synagogues on the Sabbath and thus may have gathered for their meetings at various times.

Bacchiocchi finds Sunday observance coming about as part of an anti-Jewish reaction, in which Sabbath was even seen as a temporary institution imposed as a trademark of the divine reprobation of the Jewish race. At any rate, there is no biblical evidence to suggest that Sabbath does not have its value as a sign of God's continued covenant with Israel, originally made with Abraham.

For a *Messianic Jew, it is a day that celebrates the Sabbath rest that is ours in Yeshua who is Lord of the Sabbath.*

The Catechism of the Catholic Church, actually a new catechism from 1996, argues that the seventh day Sabbath has not been abrogated and is still the appropriate observance for Jews. It then goes on to defend Sunday as proper to Christians.[4]

Messianic Jews must avoid a legalistic approach to Sabbath, where rules are imposed ad infinitum. However, if Sabbath is to be taken seriously, there are some basic principles that may be applied by our people.

First, Sabbath should be a day of freedom from work, especially that work which is required for our economic and material security. Judaism has always recognized that professions providing help in emergency (doctors, firemen, etc.) must be exceptions. Even these people, however, need the principle of renewal and should seek a period of rest.

Second, it is of spiritual value to mark the day off from other days by a special Friday evening meal, the lighting of candles and prayer. This makes us conscious of entering into a special period of time. Some Messianic Jews give special recognition to Yeshua, who is the light of the world, in their lighting the lights before the Friday evening Sabbath meal. Blessings over bread and wine for Sabbath are helpful additions along with the content of the Sabbath *Kiddush.* As Yeshua according to Luke took the wine as symbolizing His blood after the meal and not as part of the Passover Kiddush, I do not think it is necessary that Messianic Jews make their *Kiddush* into communion.

Sabbath is also an appropriate day to gather for worship and to hear the Word exposited. It is a time as well for friends, fellowship, and family. It is a wonderful time for those restful activities that we might otherwise overlook. Reading biblical stories together, quieter games, and napping can all be interwoven to make Sabbath a joy. The Sabbath also may be ended with special prayer. The *Havdalah* service is a meaningful way. *Havdalah* means a *separation* from Sabbath. A special candle is lit and extinguished in wine. Sweet spices are shaken in a spice box and sniffed by all as a reminder of the sweetness of Sabbath.

Of primary importance is that our activity be a true renewal of life in God. We need not be overly detailed in defining what constitutes work. Activity that is wearing on us, which depresses, which is related to material security, should be avoided. Sabbath should be a *real contrast* from other days. Congregations with Sabbath schedules ought as well be careful to not tax their people with too much activity. To make Sabbath a delight, may our celebrations be creative.

Much material on Sabbath is available from Jewish publishers. Take note as well of the *Jewish Catalogue*, a fine source for all the holidays.[5]

The Feasts of Israel

Passover

Passover is the great feast that recalls the Exodus from Egyptian bondage. It recalls the birth of Israel as a nation and our nation entering into freedom. As a great feast of remembrance, Passover is without equal. It is full of meanings that are also relevant to all followers of the Messiah. The Exodus is a type or image pattern of God's redemptive acts and even of the final redemption and the establishment of God's Kingdom. Hence, we note these salient facts.

1. The slaughter of the Passover lamb sacrifice and the placing of its blood on the doorpost and on the lintel is used in the New Testament as the background for understanding the death of Yeshua. As the angel of death *passed over* the houses of the Israelites who were protected by the blood of the lamb, even so we are passed from death unto life by the atonement blood of Yeshua. Hence, Yeshua dies on the eve of Passover in

John 19, for He is "our Passover lamb" who is slain (see 1 Cor. 5:7ff). In the Corinthian passage, we are enjoined to purge out the leaven of malice and wickedness.

Your boasting is not good. Don't you know that a little yeast works through the whole batch of dough? Get rid of the old yeast that you may be a new batch without yeast— as you really are. For [Messiah], our Passover lamb, has been sacrificed. Therefore let us keep the Festival, not with the old yeast, the yeast of malice and wickedness, but with bread without yeast, the bread of sincerity and truth (1 Corinthians 5:6-8).

Leaven was not eaten by Israel when they left Egypt because the dough had no time to rise. Leaven also became a symbol of that indwelling evil which pervades and affects life. Passover symbolism is central to Paul's exposition of the meaning of Messiah Jesus.

2. The 5,000 Israelites ate the loaves that were multiplied by the supernatural power of God in Yeshua. The feeding of the 5,000 is fraught with the Passover symbolism, recalling the manna in the Wilderness.

3. The early believers—both Jew and non-Jew—celebrated the resurrection of the Messiah on Passover that began the eight-day Feast of Unleavened Bread. He replaced the sacrificial lamb that was absent in their celebration.

4. The Messiah's memorial meal (the Last Supper) was a Passover meal in which Yeshua made the wine of the cup of redemption (probably the third cup) and the bread of the *afikomen* (dessert) symbolize His broken body and shed blood. Therefore, He was telling His disciples to make the bread and wine of the Passover meal a pointer to His redemption and a participation in its power and meaning.[6]

In the light of this, we see how Passover is celebrated by Messianic Jews. They, of course, rejoice in the eight-day festival in thanksgiving to God for their redemption from Egyptian bondage, their birth as a nation, and their continued preservation. Eating only unleavened bread for eight days, special services, and the Passover meal itself on the 14th/15th of Nisan are all a joyous part of their celebration! However, their celebration also incorporates all of the meanings of Yeshua's life in us. The bread and wine would stand for Him. He would be seen in all of the sacrificial images which were part of Passover.

This is a great annual teaching time for the family. The family and its guests gather for the meal on the 14th/15th of Nisan. Each family would have a Seder (order) or Passover meal, reading the stories of the Exodus and of our redemption in Yeshua. The festival would be a seven-day celebration of the resurrection with special days off from work to gather as a congregation on the first and seventh days as enjoined in Leviticus 23.

Passover is a great celebration of God's grace in both Old and New Testament times! We should note that, in our view, the proscription of guests who are not circumcised at the meal is not applicable to any believer who is clean (circumcised in heart) in Yeshua (see Acts 10). However, it would imply that the elements of the Messiah's Supper are not to be given to those who are not believers.

Passover celebrates the fulfillment of God's promise to Abraham to make him a great nation and to bring Messiah from his seed. Thousands of Messianic Jews around the world now celebrate Passover in this way.

The eschatological meaning of Passover is important and should be brought out in Messianic Jewish celebration. Passover looks forward to all nations entering into a promised land prepared for them. As Israel is established in her promised, so all nations will be so established. The feast looks forward to the ultimate Promised Land for all peoples, the New Heavens and New

Earth and the New Jerusalem (see Rev. 21). Just as in Passover, the promise is preceded by plagues of God on the world with Egypt, culminating with the ultimate deliverance of Israel, the Body of the Messiah, and finally the conversion of the nations (see Isa. 2; 11). The Book of Revelation is thus very relevant for reading and explaining in the context of Passover.

First Fruits—Counting the Omer

In Leviticus 23:9-14, we read about the Feast of First Fruits, celebrated on the day after the Sabbath that follows Passover. The Feast includes an offering to God of the first produce of the year. As stated previously, Yeshua the Messiah now takes the place of all of the *sacrificial* dimensions of all the feasts. Although this feast is not as "major" in the Hebrew Scriptures as other feasts, it does have important significance. Indeed, it is the celebration of the resurrection. We read in First Corinthians 15:20,22b—"But now [Messiah] is risen from the dead...the first fruits of those who have fallen so in [the Messiah] all shall be made alive."

The meaning of First Fruits is the promise of more to come. Because He rose, there is more to come, namely the resurrection of all followers of Yeshua. Thus, we might recommend as part of Messianic Jewish practice, a gathering of the congregation for worship. Reading Leviticus 23:9-14 and First Corinthians 15 on the resurrection would be excellent. In addition, a special offering could be taken in our congregations or for other worthy spiritual ministries to show that all we have is God's.

In ancient Israel, First Fruits celebrated the beginning of fruit trees and the first of the barley harvest. We, in remembering this, tie ourselves to our people and its land.

Shavuot (Weeks)—Pentecost (50)

We are enjoined to count forty-nine days—or seven weeks—after First Fruits to commemorate the Feast of *Shavuot*. These days are actually counted in synagogues in Jewish liturgy. This is called the "counting of the Omer," a sheaf of wheat. The fiftieth day is the celebration of *Shavuot*, one of the three major festivals during which men (often with families, if possible) presented themselves before God at Jerusalem.

In biblical times, Shavuot originally signified thanksgiving for the first harvest of wheat. However, by the time of Yeshua, this ancient feast was connected by rabbinic calculation to the time of the giving of God's revelation on Sinai. It is valuable to connect to the land through this feast as well as to celebrate the giving of the Law in our worship. The rabbinical calculation is reasonable.

However, there is a central meaning for Messianic Jews and Christians who have adopted this Holy Day as one of their own; for on this day, God in His sovereignty chose to give the Holy Spirit *(Ruach ha Kodesh)* to Yeshua's gathered followers. In Acts 2, we read the marvelous story of how the Apostles preached the Gospel supernaturally to Jewish people from many lands in many languages. The followers of Yeshua were able to communicate in these languages, even though they had never learned them, the news of salvation in Yeshua. A great harvest of people was gathered into the new community of Yeshua's followers.

It is significant that God providentially gave His Spirit on this day, for it is only through the power of the Spirit that we can we do God's will or obey the Law. It is by the Spirit that God's Law is written on our hearts (see Ezek. 36:25-27; Heb. 10:16).

As with all the feasts, Shavuot is fraught with eschatological meaning and looks forward to the day when the Spirit is poured out on the whole world and the Age of the Spirit is fully established.

Shavuot is thus a great celebration of many biblical meanings and events. It is a day of rest and worship. Homes and congregational buildings may be decorated with greens. The services of worship at home and in congregations will emphasize the truths of the relationship of the Law of God and the Spirit of God who inspired the writings of the Law. Special gifts to worthy ministries and needy people are also ways of showing gratitude to God.

Furthermore, it is ideal to recommit ourselves to walk in the Spirit and to seek to be filled anew by the Spirit. We sometimes had all-night prayer and worship times for this feast.

Rosh Hashana

The Feast of Trumpets—the Jewish New Year—takes place in the autumn, on the first of *Tishri,* on the Israeli calendar. Originally this day was not celebrated as a new year, but rabbinic calculation fixed the anniversary of the Creation of the world on this day.

Actually, Israel was originally to observe this as the day of the blowing of the Shofar (ram's horn) in preparation for Yom Kippur. Hence, Jewish tradition rightly incorporates prayers seeking forgiveness on this day as well as New Year memorials. Scripturally, our people were told to celebrate the month of the Feast of Passover as their new year. Tishri in the fall was actually the New Year festival of the surrounding nations of the Near East, just as January first would be our parallel today. There is nothing wrong with remembering the Creation of the world on this day, too, as long as we do not lose sight of the day as an *entrance into the days of self-examination and repentance before God.*

The Feast of Trumpets also reminds us of the return of Yeshua the Messiah to rule and reign. In First Thessalonians 4:16-18, we learn:

> *The Lord himself shall descend from heaven with a shout, with the voice of the archangel, and the* [shofar] *of God: and the dead in* [the Messiah] *shall rise first: then we which are alive and remain shall be caught up together with them in the clouds...and so shall we ever be with the Lord. Wherefore comfort one another with these words* (KJV).

We also read in First Corinthians 15 that we shall be changed in a moment at the resurrection, at the *last shofar,* in the twinkling of an eye.

Messianic Jews, therefore, celebrate Rosh Hashana as a day of rest, with services of worship emphasizing preparation for the return of the Messiah and the resurrection, as well as a preparation for Yom Kippur. Traditional and modern worship material may be creatively adapted to this end. The traditional Jewish emphasis of God as King and Judge are quite fitting for emphasis on this day.

YOM KIPPUR—(THE DAY OF ATONEMENT)

Yom Kippur is the holiest day of the Jewish year. In ancient Israel, Yom Kippur was the day on which atonement was made for the whole nation (see Lev. 16). On this day, the high priest went into the Holy of Holies with the sacrificial blood to make atonement for the people's sins. He sprinkled this blood on the Ark of the Covenant. Prominent at Yom Kippur as well was the ceremony of the scapegoat. The priest laid his hands on the head of the animal, which then symbolically carried away the sins of the people. This is the only day in Torah specified as a day of self-affliction (fasting). On this day, the nation was to "afflict itself" in repentance for sin. Traditional Judaism incorporates many great prayers of repentance for seeking forgiveness, some of which are fraught with Messianic significance. For example, the merit of the Messiah is appealed to for forgiveness.[7] Forgiveness is also asked on the basis of Abraham's offering of Isaac as a sacrifice (which Messianic Jews know to be a foreshadowing of the sacrifice of the Messiah Yeshua). (This is the case with daily services as well.)

Yom Kippur also has important significance in Messianic Judaism. It is not that we seek atonement through our prayers or by the observance of a day: Yeshua the Messiah is our High Priest, our atonement, and our scapegoat! The central chapters of the Book of Hebrews explain the meaning of Yeshua in the light of Yom Kippur and are central passages for us on this day.

Yom Kippur is a day incorporating several meanings:

1. It is the central celebration of the fulfillment of the biblical meaning of *Priest* and *Sacrifice* in Yeshua.

2. It is a day of prayer, fasting, and intercession for Israel, our people.

3. It is a day of self-examination and turning from sin in our own lives. Scripture enjoins us to "examine ourselves" (see 1 Cor. 11:28; 1 John 1:8-9).

It is a day to worship in community as well as to be apart, to examine our lives from the past year. Where have we missed God's direction? Where have we grown? Where have we slipped? As James 4:6-11 enjoins us, we are to repent and turn from these sins unto God. Confession and forgiveness form a daily part of our life in Yeshua. However, as individuals and as a community, it is of value to have a special season for this purpose as well.

The services for Yom Kippur emphasize Messianic fulfillment as well. The breakfast is a special time of rejoicing and celebration for our forgiveness in Yeshua.

Two areas of special misunderstanding are worth noting in relation to Yom Kippur. One is *"Kol Nidre"* (All Vows), a chant which begins the first evening service, called the *Kol Nidre* service. This particular chant asks forgiveness for all past and future vows which we might make and break. It is not that Jewish people intended to break vows, but under extreme duress and torture, Jews were often forced to take vows which they could not keep and yet be loyal to God. Messianic Jews have the promise of God's grace and the command of Yeshua to be totally truthful. Our Yom Kippur observance needs to emphasize this.

Second, both Rosh Hashana and Yom Kippur services have us pray to be inscribed in the Book of Life (for the coming year). Some followers of Yeshua have sometimes had difficulty with both the prayer and the Rosh Hashana greeting, "May you be inscribed (in the Book of life)."

The Book of Life may refer to several books within Judaism. Some have thought that the reference must be to the symbolic book of eternal life found in the Book of Revelation. Other references, however, are only to the Book of Life in the sense of God's decrees concerning those who will be kept in life and health for the coming year. In the latter sense, there is no problem with the greeting.

Some Messianic Jewish congregations fittingly conclude the Yom Kippur Fast with a communion celebration since Yeshua gave His blood for us in the symbolism on this feast.

SUCCOT—(BOOTHS OR TABERNACLES)

Soon after Yom Kippur, the Feast of Succot begins. It is the third major feast in which the men of Israel were required to travel to Jerusalem. Bringing the family was ideal. This is an eight-day festival during which the people of Israel dwelled in tents to recall their wilderness wanderings, when they had little in the way of possessions, permanent dwellings, or natural provision for food. God supernaturally provided for their needs of food, clothing, and shelter. To dwell in tents is a vivid reminder of God's grace. When Israel dwelt in tents, they remembered that, although they might have homes and land and other measures of wealth, their lives were just as dependent upon God. Security was not in possessions. Nor was Israel to think that its might or wealth was a product of its self-righteousness or power (see Deut. 8–10). Israel was to love and trust God first and only. The eight-day celebration of *Succot* was to be a vivid reminder of all of these truths.

The Feast of Succot was also a celebration of the last major harvest in Israel. It was a great festival of thanksgiving. Part of the tradition of this feast was the recitation of the Hallel Psalms 113–118 and the waving of fruit (etrog) and branches of palm, myrtle, and willow (lulav) before God (see Lev. 23). This is called the Four Species. Waiving them in the four directions of the compass and up and down proclaim God's Kingship and, for us, Yeshua's Kingship over all the earth.

Hospitality is an essential part of observing Succot. In gratitude for God's provision, we share with others. The first day and eighth day of the festival are assemblies of worship.

The Feast of Tabernacles is also full of Messianic significance. In John 7–9, the teaching of Yeshua is best understood in the context of the feast of Succot. The last Day of Succot was the context of Yeshua's statement:

> If any one thirst let him come to me and drink. He who believes in me, as the scripture has said, "Out of his heart shall flow rivers of living water." Now this he said about the Spirit... (John 7:37-39 RSV).

We know from the description of Succot in the Talmud that this was the day in which a great ceremony of pouring out waters of libation took place.

The joyful ceremonial of festival reached its climax in Temple times when the procedure known as "the joy of water drawing" began on the second night of Succot and lasted for six days. Each morning a libation offering of water was made. It was taken in a golden ewer from the pool of Siloam, carried with great pomp and ceremony, and poured into a perforated silver bowl placed on the west side of the altar, symbolizing the abundant rain for which the people prayed. Bonfires were lit and men of piety danced, holding lighted torches and singing songs and hymns to the accompaniment of harps, lyres, cymbals, and trumpets played by Levites.[8]

During the last day of the feast there was a magnificent lamp-lighting ceremony in the Court of the Women. The Temple thus shone with an incredible brightness of light. This, in all probability, was the context of Yeshua's statement, "I am the light of the world" (John 8:12).

Matthew 6 is also an excellent chapter as well to remember at *Succot* time, for it supremely recounts to us the nature of God's fatherly care.

Lastly, we should note that some argue on the basis of the dates for the course of the priests and the vision given to Zacharius and the prophecy of the conception of John, that Yeshua was born on Succot. That there was no room in the inns could be due to the many who came for the feast. Many scholars do argue for an autumn date for the birth of Yeshua.

How is *Succot* best celebrated by Messianic Jews? There are a variety of creative ways: First, as in all the feasts, the sacrificial dimensions are replaced by the centrality of Yeshua's sacrifice. In addition, services on the first and last days of *Succot* are a time for the gathered community to give thanks, to wave fruit and branches in thanksgiving, to read the *Hallel* Psalms 113–118, and to creatively worship using traditional and modern material. Evenings should be times of special fellowship through the sharing of meals and reading the Scriptures we have mentioned.

One of our dilemmas, of course, relates to the biblical stipulation to dwell in tents: In Israel, with a warm climate, the practice is not only beautiful but practical. In some Diaspora climates, this becomes less possible. The rabbis, in realizing this, have sought to instill the practice of building a *succah* and at least taking meals in the Succah.

As we look at Messianic Jewish practice, we note as well the importance of conveying the meaning of this feast in an enjoyable way, recognizing that the command to dwell in tents was given for the nation dwelling in its land in a warmer climate and possessing houses and security. In the Diaspora, there is a great measure of freedom. Climate permitting, we would indeed recommend the building of a *succah* by families, as well as sleeping and the eating of meals in it.[9] Decorating the *succah* is a great joy to children; a festive spirit prevails. Some Messianic Jews have sought to take a camping trip during part of Succot so as to really get a greater sense of the bare necessities and of God's provision for us through the produce of the land, for He gives the rain and sunshine. The first and last days of the eight-day festival are special days of rest and community gathering for worship celebration. Traditionally, this was a period of especially looking forward to the Messianic Kingdom. God will someday be seen as the provider for all the earth; hence, according to Zechariah 14, this feast is to be universally observed.

All nations will send representatives to Jerusalem to observe this feast with Israel. We waive the *lulav* and *etrog* in all four directions and up and down to proclaim the universal dominion of Yeshua. If Rosh Hoshana and Yom Kippur are connected to the second coming of Yeshua, the first Feast of Succot after his return could well fit the eschatological vision of the Marriage Supper of the Lamb. It is important to note that the rabbis taught that the seventy bulls offered during the week of Succot were for the sins of the nations. This connects well to the universality of the feast. Succot was the greatest feast on the ancient Jewish calendar.

MINOR FEASTS AND FASTS

Simchat Torah (Rejoicing of the Torah)—Since we have just described *Succot,* it is fitting to describe Simchat Torah as well. *Simchat Torah* is not a biblically prescribed feast. It occurs immediately after Succot and celebrates the transition from the last to the first reading of the annual Torah cycle. The Jewish community created a festival of joy on a day that could have been only a day of the tedious rerolling of the community's scrolls from the end to the beginning. We might also ask, is it not a cause for rejoicing to complete a reading of the Scriptures by the community and to have the opportunity to begin reading again!

The festival includes music and dancing with the Torah scrolls. Among some of the Orthodox Hasidic communities, the celebration soars into great heights of joy and energy. For Messianic Jews, there is further cause of rejoicing—for in the Messiah we are accounted righteous and have the joy of God's Torah written on our hearts by His Spirit.

Purim—celebrates the deliverance of Israel from a wicked plot of annihilation during the days of the Persian Empire. The Book of Esther records the account of the wicked plans of Haman and the efforts of the Jewish Queen Esther (Hadasah) to influence the king to save her people. Purim falls near the end of winter in the month of Adar. It is characterized by plays, songs, costumes, and the reading of the Scroll of Esther (the Megillah) during which children make noise with "gregors" to drown out the name of Haman. Other great periods of danger and deliverance in Israel's history are also recalled. The creative possibilities of the Messianic Jewish celebration of this day are unlimited. Special plays, dialogues, concerts, spiritual parties, and more have been successfully undertaken.

Yom Ha Shoah (Day of Calamity)—This day, occurring in the spring on the 25th of Nisan, recalls the destruction of European Jewry under the unspeakable horrors of the reign of the Nazis. The day is marked in both synagogues and larger communities by services that include memorial prayers, readings from concentration camp poetry and literature, and recommitment to the survival of Israel. Messianic Jews join in mourning and memory with the whole Jewish community on this day as well as affirming the ultimate hope of justice and peace in the reign of the Messiah.

Lutheran Franklin Littell also suggests a service for Christian churches in his book, *The Crucifixion of the Jews.*[10] The Church would thereby repent of its past silence in the face of this atrocity while yet showing a solidarity of mourning and memory with the Jewish community.

Israel Independence Day *(Yom Ha Atzmaoot)*—Later in the spring, the 5th of Iyar marks the rebirth of the State of Israel in 1948. It is a day of prophetic fulfillment and celebration. Congregations and communities all over the world celebrate this miracle! However, we should temper Zionism, our support for the return to the Land, with the understanding that Israel has not embraced Yeshua. There is corruption, sin, and injustice as in other Western nations. We will not see Israel come into the fullness of her promise until she embraces Yeshua.

Tisha B'Av (The 9th of Av)—This date, which occurs in midsummer, is a day of fasting and sadness. On this day, supernaturally—by any standard of unbiased reasoning—the first Temple of Israel was destroyed in 586 B.C.E. by the Babylonians and the second Temple was destroyed in 70 c.e. by Titus. Incredible as it seems, both Temples were destroyed on the same date 656 years apart! Also on this day, the decree of the expulsion of the Jewish community from Spain in 1492 went into effect. Other tragedies occurred on this day.

Messianic Jews should seek identity with their people, mourning in prayerful intercession as we reflect on such judgments. We should also note the passages of comfort and hope in the Scripture. Let us pray for the peace of Jerusalem as well as for the salvation of friends and of all of Israel.

Chanukah (*Hanukkah*, The Feast of Dedication)— This feast celebrates the amazing victories in Israel's overthrow of its tyrannical Syrio-Greek rulers during the days of the Maccabees. The Syrio-Greek Empire sought not only to rule Israel, but to destroy Israel's unique religious fidelity to Scripture. They imposed pagan customs and rites on Israel, even in the Temple itself. Many were martyred for their faith. Hence, in the 160s b.c.e., the Maccabee family led a great revolt, eventually culminating in the rededication of the Temple and the independence of Israel for the first time in over 400 years. Chanukah itself, which usually falls in early winter—on the 25th of Chislev—marks the rededication of the Temple. Prominent during the eight-day festival is the lighting of the candles of an eight-branched menorah. Every day, one more candle is lit. This recalls the reported miracle of oil in the Temple lamps. When the Temple lamps were relit, there was only enough to last for a day, yet the light burned for eight days until new oil could be obtained. Messianic Jews celebrate the victories of those days with the rest of the Jewish community. They retell the stories of Chanukah from the books of the Maccabees as well as reliving these events through Chanukah plays. Another reason for the eight days was that Chanukah was a belated celebration of Succot, which also lasts eight days. The symbols of both feasts have parallels.

Messianic Jews would do well to also recall that this feast was the occasion of Yeshua's profound teaching on the relationship between Himself as the Good Shepherd and the rest of His sheep who "hear His voice," know Him, and follow Him (see John 10).

We note that Chanukah played an enormous part in the consciousness of first-century Jews. The names of the Maccabee family were the most common names at that time, as represented by Yeshua's disciples.[11] Indeed, false Messiahs looked to the victories of that period as the model for what they would do in leading the revolt against Rome. Yeshua consistently warned against such a direction. These were the false Messiahs of John 10, in the context of Chanukah. Yeshua is the true Messiah that will deliver Israel in much greater supernatural deliverance than was obtained under the Maccabees.

We cannot overlook the fact that it is in this season that most Christians celebrate Christmas. Although there is no ambivalence among Messianic Jews toward the biblical meaning of Christmas—the entrance into this world of the Messiah Jesus—Christmas itself brings ambivalent feelings to Messianic Jews. First, scholars usually hold that this date is *not* the time of the birth of the Messiah. Usually, the date is explained as one that correlated to the old pagan winter solstice festival in which pagans symbolically sought to magically assure the resurrection of spring. Perhaps the reason for the Church's date was to counter such paganism with a Christian holiday. Yet the ambivalence persists. The Puritan Christians forbade the celebration of Christmas in the sixteenth and seventeenth centuries because of supposed pagan connections. On the other hand, we should note that the Jewish feasts are connected to the changes of the seasons, equinox, and solstice. Chanukah fills in the one such period where there was not a feast in Torah.

The Jewish community has actually tended to emphasize Chanukah, which was a minor feast, to counter the influence of Christmas by having a parallel gift-giving holiday. The story does not end here, for recently Cardinal Jean Danielou proposed the opinion that the reason December 25th (a solar calendar date) could be proposed as a date for the birth of the Messiah, despite its pagan connections, must be sought in the fact that the 25th *of Chislev* (a lunar calendar date) already possessed great significance to Messianic Jews. In latter times, this connection was lost and the 25th of Chislev became identified with the 25th of December and the birth of Yeshua. Danielou holds that the 25th of Chislev was the birth of James the apostle (Jacob).[12] It should be noted that if Yeshua was born on Succot, a very possible date as explained above, then the miracle stories in Luke and his conception would have been at this time, so incarnation meaning may have been remembered for this season, but later identified with his birth. John Fisher, one of the fathers of the modern Messianic Jewish movement, argues from Hippolytus that Yeshua really was born on the 25th of December.

Is there a solution to the problem of these dates and the ambivalence they cause, a solution that also meets the special need to recognize the birth of Yeshua as well as reading with special festivity the passages so profoundly recording the details of his conception and birth (see Matt. 1–2; Luke 1–2)?

If we note the practice of Messianic Jews of today and yesteryear in celebrating the resurrection of Yeshua, we might gain a hint at a solution. Messianic Jews celebrate the resurrection in connection to the 14th of Nisan, which is Passover. Thus they follow the Jewish lunar calendar for religious observance. If we note that there is no agreement on the date of the birth of the Messiah, we can perhaps make some creative new suggestions.

Without Chanukah and the preservation of the Jewish community by God, Yeshua would never have come according to the prophecies. Chanukah is a festival of lights, and Yeshua is the light of the world. Perhaps then for Messianic Jews, the climax of Chanukah could be the celebration of the birth of Yeshua. However, this celebration would be set by the Jewish lunar date of the 25th of Chislev. It would also be well to then read the birth narratives. Also, during Chanukah, the life of James (Jacob), the great leader of the Messianic Jewish community in Jerusalem, can be recalled. Messianic Jews need to produce story books and celebration ideas incorporating all of these significant events in the light of Yeshua. These books would then be of help to families and congregations. Messianic Jews might also want to include the birth of Yeshua at Succot, as a significant part of this celebration as well. These are only suggestions, but it is put forth with the hope that it has merit.

OTHER COMMON WORSHIP PRACTICES

The Tzizit (Fringes)

The Lord said to Moses, "Speak to the Israelites and say to them: 'Throughout the generations to come you are to make tassels on the corners of your garments, with a blue cord on each tassel. You will have these tassels to look at and so you will remember all the commands of the Lord, that you may obey them and not prostitute yourselves by going after the lusts of your own hearts and eyes. Then you will remember to obey all my commands and will be consecrated to your God. I am the Lord your God... (Numbers 15:37-41).

The meaning of this command is quite simple. The ancient Israelites wore four-cornered garments, almost like a sheet with cutouts for head and arms. Upon each corner of the garment was to be sewn a fringe or tassel with a cord of blue. This cord of blue was to be a memory tool to remember to do all in commitment to God, not for selfish desire, to be consecrated to God, and to obey all His commands. Whenever it was looked upon, it was to call the Israelite to his commitment. In addition, some years ago, the famous Jewish archaeologist, Cyrus Gordon, argued that the fringes were a symbol of royalty in the ancient world. Hence, Jews were to see the fringe, be reminded that they were a royal priesthood, and to live as fitting to that calling.[13]

Our desire as Messianic Jews is to recapture the *Spirit* (the reason and application for today) of the Law and not just the letter. This command does not mean that we as Western twenty-first-century people have to return to the dress of 3,500 years ago and sew tassels on the corners of our garments. It does mean that we should seek means of constantly reminding ourselves of our commitment to God and to His commandments, that the love of God and love for God be constantly remembered.

Messianic Jews may find value in the prayer shawl (Tallit), a garment developed for the purpose of keeping this command, even though we do not wear four-cornered garments today. As they place the prayer shawl upon themselves, they return to their first love. Some Messianic Jews find value in the Tallit Katan, worn under the shirt so that fringes are worn in all waking hours. We recall the words of Yeshua, "If you love me, keep my commandments." Thus the fringes still have value. However, it is the principle of memory that counts, not enforcing the particular means of memory. Some Messianic Jews who wear fringes use blue fringes that are now used in some Chasidic sects.

The fringes were worn by Yeshua, and those who sought healing from Him would seek to touch the fringes of His garment (see Mark 5:28; 6:56). Some also use the Tallit as a symbol of being clothed upon with the righteousness of Yeshua, in whom we are accounted righteous. By His power in us, we fulfill God's commands.

H.L. Ellison argued that Paul certainly wore fringes all of the time or would not have been heard at all in the synagogues.[14]

Tefillin (Phylactries)—In Deuteronomy 6:4ff—"the Sh'ma Passage"—we read the words: "You shall "love the Lord with all your heart and with all your soul and with all your strength," and that these words should be bound "as a sign upon your hand" and as a sign "on your foreheads." They are to be written "on the doorframes of your houses and…gates" as well.

The traditional means of fulfilling this command is a small box with leather straps that is placed on the arm, the straps being woven around the arm and hand. Another box with leather straps is placed upon the head. The command in relation to gates and doorposts is fulfilled through use of the *mezuzah,* a small container affixed in the proper place on the door. All three contain the biblical verses enjoined by Scripture. The *tefillin* is worn daily during daytime prayer services.

Again we have a significant memory device in Scripture. Jewish tradition rejects the use of *tefillin* on Sabbath because Sabbath is also called a "sign" between God and Israel of God's covenant with Israel. Jewish reasoning eschews the use of signs in a way that one sign could detract from the significance of the other; the tefillin are also taken to be a covenant sign. It should be noted that some have interpreted the boxes to be symbolic and not intended literally. Others do argue for a literal interpretation.

The spirit of the Law allows freedom in the usage of these memory practices and emphasizes the memory purpose of the command. Perhaps a modern rendition would be to write the Sh'ma on our dashboards so as to remember it while driving to work or to place it in other visible spots (e.g., the bathroom mirror while shaving). We are strictly warned to not make any sign as an ostentatious display to call attention to ourselves (see Matt. 23:5-6).

The Yarmulke (the Kippah, Head Cap)—The head cap is an essentially nonbiblical tradition that is also a sign of reverence and Jewish identification among orthodox Jews. Conservative Jews and Reform Jews mostly use this symbol in their worship services. Freedom prevails in such usage. However, there is some question as to whether the *kippah* is allowable in prayer since First Corinthians 11:7 says that a man who prays "ought not to cover his head, since he is the image and glory of God" (NKJV). However, we need to remember that various cultures give opposite meanings to various objects of use; we cannot universally say that a head covering shows submission and self-abnegation as in Paul's day. In one tribe in Africa, sticking out one's tongue is a friendly greeting, but Paul might have forbidden it among believers in America.

The cultural meaning of head coverings is no longer understood as conveying anything in some cultures, but in Paul's day the meaning was a part of their symbolic language structure. The spirit of the Law principle applies here as well. We are to show the proper reflection of God's image and His forgiveness in the Messiah as men and not to act as though we are unforgiven and rejected before God. This is the essence of Paul's meaning, and if the *kippah* does not convey a contradiction of this meaning to our culture, it can be worn. Indeed, it is very unlikely that Paul was precluding the *kippah* since priests wore hats in the Temple.

The following passage from *The American Messianic Jew*, Spring, 1979, is republished here to bring out the probability that there is little relationship between the head covering of Paul's day and the kippah:

The "Yarmulke" from The American Messianic Jew:

> One of the symbols of Jewish piety has been the *yarmulke*. This head cap, required in Orthodox Jewish circles, is a sign of reverence before God. In Jewish Reform circles, it is now becoming common as a symbol of identity with Israel and the Jewish people. This practice has become popular also with some Messianic Jews.
>
> Recently, some have raised objections to its use on the basis of the Scriptures. Some Christians have rebuked Messianic Jews for this practice, and some "babes" in the Messiah become confused by the interpretation of the biblical evidence, for they were told that they could keep their Jewish identity in the New Covenant faith. Since Scripture is our ultimate authority, only a deeper look into the passages at issue can solve the problem.
>
> The passage in question is 1 Corinthians 11:4-15. Paul is here arguing for the distinction between the sexes, based upon the Creation order. He speaks of hair length

as a reflection of the Creation order, and then goes on to speak of head coverings as another reflection of this order. Although the yarmulke was not in vogue at the time, we still need to see whether the passage has relevance to this issue and summarize it for this purpose:

"...but any man who prays or prophesies with his head covered dishonors his head..." (v. 4 ff). "If a woman will not veil herself, then she should cut off her hair; but if it is disgraceful for a woman to be shorn or shaven, let her wear a veil. For a man ought not to cover his head, since the image and glory of God is he; but the woman is the glory of man. Neither was man created for woman, but woman for man. That is why a woman ought to have a veil on her head, because of the angels...Judge for yourself, is it proper for a woman to pray to God with her head uncovered? Does not nature itself teach you that for a man to wear long hair is degrading to him, but if a woman has long hair, it is her pride."

As we look into this passage, the first thing we notice is the inconsistency of those who criticize the practice of wearing the yarmulke. These people do not require women to cover their heads as required by this interpretation.

TEXT AND CONTEXT

One of the first rules for Biblical understanding is that we must understand the passage in its original historical and cultural context. This text involves the whole gamut of issues relating to male and female distinctions, including styles of dress and grooming. The question is what Paul meant by the veil or headcovering and its relationship to hair length. The evidence is very strong that Paul was not speaking to anything relating to the yarmulke. Rather, he was speaking of a particular kind of veil, a large size veil that would cover all of the woman's hair. The hair of a woman was considered her glory as a covering. It was her glory because it was itself beautiful and attractive while gracing and covering her head. A woman's hair was not to be let loose for this was indicative of a loose woman. Jewish literature is clear on this point (Isaiah 3:17; Numbers 5:18; III Macabees 4:6; Talmud Ned. 30b; Numb. R. 9:101). If a woman walked bare-headed, the husband could divorce her without question (Ketubot 7:6). Women were not to have their heads uncovered after marriage (Ketubot 2:1). Indeed, Talmud Berachot 24a compares the exposure of hair to be like an exposure of one's private parts. There is even the concept that beautiful uncovered hair tempted the angels. Thus Paul probably had in mind a total head covering that would cover the face also, to be used while praying, and speaking in the public meeting.

How are we to apply our evidence? The rule is that we must follow that which the Biblical writer intended to teach. A majority of Biblical exegetes believe that there are two levels of intent in this passage: There is a universal principle that male and female distinctions are part of the Creation order. These distinctions are to be reflected in dress and action. Such is a valid principle for all times. However, there is also a particular application. In Paul's day, the way to maintain this order was by the headcoverings and other symbols which reflected sexual distinctions and purity. If a man was to wear a woman's full headcover, this (at the time) would have been a blatant "transvestite" act. Paul did not intend his particular instructions to be binding for all times. Therefore, the yarmulke is permitted under the concept of Biblical liberty. We trust that liberty in the Messiah shall prevail. It seems that the head covering of Paul's day has little relation to the yarmulke.

Of greater concern is the danger that wearing a yarmulke might profess submission to Rabbinic authority and orthodoxy (especially in Israel). Messianic Jews need to weigh this in their practice.

BIBLICAL FOOD AND CLEANLINESS LAWS (LEV. 11–16; DEUT. 14)

It is a difficult task to understand the food and cleanliness laws of these chapters. There are many possibilities of interpretation. There is the "health" explanation repeated by Elmer Josephson in *God's Key to Health and Happiness,* as well as in many other publications. This view holds that the avoidance of the foods on these lists prevented disease since the various animals forbidden as unclean were dangerous for human consumption. The ban against touching dead bodies, animals, and the rule of uncleanness in regard to issues of blood, leprosy, and emissions of all kinds are interpreted as safeguards against contamination and possible disease. Some animals on the list are known today to have adverse health effects. Some critics argue that even the best preparation of pork does not prevent trichinosis. However, although God's stipulations here do have a connection with health, one has to stretch the argument a bit far to find hygienic reasons for every rule. Why for example, is a mother unclean only thirty-three days after giving birth to a male, but sixty-six days after giving birth to a female? Other laws in the list are also problematic. Why is one unclean after sexual intercourse?

A second explanation, which is still held widely, was given great scholarly support in the *Old Testament Commentaries* of Keil and Deiletch. They argued that the clean and unclean distinctions were symbolic reminders of sin or fallenness. Since death entered the world through sin, and all those born since Adam would be transgressors, all things connected with birth and death render one unclean. Unclean animals are scavengers; they feed off death. Touching that which is dead is an intimate contact with "the wages of sin." Sexual intercourse is itself not sinful, but will be the means of perpetuating a race that is fallen, although in the light of redemption such perpetuation is desirable. In addition, birth falls under the same symbol of making unclean. Leprosy is symbolic of that indwelling sinful nature. Other disease conditions also reflect fallenness and render one unclean. The woman sinned first, so a sixty-six-day period of uncleanness is a reminder of this fact, while a thirty-three-day period reminds us of Adam's sin.

A third explanation is that of Mary Douglas, who holds that the lists reflect something of a distinction between the ancient ideas of wholeness and "fit" and "that which did not fit" and was, therefore, abhorrent. Hence, fish have scales, but that which is like a fish, but lacks scales is lacking in wholeness. (It should be noted that this explanation, widely embraced by scholars, was repudiated by Mary Douglas in her last writings on the subject! Her last view was an ecological theology of Leviticus where unclean means that humans are to not make use of everything in creation, but some things are to be seen as being allowed to live in their natural state and are not for human use. I think it is a stretch to see all the laws on unclean foods as fitting this explanation.)

Perhaps these three explanations for the clean-unclean distinctions and the forbidden food lists all have some value. The evidence is certainly not so clear as to justify dogmatism. We should note, however, that the unclean person was in some cases isolated, a clear disease preventative, and was *forbidden during the specified period from participation in the Temple and its sacrificial system*. This system was to reflect purity, holiness, and the wholeness of redemption. One could be unclean until evening and then take a bath and become clean, or unclean seven days, or for the duration of the disease. In some aspects, therefore, the clean-unclean distinctions are for the age of the Temple that has been superseded for us in Yeshua. However, the eating of blood, including intentional intercourse during a women's period, were moral violations that required one to be cut off from his people. This is a universal command for today.

THE IMPORTANCE OF MESSIANIC JEWISH CONGREGATIONS

Some, having read thus far, might conclude with us that it is valid and expedient for Messianic Jews to maintain their Jewish identity and practice. They would, however, question why it is important for Messianic Jews to form congregations. Wouldn't it be possible for Messianic Jews to be part of non-Jewish New Testament fellowships while maintaining their individual and family Jewish identity as well as their involvement in the Jewish community? Yes it is possible. There are some strong individuals who have done this, even maintaining regular synagogue attendance. We do not desire to dissuade these people from their patterns, but invite them to simply weigh their stance in terms of effectiveness for God's Kingdom.

For most people, however, such a strong individualistic stance is simply not practical. Messianic congregations can provide many necessary functions for God's Kingdom expression. They provide a unique corporate witness of the Messiahship of Yeshua to the Jewish community. They are the most forceful visible testimony that Jewish believers have not forsaken their love of Israel in that their lifestyle and worship is Judaic. They also testify—by the presence of non-Jewish members—that Jew and Gentile are one in the Messiah.

In addition, Messianic congregations can uniquely provide for the special ongoing discipleship needs of Jewish believers who wrestle with the questions of their Jewish identity and practice *vis-a-vis* New Testament faith.

The Messianic congregation has the potential to provide the worship, social, and educational context for raising children of Jewish New Covenant believers as Jews with a strong and secure identity in Yeshua. Additionally, Messianic Jewish congregations provide the practical means of an ongoing and growing lay witness for Yeshua in the Jewish community. For most people, it would be simply too difficult to give adequate time to their Jewish heritage and Jewish community involvements as well as to be adequately involved in a non-Jewish congregation. But in a Messianic congregation, one is in the Body of believers locally and his involvement dovetails with his call as a Jew. The eventual end for many not in Messianic congregations would be slippage from a Jewish life resulting in a significant chance of assimilation, especially for the children of these Jewish believers in Yeshua. Many Jewish practices are congregational in nature. The only corporate model other than the Messianic Jewish congregation that is practical is a congregation that is not Jewish, but has a Jewish wing of believers in Yeshua who maintain their Jewish life together though home groups and special services. Some non-Yeshua-believing Jews would not respond to this as well since one of the great testimonies of Messianic congregations is that they are self-supporting and not a missionary arm or "front" for a non-Jewish group. Yet this certainly is a valid biblical model.

The studies in missionology in recent times have shown that the greatest potential for the spread of the Gospel is the planting of indigenous congregations adapted to the culture of the people whom they seek to reach. If such indigenous congregations have a strong emphasis on witnessing and discipleship, they are far and away the most effective means of spreading the Kingdom to the Jewish community. The biblical method of spreading the Gospel was just this, to plant congregations that were able to adapt to the needs of the various cultural communities in which they were planted.[15]

Since the first publication of *Jewish Roots*, I have been reflecting on the possibility of another model for Messianic Jews, which I call dual expression congregations. This model arises from several factors. The first is that there are many Jews in churches, and they show no inclination to leave their churches and join Messianic Jewish congregations. Second, some Messianic Jewish congregations are weak in discipleship formation and other programs. Jewish followers of Yeshua are not impressed. Third, for the last two decades, many Gentiles have joined Messianic congregations for the wrong reason, as if it was the ideal form of congregational life to which all congregations should ideally conform. I do not hold this view and will argue against this in a later chapter as one of the aberrations from the Messianic movement. I affirm the legitimacy of the forms and heritage of expressions in Protestant Christianity. Fourth, many Jews are not only looking for those who are like them in Jewish identity, but who are like them in professional and social status. They will feel more at home in a congregation of achieving Gentiles than one made up of mostly Gentiles who think they are in the ideal form of the Church.

So what if a strong church has a pastor who has really studied and understands Jewish calling and creates as part of his church a Jewish expression or expressions including weekly Jewish services for Jewish members and others who desire to experience it, Jewish home (chavurah) groups, feast celebration services, and discipleship in Jewish life and also maintains a vibrant Christian service that fully honors the Christian heritage of symbol and calendar. This could fill a gap. We now have Jewish pastors of churches that have come to embrace their Jewish calling and are trying to do just this. We know of two large churches pastored by Gentiles who have taken Jewish leaders on staff to do this. Such an orientation could challenge the tens of thousands of assimilating Jewish believers in churches with regard to their irrevocable calling as Jews. I think it is important to link such Jewish expressions and make a place for them in the Messianic Jewish movement.

LIFE IN A MESSIANIC CONGREGATION

A Messianic congregation is involved in all the tasks of any truly biblical congregation. It seeks to provide a home of fellowship for its members. This congregational home should be a central focus of the commitment of each member. Indeed, the questions of where we live and work and how we spend our time and money should relate to our primary involvement in the congregation. We are to seek to become one in love, fellowship, and mutual ministry. Second, we need to use our gifts to build up the Body. We applaud the nationwide movement of believers to live in proximity to one another and to share their lives more deeply on a day-to-day basis.

Additionally, we as congregations need to be witnesses of our faith through a high quality of life in the community of faith. We seek to disciple others in the Scriptures as well as to find the best means to spread the Good News.

The congregational tasks of education, worship services, preaching, and counseling are ours as well. Indeed, the Messianic congregation needs to provide the full-orbed means of healing and growth, which is part of biblical congregational life. Physical healing, inner healing, freedom from oppression, the Messiah's Supper, and the Mikvah of Yeshua (Baptism) are all intrinsic parts of congregational life.

We believe very deeply that life in the Body—with the operation of the ministry gifts of the Spirit in the Body through love (see Eph. 4:11ff; 1 Cor. 12–14)—are means of growth which a believer in Yeshua must not forego. Congregational life is the means used by God to encourage, correct, and enable us to grow into maturity, to be like the Messiah! Elder leadership in congregational life is necessary as well to give the congregation direction. Within the bounds of scriptural truth, we are called to be accountable to one another and to our leaders (see Heb. 13:7,17; 1 Pet. 5). Hence, elder insight and counsel should be a crucial part of our growth and decision-making. Our desire is to teach the walk of faith and to confess the Scriptures so that God's gifts and promises would be ours. The victory is ours in Yeshua.

RABBIS, SCHOOLING, AUTHENTICITY

Many have questioned the nature of training for spiritual leaders or congregational leaders who would need to be thoroughly trained in biblical studies, practical leadership, and Jewish studies. There are both institutional and noninstitutional means of such training. Presently, many congregations have leadership training and independent supervised study as part of their program. However, we should not eschew the value of an intensive period of study in the best of Jewish and Christian institutions. While we reject intellectual pride, we also recoil from the pride of ignorance, the sin of those who presume to know and cannot see the value of a "formal" education. It is true that a congregational leader is not made by academic training. He must have a call from God that is recognized in the Body. However, superior training for the one so called can produce greater quality, a person with a deeper understanding of the complexity of life and biblical issues. Such a person should be one of deep convictions without dogmatic narrow-mindedness. Liberal Arts training from a biblical point of view as well as graduate level theological training can be very helpful in producing a person who can relate to others from all walks of life.

The interpretation of difficult biblical passages, for example, is aided by an understanding of the meaning of the language of the passage(s) in their cultural-semantic context of meaning usage. Archaeological and linguistic studies are helpful. Further help is available in seeing how others have perceived the passage throughout history. This will lead to a prayerful conclusion that has a degree of objectivity.

If we are to test the Spirit by the Word, objective means of interpretation are crucial. Such information is required by our very biblical translators in their work, so we eschew such study to our detriment (as the proverbial man who saws off the limb on which he sits).

A knowledge of Jewish and Christian history provides us with a knowledge of the gains and mistakes of the past, even vividly illustrating the terrible results of destructive paths of interpretation and action. God has worked in the history of His people, and he who will not learn from history is bound to repeat its errors.

At present there are several schools. A list of schooling opportunities is available through the Union of Messianic Jewish Congregations. The Union also sponsors its own summer program. Those who do not choose such options must prayerfully seek the best education they can receive in the various needed areas of theology, Bible, Judaica, and practical leadership. Reading, courses at nearby schools, and guidance from a spiritual leader all can be part of a general program of training. We would suggest that the trainee and his mentor keep a record of all practical and theoretical training.

Should Messianic leaders be called rabbis if they have adequate training and fulfill the leadership position? The title originally implied "Master," "my great one," and is applied today to ordained Jewish spiritual leaders. In seeking a close identification with Jewish community practice, some believers might desire to call their leaders Rabbi. Yeshua, however, said:

> But you are not to be called rabbi, for you have one teacher, and you are all brethren. And call no man father on earth; for you have one Father, who is in heaven. Neither be called masters, for you have one Master, [the Messiah]. He who is greatest among you shall be your servant, whoever exalts himself will be humbled, and whoever humbles himself will be exalted (Matthew 23:8-12).

Some Messianic Jews have held that such a structure was given in the light of those who sought the title for pride, but most Messianic Jews use the term only out of love for the Jewish community.

Furthermore, they argue the term today connotes teacher and elder, not "great one."

Men desire titles of acclaim. Yeshua teaches us to forego them. Perhaps Messianic Judaism is meant to contrast with other forms of Judaism in regard to titles. We, at least, should feel a sense of uneasiness in the use of titles in the light of Yeshua's teaching. Elder brothers seem to be the highest titles of use among the first Jewish believers. Because of Matthew 23:8, perhaps we would do well to follow their example. If the term Rabbi is used with this in mind, in a humble context, we would not, however, object.

I would urge that those who would use such a title receive ordination only after the completion of a serious educational program. For most Jewish streams from modern Orthodoxy to Reform, this is a masters level of education. Rabbinic education is very strong in Rabbinic literature. Messianic Jewish education will have a much stronger emphasis on the Bible and biblical theology and the history of New Covenant interpretation. However, a basic knowledge of Rabbnic Judaism is important for one who would use such a title, including the ability to use the languages of Judaism.

Chapter Eight

EXTRA-BIBLICAL PRACTICES

WHEN DEALING WITH EXTRA-BIBLICAL PRACTICES, the rule for any culture is that those practices that are good, beautiful, and true by the standard of cohering with the New Covenant order are to be honored and embraced as people are led by the Spirit. Some have argued that we should embrace everything practiced by Orthodox Jewry as long as it does not contradict the Bible. However, cohering with the spirit of the New Covenant is a broader and more adequate test. This includes a degree of liberty in the Spirit that precludes such a rule. In addition, our evaluation of calling, adjusting to contemporary life, and more make the Orthodox life not feasible except for those who have a special call to it. We are not bound by tradition as a legalistic straitjacket, but follow the leading of the Spirit in practical reflection.

However, I believe that if one eliminates the heritage of Rabbinic Judaism, one is left with a Messianic Judaism with little texture and color. Even those who profess to want to abandon Rabbinic Judaism, while yet maintaining Jewish life with Sabbath and feasts, do much more that is rabbinic than they profess. From weddings to Passover *seders*, rabbinic practices are embraced as part of the common usages of our people. It is better to have evaluation criteria than a wholesale rejection or acceptance. We ask again, what are those practices that do cohere with the New Covenant revelation?

From the lighting of candles to inaugurate Shabbat to an order of prescribed liturgical services, Judaism has developed many extra-biblical traditional practices. In addition, Jewish rabbinic leadership has developed a host of applications of Torah, as recorded in the Talmud and the Responsa (body of rabbinic literature in response to community questions). This application material is known as Halakah (way).

For example, Orthodox Judaism prescribes the number of daily services so as to keep accord with the periods of sacrifice in the ancient Temple. Must Messianic Jews be concerned to keep Shacharit (morning) and Maariv (evening) services according to the rabbinic directives? We could perhaps conceive of a situation in an Orthodox community where Messianic Jews would desire to do so, especially remembering how all the sacrificial periods find their locus of meaning in Yeshua. However, for most Messianic Jews, it is not practical or desirable to be so ordered. Each community of faith must seek God's leading in ministering to the unique situation it serves.

Messianic Jews should respect the Jewish application of the Torah, *Halakah*, while at the same time reserving the right to criticize. Yeshua Himself warned, "You make vain the Word of God by your traditions." Traditions must never blind us to the heart intent of the Word. They would then become more foundational than the Word.

There are some guidelines for approaching Halakah: The reapplication of scriptural teaching for new situations *is an* absolutely *necessary task in every generation*. A little maturity of thought shows this to be the case. Scripture commands us to build a fence on our roofs (see Deut. 22:8). It also advises a full veil over the head and face for women who give prophecy (see 1 Cor. 11:5). Most believers today follow neither of these commands literally. Why? Because Scripture advises us *to follow the spirit of the Law*, which gives life, not the letter, which kills. We recognize that the command of fence-building was given for those who lived in flat-roofed homes and used the roofs like porches. This law was an application of the command to "love thy neighbor" (Lev. 19:18 KJV). We would apply the Law today by advising the repair of sidewalks and keeping them free from ice in winter.

The head veil was commended in an age when, for many, it was an important symbol of marital faithfulness and submission. The foregoing of the veil caused new believers in Yeshua to be spoken of negatively by the unbelieving community and brought shame. With no such common connection of the veil to fidelity or to submission, some communities today forego the practice as of no modern relevance. Others have advised, instead, a small symbolic head covering to recall what they see as a truth concerning fidelity and submission. In all of these examples, the believing communities have sought the spirit—or heart intent—of the Scriptures in their application of the Law. In other words, they have engaged in *halakic* reasoning.

Halakic reasoning is as necessary today as ever. Halakic reasoning is pre-Yeshuic: Since Moses, Jewish leaders have applied the principles introduced in the Law to new situations. The body of Oral Law found in the Talmud is sometimes ancient and at other times reflects later applications (first–fifth centuries). Although the principles of *halakic* reasoning date back to Moses, by his designation of judges, who would produce a tradition of legal applications (just as the record of judicial precedent in the United States), we cannot hold the belief that is held by some Orthodox Jews that the basic content of the whole *Mishnah* (the early part of the Talmud) was orally delivered by Moses and passed on generation to generation. This is an incoherent mythology. We respect some *Halakah* as ancient and some as wise, but never as Scripture's equal.

We must also note that the halakic tradition is a "mixed bag." Sometimes there are brilliant applications of the scriptural heart intent of the Law. At other times, the tradition seeks to maintain the letter and multiples strictures and minutiae and directions that tend to contradict the very intent of Scripture. Yeshua, for example, saw the multiplication of non-biblical Sabbath restrictions as destroying the intended joy and peace of the seventh day. On the other hand, there are rabbinic applications of justice in business dealings that are brilliant in maintaining a true sense of Scripture's call for just weights and measures.

How does a Messianic Jew approach *Halakah?* He seeks to return to the original biblical teaching and understand it in context. Is the Law (or command) a direct universal moral principle (e.g., "Thou shalt not commit adultery"), or is it an application of moral principle as building a fence on the roof (see Deut. 22:8)? Universal moral principles are to guide all believers in the Spirit. This holds for both Old and New Testament commandments.

Is the particular Law part of Israel's heritage in celebrating God's grace in her history? Is it part of Israel's God-given, national-cultural identity rooted in the Abrahamic Covenant (feasts, Shabbat, circumcision) that has application to Jews today? Can it be followed practically both in the land and in the Diaspora? Is it so intended?

Or, is the specific law part of Israel's priestly Temple sacrificial system, which has been fulfilled during this age in Yeshua and in this age is observed by recalling how His work is the essence of the practice?

Having ascertained the basic sense of the biblical teaching in the light of its original historical context and New Testament teaching, we can next look at rabbinic conclusions. We may find an illustration of the *wrong* road to take. This would be helpful in clarifying our direction. Or we may find a brilliant application that helps us to appropriate the teaching in our day. The issues of our society—medical-ethical issues, divorce, environmental concerns, food adulteration, war and vast weapon systems, community destruction—all require our best logical and prayerful efforts as mature believers.

In a sense, the Christian Church has its own *halakic* tradition, and we need to recognize its particular historic involvement in seeking to apply Old and New Testament scriptural truth. Our approach should also take into account the Christian tradition, recognizing its strengths as well as its departures from a more biblical approach to the issues involved. A comparison of Jewish and Christian interpretations and applications can, therefore, be most instructive.

Our goal, however, should always be to discern in the Spirit. Our minds should be submissive to the Word of God, humbly seeking God's direction—without pride or narrow dogmatism. If we love Israel, our involvement will show respect as well as disagreement.

Kashrut—"Do you keep kosher?" This is a common question addressed to Messianic Jews. The usual answer is yes, but not rabbinical kosher—biblical kosher! Keeping biblical *kashrut* was explained in the last chapter and mainly involves avoiding the forbidden foods listed in Leviticus and Deuteronomy.

Some Messianic Jews, who are more oriented to an Orthodox practice, decry the concept of biblical kosher as not related to Jewish meaning and understanding. However, the concept is quite coherent. Recently, the leader of the American Conservative Jewish movement called on all Conservative Jews to at least keep biblical kosher. He had no problem understanding it and calling for it.[1] However, the rabbinical meaning of the word *kashrut* or kosher is much more extensive. Rabbinical *kashrut* is built on the command, "You shall not boil a kid in its mother's milk" (Exod. 23:19 RSV).

The ancient rabbis adopted the principle of building a fence around the Torah. This meant creating additional laws—which were more rigid than the Torah—to prevent the breaking of Torah command itself. This produced what many see as a burdensome legalism. The reasoning went as follows: How can we know for sure that the animal we cook in milk is not the offspring of the mother from whom we got the milk? Couldn't this accidentally happen? Well, it is remote, but possible! Therefore, we will never cook meat in milk. However, to make sure we don't cook meat in milk, we should perhaps avoid eating meat and milk together because digestion is like cooking in our stomachs. But what constitutes eating meat and milk together? There may be a particle of a dairy product left on the plate that mixes with a meat product. To avoid this, why not separate dishes for meat and for milk? Furthermore, a prescribed number of hours between meat and milk meals should be followed to avoid mixing milk and meat by mouth. A Kosher product, therefore, has no blood and no mixture of milk and meat in it. This is the progression of reasoning.

As for *kashrut* in this rabbinical sense, we believe that everyone should be led by the Spirit. Is God leading the person to a special level of identification whereby he or she will practice the full rules of *rabbinic kashrut?* Or would this be too restrictive even for our general social relationships in the Jewish community in which we minister? Everyone must seek God in this. Certainly there is no requirement in these matters for Messianic Jews. If people desire to entertain Orthodox Jews in their home, rabbinic *kashrut* becomes a necessity.

The Life Cycle (Birth, Puberty, Marriage, Death)—As in many cultures, Judaism has developed its "rites of passage." These are traditions and ceremonies that mark the passage from one stage of life to another. Such ceremonies and traditions enhance the meaning of these events.

The first of these rites are connected to birth. They include circumcision for the male on the eighth day and synagogue dedication for the female. In both cases, the child is offered to the service of God. Messianic Jewish parents commit themselves to raise the child as part of Israel as well as in the *fullness* of New Covenant faith and life. This is a time for the whole community to rejoice.

The *pidyon ha ben* (redemption of the firstborn son) is a ceremony recalling the redemption of the first son in the Torah. In ancient Egypt, the firstborn of Israel were spared in the judgment of God on the land of Egypt. The destroying angel *passed over* (Passover) the homes that had the Passover lambs' blood upon the doors. Later, the Levites, tribe was chosen to serve God in the work of ministry in place of all the firstborn sons of Israel. God also commanded a special gift and sacrifice for the redemption of the firstborn. The Jewish tradition symbolically enacts the payment of five coins to a *cohen* (priest) as the redemption of the firstborn son. This reminds us that the ancient sacrifices and offerings were used for sustaining the priesthood.

Messianic Jews may symbolically engage in the *pidyon ha ben* as well, recalling that the ancient Israelites were given a system of sacrifice whose central meaning was to point to Yeshua. We recall the Passover in Egypt when the firstborn sons, our ancestors, were spared. Our rite should extol the fact that Yeshua is now our redemptive sacrifice and our Passover. He is our High Priest and, in Him, not only our firstborn, but all who come to Him in faith may have redemption.

The second rite of passage is from childhood to adulthood. Most cultures mark this time at the age of twelve or thirteen, when children reach puberty. It is the age of early sexual maturity wherein the children, if married, would be capable of producing offspring. Maturity should be not only physical, but an entrance into adult responsibility. After a period of training in Scripture and Judaism, the young person is invited to participate in the Sabbath service as an adult, to read the Torah, and to affirm that he has made Israel's faith and responsibility his own. He is "bar mitzvah" or "son of the Commandment." "Bat Mitzvah," "daughter of the Commandment," is also applied to young women in Reform and Conservative traditions. In a Messianic Jewish context, we seek to avoid the greed and materialism that have become so common in the post–Bar Mitzvah reception.

Rather, it should be a time where the child is seriously, in conscience, confirming his faith in God and Yeshua. He would then be committing himself to live in accordance with the Scriptures.

The Bar or Bat Mitzvah child should have a basic scriptural and Jewish knowledge. The involvement in parts of the service is a recognition of the child's commitment and our renewed desire to respect him or her as a young adult. Specific materials for training in Hebrew and Jewish life are readily available at Jewish bookstores. I also believe that the young person should be immersed in the name of Yeshua before the time of the Bar Mitzvah to be fully committed to our faith as a responsible adult.

One significant question is the need for rites of passage for the non-Jewish members of the Messianic congregation. Non-Jewish babies should also be dedicated *to* God. In addition, because we are one in the Messiah, the non-Jewish child should be confirmed, not as a Jew, but as one who is a spiritual child of Abraham, an ingrafted branch. Commitment to God can thereby be expressed. The child also can participate in those parts of the service that are not specifically affirming a Jewish identity. Such a child is affirming his support of God's work in the world through Israel, his special call of love and solidarity with Messianic Jews, and his faith in God's work in the true Christian Church.

Marriage is the next major rite of passage. It is in marriage that a man and a woman leave their parents to cleave unto one another and become "echad," one flesh. In the Jewish tradition, marriage is a gala joyous event. Ancient customs have become a significant part of Jewish weddings. Some of these are:

The Vows of Betrothal, which are today incorporated into the marriage vows themselves. However, in ancient times, the betrothal (engagement) took place a year before the marriage. It was as binding as marriage, even though the couple did not marry and consummate their relationship until a year later. Unfaithfulness during betrothal was considered adultery. Thus, we find that when Joseph discovered his betrothed Miriam (Mary) was pregnant before they had come together, he was desirous of divorcing her privately. Later of course, he found that the child was a supernatural product of the Spirit of God.

The Hupah is a very special canopy under which the marrying couple exchanges vows. It is either freestanding or held up by the groom's attendants. His prayer tallit would be on top of the canopy. This symbolizes the groom taking the bride under his roof; she becoming part of his house. It also symbolizes their desire to be a faithful family of Israel.

The Ring symbolizes permanent covenanting and may be connected to ancient rights where a covenant was cut and a scar marked the evidence.

The Seven Benedictions are also chanted. They prayerfully give thanks for the marriage as well as voicing special hopes for the family and the community.

The Blessing Over the Wine, a symbol of joy, enhances the wedding as one of the most joyous events in Israel.

The Breaking of the Glass at the end of the wedding by the groom is an ancient symbol of sorrow. Even in the midst of our joy, we are not to forget the destruction of the Temple and of Jerusalem. Others have interpreted the shattering of glass a symbol of the finality in which the marriage vows are expressed.

In a Messianic Jewish context, such symbols are present, along with scriptural material pertaining to marriage. Ephesians 5, on the meaning of marriage and the Messiah and his congregation, is often read. The couple also may tailor their ceremony to individually express themselves as well as their faith in Yeshua. The congregational spiritual leader guides them in this process.

The Ketubah is a marriage covenant agreement that now comes in several forms. In ancient times, the *ketubah* emphasized the promissory price to be paid to the bride in the event of divorce. Such was meant to be a preventative in the light of a looser Jewish interpretation of the meaning of divorce than found in the New Testament. Yeshua only excepted divorce between believers on the ground of adultery (see Matt. 5:31-32).

The largest question in Messianic Judaism, as regards marriage, is the question of intermarriage: Jews were forbidden to marry "pagans" and assimilate. However, a follower of Yeshua is no longer unclean and is certainly not to be considered a pagan. Many have been hurt by what have been taken as insensitive statements against Gentile singles seeking to marry Jews.

In the Messiah, the primary question is one of calling, not physical origin. Since Jews are called to maintain their identity with Israel, the main question is: Is God truly leading the non-Jewish person to take up a Jewish lifestyle and adopt a Jewish family as a lifetime commitment? We cannot preclude such a match because of physical origins any more than the match of Ruth and Boaz. Each couple and individual should prayerfully seek God's leading for their life in this serious step. For the non-Jewish partner, this entails a public commitment to identify as Ruth ("your people shall be my people"). For the man, I believe it entails circumcision. Care must be taken to assure that the calling is from God and not a rationalization of some romantic or marital desire.

It is very possible that God's Spirit may lead many to marry only those with physical Jewish roots as a witness to Jewish people, who might not accept the Jewish calling of a non-Jewish believer. I think this should be the proclivity of Messianic Jews. However, this should be by the leading of the Spirit, not by legal requirement. We, both Jews and Gentiles, are one in the Messiah. In Him we are called to different lifestyles and to perhaps witness to and through different communities. However, we must be "up front" in our witness and honestly convey that we are New Covenant congregations where Jew and Gentile have become one in the Messiah.

Special recognition of commitment to Jewish identity for a non-Jewish partner (conversion) is presently a matter of debate. At the present time, there is no one authority or type of authority that is accepted for such conversions in the Messianic Jewish movement. Such conversion in the New Covenant is very problematic (see Gal. 5). Opening this door could lead to a great number of people converting and claiming to be Jewish for the wrong reasons and under a system of poor standards. I believe it is much better to have a commitment of the Gentile to join with Israel through the Messianic community as a lifetime commitment, but not to call it conversion or to claim Jewish identity.

Death—The last great rite of passage in Judaism is, of course, death. Many of the practices surrounding death are for the benefit of those who are left behind to carry on in this realm of space and time.

In no area do we find the Jewish traditions more consistent with biblical values than in the case of the treatment of the bereaved in death, though there are a few matters that are not biblically coherent. We reject, for example, the Jewish practice of praying for the dead since the Scripture indicates that our destiny is fixed in this life.

Judaism prescribes simplicity in funeral practices. When a relative dies, the family is not to seek an ostentatious funeral. Expenses are to be kept to a minimum to reflect that in death all are equal. We brought nothing into the world, and we can take nothing out of the world. It is thus traditional to bury the deceased body in a white shroud; and, although this is not necessary, to do so is in accord with the spirit of the Bible. It is also culturally traditional to only have the closest friends and relatives involved with the mourner during the period just after the memorial service and burial. Many Jewish communities have burial societies that will voluntarily prepare the body. This is considered a great privilege. The burial takes place as soon as possible, and the body is not embalmed. Preserving our old bodies is not a Jewish value, but treating the body with reverence is a Jewish value.

The Jewish funeral is a closed casket memorial service. Since the person is no longer in the body, it is taught that we should not seek to glorify and attach ourselves to the body. Instead of flowers, it is recommended that gifts in memorial of the deceased be given to charity or worthy causes.

During the mourning period, it is customary for the closest friends to bring meals to the immediate family.

After the funeral, a friend would often organize meals and hospitality to those who come from out of town. Another friend would provide a meal for only the closest friends and relatives of the immediate family. This shelters the mourners from dealing with crowds of people. The first mourner's meal is usually simple, an egg traditionally being the first food (the egg is a symbol of mourning and sacrifice). The funeral service includes the reading of Scriptures and a time to recall the life of the deceased.

The seven days after burial are the *shivah* period. During this time, the mourner receives callers at home for comfort. The institution of a mourning period is Judaism's recognition that, although the deceased lives with God, the separation is a difficult trial. The separation of death is not natural, but is part of the fall. Rather than suppressing mourning by spiritual platitudes, we need to be able to honestly cry, to face the hurt of loss, and to share this burden with others. The New Covenant Scriptures, for example, never teach that we are not to mourn, but that because of the hope of the resurrection, "we mourn not as those who have no hope" (cf. 1 Cor. 15:19; 1 Thess. 4:3-18).

The practice of saying *kaddish* is a universal Jewish tradition. The *kaddish* is not a prayer for the dead and was not instituted to be a prayer for the dead. It is a prayer of praise to God and of longing for His Kingdom. It was instituted to teach that we are to praise God at all times, whether in joy or in sorrow. Thus, the *kaddish* gives glory to God and reflects well upon those who have died if prayed with this understanding. Rather than saying *kaddish for* the deceased by a son, etc., Messianic Jews need to recover these original intents of the *kaddish*. Any mourner may say the *kaddish* in praise to God: husband, wife, child, parent, or friend. The *kaddish* is here translated:

Glorified and sanctified be the Great name of God in the world which He has created according to His will. May He establish His Kingdom during your days and during the days of the whole house of Israel at a near time speedily and soon, and say Amen.

May His Great name be praised forever, glorified and exalted, extolled and honored, and praised and magnified be the Name of the Holy One, blessed be He, whose glory transcends, yea is beyond all blessing and praise and consolation which is uttered in the world, and say Amen.

May there be great peace from heavens upon us and upon all Israel, and say Amen.

May He who makes peace from the heavens, grant peace upon us and upon all Israel, and say Amen.

The Jewish idea that the saying of the *kaddish* has merit that shortens the time in purgatory should be rejected by Messianic Jews.

The basic structure of the *kaddish* is ancient. Yeshua Himself repeated the content of the first two lines of the kaddish when he taught His disciples to pray saying, "Our Father who art in heaven, hallowed be thy name. Thy Kingdom come. Thy will be done, on earth as it is in heaven" (Matt. 6:9-10 KJV). Yeshua's prayer is a modification, since the Kingdom was inaugurated with His coming and our prayer is a prayer for the present extension of it.

It is traditional for the *kaddish* to be said by the closest appropriate kin for eleven months, but there need be no limit to its use in a Messianic context. Messianic Jews may see the Lord's Prayer as appropriate along with the *kaddish*. I have composed a New Covenant *kaddish* combining the prayer of Yeshua with the *kaddish*. I should note that the *mourners kaddish* is one form of the prayer and other forms of the prayer are used for different parts of the Jewish prayer service.

After the seven-day mourning period, the mourner enters back into a more normal pattern of life, albeit a quieter life. In this period, other friends may visit. This lasts for a month. For eleven months the mourner is especially reminded to praise God and recall his loss. After eleven months, the mourning period ends.

The spiritual meaning and psychological value of these practices is incalculable. It recognizes our need to express our loss, to be emotionally and mentally honest. We know that suppressing mourning produces later emotional and psychological damage. The New Covenant directs us to look to God for comfort, to trust Him and praise Him despite our loss. In Yeshua, this is possible because of the clearer knowledge of the resurrection to eternal life in Him. I repeat, Judaism counsels us to have a real period of mourning, intense for seven days, moderate for thirty days, and eleven months for progressively coming out of our mourning. However, after eleven months, the mourning period is over. The New Covenant shows us not to wallow in sadness forever, but to get on with the business of living and loving God!

Judaism also includes *Yiskor* or memorial services during various holiday seasons as well as memorial on the anniversary of death. The New Covenant reminds us of departed saints to inspire us with the memory of those whose lives are spiritual examples to us.

KABBALISM AND HASIDISM

The *Kabbalah* is an ancient Jewish mystical tradition. This tradition is primarily based in the *Zohar*, a late Middle-Age compilation of mystical ideas of God and creation, numerology, concepts of redemption, and magic. From the Messianic Jewish perspective, the *kabbalistic* tradition is a mixed bag. The *kabbalistic* tradition sometimes presents us with profound and biblically valid thoughts on everything from the Messiah's suffering for sin to even a Triune concept of the unity of God. However, Kabbalism also contains concepts from magic and paganism.

Gershom Shalom, in his monumental book, *Major Trends in Jewish Mysticism,* shows that Kabbalism has roots in second- and third-century *Gnosticism.* Gnosticism was a religious approach from paganism that influenced *heterodox* Christianity and Judaism. Gnosticism was a system that taught salvation by the way of a secret knowledge of spiritual and magical realities which was only conveyed to initiates. This secret knowledge assured passage after death unto salvation as well as a means to tap into spiritual powers whereby current events and situations could be manipulated. When the *Kabbalah* sets forth these magical and gnostic viewpoints, the Messianic Jew judges it as dangerously occult and to be avoided. Yet not everything in *Kabbalism* is of this nature. No one but the most spiritually mature should seek to discern the difference between the strands of this tradition.

The Chasidic Movement flourished in the eighteenth century and continues to this day. It traces its origins to the Baal Shem Tov, the Lord of the Good Name. Today's *Chasidim* are strictly Orthodox Jews, but in the beginning, the Chasidic Movement was considered to be heterodox. Martin Buber sought to give us an appreciation for this movement.

Chasidism was a renewal movement within Judaism that brought exuberance, passion, and dance back into a religion that many considered arid. However, the Chasidic leaders, although greatly interested in Torah and Talmud (traditional Jewish areas of study and practice), also were greatly influenced by and involved in *Kabbalism.* The *Misnagdeem,* the Orthodox establishment of the day, condemned Chasidism. Usually a picture is painted of the *Misnagdeem* as dry scholars with no spiritual life who rejected the Chasidim, who were full of love, fervor, and energy. It was not so simple. The *Misnagdeem* not only recoiled at the untraditional actions in Chasidic life and worship, but at what they considered involvement in magic and heretical concepts!

In the Chasidic literature, we find stories of rabbis who lost their minds in practicing *kabbalistic* magic. Some who dabbled in magic did not. However, there were other leaders who eschewed the magical aspects of Chasidism. Stories in the literature note the extreme dangers for even the most spiritual from the lesson of those who indulged in magical means to produce certain ends or to bring the Kingdom of God. Some even lost their lives. The dangers of *Kabbalism* are certainly reflected in these stories, yet, via the *Zohar* and other literature, the dangers exist even to the present day.

The Chasidic stories also recount teaching and examples that are closer to New Testament teachings and attitudes than other contemporary Jewish literature. The incredible example of Zusia, who allows himself to be abused for the sake of others, but thoroughly loves his enemies, is a primary example. The love of God and of neighbor and mercy and justice are reflected in profound yet simple stories of great beauty. These aspects of Chasidism make it a great attraction to the rootless young today.

CHAPTER NINE

JEWISH AND BIBLICAL WORSHIP

JEWISH WORSHIP HISTORICALLY HAS BEEN based on a traditional prayer book, the *Siddur*. However, the earliest Talmudic statements also call for recognizing the importance of spontaneous prayer as well. The Talmud eschews the use of written prayers in a rote way, requiring that in our meditations, the prayer truly becomes the prayer of our hearts. Today's society is anti-institutional. Organized religion is rejected, and so are its trappings. A prayer book to many is just one of those expendable items from "dead" institutional religion. This is especially the case for those who grew up in Judaism and heard and partly recited the prayers in Hebrew without understanding what they were saying. The viewpoint that arises from such experiences is biased. Action taken on this basis is unbalanced.

Our age is media-crazed and entertainment-oriented. Entertainment is fast-paced and active. Many have no patience for more delicate pleasures and subtle joys. We require the ubiquitous television—not a good biography; a pummeling drumbeat, not classical Mozart. This, in part, influences our disenfranchisement with traditional worship forms that use prescribed materials.

Biblical worship has a place for dance and exuberance, but it *also* has a place for the softer joys of quiet reflection and written prayer.

God has revealed Himself in a written Word, in classical communication. Closeness to God requires recapturing a reading and meditative ability that our culture has lost. Our mass media culture produces shallow people who cannot think for themselves, who are easily manipulated. This culture is opposed to the values of the Word of God.

God Himself gave the first prayer book, the Book of Psalms. Why are there written prayers to be recited, memorized, chanted, and sung? So that we might learn to pray more deeply, with a greater content to praise and intercession! The Psalms teach us from one of the greatest praying giants in history, King David. They also teach us from the best of Israel's prayer warriors. Evidently, God considers written prayer of value. Nothing is so boring as the same "spontaneous prayer" without depth, rotely repeated week after week! Written and spontaneous prayers can both be rote!

We note, first, that the Psalms make up a good bulk of the *Siddur.* The second greatest concentration is made up of prayers composed of *scriptural* verses and phrases interwoven. The rest of the *Siddur* is comprised of prayers composed by various leaders throughout Jewish history. Some of these prayers are truly in the spirit of the Scriptures; others are not. In responding to these non-biblical prayers, we must use discernment.

A few sentiments expressed arise from a *kabbalistic* background: When a person uses the *content* of the Siddur in Messianic Jewish worship, he should only pray with scripturally-based content.

Having noted this warning, the bulk of the Jewish prayer book, and I would also add the High Holiday prayer book, is amazing for its correct theology and is assertions concerning the grace and mercy of God as the only basis for our hope and salvation.

"Teach us to pray," the disciples asked Yeshua. Yeshua then taught them the prayer recorded in Matthew 6:9-13, "Our Father who art in heaven, hallowed by thy name..." (KJV). The value of the *Siddur's* prayers and the Psalms as well as other prayers that Messianic Jews may compose is that they teach us to pray with a depth of scriptural *content* and beauty that improve the level of our own spontaneous prayer. Scripture teaches, "...if we ask anything according to his will, he hears us, and we know that if he hears us, we know that we have obtained the things requested of Him" (1 John 5:14-15). As our heart in prayer is akin to God's heart, we pray in His will. We are aided in praying in His will if we learn to pray according to the Word.

There is one more important issue concerning Messianic Jewish prayer and worship. In John 5, Yeshua makes the bold statement that the Father desires that we honor the Son as we honor the Father. There is a great problem with the Jewish prayer books. It is what is absent. The Jewish prayer books pray from a pre-Yeshua point of view, as if Yeshua never came. New Covenant worship in Spirit and truth should center on Yeshua and what God has done for us in His life, death, resurrection, present ministry, coming again, and future reign. As the Psalms are filled with content based on Passover and Exodus, so Messianic Jewish worship should be pervasively oriented to Yeshua and New Covenant content and realities. Sometimes Messianic Jewish worship, even with new material, has little of this content. I believe it is part of the reason that we do not experience His powerful presence. The presence of God to renew us and heal us is, I believe, dependant on pleasing God in our worship. We cannot do this unless God is fully extolled for His greatest work in history. Messianic Jewish worship and preaching should be pervasively New Covenantal without at all demeaning the pre-New Covenant work of God and the value of the *Siddur.*

In this regard, there is important content in Scripture that scholars believe was part of first century Messianic Jewish liturgy. Using these passages as faith confessions is very helpful in supplying the Yeshua-centered dimension in our worship. Philippians 2:6-11, Colossians 1:15-20, First Corinthians 15:3-7, and Hebrews 1:1-3 are powerful worship material and keep our services Yeshua-centered.

In addition, one of the most important things that a Messinanic Jewish congregation can do to assure the centrality of God's work through Yeshua in our testimony and worship is to have a regular quality celebration of the Messiah's Supper. The central text in First Corinthians 11 states that in celebrating we show the Lord's death until He comes. I believe, in the light of the words of Colossians 2:15, that we are showing His death to the princes of darkness and, once again, nullifying their power over us. In addition, first century Jews would not practice ritual only for its teaching value, but would believe that they really received life and affected the world by so doing. This means that we really receive the renewal in us of the power of His body given for us and His blood shed for us. Generally, the celebration is the celebration of the Body under elders, though a case can be made for family celebration, especially at Passover. Key elements for celebration are reading the text of First Corinthians 11 and warnings to not take the meal in an unworthy way, but to truly confess sin and to make a full recommitment to Yeshua. Time for confession and worship preparation are very important. The Hebrew blessings over the bread and wine in a Messianic Jewish context precede the declaration over the elements that they now convey to us the meaning of His body given for us and His blood shed for us.

Messianic Jewish worship should, therefore, incorporate the best biblical content of ancient prayer and biblically-based hymns from the ancient Psalms to new Messianic Jewish compositions, both liturgical and free form, that center on Yeshua. This material may be used with modern Jewish music.[1] The material can be used in Hebrew or English. It is important that the material conveys *meaningful content*. We should recognize that forms are relative.

We need to stop asserting our preferences for different forms as if they are objectively superior. However, the content of worship is not a relative matter, but the objective center of our worship.

Traditionalism, as contrasted with drawing upon rich traditions, feels constrained to maintain the same prayer forms with exactitude—week after week. Those under the power of traditionalism are offended if the ancient material is used in new ways. For most Jewish people today— especially in America—there must be freshness in worship. There should be a place for celebration, spontaneous worship, and praise, as well as using traditional content in new ways. We can vary which traditional content is included in services and how it is used as the Spirit leads worship. Will it be a choral piece or a meditation or a chant? Stuart Dauermann, the former musical director of Jews for Jesus, was working on putting the Amidah, the great ancient Jewish prayer of nineteen benedictions, to modern-sounding Jewish music. His rendition of the second benediction on the promise of the resurrection, called *"Melek Ozair,"* is a beautiful worship song. It is almost a classic of the Messianic Jewish movement. Hebrew and English are both sung in this song. David and Lisa Lodan from Israel have also put parts of the Amidah and other Jewish prayers to music for congregations. We can indeed mediate valuable ancient content in new ways. The writing and music of Paul Wilbur and Mark Chopinsky, formerly of Israel's Hope, and Steve McConnel, have been a great boon to the movement. So also some of the songs of Joel Chernoff. Today, young Israeli writers are composing beautiful material in Hebrew that center on New Covenant realities. Judah and Jennifer Morrison are one example.

It is important for Messianic Jews to seek a balance between the values of tradition and that of spontaneity. We must neither fall into rote traditionalism nor contentless emotionalism in worship. We must flow with the Spirit while allowing the richness of the biblical and Jewish heritage to take root among us. Those with differing gifts can blend harmoniously. The modern guitarist can be used as well as the cantor to bring an offering in righteousness to the Lord. The spontaneous, when really of the Spirit, is very impacting, especially when it plays off of the normal flow of familiar material.

A few words should be said about the specific nature of prayer in the Jewish tradition. The pre-second century Jewish tradition is well in accord with Philippians 4:6-9, which teaches to give thanks in all things. Hence, the basic form of Jewish prayer is the benediction which begins with this opening: "Blessed are you, O Lord our God, King of the universe, who..." and then adds the content of the praise or the request. The prayer closes with a *seal*, which repeats the "Blessed are you, O Lord, king of the universe..." and ends with a phrase in accord with the basic prayer. If the blessings are part of one prayer—as in the great prayer known as the Amidah—an opening will suffice for a whole group of blessings and only the seal will be included to end the blessing before new content begins the next blessing. *Ancient Judaism's prayers were faith confessions. God is not just requested to heal the sick; He is blessed as the healer of the sick: It shall be done, since it is according to God's character and promise.* God is not just requested to restore Jerusalem, but is thanked for that restoration since it is assured in His promises.

Most basic to Jewish prayer are the Psalms. Central to all Jewish services are Scripture portions known as the *Sh'ma*, which incorporate Deuteronomy 6:4ff, Deuteronomy 11:13-21, and Numbers 15:37-41. Israel is herein reminded to remember that the Lord alone is God and that we are to love the Lord with all our heart, soul, and might. These passages also call the nation to obedience to God in every area of life. Two blessings from the first century lead to the *Sh'ma* and praise God for His love and wisdom. They are "Creator of Luminaries" and "With Abounding Love."

The prayer known as the *"Amidah"* or *"Shemoneh Esreh,"* also known as *the prayer,* is similarly central to Jewish worship. This prayer of Eighteen Blessings (actually nineteen since the one on rebuilding the Temple was later added), praises God for His faithfulness as the God of our fathers, for the resurrection, for His healing, for His restoration of Israel, and much else. The *Sh'ma* and the *Amidah* constitute Israel's basic faith confessions. In spite of the claim that Judaism is a religion of deeds and not creeds (a foolish and simplistic statement), these two prayers are the most basic and ancient of faith confessions that have united the Jewish people and are a summary of the Jewish faith. The *Amidah* is biblical, but in a pre-Yeshua context.

Other great prayers or chants which are part of the service are: the *"Kaddish,"* the prayer of praise said by mourners in one version as well as by the congregation in various parts of the service in other versions; the *"Yigdal,"* the confession of faith, based on Maimonides' Thirteen Articles of Faith, which has been revised in Christian tradition in "The God of Abraham Praise"; the *"Alenu,"* a prayer of praise and call to responsibility for Israel as a witness people; the *"Adon Olam"* hymn on the majesty of God and His faithfulness; and many others. The Yigdal is problematic in its confession of the absolute unity of God.

In summary, the major traditional service elements would, in order, be: the Psalms, the *Sh'ma*, the *Amidah*, the *Kaddish*, the *Yigdal*, the *Alenu*, and the *Adon Olam*. Also central to Jewish worship on Shabbat, Monday, and Thursday is the Torah service. This includes blessings that praise God for giving the Torah as well as ancient songs which celebrate the giving of the Law. The prophets *(Haftorah)* are also read and, in Messianic Jewish congregations, New Covenant readings are added. Messianic congregations that have a Torah service tailor various elements of ancient and modern worship into a meaningful period of praise. The Scriptures are read in Hebrew or English, sometimes concurrently. A commentary ties together the readings in the light of New Testament fulfillment.

Many prayers of confession and praise are also especially used on holy days, and the special prayer book, known as the *Matzor,* has been issued for these holidays. It incorporates the daily and Shabbat content with all the Holy Day additions.

Some of the High Holy Day prayers are especially noteworthy. After the *"Al Het"* (for the sin) prayer of confession, congregants ask to be forgiven in the light of Abraham's merit and the sacrifice of Isaac. The sacrifice of Isaac is a great pointer to the sacrifice of Yeshua and the truth of the Messiah's suffering for sin. Prayers of confession are the purpose of self-examination, as required by Scripture (see 1 Cor. 11:28, "Let a man examine himself..."). The *Al Het* is the most comprehensive catalogue of sins in print. We pray for forgiveness, not only for ourselves, but for the whole community of Israel which has sinned. We should always remember that Jewish prayer is mostly corporate and intercessory, praying for the community and the redemption of the world. We do not pray as those whose forgiveness is in question, for the Scriptures say, "If we confess our sins, he is faithful and just to forgive us our sins and to cleanse us from all unrighteousness" (1 John 1:9 KJV). Scripture calls us, as believers, to confess our sin. Such times of prayer can be used as meaningful occasions for the Holy Spirit to search our hearts by the Word and by these biblically-based prayers. The time can also be used to redirect our steps, priorities, and commitments on a more solidly biblical basis for the following year in the light of a self-examination of the previous year.

Messianic Judaism is developing worship "in Spirit and in truth" that truly reflects Messianic Jewish calling and identity. It is a worship that primarily glorifies God and His Messiah. It has the verve and exuberance of the Spirit along with the depth of biblical content. It avoids only providing simple choruses for worship (that has its place) without recounting great scriptural truths.

The times of Orthodox Jewish worship services parallel the times of various ancient sacrifices in the Temple. *"Musaf,"* the additional service, for example, parallels the additional sacrifice on Shabbat. Most Messianic Jews have not tied themselves to these times. However, if they do gather at any of the traditional times—such as the *Shachreet* (morning sacrifice) service—they would do well to recall the times of sacrifice as an occasion to remember Yeshua's sacrifice and His fulfillment of the meaning of sacrifices.

The daily service also includes the reading of Genesis 22, the sacrifice of Isaac, which is considered to be a sacrifice that merits our forgiveness. This is a harbinger of Yeshua's sacrifice, in detail, and easily causes us to rejoice in Him. Prayers for grace after meals also appeal to the memory of Messiah for forgiveness.

CHAPTER TEN

DANGERS TO BE FACED

MESSIANIC JUDAISM FACES MANY DANGERS. As a relatively new—yet ancient rooted—movement, the presence of mature, discerning leaders and congregants is proportionately lower than in some other groups. There is a need for theological maturity so that the Scriptures will be a solid foundation for all our endeavors.

These dangers are intrinsic to the fledgling Messianic Jewish movement:

Legalism—In some quarters, a legalistic sense of "ought" in relation to tradition has taken root. Indeed, we should draw upon the richness of the Jewish traditions. However, we must, under the Spirit, choose our use of the traditions as He leads. Tradition must not rule us. Rules as to how much tradition to adopt or not adopt are not in accord with the New Covenant Age of the Spirit. When the latter occurs, there is a sense of "must" which destroys a sense of freedom and joy. *Must* is a word for biblical commands; *expedient* is a word for nonbiblical but recommended practices. Even for biblical commands, obedience must flow from the power of the Spirit in us and our identification with the Messiah.

This sense of "must" produces a feeling of restraint. Members of the Body who have a legalistic, critical bent (which is all too common among human beings) use conformity to a tradition as the basis for judging others. If a phrase is changed in a service or a substitution made, or if a particular order is changed, there is a response of anger and intolerance. Others buckle under and conform. However, it will be with a diminished joy and a sense of feeling manipulated. Most Jewish people today are not desirous of a demand for regular conformity in all of the details of their lives and worship. In addition, judgmentalism and rigid conformity requirements in life and worship destroy creativity. Where will there then be room for new prayers, songs, drama, and dance that God would desire in our midst?

Worship material of value can be produced today as well as a thousand years ago. New material and style reflects our identity and expression *today* as Messianic Jews. It is also necessary. Ancient material roots us in our history; new material shows the creative.

Love should predominate in our midst. We should allow the Spirit of God to inspire one another toward the practices He lays on our hearts. It should be at God's pace, not by peer pressure. I personally may not eat shrimp, but if another Messianic Jew does, not thinking that the food lists have continuing application today, I should not look at him with an eye of disapproval. We can share our reasons and our leading in the Lord, but we must seek obedience or conformity only in clear biblical directions. Legalism says "my way is the only right way," whether that way be modern or ancient. Legalism seeks to control others and cannot trust the Spirit to bring about God's desired ends. We must be on guard.

Shallowness—Another danger in Messianic Judaism can be shallowness. There is, in some Messianic Jewish quarters, a desire to be free of all tradition. However, this goes to such an extreme that the richness of our Jewish heritage as well as the value of historical Christian theology and tradition is ignored. Messianic Judaism would, therefore, not have the capacity to recognize the theological and methodological pitfalls of the past. The greatest minds and pious saints of history are ignored, leaving Messianic Judaism shallow and bereft. Shallowness is reflected in all areas of life. Worship becomes a mix of fast-paced choruses, which are great fun, but that do not convey either the depth of Scripture or the wisdom of Judaism in its biblical dimensions. Our theology becomes overly simplistic. We are unable to grapple with the complexity of the issues we face. Having eschewed scholarship, we misinterpret the Bible, not gaining an accurate sense of the cultural-linguistic background of the text. Without this background, we sometimes cannot understand the meaning as it would have been grasped by the original readers of Scripture.

The rejection of education causes a corresponding inability to be broad-minded, to be able to understand with love a wide variety of peoples, and to respond to the social, political, and aesthetic issues of our day with a biblical perspective. Instead of being salt and light in the world, we isolate ourselves by our attitudes and bring little of value to the daily marketplace of living.

Having given this warning, I also want to note that intellectual pride can be just as much of a danger.

In some quarters, this shallowness manifests itself in anti-institutionalization. The spiritual way is thought to be apart from having anything to gain from Jewish and Christian agencies, colleges, and seminaries. Yes, God can prepare a congregational leader outside of the means of traditional institutions. To this we should be open. A person's position in the Body should be by calling, not by an academic degree. Yet, a period of intensive study under the best biblical and theological scholars is valuable!

Separatism—Although Messianic Jews have a distinct calling from God, they *are* part of the Body of the Messiah universal! We cannot fall into the danger of compromising biblical truth for the sake of cultural identity. This is manifest by words and deeds. Words can be used to put distance between Messianic Jews and other believers so that the Jewish community will not perceive us to be one with the Body. *But we are one with the whole Body of the Messiah.* Jews and Gentiles are one in Him, and a Messianic congregation has non-Jewish members, too. Although we seek to be part of Israel, we are also one with the Body of Messiah Jesus. Our words should reflect this. Our deeds should reflect this as well. There should be joint services and cooperative fellowship with leaders, etc. We can learn from the whole Body as we hopefully enrich it as well.

Heresy—The danger of heresy comes from several factors: First, the desire to identify with the Jewish community could be so strong that it would influence us to compromise our biblical values and views because such views are incompatible with Jewish thinking. The Scriptures must remain our final authority. Under this danger we would place Ebiontism, which denies the deity of Yeshua. The denial of the substitutionary atonement of Yeshua for a doctrine that explains the value of Yeshua's life and death only in terms of moral influence is another example of heresy. Yeshua is not just our perfect pattern; "He died for our sins according to the Scriptures." Second, there is also danger from those who do not test prophetic gifts rigorously by the Scripture. It is common today in some groups to form doctrine by a prophetic sense that spiritualizes the Scriptures and finds allegorical meanings not intended in the text! This is the root of strange heretical doctrines. If the Scripture, in context, is not the basis for testing, then we enter into a subjective mode of doctrinal formation that leads to chaos. We should hold as suspect all teachings that pull phrases out of Scripture to show some great new revelation not intrinsically present in the Scriptures. This is not to demean prophecy today, where the Spirit speaks by prophetic analogies and the Bible is a jumping-off point. However, doctrine must never be built though such prophecy.

Control—Messianic Judaism is a movement of the Spirit. The Spirit has independently brought many of us to see the same truths. He will also unify. One of the dangers in the national and international scene is a feeling that *we* have *the right* sense. When a group has the *attitude* of superiority, even if they *are* superior (in age, by numbers, etc.), they alienate others. We all have much to learn from one another. God can unify and blend us without any group or individual controlling and manipulating others. Prayer and sharing will bind us together. If we talk and act as if our group alone is of importance, if we do not seek concrete means to edify other groups or seek in to benefit our group to the hurt of others, we produce alienation.

If there are heresies inherent to Christianity, there will be heresies from Messianic Judaism as well. May God guard us from these dangers and many others that are not yet clear to us. May He guard us from gullibility as we seek to apply the Word with maturity.

Chapter Eleven

ABERRATIONS: JEWISH ROOTS MOVEMENTS, ONE LAW MOVEMENTS, THE EPHRAIMITE MOVEMENT

Since the original edition of this book, Messianic Judaism has become popular in some circles. Aberrant teaching and movements have been fostered. Three movements are especially important. The errors of these movements have overlapping wrong teaching.

THE JEWISH ROOTS MOVEMENTS

There has been a cry to return to Jewish roots in many circles that has spawned Jewish roots movements and organizations. There are some very good Jewish roots organizations, and there is good Jewish roots teaching. On the other hand, there are bad teachings and dangerous organizations. I will not name any such organizations, but will note the difference between good and bad teaching.

The quest to understand the New Covenant Scriptures in the original first-century Jewish context has been the essence of good Jewish roots teaching. Studies in first-century Judaism, commonly known today as Second Temple Judaism, is now common in the

academic world. This is enormously helpful. Much of the scholarship agrees with the teaching of this book. The best of Jewish roots
study restores our understanding of the message of the Gospel of
the Kingdom in the preaching of Yeshua by placing this message
in the context of first-century expectations among Pharisees, Essenes, and Zealots. Jewish roots studies have given us insight into
the meaning of the feasts of Judaism in the life and teaching of
Yeshua and the Apostles. The feasts have their fullness in Him.
Such teaching restores the importance of the understanding of
the Jewish feasts in the teaching of the Church and their ongoing
significance. Such studies also show us the hope of the salvation
of the Jewish people, their connection to the Church, and the
importance of the saved remnant of the Jewish people through the
context of the teaching of Paul. The book by Norwegian Lutheran
theologian Oscar Skarsaune, *In the Shadow of the Temple*, is a good
example of the best of Jewish roots teaching.

Jewish roots teaching also provides us with a better understanding of God, a less abstract view of God due to the influence
of Greek philosophy on historic Church theologians. God is
personal, responsive, and best understood through the anthropo-
morphic metaphors as noted by many, though such metaphors are
qualified by His nonfinite reality.

Some who teach Jewish roots say that the Church would
be well served by feast celebrations in connection to the Jewish
community during the seasons of the feasts, though they do not
call for a Sabbath rest on the actual day of the feast as necessary
for Christians.

All of the above is to the good. However, a number of people
who claim to be in the Jewish roots movement and are teaching on
Jewish roots have a very wrong and negative view of the Church.
They claim that the historic Church compromised with paganism,
embraces pagan practices, and in addition, changed the calendar.
They are said to celebrate on illegitimate days, first in Sunday
gatherings for worship and keeping Sunday as a day of rest. The

Church is condemned for celebrating Christmas and replacing Passover with Good Friday and Easter, which is said to be the feast of the goddess Ishtar. The implication is that the Church should keep the biblical Sabbaths and feasts. In addition, the Church is condemned for statues as aids to worship, worshipping Mary and the Saints and much more. In addition, the Church is condemned because they do not teach their members the benefits of keeping the whole Law or Torah. All of this is said to be part of the anti-Semitism fostered in the historic Churches. Emperor Constantine is considered a devilish figure who brought about massive change and the embrace of these errors.

There is some truth in these false teachings, but mixed with much error. First of all, I do not want to defend all the practices of Catholic and Eastern Orthodox Churches. I have never been part of these communions and will leave it to them to defend themselves. I cannot defend statues as aids to worship or praying to Mary and the Saints as ways to aid our intercession. My Catholic friends have tried to convince me. Though I will not defend the specifically Catholic and Orthodox practices, I want to respond with regard to historic Protestantism. Historic Protestantism removed the offending practices. It is very wide of the mark to claim that Protestantism is pagan! What is paganism? Its essence is polytheism and occult practices.

There are two primary problems with those fostering the wrong Jewish roots teaching. The first is not recognizing that practices and symbols inherited from Judaism are part of the Church. It is not so much that the Church did not have such practices, but that it did not acknowledge and recognize the source with thanksgiving to the Jewish people. The second is that the Church-bashing Jewish roots teacher commits what philosophers call the genetic fallacy where the origin of a practice defines and determines its present usage and legitimacy. The third issue is the view that the Church rejected the Law. I will speak to this in the next section dealing with *one law movements*. At any rate, much of the extreme criticism fails to understand the Church and to differentiate between different denominations and streams.

It should be noted that with regard to the Sabbath and the feasts, it is quite clear that the Apostles never called those from among the nations to be responsible for the seventh-day Sabbath or to celebrate the biblical Jewish Feasts as days of rest on the Torah-prescribed days. The Roman Empire did not yet even have a seven-day week. This is not to say that the Church should not have a responsibility to support the Jewish people in their practice of the Sabbath and feasts and to embrace the teaching importance of the Sabbath and the feasts. Of course, Christians are free to celebrate the feasts.

In reality, however, the Church embraced three important Jewish feasts and celebrated them in their meaning in Yeshua. Passover was kept on Good Friday as the day of His crucifixion. It was understood that He was the Passover Lamb for the whole world. The following Sunday was the day of resurrection or First Fruits, for Yeshua rose from the dead on this Jewish feast and is the first fruits of those who sleep and the proof that we shall be resurrected. Fifty days later, the Church celebrated Pentecost, the date of the Jewish Feast of Shavuot. It is true that it is not celebrated as the day of the giving of the Torah or as the harvest that takes place in Israel. We would like the Church to remember the full context of the fulfillment in Yeshua and the fulfillment yet to come.

The extreme teachers say that the Church celebrates on the wrong days, but the exact day is a controversial question. Elat Mazir, the excavator of the probable palace of King David near the Old City of Jerusalem, argues that the original Temple calendar was solar, meaning that the monthly cycles of the moon were reconciled every year to the solar year. If so, the dates of the Church coincide with the biblical calendar more than the rabbinic calendar! Though there were anti-Jewish motives in Church calendar decisions, the debates in the early centuries also show a deep concern to really choose the accurate days for celebrations according to the best mathematics and astronomy. No one really knows for sure the exact days of the biblical feasts. Judaism well knows and teaches that the Sabbath was set by God and is consistent and sure, but the feasts are set by man because there is *no biblical directive on how to reconcile the solar year with lunar months.* The rabbinic Jewish solution was to add a month to the calendar every few years. It is a legalistic mistake to think we have to have the exact days right. Some are so extreme that they think that both the rabbinic calendar and the Church calendar must be rejected. They claim to have returned to the real biblical calendar.

In addition, I want to argue that the meaning of the days of celebration in the Church are what the Church tells us that the celebration means, nothing more and nothing less. The genetic fallacy tells us that the meaning is some ancient parallel. Christians celebrate the incarnation, the birth of Yeshua, on Christmas (in the Eastern Church, it is early January). This is said to involve them in the festival of Saturnalia, a Roman Winter Solstice festival. That may have been the origin of the date, but it is now irrelevant. Though I argue for a birth during Tabernacles, *Succot,* there are some that argue that Yeshua was really born on December 25th. John Fischer, a patriarch in the Messianic Jewish movement in America, argues for this in a taped teaching. At any rate, the meaning of Christmas in a Church context is according to the meaning given in the Church that is well expressed by the carols and hymns for the season. The accusation against Easter is even more far afield since by some calculations it is the right day to celebrate. In Europe, it is still called Pasca, after Passover, so the name change to Easter is by no means universal in the Church. Sunday is as well the celebration of the resurrection, for Yeshua did rise from the dead on the first day of the week. To claim that resting and or worshipping on Sunday is an embrace of paganism and sun worship is really a bizarre claim, but is regularly made by some of these teachers.

The result is that some claim that the Messianic Jewish congregation is the ideal form of the Church. They seek to see all churches look like Messianic Jewish synagogues. Somehow, among some, Jewish and rabbinic cultural practices are embraced without serious defense or evaluation as to the wisdom to do so in a Gentile or non-Jewish context.

The Church has derived much from the Synagogue and the Temple. The seven-branched lamps and candelabras are from Temple and Synagogue as is the eternal light, a separate reading podium, blessings before and after Scripture readings, the use of psalms, the architecture of the Church into three parts like the Temple (entry way, the sanctuary, and the front portion, which is holy and the Table for the Lord's Supper in the between area like the ancient altar). Even churches that use liturgical garments show rooting in the ancient priesthood of Israel. In addition, the basic elements of the Eucharistic liturgy of the Church derived from Jewish prayers. In a stunning presentation, Fr. Louis Bouyer demonstrated that this communion liturgy derived from a combination of several Jewish sources. This included the preliminary blessings that are recited in the Synagogue before singing the Sh'ma, three of the grace after meals blessings in the home table liturgy combined with ancient Passover liturgy, and finally several of the blessings of the Amidah, or the Shemoneh Esreh. This is especially important since the Amidah prayer is said to connect the Jewish worshipper to the ancient sacrifices as part of their intercession. The Christian service is connecting worshippers to the sacrifice of Yeshua.[1] This basic communion liturgy is common in Catholic, Eastern Orthodox, Lutheran, and Methodist congregations.

It is sad that the Church embraced Jewish elements in a context of replacement theology, that the Church replaced Israel and was the new and true Israel. We do desire the Church to embrace Israel and the Messianic Jewish community. We do desire that they teach on the feasts near to the seasons of their occurrence. However the basic practice of the Protestant churches is legitimate. The best form of the Church is not the Messianic Jewish synagogue, but is that form and expression that is true to biblical teaching and can best establish the Church in the culture of its location.

ONE LAW MOVEMENTS

I will not repeat the detail from above concerning the false teaching of One Law movements. One Law movements teach that the Gentiles and Jews in Yeshua have the same responsibility to the whole Torah; that there is no difference. Most, but not all, make an exception with regard to circumcision, but this is inconsistent with the rest of the teaching. Generally they misrepresent the teaching of the Church on the Law, perhaps out of ignorance. Usually they represent the Church as anti-law or antinomian. This is true with regard to some streams of the Church, but certainly is not true of historic Calvinist denominations (Reformed and Presbyterian), Anglicans, and Methodists. Most of these streams realize that the Law must be applied as is fitting to the New Covenant order in which we now live. They made a distinction between ceremonial law, which is to no longer be kept since it was fulfilled in Jesus, and universal moral law. The truth, in my view, is as expressed in this book, that the distinction between moral and ceremonial law is too simple. There is a distinction between universal Torah that is for all people and Jewish specific law that is part of the calling of the Jewish people. This distinction goes back to Rabbi Hillel, an older contemporary of Jesus. More exacting distinctions have to be made concerning universals, including principles for civil law, business law, and more. In addition, Jewish law has to be sorted by that which is so connected to Temple practice that it can no longer be practiced appropriately and that which is part of the Jewish pattern of national life (Sabbath, feasts, circumcision, avoiding pork and shellfish, etc.).

One Law teaching tends to obliterate the distinctive call of the Jewish people and in an inadvertent way (I do not believe it is usually intentional) ends up being a partial replacement theology.

I have written an extensive paper on this available from the Union of Messianic Jewish Congregations.[2]

THE EPHRAMITE MOVEMENT
(TWO HOUSE MOVEMENT)

Ephraim is the name of one of the northern tribes of Israel and became a name in Scripture designating the northern tribes of ancient Israel. This strange movement claims that most born-again Christians are the lost tribes of Israel. They mean this literally in the physical sense of blood descent. There is a variant that claims that the true Christians have a significant and undetermined number of lost tribes people as a percentage that could be a majority or may not be a majority.[3] Because the true believers who are not Jewish are lost tribes people, they are called to return to the Torah and keep the Sabbath and feasts and, according to a minority of teachers, even to circumcise their sons. The prediction of Ezekiel 37 that the two sticks would become one is said to be the reconciliation of true Christians (Ephraim) with the Jews, though Yeshua.

The grounds for this strange view is the mystery of those passages in the prophets that speak of the return of the tribes of Israel to the land of Israel. Now placing a billion Christians in the land could be a problem, even with the most generous borders, so perhaps the proponent believes that the number of true believers is much smaller. The texts that state that members of the other tribes joined Judah during the revivals of Hezekiah and Josiah and the evidence that members of other tribes returned with Judah, is not credited. In addition, there is evidence that Orthodox Rabbis and Messianic Jewish leaders are finding real lost tribes people in Pakistan, India, South Africa, and Zimbabwe. The Ephraimite or Two House people emphasize that the scattering was to all nations and thus those who become Christians in these nations are really lost tribes people.

This teaching ignores the constant and consistent emphasis in the New Covenant Scriptures that salvation is now brought to the nations and not just to lost tribes people. This understanding begins with Peter's statement in Acts 10:34, which includes the righteous in all nations. Those who are in the Messiah are in Abraham according to Galatians 3, and assuming that they are from lost tribes is really irrelevant. That they are not to be circumcised (see Gal. 5) proves that they were not considered descendants of the lost tribes.

I also have a more extensive article on this movement that is available from the Union of Messianic Jewish Congregations.

People who are part of the One Law movements and the Ephramite movement tend to bash the Church as pagan and not respecting the Torah. It is easy to see the overlap in these movements. One of the sad aspects of these movements is that Church leaders sometimes think that they represent the Messianic Jewish movement, whereas the mainstream of the Messianic Jewish movement in Israel and every continent has rejected these false teaching.

CHAPTER TWELVE

THE MESSIANIC JEWISH MOVEMENT AFTER FORTY YEARS

I HAVE BEEN SERVING IN THE Messianic Jewish movement for over forty years. Therefore, I desire to give some perspective and to evaluate the movement. Since I am now in my sixties as I write, I hope I do not have an axe to grind and that my evaluations will aid leaders who will come after me. There is no way to avoid an obvious truism. We evaluate on the basis of what we believe, the set of values we have come to embrace. Naturally, therefore, my evaluation is on the basis of those values and beliefs. I embrace these distinctive beliefs. First is that we are called to a Jewish expression of New Covenant faith that applies the Torah as is fitting in the New Covenant. In addition, we are called to honor the rabbinic heritage where it is true and faithful to the Spirit of the Bible, but not to fall into an over-adulation of this tradition, which at times seriously departs from what I perceive to be biblical emphases. I am committed to a Messianic Judaism that embraces the power of the Spirit and all of the gifts and manifestations of the Spirit that are based in a scriptural theology of the Spirit. In this regard, I am oriented to revival and outpourings of the Spirit as a key to Messianic Jewish progress. In addition, I embrace the importance of congregations being linked in mutual accountability in associations of congregations and leaders. These associations should give authority to all its leader representatives while recognizing God's chosen leaders for associational leadership. In this regard, I am committed to an understanding of what I call fivefold leadership, where roles of apostles, prophets, evangelists, pastors, and teachers are to be recognized and placed in positions where they can most effectively equip congregations. This means that real qualities of leadership are needed to further the movement. I believe in the importance of an educated leadership, but also want to make sure that our education is based on a commitment to the authority of the Word and the power of the Spirit. It is crucial that we do not fall into Western enlightenment influences that tend to dampen real faith and power in the Spirit, cutting off the miraculous and leading to skepticism. So I will be evaluating our movement with these views in mind.

THE MESSIANIC JEWISH MOVEMENT IN THE DIASPORA AND THE GENTILE INFLUX

In the 1980s, the Messianic Jewish congregational movement in the Diaspora consisted of a majority of Jews. Gentiles were a large minority. I do not think that most of us in leadership ever anticipated the great influx of Gentiles from the 1990s and into the second decade of the twenty-first century. This has both positive and negative repercussions.

The Gentiles who join Messianic Jewish congregations are there for three primary reasons. Some have joined because they believe we are the ideal form of New Covenant congregation (I sometimes say the ideal form of the Church). The controlling idea is that it would be better if all churches were like Messianic synagogues. This is not a right reason to be in a Messianic Jewish congregation. It betrays a profound misunderstanding of the value and depth of the churches and their practices. In the section on Jewish Roots Movements, I share that churches do need correction to become Jewishly rooted, but this is not to throw out their enriching traditions and to become like Messianic Jewish synagogues. This reason will cause division with the churches with which we desire to be in unity and will also be a barrier to Jewish people. When they come to our congregations and see few Jews, but many Gentiles who are living a Jewish life, it will cause confusion. The reaction to this among some Messianic Jewish leaders in North America is to limit membership so that the majority of the congregation will remain Jewish. I am sympathetic to these leaders, but do not believe that this is the best way to handle the issue. Rather, we need to teach on the legitimacy of the churches and a right approach to Jewish roots. In addition, I support Jewish expression in larger churches for their Jewish members as a way to not lose the many Jews in churches that are not open to leaving their churches and joining the Messianic Jewish congregations. For this to succeed, head pastors will need to have conviction that their Jewish members are called to identify and live as Jews and to support Jewish expressions in services and/or fellowship home groups. In addition, we need to emphasize the right reasons for Gentiles to join Messianic Jewish congregations to help those join who are really called and to see those move on who are not. I believe that Gentiles with a negative Church-bashing orientation are bad for our congregations, and unless they change in their views, they need to be sent out from us to find other fellowships, for they are not in accord with our vision and values.

The second reason for joining us is that the Gentile just loves Jewish life and cultural expression, not that he or she thinks it is superior. This can be part of a good motivation, but unless it connects to the third motivation, it will not produce the right orientation either. Some in this second orientation will be so oriented to Jewish culture that they will seek to blur the lines of distinctive Jewish calling and seek to take on the full dimensions of Jewish responsibility. Where Gentiles join in Jewish life, there needs to be sensitivity to maintain the distinction of Jewish ethnic calling and a profession and practice of unity with distinction.

The third reason is a passionate love for the Jewish people and that one wants to live New Covenant life with and before the Jewish community so as to win Jewish people to Yeshua. Such people do need to have a love for the good things in Jewish life and culture. When this is the orientation of Gentile members, Jewish people will be won to Yeshua and congregations with a majority of Gentile members can be sensitive and effective. Congregations with such memberships do not feel strange and off-putting to Jewish visitors, but healthy Gentiles actually attract them to the congregation.

THE DECLINE IN NORTH AMERICA

While the Messianic Jewish Movement continues to grow slowly in South America, significantly in Russian-speaking Jewish populations in the countries that were in the Soviet Union, and also in Germany, the movement in North America is in plateau or decline. To understand this, we need to evaluate the main organizations of the Messianic Jewish Movement in North America and their effectiveness. I also note that the Messianic Jewish movement has tracked with the plateau and decline of the Church in North America. I think they are related.

THE MESSIANIC JEWISH ALLIANCE AND THE INTERNATIONAL ALLIANCE OF MESSIANIC JEWISH CONGREGATIONS AND SYNAGOGUES

The above named organization originally brought Messianic Judaism to prominence in 1975. Leaders such as Manny Brotman, founder of the Messianic Jewish Movement Int.; Marty Chernoff and his family pastoring in Cincinnati; Joe Finklestein and Herb Links in Philadelphia at Beth Messiah Congregation; Manny Brotman, Sid Roth, and Paul Liberman at Beth Messiah in Washington, D. C.; John Fischer at B'nai Maccabi in Highland Park, Illinois; and myself at Adat HaTikvah in Chicago brought sufficient numbers *to change the name of the Hebrew Christian Alliance of America to the Messianic Jewish Alliance.* This was to affirm that Jews who come to faith in Yeshua are called to identify and live as Jews and to affirm the importance of Messianic Jewish congregations.

In 1976, the Messianic Jewish Alliance Board called for the formation of a union of Messianic Jewish congregations, but stated that it should not be legally under the Alliance since the Alliance was an organization of individual Jewish believers in Yeshua of all stripes in churches or Messianic Jewish congregations. Instead they called for a union to be formed as a separate organization, but in fraternal relationship to the Alliance. In 1979, a newly elected board in the Alliance rejected the policy of the 1976 board so that the new union was formed in tension with the Alliance board, which did not embrace the idea of an official government structure of leader delegates to govern an official association. This had and still has important repercussions for the North American Messianic Jewish Movement. Thankfully a fifteen-year division over this issue was overcome and a reconciliation agreement was signed in the 1990s.

In 1984, the Messianic Jewish Alliance decided to foster their own congregational association, but embraced an unusual type of government for which there was no precedent in either synagogue associations or church associations. The Jewish only membership of the Messianic Jewish Alliance of America elects the board and officers of the Alliance as it has for its whole history since 1915. The new direction was that the President of the Alliance would appoint the leader of the congregational association as well as a steering committee. Thus, International Alliance of Messianic Congregations and Synagogues is fully under the government of the MJAA members and board. Its members from other countries do not have governmental vote, but their congregations join a fully American-governed organization.

It should be noted that IAMCS enforces foundational moral and doctrinal standards in their membership. This is a gain. Other than requiring such standards for members, the IAMCS is completely nonintrusive in the life of its member congregations. Some like this, and others think this is too loose. The IAMCS also maintains a very basic program for ordaining Messianic rabbis.

The response of the International Messianic Jewish Alliance to this step was to question the American Alliance in its creating an international organization under the American corporation when there was an International Alliance (since 1925) that tied together national Alliances. They, therefore, fostered an alternative Alliance in America called the Association of Messianic Jewish Believers connected to the Union of Messianic Jewish congregations (see below). This has remained the situation to the present day.

The MJAA and IAMCS are important and do do very valuable work.

I first want to list what I think are the strengths of the Messianic Jewish Alliance in America. *The Messianic Jewish Alliance has maintained a very strong emphasis on revival and prayer for revival.* Their orientation to revival was inspired by the writings of Charles Finney from the nineteenth century. There are strengths and weaknesses in these writings, and evaluating this would take us too far afield. However, I believe that MJAA leaders are right in that we will only succeed through outpourings of the Holy Spirit and revival. Without this supernatural empowerment, we simply will not succeed. The Chernoff family has latched onto this like a bulldog and will not let any other emphasis displace this one. I give them credit and believe the whole movement needs to follow them in this.

The American Alliance has wonderful events and conferences for encouraging the movement. Alliance gatherings are like one massive prophetic encouragement for the goals of the Messianic Jewish movement, namely that Jews will come to faith, that they will still live and identify as Jews and will be in Messianic Jewish congregations, and that all Israel will be saved. The American Alliance is committed to the charismatic dimension, which to me is essential and biblical. Rabbis' conferences provide encouragement and mutual sharing and prayer. General conferences provide powerful praise, dance, and exhortation. No one should doubt that the Alliance has been and will continue to be a major player in fostering the movement in North America. Some claim it is the major player.

However, there are weaknesses in the Alliance that may hinder the goals. The government structure for the congregations does not empower the leaders of the congregations to have real input and government in the organization. Empowering the leaders provides the culture for change and input that strengthens a movement and its leaders. Furthermore, the Alliance has two bents that are not helpful. One is anti-intellectualism and an anti-Rabbinic thrust among some of the most influential leaders. This can lead to theological shallowness. So the Alliance has few if any earned PhDs or ThDs in relevant subjects. Most would struggle to fit into the Alliance culture. While I warn against an over-embrace of rabbinic authority and law, I do want to give honor where honor is due according to New Covenant standards.

This orientation produces a weakness in programs for the training of rabbis. With a small number of courses, one can be ordained a rabbi in the Alliance. If the education standards become known in the larger Jewish community, I think it will undercut our credibility in this community. I think it is better to not use the title Rabbi unless there is significant higher education, as is the case in the Jewish community. There is a great need to further training in the whole movement, Alliance, Union, and beyond—how to lead, disciple, do small groups, counsel, and bring healing. Training, training, and more training is the order of the day.

I personally believe that the government structure of the International Alliance of Messianic Congregations and Synagogues is problematic and that the leaders of the congregations should have governmental responsibility for a congregational association as is the case in most synagogue associations outside of the ultra-Orthodox and in almost all church associations. It is problematic that the American organization seeks to link congregations in other nations to an American organization where they have no governmental role. There is an International Messianic Jewish Alliance was well, and there are other national alliances, but only one alliance association of congregations. However, I think it is better that there be membership in such an association of congregations than no association at all. Hence, I support those who in conscience choose to associate with the IAMCS, though it does not fit my understanding of right government.

When I think of the hindrance to revival, I think in terms of the greater unity that I believe is the desire of God in our movement. When we look at the strengths and weaknesses of the Union of Messianic Jewish Congregations and the MJAA-IAMCS, I think we will see that greater unity would greatly move us toward the revival, but to do this, each side may have to give on some things that have divided us.

The large Alliance gatherings sometimes tend toward triumphalism and speaking as if we are already in revival. We are not. Yes it is good to draw 2,000 to a conference, but 1,400 perhaps are not Jewish. It is important to face the reality on the ground in our congregations. There are many that are marginal congregations, and most are not significantly growing. Our prayers for revival must include crying out on the basis of this reality. The big rally is not adequate to producing real growth on the ground.

I think one issue is important in both the Alliance and other organizations is to see equipping evangelists raised up. This is a reason for much prayer—equipping evangelists who will enable the people of the movement to be much more effective in winning Jewish people to Yeshua. This is a foundational need.

THE UNION OF MESSIANIC JEWISH CONGREGATIONS

A serious attempt to form the Union of Messianic Jewish Congregations occurred in 1976 under Manny Brotman and Jim Hutchins, but due to lack of a strong response, a new effort in 1978 was begun. It was successful and led to an incorporation meeting in 1979. The Union grew rapidly as the only congregational association of Messianic Jewish congregations until 1984.

In the first decade of the UMJCs existence, a strong charismatic thrust was part of teaching and conferences. However, this changed in the late 1980s due to controversy over prophetic input and manifestations of the Spirit (which not all agreed were manifestations of the Spirit).

The great strength of the UMJC is its delegate structure of government. Every leader of every full member congregation plus one elder is a full governing delegate of the UMJC. The gathered delegates are the highest authority of the UMJC. Thus leaders are empowered. The direction of the UMJC comes from leaders who care enough about it to be committed to invest in it. In this context the UMJC has developed strong standards for discipline for leaders and congregations that fall into sin or error. There are clear and fair due process standards under leaders who are wise in eldership judicial functions.

Yet this very strength produces a weakness. Despite my own commitment to the Union and early belief that such a structure would recognize the best leaders in our midst to take us forward, this has not always been the case. We have sometimes had capable leadership, but not always. This is because we sometimes do not recognize the difference between leadership and scholarship and between those who manage and those who are called to lead. I call this the lack of understanding fivefold leadership (which is also a weakness in the MJAA structure), where leadership is given to fruitful leaders who are apostles, prophets, evangelists, pastors, and teachers (see Eph. 5:11ff). The leaders of the UMJC should be those who have been most fruitful in local and trans-local ministries based in congregations. This would produce impartation and equipping for other leaders to gain in effectiveness and for the whole Union to gain in effectiveness. The lack of understanding leadership has been a factor in the UMJC's present lack of growth and in its loss of members, but there are other factors. The lack of leadership has allowed people lacking in diplomacy to foster views in the Union that were way beyond the common consensus, thus producing division. There has been shaking on how we see scriptural authority, salvation, and Rabbinic Judaism. Most of this has been finally dealt with to the good of the Union. However, strong leadership could have prevented the level of shaking that had taken place. The Union does find itself struggling between the progressives who connect to Hashiveinu and the conservatives in Dayainu. I will write more on this below.

The UMJC is strong in scholarship and most PhDs or ThDs in the North American Messianic Jewish movement are connected to the UMJC. The UMJC has produced a Rabbinical ordination program that is the most credible in the Messianic Jewish world. However, the emphasis on scholarship (which I affirm) can sometimes become intellectualism in such a way that the important emphasis on revival and the power of the Spirit is lost. We are sunk without this emphasis.

Hashiveinu is a fellowship of good men and women who seek greater Jewish or rabbinic authenticity in our movement. Some think the leadership of Hashiveinu foster orthodoxy, but their Jewish orientation is probably more like classical American Conservative Judaism. Their thrust has sometimes, in my view, been an over-adulation of Rabbinic Judaism, where even some negative aspects of Rabbinic Judaism are defended. In addition, sometimes prayer expressions are fostered that are thin in the New Covenant content. Some have questioned the objectivity of Scripture and have overemphasized that our interpretations are communally influenced (almost determined?). Everyone who engages scholarship knows the issue of communal influence. It is a truism today. Yet, our hope is that prayer, the leading of the Spirit, and research with intercommunal dialogue can enable us to progressively transcend communal limitations and gain a more accurate scriptural understanding.

In addition, there is in my view an overemphasis on the adequacy of Judaism for our people. I have argued that Judaism does preserve the basics of salvation, grace, faith-faithfulness, and more from *a pre-Yeshua perspective*. However, this does not mean that our people, both religious and nonreligious, do not need to embrace Yeshua to ensure personal salvation. Mark Kinzer is one of the key thinkers in our movement and a key part of Hashainu. The title of Mark Kinzer's book, which has many fine features, is *Post Missionary Messianic Judaism*. If this means that we do not want to see an assimilation type of evangelism, I agree. If it means that our calling to Jewish life is not only for the sake of evangelism, but is our Jewish calling for its own sake, I also agree. I have argued this for forty years. However, for some, this means a change in evangelism whereby the Jewish person is not looked upon as one who needs to embrace Yeshua for personal salvation, but for other goals, such as coming into fuller truth or hastening the day of the coming of the Messiah. These motives are important, but the motivation toward the personal salvation of Jewish people is also crucial.

Yet, there are very important things that are being said and good challenges to the movement to understand and at least appreciate the good things in Rabbinic Judaism. There is a real concern to overcome shallowness and to avoid creating a Messianic Jewish ghetto that is unrecognizable as a Jewish movement by the larger Jewish community.

Dayainu was a coalition formed in the Union to make sure that the UMJC was clear on the authority of Scripture as God's inerrant and trustworthy revelation, an objective revelation, and that a personal faith decision to embrace Yeshua was crucial for assuring individuals of the final good end of everlasting life. This emphasis was important in ending the shaking that was taking place in the UMJC.

What would I like to see in the UMJC? I would love to see a greater emphasis on revival, the power of the Spirit, the gifts of the Spirit, and the understanding and application of fivefold leadership. There is potential for more training in the UMJC, and seminars do emphasize training for leaders. We need much more training for leaders.

In addition, we need a great thrust for praying for and then seeing a contingent of equipping evangelists becoming more significant in our movement. Without this, we will not go forward with strong growth. Those who have this gift in large measure are sometimes offensive to the scholars in our midst. They seem too black and white. Yet they carry an anointing that is remarkable and essential.

When I see the emphases of the UMJC and the MJAA, I think that the greater balance and wholeness would be in the thrust of both together. Think of the thrust in the Alliance for revival and the charismatic, the UMJC toward education, due process, and a government of delegate leaders. Both need to understand and embrace a fivefold understanding and philosophy of leadership.

RUSSIA, UKRAINE, AND EUROPE

The movement in Russia and Ukraine was launched in a major way under the leadership of Jonathan Bernis in the mid-1990s. His organization at that time was called Hear O Israel. After an amazing success of musical festivals (tens of thousands attended and many thousands of Jews professed faith in Yeshua), congregations were planted. Jonathan Bernis taught a fivefold understanding of leadership and the importance of charismatic gifts with Holy Spirit power from the very first. The movement that came out of these festivals thus tends to continue in the same orientation. In

Ukraine, the largest Messianic Jewish congregation in the world is led by Boris Grenshenko, who inherited the leadership of the movement in Ukraine. They have regular leadership-equipping conferences. There is a very strong anointing in the Kiev congregation, led by Boris Grenshenko, who has fostered the planting of several new congregations.

In addition, a Messianic Jewish Bible Institute school was planted by Wayne Wilks and is now led by Valintine Sviontec. The school has been full-time for many years now and graduates people with a clear Messianic Jewish theology to serve in both churches and Messianic Jewish congregations.

My primary comment is that I would like to see the movement have a greater embrace of the good things in Jewish expression and practice and many more from the whole network connected to schooling.

In Russia, Michael Becker, who was part of the founding of the Moscow congregation that was planted after the festival, spurred the formation of a Union of Messianic Jewish Congregations of Russia. This Union embraces fivefold ministry and charismatic Holy Spirit power. I would like to see them do much more in equipping. There is also a Messianic Jewish Bible Institute program in St. Petersburg, led by Yura Molkert, who also is part of the leadership to the UMJC of Russia.

The main strength of the movement in Europe is in the Russian Jewish population. These congregations are growing and are connected through the leadership of Vladimer Pikman in Berlin. There is a congregation in Paris that has held forth a good witness for many years as well.

While there are other movements and congregations in Russia, Ukraine, and Germany, most are more traditional and do not have the same emphasis on the power of the Holy Spirit.

The movement in England has been quite weak and there is great need of new planting and new capable leaders.

SOUTH AMERICA

In Brazil, the most significant congregation is led by Marcello Guimares and his son Matthew. It is made up of Jews, Morranos (those who were forced to convert to Christianity in centuries past, but are returning to their Jewish heritage), and Gentiles. The congregation and a loose network connected to Marcello embraces the gifts and power of the Holy Spirit, fivefold ministry, and a commitment to Jewish life. There is good balance. The congregation in Brazil fostered a Messianic Jewish Bible Institute campus and now does much in the way of video and correspondence education. Joseph Shulam from Jerusalem has been a major figure in teaching the foundations of Jewish life in the context of a Jewish biblical theology. They recently formed a network of congregations.

A congregation and Messianic Jewish Bible Institute has also been planted under Jorge Goldstein in Buenos Aries. This ministry has spurred groups in other South American countries. The challenge is growing in Jewish understanding and depth. Leaders from the United States are helping them grow in this understanding and ability.

JONATHAN BERNIS AND OTHER MOVEMENTS

Jonathan Bernis has continued to make pioneering progress for the Messianic Jewish Movement. He has now planted a movement in Ethiopia. Beginning with medical missions trips, there are, at the time of this writing, three congregations among the black Jews of Ethiopia. A Messianic Jewish Bible Institute has also been established that is now training near two hundred in three locations. This is one of the more amazing happenings. The ministry there is led by Mezmor Zimichael and reflects the orientation of Jonathan Bernis, with whom I share great agreement. It has been my privilege to teach in the Messianic Jewish Bible Institute programs in Ethiopia. A new movement has also begun among the Lemba black Jews (really genetically Jewish) in South Africa and Zimbabwe.

The congregations and networks that came from the work of Jonathan Bernis, with whom we are in close cooperation, foster a strong orientation to indigenous leadership and networks. We seek to see networks that are self-governing in the countries or language regions of the different parts of the world. Despite possible financial inducements, we do not believe it is good for congregations to join American-based organizations, but would very much like to see an international association of networks from these various nations or language groups and regions.

TIKKUN, THE AMERICAN NETWORK

Tikkun International originally was formed to send and establish two senior leaders from our American network of Messianic Jewish congregations to Israel. (Before this sending, we formed a network of congregations known as Beth Messiah Apostolic Ministries.) The hope in sending our leaders was that they would plant congregations. There are now eight congregations linked from their efforts, one called Ohalai Rachamim and the other Revive Israel. The American network leaders requested to be included under the incorporation of Tikkun and not the corporation of a local Messianic Jewish congregation. The American network is called Tikkun America and the networks of Ohalai Rachamim (Tents of Mercy) and Revive Israel are explicitly committed to the fivefold understanding of leadership. We are all committed to Jewish life, Holy Spirit power, and fivefold ministry and networks.

The American network at this time of writing includes twenty congregations. We do not recruit, but seek only to join with those called together with us. We emphasize equipping visits, conferences, and institutes for leaders, and we have one general conference for congregational members once per year. We have also joined to the educational programs of Messianic Jewish Bible Institute through our affiliated school in America, Messianic Life

Institute in Northern Virginia under Dr. Michael Rudolph. Our accredited program is with The King's University in Van Nuys, California, founded by Dr. Jack Hayford. This is a joint program with Messianic Jewish Bible Institute. We care about education, but desire MJBI to be in an impartation model where the teachers model the presence and power of the Spirit, solid and godly character, fruitful ministry, and good scholarship. We were part of the formation of the MJBI schools.

The American Network believes that it is important for us to relate to and support the larger movement. Most of our congregations are members also of the Union of Messianic Congregations. We have a few that are in the International Alliance of Messianic Congregations and Synagogues.

JEWISH VOICE: VISITING AND EQUIPPING

Jonathan Bernis accepted the leadership of Jewish Voice Ministries, a television ministry. He has built this into a strong voice, but has done much more through this ministry, including continued ministry in Russian-speaking lands, Ethiopia, and also to communities descended from ancient Israel and the Jewish people in India. He recently committed himself to foster an American network built on similar principles of Tikkun America. This could be an important development for the American Messianic Jewish Movement since his anointing and leadership could greatly help us see new growth.

ISRAEL AND OLIVE TREE

The Messianic Jewish Movement in Israel is quite different from the Diaspora or North America. There are about 100 congregations from very small house congregations to good size congregations of many hundreds. Some are charismatic and some are not. The Russian Jewish Aliya brought many Jewish believers to Israel, swelled some congregations, and fostered the planting of several. Most do not see the importance of including Jewish tradition in their weekly gatherings. However, there are important exceptions. However, all keep the feasts and the Sabbath in some way. Hebrew is an important point of identity through shared language. Living in the land of Israel is also an important part of Jewish identity. However, I do think it is a mistake to not know about or embrace the good things in our Jewish heritage. As secular Israelis, many think Rabbinic Judaism is a product of Babylon, but the orientation of the Pharisees and the early Rabbinic Jews was in the land of Israel, though after the fall of Jerusalem, Babylon became the stronger center over the next centuries. Some traditions of prayer were contemporary to Yeshua and are very biblical. Most Israeli congregations follow a model of congregational government that is like Baptist independent congregations. However, there are some loose pastors' affiliations that seek to deal with major issues of morals and heresy.

A few senior brothers in Jerusalem have started a fellowship of leaders called Olive Tree. It is their desire to foster a different orientation that would include a charismatic orientation, an embrace of the place of fivefold ministry, and finally, a deeper theology of Jewish calling and identity. Olive Tree could move beyond a discussion forum and actually become a cooperative network of congregations. This could be very important for the Israel movement.

CHOSEN PEOPLE

The old Jewish missions tended to be negative to the Messianic Jewish movement. When the movement began in the early Seventies, Chosen People Ministries (at that time the American Board of Missions to the Jews) took a moderately negative stand, but did not actually oppose the movement. This slowly developed until planting congregations was embraced. Under the leadership of Mitch Glaser, the Messianic Jewish movement was embraced. Dr. Glaser has fostered a mission organization that embraces leaders of very different orientations, charismatic, non-charismatic, Jewish tradition-oriented, and not so oriented. Dr. Glaser has led Chosen People to become a very important organization and has been able to expand in leaders, planters, evangelists, and in funds and facilities. He also established a Messianic training program called the Feinburg Institute as part of Talbot Seminary. Chosen People links leaders who lead congregations in Israel, America, and Europe. There is a strong emphasis on their leaders getting a strong education in the movement. CPM's growth has been an important development.

JEWS FOR JESUS

The late Moishe Rosen, the former director of missionary training for the American Board of Missions to the Jews, founded Jews for Jesus in San Francisco in the early 1970s. Jews for Jesus is an evangelistic mission organization. Jews for Jesus became so well known that most Jews who are not followers of Yeshua call all Jewish believers in Yeshua Jews for Jesus. This is irksome to some Messianic Jews, who do not want to be known as related to the public types of street evangelism for which Jews for Jesus became known. Rosen refused to go along with the desire of traditional Jewish missions to condemn the Messianic Jewish Movement. He showed support for our congregations. A small number of Jews for Jesus leaders did connect to Messianic Jewish congregations. Jews for Jesus considered planting and did foster two congregations, one in New York and one in San Francisco, but then decided that this was not their calling. Jews for Jesus was really a bridge in time and an overlap between the old missions and the Messianic Jewish congregations. They pioneered Jewish Gospel music through the Liberated Wailing Wall musical group. Jews for Jesus has been a disciplined band of Jewish evangelists.

Most Messianic Jewish leaders have been concerned that Jews for Jesus does not share the concern of the movement in regard to assimilation, but that assimilation in the churches is an acceptable option to them. However, in the appendix of the book by Rich Robinson, *The Messianic Movement: A Field Guide for Evangelical Christians*, David Brickner has called for Jewish believers to not assimilate, but to maintain Jewish identity and life. It will be interesting to see how Jews for Jesus develops in the years ahead.

THE MESSIANIC JEWISH RABBINICAL COUNCIL

A few years ago, a council of Messianic Jewish congregational leaders and scholars formed the Messianic Jewish Rabbinical Council. The council is dealing with the important issue of seeking consensus for Messianic Jewish practices. I called for *halakhic thinking* in the first edition of this book some twenty-five years ago with the hope that a consensus would grow in our movement toward basic Jewish practice. The MJRC is clear that they do not see themselves as setting *halakha*, or authoritative rulings for the Messianic Jewish movement, but guidelines for those who will follow them. Generally, it seems that the decisions on Jewish practice are close to the Conservative Jewish Movement, but not where Conservatives have recently veered from biblical norms in such matters as homosexual practice. Generally, the guidelines of the MJRC are reasonable, though some will take issue with how they would interpret and apply Jewish practices. Because the group is small, I would prefer that the UMJC had such a body and would have greater influence in our movement as a whole. Even then, congregations that are not UMJC connected would not subscribe, but might be influenced. In addition, I would note that the UMJC does give guidance through the theology committee and guideline papers on such issues as gender equality, conversion, and more. In addition, Tikkun America does also seek to give guidelines for practice.

One direction of the MJRC has been of great concern to me, and I hope to write more extensively on this. This is the issue of the MJRC embracing the conversion of Gentiles under Messianic Jewish auspices and specifically the MJRC. I believe that the movement would be best served if we took a strong stand against the conversion of Gentiles. Why? So our book will not be too long, I will list my reasons. I first want to note my deep respect for the people who constitute the MJRC.

1. I believe that the weight of Scripture is strongly against the conversion of Gentiles to become Jews. An essential change has taken place with the establishment of the New Covenant and that is that Gentiles are offered status as priests though Yeshua, who now can stand shoulder-to-shoulder with Messianic Jews as equals. Yes, there is still distinctive calling of Jews that continues, but status in Yeshua is central to New Covenant theology. The statements of the New Covenant Scriptures, in Acts 15 and Galatians 5, are especially strong, and in the case of the Galatians passage, it seems to almost be a commandment against it. I understand the interpretation that this is only due to the wrong reasons for conversion, but I think it is not so. In addition, the rule of the congregations for the New Covenant is not to change one's position from Jewish or Gentile callings. David J. Rudolph has a very strong position on this in his book *A Jew to the Jews*. His PhD dissertation at Cambridge gives a very full exposition of First Corinthians 7. I would not stand against exceptions for one called to marry a Jew or for one seeking to reconfirm Jewish identity from a Jewish grandparent. However, in the former case, I think it is also good to have the status of *kiruv Israel*, one that has come to be part of the people without claiming the identity of being a Jew. This opens up marriage to a Jew and Jewish life without the confusion of a conversion. This is the policy

of Tikkun International. I know there are emotional arguments to yield to Gentiles in our midst who want to be Jews and have full access to Jewish practices and identity, but I think it is a mistake on their part, and they miss their God-intended calling to be supportive Gentiles if called to the movement. It must be stated in support of the MJRC that they do not think it is generally good for Gentiles to convert. It is the exception, and most are to be dissuaded from this direction.

2. I think conversion will debase the authenticity of the Jewishness of our movement in the view of the Jewish community. I know the thought is that we are more like the rest of the Jewish community if we convert Gentiles because they do this. However, they certainly will not recognize our conversions, but some do recognize Messianic Jews as still Jews. No doubt they will even more claim that we are Gentiles masquerading as Jews.

3. It will make our relationship with the Christian community more difficult, for most will conclude that we have violated Scripture and are practicing the Galatians heresy.

4. It assumes that a group can form a *bet din*, a judicial court, with sufficient authority to declare a Gentile to have so proven himself or herself as to now be declared a Jew. Can we really think that such authority has been given in the Messianic Jewish movement? Is there any precedent in the New Covenant Scriptures for such a major step? I do not think there is.

5. It sets a precedent for conversion to Judaism under Messianic Jewish auspices and will be used by others who will declare themselves *bet din* and will convert

others with much lower standards than the MJRC. This is already happening, even to the bizarre situation of some in England who self-converted and now have declared themselves a *bet din* and are converting Gentiles. They do not believe in limited conversions as the MJRC. Others will also do conversions, and we will say that their standards were too low, for the MJRC does have high standards. Yet the only way to stand against these trivialized conversions in my view is to stand against conversion in general. Otherwise, we will have to declare some to be Jews who have what some think is an authentic conversion and others to not be Jews. It is far better that none convert and be called Jews unless they have a Jewish grandparent for this is sufficient Jewish rooting for citizenship in the nation of Israel. I see no way to prevent the harm to the movement unless we stand united against conversion.

6. The Jewish community has an overwhelming consensus on the legitimacy of conversions. However, even then, the Orthodox do not accept Reform and Conservative conversions. Yet the State of Israel does accept them. However, the Messianic Jewish community has no such consensus. In fact, the overwhelming consensus is against conversions, in the United States, Russia, Ukraine, Europe, and especially Israel. This makes the place of the convert so tenuous that I believe it is a pastoral mistake. It is also a mistake of policy to break from such a strong consensus in a matter so as to actually change the calling of a person from a Gentile to a Jew.

7. I am concerned that this is dividing and will divide our movement. Most in Israel, Russia, and in the MJAA are very negative about this idea. I do not think we have near sufficient consensus in the movement to do it.

In conclusion, the original guidance paper from the UMJC, which is still the official position of the UMJC, is the correct position.

I write these words with some degree of pain since I do want to affirm the MJRC as much as I can, and the brothers who are in leadership of the MJRC are my friends and very good people.

EDUCATIONAL INSTITUTIONS

There are several educational institutions in the Messianic Jewish movement. One of the first was Messiah Yeshiva, which became Messiah Biblical Institute in suburban Washington, D.C. The program offered graduate and undergraduate studies and had a credit agreement with Regent University in Virginia and later Oral Robert's University Graduate School. Some have gone on to advanced degrees at other institutions. The school maintained strong impartation and practical training emphases. The program today continues as Messianic Life Institute, which is today a correspondence and Video school under the direction of Dr. Michael Rudolph.

The MBI program in part spurred the founding of Messianic Jewish Bible Institute that has the same emphases as MBI. MJBI programs are established in several countries—Ukraine, the first and still very successful full-time school, Russia, Brazil, and Argentina. Teachers travel from North America and Israel to serve these school, and indigenous teachers have also been trained. The MJBI program is an undergraduate program for a two-year certificate.

Messianic Jewish Theological Institute was founded by leaders who were also in the Union of Messianic Jewish Congregations. The Union Yeshiva program, founded in 1983, then merged with MJTI. For a season it was under the authority of the UMJC. It later became independent. Today its program is mostly a web-based program. It is a graduate program that is very serious in academic quality and offers a masters degree. However, in my view, many more courses of a practical nature are needed for Messianic Jewish Rabbis to enable them to more capably fulfill their leadership callings.

There are a number of schools that are in partnership with Christian Seminaries. The first, to my knowledge, was *Netzer David*, led by Dr. John Fischer, one of the fathers of the Messianic Jewish movement. Netzer is a graduate program that is affiliated with St. Petersburg Theological Seminary, of which John is the dean. He is the important professor in the Jewish program. His courses are full of valuable content.

The Feinburg School was founded under the leadership of Dr. Mitch Glazer of Chosen People and is affiliated with Talbot Theological Seminary. Its program would, therefore, be more dispensational.

Denver Seminary also has a program for Jewish studies connected to Messianic Jewish Rabbis Burt Yellin and Chaim Urbach in Denver. This is part of the seminary graduate program.

Finally Messianic Jewish Bible Institute has established a joint program with The King's University for both graduate and undergraduate degrees with a Jewish studies emphasis. The program is web-based, accredited, and requires some on-campus intensive seminars of one week in Van Nuys, California. The program fosters a charismatic view of the fullness of the Spirit.

With so many programs, we might ask how it is possible to find qualified teaching staff for them all. This is a problem, and I do have concern that the number of programs with the current size of the movement could really be a stretch. I personally cannot fill near the number of requests for teaching in these schools. However, it is a gain that education that is Messianic Jewish oriented is growing in both independent programs and programs with Christian seminaries.

CONCLUSION

The Messianic Jewish movement will succeed, I believe, because it is a prophetic and scriptural necessity in preparation for the return of Yeshua. However, this does not mean that we do not have challenges. It is best to face the challenges. The decline in North America, the gains in Russia and Ukraine, with their strengths and weaknesses, and the movement in Israel, with its very youthful quality, and again strengths and weakness, has to be understood. We must honestly evaluate to move forward. Europe and South America still have potential, but need development. The honest evaluation of this chapter is a hopeful evaluation. I believe we will address and overcome the weaknesses. We will grow. The largest weakness, where the movement is a good size, is in North America due to the need of a younger generation of leaders to replace our aging leaders. There are some young capable leaders. This should be a primary cause of prayer.

CHAPTER THIRTEEN

A MESSIANIC JEWISH VISION

WHEN ONE SPEAKS OF A vision, he has in mind the basic picture to be painted on the canvas of living. Messianic Judaism is, as yet, in its childhood stage. Without a vision, it will not have direction for growth. What is our vision of Messianic Judaism?

It is nothing less than to recover the dynamic power of the Gospel in the midst of the Jewish community. From the spread of the Good News in the context of Jewish loyalty will come an authentic Jewish expression of the New Testament faith. This expression will take various forms from independent congregations to Jewish wings of other New Testament groups. Yet it is our hope that all of these groups will grow over time in an affirmation and practice that has continuity with the beginnings of the faith in the first century. In the beginning, we read in Acts 2:44-47 that the Jewish believers gave themselves to the Apostles' teaching, to prayer, and to the breaking of bread in the homes of one another. Let us expand upon these themes.

First, may there be a dedication to apostolic teaching. We should seek to understand the Word in its original context of language and culture and to apply it to our lives. To love in the power of the Word and the Spirit as a demonstration of the present reality of God's Kingdom is truly our call.

Second, the first believers gave themselves to "the prayers." This includes praises, written prayer as teaching models, intercession, and fellowship with God in prayer. We must truly be a praying community.

Third, they were found in one another's homes, breaking bread. These early Jewish believers in Yeshua shared their lives. They sold property and moved to be near one another and under apostolic teaching. In a day of anonymity, a day in which the economic motive determines where we live and how, we need to recapture the sense of community demonstrated by the early followers in Yeshua. We ought to consider it to be of prime importance to choose where we live, where we work, and how we spend our time in relationship to how we can best serve God in the community. If we are to truly share, be available, and be involved, distance from *one another* is to be avoided. Moving for selfish reasons, without being led to another congregation, should also be questioned. Why do we consider our relationships so expendable and our part in the community of such little consequence to our decisions? This is certainly not in accord with Scripture. We ought rather be giving ourselves to build that spiritual, healing community in which the life of God can be recognized in the Body; we are to do the work of the Messiah while there is still time. In the Body, we are accountable to one another without binding each other's conscience. We seek to build up one another. From the Body, we reach out to others. This is the clear model of John 17 and Acts 2:44-47. When we love deeply, then the world will know the truth according to Yeshua's teaching. If we love, we no longer act as isolated individualists. We *are* our brothers' keepers, and we no longer direct our lives without sharing our directions any more than we would ignore our immediate families in such matters.

What of the Jewish heritage? I will fight the views of those who would make this heritage a legalistic burden. We should be free to experiment, to use new tunes, to use English as well as Hebrew in English-speaking lands, to use music, drama, and dance in new ways. However, my vision is that, if we truly love Israel—*past, present, and future*—we will have a heart desire to identify in a biblical way with our people's heritage.

Messianic Jews ought to be zealous to learn Hebrew; this is our national language. If Ben Yehuda could revive a Hebrew-speaking nation, surely we can develop Hebrew as a second language. Surely we can learn to appreciate singing and praying in Hebrew as well as in English. Anyone who loves France studies French and learns French literature and culture. Isn't this obvious? Hebrew is the language of the *Tenach* itself! We should have a Messiah-given love for our people far beyond our compatriots.

Second, we should see a *creative* appropriation of Jewish heritage to the extent that it is consistent with Scriptures and can be used to extol the grace of God in history and the fulfillment in the Messiah Yeshua. We could have leaders who foster times of joy. We could have a love of traditional melody, in *identification* with *the historic expression and experience of our people.* Our involvement would be with understanding! However, we could develop new expressions of music, dance, and drama drawing from the Scriptures and Jewish tradition. Because of the Holy Spirit, we could be an expression of our heritage that has life, verve, meaning, and joy to such an extent that our people would say, "It is Jewish, but it is so much more full of life!"

Our desire is not to destroy the Jewish community, but to recover the means by which Jewish people could be part of the universal Body of believers, while yet remaining part of their people and the nation of Israel. It is not true that the Jewish nation must be separated from the universal Body of the Messiah to assure their distinctive continuance. Rather, all that is required is an expression of the Body which is Jewish and maintains the ethnic identity and call of Israel.

As we have said, Messianic Judaism is in a childhood state. How shall we judge it? Hopefully, with broadness and tolerance! We need the help of all New Covenant believers; we need their input and wisdom, not just to be shunned as odd. The Scripture says, "By their fruits ye shall know them" (Matt. 7:20 KJV). What are the fruits of Messianic Judaism, fairly judged?

First, in comparison with congregations and movements that have been in existence for centuries and have mature, seasoned believers, we could seem as though we are lacking in fruit. Congregations of predominantly new believers in Yeshua, without trained leadership, are not going to match up to that which is seasoned. Indeed, things are said and done in ignorance, and controversy is engendered. But let us not forget that this is the case with all new religious movements. The Corinthian congregation was so full of division and carnality that it makes us look quite good! Yet Paul did not dismiss the Corinthian Church as not of God. He called them to maturity.

The Reformation was a great back-to-the-Bible movement. Some of the great reformers would not speak to one another. Religious wars followed the Reformation in which thousands were killed. Messianic Judaism has not fostered war or immorality. Do we really judge this new movement fairly from the outside? Yes, I know of tendencies to error, but allow me to make a personal statement from my own observations of the real inner fruit of Messianic Judaism:

When I began my work in the ministry, I had occasion to observe the practice of the old Christian missions to the Jews in Chicago. Praise God, many have changed dramatically since those days. In those days, many of the people who attended were spiritually and socially crippled. Some even hated themselves for being Jews, but felt they could not gain acceptance in the Jewish community. Being in the Hebrew-Christian mission was the closest to their desire to mediate between their self-hatred and their fear of Jewish rejection. How few were those coming to know Yeshua! Pathetically, we would see the same group of people make the rounds of all four missions in town. Each mission would print the stories of the same person as if it was responsible for the "conversion."

At that time, I did some figuring in regard to the budget of a large mission. From their own statement of finance and "conversion," we found their cost to be approximately $30,000–$40,000 per convert in 1970s dollars. Yes, it is a small fee to pay for a person's eternal life! However, how many of the reported decisions resulted in lasting commitment?

When I fairly judge the fruits of Messianic Judaism, I must keep all this in mind.

These have been my experiences in Messianic Judaism: First, Messianic Judaism is not a heresy, but affirms the clear doctrines of the New Testament as do all believing historic Christian groups. Second, people are being won to Yeshua, both Jew and non-Jew, because of Messianic Judaism. During one year, my own congregation saw over fifty people commit their lives in the waters of the covenant. Over two-thirds were Jewish, and most remained as members and attendees of the congregation. Proportionately, in my previous congregation, our results were also good, though not quite up to that level. Those ambivalent to their Jewish identity cannot find a comfortable niche among us unless they work through their self-rejection. Because of this, people become healthier. What was the cost of this response? We estimated $1,500 per person on the basis of total congregational budget.

What are some other fruits besides that of salvation? Let's look at the inner evidence: We have seen dozens of mixed-up kids forsake the occult, drugs, and Eastern religions. We have seen such kids reunited with their families and their families accepting them because of their renewed involvement with their Jewish heritage. What a joy to see whole families in Yeshua. I remember the tears of one young woman when we saw her father embrace Yeshua. The whole family cried. He taught Hebrew for the United States State Department.

Time does not permit us to recount the stories of some who were healed of paranoia, schizophrenia, depression, anger, and all sorts of confusion. Then there are the healed families. In years of Jewish congregational ministry, we have seen broken homes united and unstable marriages stabilized. I don't know of many who could say this, but in those years of ministry, we rarely had any marriage end in divorce! Most marriages that have taken place seem solid. Yes, we did have a strong emphasis on discipleship. We saw people moving to be closer to one another, to help, and to serve. My time in the leadership of congregations did reveal at least part of what could be done.

Have there been problems? Of course! Immature Jewish believers, not recognizing the equality of non-Jews in the Messiah, have made statements which have hurt. Some have misunderstood. Yet, I have no doubt that the fruit outweighs the dross. People are growing to be more like Yeshua!

As I look at the people of our congregations, we see people from all walks of life; what a miracle! We have homemakers, secretaries, government bureaucrats, doctors, corporate executives, repairmen, a tow truck driver, lawyers, biologists, social workers, an editor, teachers, a professor of traffic engineering, a real estate entrepreneur, etc. Here is an incredibly diverse group being made one in the Messiah! I, for one, am convinced that the fruits are good and shall remain so, and shall improve, if we keep our eyes on Yeshua and discipline ourselves by the Word, keeping an open mind to learn from all streams in the Body.

Messianic Judaism must be an ensign of the final redemption and of the uniting of the Jewish community to the Body of believers, while preserving Israel and its unique contributions to the Body. Praise God for all His work, for His consistent revelation in the Word. "For the gifts and calling of God are without repentance" (Rom. 11:29).

When God speaks, there is no double tongue in His promises, calling, or purpose. It is His desire to have mercy on all. To that end, He has and will use Israel; to that end, He has and will use the Church. May we all be in accord with His purpose. May we be light and salt in the Jewish community, a visible representation of Yeshua's Kingdom. May we be salt and light to the world.

A MESSIANIC JEWISH VISION

THE 613 LAWS

There are over 1,000 New Testament commands. Some are of difficult application, but most are clear. Paul, however, taught that *all* Scripture is profitable for doctrine, reproof, for instruction in righteousness. This includes Torah commands. Therefore we seek to know how to apply the 613 Torah commands to our lives. Following is a brief delineation categorizing these laws by purpose to facilitate their application.

Key:

T (Temple)—Part of the Temple sacrificial system replaced by Yeshua's priesthood and sacrifice. Of teaching value in pointing to Him; but can only be kept during this age through receiving Him, no longer by practice. (For example, Thanksgiving sacrifices are paralleled by prayer and offerings during this age).

U.M. (Moral Universal)—Direct commands of personal and social morality which either apply directly to us or have underlying principles which do apply to us.

U.R. (Universal, but *revised*)—Intensified and deepened in New Testament. (For example, *Swear by His name* Deuteronomy 10:20. *Swear not but say yes, yes, and mean it.* Matthew 5:37.)

J (*Jewish*)—Part of the Jewish heritage which celebrates

God's fulfillment of His promise to make Israel a nation. Valid as part of Israel's national and cultural identity when done so as to show Yeshua's fulfillment, Yeshua replacing the sacrificial dimensions of the practice.

J (Ancient)—Applies to ancient nation.

?—Unclear as to the purpose or application—at least in part.

C (Combination)—A combination of above categories: (e.g., 1) food lists may have a moral dimension if they are valid for health reasons; may be part of a cultural distinction in Israel; and may be part of the Temple sacrificial system by making a person unclean. (e.g., 2) Sabbath is both J as well as having a moral significance for all people who need to rest one day in seven on some day of the week.

N.A.—No longer can any application be found.

There are also over 1,050 New Testament commands. Neither the continuingly valid commands from the Torah or the New Testament commands can be approached for merit or as if we seek to fulfill them in our own power. Only dependence on God's grace and atonement—resurrection power—enables us to obey from the heart. Commands deepen our humility and sense of dependence on God's mercy and power.

MANDATORY COMMANDMENTS

[1]Ex. 20:2   UM **God**

[2]Dt. 6:4   UM   The Jew is required to [1]believe that God

[3]Dt. 6:5   UM   exists and to [2]acknowledge His unity;

[4]Dt. 6:13   UM   to [3]love, [4]fear, and [5]serve Him. He is

[5]Ex. 23:25;   UM   also commanded to [6]cleave to Him (by

Dt. 11:13   associating with and imitating the wise)

(Dt. 6:13;   and to [7]swear only by His name. One

also 13:15)   must [8]imitate God and [9]sanctify His

[6]Dt. 10:20   UM   name.

[7]Dt. 10:20   UR

[8]Dt. 28:9   UM

[9]Lev. 22:32   UM

[10]Dt. 6:7   UM   **Torah**

[11]Dt. 6:7   UM   The Jew must [10]remember the Shema each

[12]Dt. 6:8   CUMJ   morning and evening and [11]study the

[13]Dt. 6:8   CUMJ   Torah and teach it to others. He should

[14]Num. 15:38   J   bind tefillin on his [12]head and [13]his arm.

[15]Dt. 6:9   J   He should make [14]zizit for his garments

[16]Dt. 31:12   J   and [15]fix a mezuzah on the door.

[17]Dt. 17:18   J   The people are to be [16]assembled every sev-

[18]Dt. 31:19   UM   enth year to hear the Torah read and

[19]Dt. 8:10   UM   [17]the king must write a special copy of

the Torah for himself. [18]Every Jew

should have a Torah scroll. One should

[19]praise God after eating.

[20]Ex. 25:8   T   **Temple and the Priests**

[21]Lev. 19:30   T   The Jews should [20]build a Temple and

[22]Num. 18:4   T   [21]respect it. It must be [22]guarded at all

[23]Num. 18:3   T   times and the [23]Levites should perform

[24]Ex. 30:19   T   their special duties in it. Before enter-

[25]Ex. 27:21   T   ing the Temple or participating in its

26Num. 6:23 T
27Ex. 25:30 T
28Ex. 30:7 T
29Lev. 6:6 T
30Lev. 6:3 T
31Num. 5:2 T
32Lev. 21:8 T
33Ex. 28:2 T
34Num. 7:9 T
35Ex. 30:31 T
36Dt. 18:6-8 T
37Lev. 21:2-3 T
38Lev. 21:13 T

service the priests [24]must wash their hands and feet; they must also [25]light the candelabrum daily. The priests are required to [26]bless Israel and to [27]set the shewbread and frankincense before the Ark. Twice daily they must [28]burn the incense on the golden altar. Fire shall be kept burning on the altar [29]continually and the ashes should be [30]removed daily. Ritually unclean persons must be [31]kept out of the Temple. Israel [32]should honor its priests, who must be [33]dressed in special priestly raiment. The priests should [34]carry the Ark on their shoulders, and the holy anointing oil [35]must be prepared according to its special formula. The priestly families should officiate in [36]rotation. In honor of certain dead close relatives the priests should [37]make themselves ritually unclean. The high priest may marry [38]only a virgin.

Sacrifices

39Num. 28:3 T
40Lev. 6:13 T
41Num. 28:9 T
42Num. 28:11 T
43Lev. 23:36 T
44Lev. 23:10 T
45Num. 28:26
   -27 T
46Lev. 23:17 T

The [39]tamid sacrifice must be offered twice daily and the [40]high priest must also offer a meal-offering twice daily. An additional sacrifice (musaf) should be offered [41]every Sabbath, [42]on the first of every month, and [43]on each of the seven days of Passover. On the second day of Passover [44]a meal offering of the first barley must also be brought. On Shavuot a [45]musaf must be offered and [46]two loaves of bread as a wave offering. The additional sacrifice must also

[47]Num. 29:1	
-2	T
[48]Num. 29:7	
-8	T
[49]Lev. 16	T
[50]Num. 29:13	T
[51]Num. 29:36	T
[52]Ex. 23:14	T
[53]Ex. 34:23;	
Dt. 16:6	J
[54]Dt. 16:14	C-JT
[55]Ex. 12:6	C-JT
[56]Ex. 12:8	T
[57]Num. 9:11	T
[58]Num. 9:11;	J
Ex. 12:8	J
[59]Num. 10:10	
Num. 10:9	T
[60]Lev. 22:27	T
[61]Lev. 22:21	T
[62]Lev. 2:13	T
[63]Lev. 1:2	T
[64]Lev. 6:18	T
[65]Lev. 7:1	T
[66]Lev. 3:1	T
[67]Lev. 2:1;	
[68]Lev. 4:13	T
[69]Lev. 4:27	T

be made on [47]Rosh Ha-Shanah and [48]on the Day of Atonement when the [49]Avodah must also be performed. On every day of the festival of [50]Sukkot a musaf must be brought as well as on the [51]eighth day thereof.

Every male Jew should make [52]pilgrimage to the Temple three times a year and [53]appear there during the three pilgrim Festivals. One should [54]rejoice on the Festivals. On the 14th of Nisan one should [55]slaughter the paschal lamb and [56]eat of its roasted flesh on the night of the 15th. Those who were ritually impure in Nisan should slaughter the paschal lamb on [57]the 14th of Iyyar and eat it with [58]mazzah and bitter herbs. Trumpets should be [59]sounded when the festive sacrifices are brought and also in times of tribulation.

Cattle to be sacrificed must be [60]at least eight days old and [61]without blemish. All offerings must be [62]salted. It is a mitzvah to perform the ritual of [63]the burnt offering, [64]the sin offering, [65]the guilt offering, [66]the peace offering and [67]the meal offering.

Should the Sanhedrin err in a decision its members [68]must bring a sin offering which offering must also be brought [69]by a person who has unwittingly transgressed a karet prohibition (i.e., one which, if done deliberately, would incur karet). When in doubt as to whether one has transgressed such a prohibi-

[70]Lev. 5:17

-18 T

[71]Lev. 5:15,
21-25;
19:20-21 T

[72]Lev. 5:1-11 T

[73]Num. 5:6-7 UM

[74]Lev. 15:13

-15 T

[75]Lev. 15:28

-29 T

[76]Lev. 12:6 T

[77]Lev. 14:10 T

[78]Lev. 27:32 T

[79]Ex. 13:2 T

[80]Ex. 22:28;
Num. 18:15 T

[81]Ex. 34:20 T

[82]Ex. 13:13 T

[83]Dt. 12:5-5 T

[84]Dt. 12:14 T

[85]Dt. 12:26 T

[86]Dt. 12:15 T

[87]Lev. 27:33 T

[88]Lev. 6:9 T

[89]Ex. 29:33 T

[90]Lev. 7:19 T

[91]Lev. 7:17 T

tion a [70]"suspensive" guilt offering must be brought.

For [71]stealing or swearing falsely and for other sins of a like nature, a guilt offering must be brought. In special circumstances the sin offering [72]can be according to one's means.

One must [73]confess one's sins before God and repent for them. A [74]man or [75]a woman who has a seminal issue must bring a sacrifice; a woman must also bring a sacrifice [76]after childbirth. A leper must [77]bring a sacrifice after he has been cleansed. One must [78]tithe one's cattle. The [79]first born of clean (i.e., permitted) cattle are holy and must be sacrificed. The firstborn of man must be [80]redeemed. The firstling of the ass must be [81]redeemed; if not [82]its neck has to be broken.

Animals set aside as offerings [83]must be brought to Jerusalem without delay and [84]may be sacrificed only in the Temple. Offerings from outside the land of Israel [85]may also be brought to the Temple. Sanctified animals [86]which have become blemished must be redeemed. A beast exchanged for an offering [87]is also holy. The priests should eat [88]the remainder of the meal offering and [89]the flesh of sin and guilt offerings; but consecrated flesh which has become [90]ritually unclean or [91]which was not eaten within its appointed time must be burned.

[92]Num. 6:5 JT
(*Acts 18*)
[93]Num. 6:18 T
[94]Dt. 23:24 UR
[95]Num. 30:3 URJ

Vows

A Nazirite must [92]let his hair grow during the period of his separation. When that period is over he must [93]shave his head and bring his sacrifice.

A man must [94]honor his vows and his oaths which a judge can [95]annul only in accordance with the Law.

[96]Lev. 11:8,
and 24 T-C
[97]Lev. 11:29
-31 T-C
[98]Lev. 11:34 T-C
[99]Lev. 15-19 T-C
[100]Lev. 12:12 T-C
[101]Lev. 13:3 T-C
[102]Lev. 13:51 T-C
[103]Lev. 14:44 T-C
[104]Lev. 15:2 T-C
[105]Lev. 15:16 T-C
[106]Lev. 15:19 T-C
[107]Num. 19:14 T-C
[108]Num. 19:13
& 21 T-C
[109]Lev. 15:16 T-C
[110]Lev. 14:2 T-C
[111]Lev. 14:9 T-C
[112]Lev. 13:45 T-C

Ritual Purity
*(Health reasons for following,
thus Temple and C.)*

Anyone who touches [96]a carcass or [97]one of the eight species of reptiles becomes ritually unclean; food becomes unclean by [98]coming into contact with a ritually unclean object.

Menstruous women [99]and those [100]lying-in after childbirth are ritually impure. A [101]leper, [102]a leprous garment, and [103]a leprous house are all ritually unclean. A man having a running issue is unclean, as is [105]semen. A woman suffering from [106]running issue is also impure. A [107]human corpse is ritually unclean. The purification water (mei nidah) purifies [108]the unclean, but it makes the clean ritually impure. It is a mitzvah to become ritually clean [109]by ritual immersion. To become cleansed of leprosy one [110]must follow the specified procedure and also [111]shave of all of one's hair. Until cleansed the leper [112]must be bareheaded with clothing in disarray so as to be easily distinguish-

[113]Num. 19:2-
9   T

[114]Lev. 27:2-8 T
[115]Lev. 27:11
-12   T
[116]Lev. 27:14 T
[117]Lev. 27:16,
22-23   T
[118]Lev. 5:16 T
[119]Lev. 19:24 T-J
[120]Lev. 19:9 UM
[121]Lev. 19:9 UM
[122]Dt. 24:19 UM
[123]Lev. 19:10 UM
[124]Lev. 19:10 UM
[125]Ex. 23:19 T
[126]Dt. 18:4 T
[127]Lev. 27:30;
Num. 18:24 T
[128]Dt. 14:22 T
[129]Num. 18:26 T
[130]Dt. 14:28 CUMJ
[131]Dt. 26:13 T

able. The ashes of [113]the red heifer are to be used in the process of ritual purification.

Donations to the Temple

If a person [114]undertakes to give his own value to the Temple he must do so. Should a man declare [115]an unclean beast, [116]a house, or [117]a field as a donation to the Temple, he must give their value in money as fixed by the priest. If one unwittingly derives benefit from Temple property [118]full restitution plus a fifth must be made.

The fruit of [119]the fourth year's growth of trees is holy and may be eaten only in Jerusalem. When you reap your fields you must leave [120]the corners, [121]the gleanings, [122]the forgotten sheaves, [123]the misformed bunches of grapes and [124]the gleanings of the grapes for the poor.

The first fruits must be [125]separated and brought to the Temple and you must also [126]separate the great heave offering (terumah) and give it to the priests. You must give [127]one tithe of your produce to the Levites and separate [128]a second tithe which is to be eaten only in Jerusalem. The Levites [129]must give a tenth of their tithe to the priests. In the third and sixth years of the seven year cycle you should [130]separate a tithe for the poor instead of the second tithe. A declaration [131]must be recited when separating the various tithes and

[132]Dt. 26:5	T	
[133]Num. 15:20	T	

[132]when bringing the first fruits to the Temple.

The first portion of the [133]dough must be given to the priest.

[134]Ex. 23:11	CJUM
[135]Ex. 34:21	CJUM
[136]Lev. 25:10	CJUM
[137]Lev. 25:9	CJUM
[138]Lev. 25:24	CJUM
[139]Lev. 25:29 -30	CJUM
[140]Lev. 25:8	CJUM
[141]Dt. 15:3	CJUM
[142]Dt. 15:3	CJUM

The Sabbatical Year

(Universal principle of care for poor and business mercy is part of 136-141)

In the seventh year (shemittah) everything that grows is [134]ownerless and available to all; the fields [135]must lie fallow and you may not till the ground. You must [136]sanctify the Jubilee year (50th) an on the Day of Atonement in that year [137]you must sound the shofar and set all Hebrew slaves free. In the Jubilee year all land is to be [138]returned to its ancestral owners and, generally, in a walled city [139]the seller has the right to buy back a house within a year of the sale.

Starting from entry into the land of Israel, the years of the Jubilee must be [140]counted and announced yearly and septennially. In the seventh year [141]all debts are annulled but [142]one may exact a debt owed by a foreigner.

[143]Dt. 18:3	T	
[144]Dt. 18:4	T	
[145]Lev. 27:21, 28	T	

Concerning Animals for Consumption

When you slaughter an animal you must [143]give the priest his share as you must also give him [144]the first of the fleece.

When a man makes a heren (a special vow) you must [145]distinguish between that which belongs to the Temple (i.e., when God's name was mentioned in the vow)

[146]Dt. 12:21 CT
UM

[147]Lev. 17:13 TUM
(Reverence for
life)—UM

[148]Dt. 22:7 UM

[149]Lev. 11:2 TC
JUM

[150]Dt. 14:11 CTJ
UM

[151]Lev. 11:21 CTJ
UM

[152]Lev. 11:21 CTJ
UM

[153]Ex. 12:2;
Dt. 16:1

and that which goes to the priests. To be fit for consumption, beast and fowl must be [146]slaughtered according to the law and if they are not of a domesticated species [147]their blood must be covered with earth after slaughter. Set the parent bird [148]free when taking the nest. Examine [149]beast, [150]fowl, [151]locusts and [152]fish to determine whether they are permitted for consumption. The Sanhedrin should [153]sanctify the first day of every month and reckon the years and the seasons.

(147–149—unclean relates to Temple (T)— food laws of health value (J) and also distinguish Jews.)

[154]Ex. 23:12 JUM **Festivals**
(Sabbath has a
univ. prin. of
rest pds.)

[155]Ex. 20:8 JUM

[156]Ex. 12:15 J

[157]Ex. 13:8 J

[158]Ex. 12:18 J

[159]Ex. 12:16 J

[160]Ex. 12:16 J

[161]Lev. 23:35 J

[162]Lev. 23 J

[163]Lev. 23:24 J

[164]Lev. 16:29 J

[165]Lev. 16:29,
1 J

[166]Lev. 23:25 J

[167]Lev. 23:36 J

You must [154]rest on the Sabbath day and [155]declare it holy at its onset and termination. On the 14th of Nisan [156]remove all leaven from your ownership and on the night of the 15th [157]relate the story of the Exodus from Egypt; on that night [158]you must also eat mazzah. On the [159]first and [160]seventh days of Passover you must rest. Starting from the day of the first sheaf (16th of Nisan) you shall [161]count 49 days. You must rest on [162]Shavuot, and on [163]Rosh Ha-Shanah; on the Day of Atonement you must [164]fast and [165]rest. You must also rest on [166]the first and [167]the eighth day of Sukkot during which festival you shall [168]dwell in booths and [169]take the

[168]Lev. 23:42	J	
[169]Lev. 23:40	J	
[170]Num. 29:1	J	

four species. On Rosh Ha-Shanah [170]you are to hear the sound of the shofar.

Community

[171]Ex. 30:12		
-13	T	
[172]Dt. 18:15	JUM	
[173]Dt. 17:15	NA	
[174]Dt. 17:11	T	
[175]Ex. 23:2	CJUM	
[176]Dt. 16:18	UM	
[177]Lev. 19:15	UM	
[178]Lev. 5:1	UM	
[179]Dt. 13:15	UM	
[180]Dt. 19:19	UM	
[181]Dt. 21:4	T	
[182]Dt. 19:3	CJUM	
[183]Num. 35:2	T	
[184]Dt. 22:8	UM	

Every male should [171]give half a shekel to the Temple annually.

You must [172]obey a prophet and [173]appoint a king. You must also [174]obey the Sanhedrin; in the case of division, [175]yield to the majority. Judges and officials shall be [176]appointed in every town and they shall judge the people [177]impartially. Whoever is aware of evidence [178]must come to court to testify. Witnesses shall be [179]examined thoroughly and, if found to be false, [18]shall have done to them what they intended to do to the accused.

When a person is found murdered and the murderer is unknown the ritual of [181]decapitating the heifer must be performed.

Six cities of refuge should be [182]established. The Levites, who have no ancestral share in the land, shall [183]be given cities to live in. You must [184]build a fence around your roof and remove potential hazards from your home.

Idolatry

[185]Dt. 12:2;		
7:5	JUM	
[186]Dt. 13:17	JUM	

Idolatry and its appurtenances [185]must be destroyed, and a city which has become perverted must be [186]treated according to the law. You are commanded to

[187]Dt. 20:17	NA	
[188]Dt. 25:19	NA	
[189]Dt. 25:17	NA	

[187]destroy the seven Canaanite nations, and [188]to blot out the memory of Amalek, and [189]to remember what they did to Israel.

[190]Dt. 20:11		
-12	T	
[191]Dt. 20:2	NA?	
[192]Dt. 23:14		
-15	UM	
[193]Dt. 23:14	UM	

War

The regulations for wars other than those commanded in the Torah [190]are to be observed and a priest should be [191]appointed for special duties in times of war. The military camp must be [192]kept in a sanitary condition. To this end, every soldier must be [193]equipped with the necessary implements.

[194]Lev. 5:23	UM	
[195]Dt. 15:8;		
Lev. 25:35		
-36	UM	
[196]Dt. 15:14	UM	
[197]Ex. 22:24	UM	
[198]Dt. 32:21	UM	
[199]Dt. 24:13;		
Ex. 22:25	UM	
[200]Dt. 24:15	UM	
[201]Dt. 23:25		
-26 UM		
[202]Ex. 23:5	UM	
[203]Dt. 22:4	UM	
[204]Dt. 22:1;		
Ex. 23:4	UM	
[205]Lev. 19:17	UM	
[206]Lev. 19:18	UM	
[207]Dt. 10:19	UM	
[208]Lev. 19:36	UM	

Social

Stolen property must be [194]restored to its owner. Give [195]charity to the poor. When a Hebrew slave goes free the owner must [196]give him gifts. Lend to [197]the poor without interest; to the foreigner you may [198]lend at interest. Restore [199]a pledge to its owner if he needs it. Pay the worker his wages [200]on time; [201]permit him to eat of the produce with which he is working. You must [202]help unload an animal when necessary, and also [203]help load man or beast. Lost property [204]must be restored to its owner. You are required [205]to reprove the sinner but you must [206]love your fellow as yourself. You are commanded [207]to love the proselyte. Your weights and measure [208]must be accurate.

[209]Lev. 19:32	UM	**Family**
[210]Ex. 20:12	UM	Respect the [209]wise; [210]honor and [211]fear your
[211]Lev. 19:3	UM	parents. You should [212]perpetuate the
[212]Gen. 1:28	UM	human race by marrying [213]according
[213]Dt. 24:1	UM	to the Law. A bridegroom is to [214]re-
[214]Dt. 24:5	UM	joice with his bride for one year. Male
[215]Gen. 17:10		children must [215]be circumcised.
Lev. 12:3	J	Should a man die childless his brother
[216]Dt. 25:5	NA?	must either [216]marry his widow or
[217]Dt. 25:9	?	[217]release her (halizah). He who vio-
[218]Dt. 22:29	UM	lated a virgin must [218]marry her and
[219]Dt. 22:18		may never divorce her. If a man unjust-
-19	UM	ly accuses his wife of premarital pro-
[220]Ex. 22:15		miscuity [219]he shall be flogged, and
-23	UM	may never divorce her. The seducer
[221]Dt. 21:11	UM	[220]must be punished according to the
[222]Dt. 24:1	UR	Law. The female captive must be
(Matt. 5)		[221]treated in accordance with her spe-
[223]Num. 5:15		cial regulations. Divorce can be exe-
-27	NA	cuted [222]only by means of a written
	TUM	document. A woman suspected of adul-

tery [223]has to submit to the required
test.

*(224-231 have a basic underlying principle of
social justice)*

[224]Dt. 25:2	UM?	**Judicial**
[225]Num. 35:25	UM	When required by Law [224]you must adminis-
[226]Ex. 21:20	UM	ter the punishment of flogging and you
[227]Ex. 21:16	UM?	must [225]exile the unwitting homicide.
[228]Lev. 20:14	UM?	Capital punishment shall be by [226]the
[229]Dt. 22:24	UM	sword, [227]strangulation, [228]fire, or [229]ston-
[230]Dt. 21:22	UM	ing, as specified. In some cases the

body of the executed [230]shall be hanged,

[231]Dt. 21:23   UM?   but it [231]must be brought to burial the same day.

(232-234—The moral principle is not endorsement of slavery but to limit hardship and apply kindness)

[232]Ex. 21:2   UM   **Slaves**
[233]Ex. 21:8   UM   Hebrew slaves [232]must be treated according
[234]Ex. 21:8   UM   to the special laws for them. The mas-
[235]Lev. 25:46   UM   ter should [233]marry his Hebrew maid-
servant or [234]redeem her. The alien slave [235]must be treated according to the regulations applying to him.

(236-245—show principles of justice)

[236]Ex. 21:18   UM   **Torts**
[237]Ex. 21:28   UM   The applicable law must be administered in
[238]Ex. 21:33   the case of injury caused by [236]a person,
-34   UM   [237]an animal or [238]a pit. Thieves [239]must
[239]Ex. 21:37-   be punished. You must render judg-
22:3   UM   ment in cases of [240]trespass by cattle,
[240]Ex. 22:4   UM   [241]arson, [242]embezzlement by an unpaid
[241]Ex. 22:5   UM   guardian and in claims against [243]a paid
[242]Ex. 22:6-8   UM   guardian, a hirer, or [244]a borrower.
[243]Ex. 22:9-12 UM   Judgment must also be rendered in
[244]Ex. 22:13   UM   disputes arising out of [245]sales, [248]inher-
[245]Lev. 25:14   UM   itance and [246]other matters generally.
[246]Ex. 22:8   UM   You are required to [247]rescue the per-
[247]Dt. 25:12   UM   secuted even if it means killing his
[248]Num. 27:8 UM   oppressor.

PROHIBITIONS

[1]Ex. 20:3	UM	**Idolatry and Related Practices**
[2]Ex. 20:4	UM	It is [1]forbidden to believe in the existence of
[3]Lev. 19:4	UM	any but the One God. You may not
[4]Ex. 20:20	UM	make images [2]for yourself or [3]for oth-
[5]Ex. 20:5	UM	ers to worship or for [4]any other purpose.
[6]Ex. 20:5	UM	You must not worship anything but God
[7]Lev. 18:21	UM	either in [5]the manner prescribed for
[8]Lev. 19:31	UM	His worship or [6]in its own manner of
[9]Lev. 19:31	UM	worship.
[10]Lev. 19:4	UM	Do not [7]sacrifice children to Molech.
[11]Dt. 16:22	UM	You may not [8]practice necromancy or [9]resort
[12]Lev. 20:1	UM	to "familiar spirits," neither should
[13]Dt. 16:21	UM	you take idolatry or its mythology [10]ser-
[14]Ex. 23:13	UM	iously. It is forbidden to construct a
[15]Ex. 23:13	UM	[11]pillar or [12]dais even for the worship of
[16]Dt. 13:12	UM	God or to [13]plant trees in the Temple.
[17]Dt. 13:9	UM	You may not [14]swear by idols or instigate an
[18]Dt. 13:9	UMJ?	idolator to do so, nor may you encour-
[19]Dt. 13:9	UMJ?	age or persuade any [15]non-Jew or [16]Jew
[20]Dt. 13:9	UM	to worship idols.
[21]Dt. 13:9	UM	You must not [17]listen to or love anyone who
[22]Dt. 7:25	UM	disseminates idolatry nor [18]should you
[23]Dt. 13:17	UM	withhold yourself from hating him. Do
[24]Dt. 13:18	UM	not [19]pity such a person. If somebody
[25]Dt. 7:26	UM	tries to convert you to idolatry [20]do not
[26]Dt. 18:20	UM	defend him or [21]conceal the fact. It is

forbidden to [22]derive any benefit from
the ornaments of idols. You may not
[23]rebuild that which has been destroyed
as a punishment for idolatry nor may
you [24]have any benefit from its wealth.
Do not [25]use anything connected with
idols or idolatry.

It is forbidden [26]to prophesy in the name of

[27]Dt. 18:20	UM	
[28]Dt. 13:3, 4	UM	
[29]Dt. 18:22	UM	
[30]Lev. 20:23	UM	
[31]Lev. 19:26		
Dt. 18:10	UM	
[32]Dt. 18:10	UM	
[33]Dt. 18:10		
-11	UM	
[34]Dt. 18:10		
-11	UM	
[35]Dt. 18:10		
-11	UM	
[36]Dt. 18:10		
-11	UM	
[37]Dt. 18:10		
-11	UM	
[38]Dt. 18:10		
-11	UM	
[39]Dt. 22:5	UM	
[40]Dt. 22:5	UM	
[41]Lev. 19:28	UM	
[42]Dt. 22:11	J	
[43]Lev. 19:27	J?	
(Ancient only?)		
[44]Lev. 19:27	J?	
(Ancient only?)		
[45]Dt. 16:1; Dt. 14:1; & Lev. 19:28	UM	
[46]Dt. 17:16	J	
[47]Num. 15:39	UM	

idols or prophesy [27]falsely in the name of God. Do not [28]listen to the one who prophesies for idols and do not [29]fear the false prophet or hinder his execution.

You must not [30]imitate the ways of idolators or practice their customs; [31]divination, [32]soothsaying, [33]enchanting, [34]sorcery, [35]charming, [36]consulting ghosts or [37]familiar spirits and [38]necromancy are forbidden. Women must not [39]wear male clothing nor men [40]that of women. Do not [41]tattoo yourself in the manner of the idolators. You may not wear [42]garments made of both wool and linen nor may you shave (with a razor) the sides of [43]your head or [44]your beard. Do not [45]lacerate yourself over your dead.

Prohibitions Resulting from Historical Events

It is forbidden to return to Egypt to [46]dwell there permanently or to [47]indulge in

[48]Ex. 23:32;	
Dt. 7:2	
[49]Dt. 20:16	
(Ancient)	J
[50]Dt. 7:2	
(Ancient	
only)	J
[51]Ex. 23:33	
(Ancient)	J
[52]Dt. 7:3	JUM
[53]Dt. 23:4	UMJ
[54]Dt. 23:8	UMJ
[55]Dt. 23:8	UMJ
[56]Dt. 23:7	
(Ancient)	J
[57]Dt. 20:19	UM
[58]Dt. 7:21	UM
[59]Dt. 25:19	
(Ancient)	J

impure thoughts or sights. You may not [48]make a pact with the seven Canaanite nations or [49]save the life an any member of them. Do not [50]show mercy to idolators, [51]permit them to dwell in the land of Israel or [52]intermarry with them. A Jewess may not [53]marry an Ammonite or Moabite even if he converts to Judaism but should not refuse (for reasons of genealogy alone) [54]a descendent of Esau or [55]an Egyptian who are proselytes. It is prohibited to [56]make peace with the Ammonite or Moabite nations. The [57]destruction of fruit trees even in times of war is forbidden as is wanton waste at any time. Do not [58]fear the enemy and do not [59]forget the evil done by Amalek.

Blasphemy

[60]Lev. 24:16	UM
(rather) Ex. 22:27	
[61]Lev. 19:12	UM
[62]Ex. 20:7	UM
[63]Lev. 22:32	UM
[64]Dt. 6:16	UM
[65]Dt. 12:4	UM
[66]Dt. 21:23	UM

You must not [60]blaspheme the Holy Name, [61]break an oath made by It, [62]take It in vain or [63]profane It. Do not [64]try the Lord God. You may not [65]erase God's name from the holy texts or destroy institutions devoted to His worship. Do not [66]allow the body of one hanged to remain so overnight.

Temple

[67]Num. 18:5	T
[68]Lev. 16:2	T
[69]Lev. 21:23	T
[70]Lev. 21:17	T

Be not [67]lax in guarding the Temple. The high priest must not enter the Temple [68]indiscriminately; a priest with a physical blemish may not [69]enter there at all or [70]serve in the sanctuary and even if

71Lev. 21:18 T
72Num. 18:3 T
73Lev. 10:9
-11 T
74Num. 18:4 T
75Lev. 22:2 T
76Lev. 21:6 T
77Num. 5:3 T
78Dt. 23:11 T
79Ex. 20:25 T
80Ex. 20:26 T
81Lev. 6:6 T
82Ex. 30:9 T
83Ex. 30:32 T
84Ex. 30:32 T
85Ex. 30:37 T
86Ex. 25:15 T
87Ex. 28:28 T
88Ex. 28:32 T

the blemish is of a temporary nature he may not [71]participate in the service there until it has passed. The Levites and the priests must not [72]interchange in their functions. Intoxicated persons may not [73]enter the sanctuary or teach the Law. It is forbidden for [74]non-priests, [75]unclean priests or [76]priests who have performed the necessary ablution but are still within the time limit of their uncleanness to serve in the Temple. No unclean person may enter [77]the Temple or [78]the Temple Mount.

The altar must not be made of [79]hewn stones nor may the ascent to it be by [80]steps. The fire on it may not be [81]extinguished nor may any other but the specified incense be [82]burned on the golden altar.

You may not [83]manufacture oil with the same ingredients and in the same proportions as the anointing oil which itself [84]may not be misused. Neither may you [85]compound incense with the same ingredients and in the same proportions as that burnt on the altar. You must not [86]remove the staves from the Ark, [87]remove the breastplate from the ephod or [88]make any incision in the upper garment of the high priest.

89Dt. 12:13
90Lev. 17:3-4 T
91Lev. 22:20 T
92Lev. 22:22 T
93Lev. 22:24 T

Sacrifices

It is forbidden to [89]offer sacrifices or [90]slaughter consecrated animals outside the Temple. You may not [91]sanctify, [92]slaughter, [93]sprinkle the blood of or

[94]Lev. 22:22	T
[95]Dt. 17:1	T
[96]Lev. 22:25	T
[97]Lev. 22:21	T
[98]Lev. 2:11	T
[99]Lev. 2:13	T
[100]Dt. 23:19	T
[101]Lev. 22:28	T
[102]Lev. 5:11	T
[103]Lev. 5:11	T
[104]Num. 5:15	T
[105]Num. 5:15	T
[106]Lev. 27:10	T
[107]Lev. 27:26	T
[108]Num. 18:17	T
[109]Lev. 27:33	T
[110]Lev. 27:28	T
[111]Lev. 27:28	T
[112]Lev. 5:8	T
[113]Dt. 15:19	T
[114]Dt. 15:19	T
[115]Ex. 34:25	T
[116]Ex. 23:10	T
[117]Ex. 12:10	T
[118]Dt. 16:4	T
[119]Num. 9:13	T
[120]Lev. 22:30	T
[121]Ex. 12:46	T
[122]Num. 9:12	T
[123]Ex. 12:46	T

[94]burn the inner parts of a blemished animal even if the blemish is [95]of a temporary nature and even if it is [96]offered by Gentiles. It is forbidden to [97]inflict a blemish on an animal consecrated for sacrifice.

Leaven or honey may not [98]be offered on the altar, neither may [99]anything unsalted. An animal received as the hire of a harlot or as the price of a dog [100]may not be offered. Do not [101]kill an animal and its young on the same day. It is forbidden to use [102]olive oil or [103]frankincense in the sin offering or [104], [105]in the jealousy offering (sotah). You may not [106]substitute sacrifices even [107]from one category to the other. You may not [108]redeem the firstborn of permitted animals. It is forbidden to [109]sell the tithe of the herd or [110]sell or [111]redeem a field consecrated by the herem vow.

When you slaughter a bird for a sin offering you may not [112]split its head.

It is forbidden to [113]work with or [114]to shear a consecrated animal. You must not slaughter the paschal lamb [115]while there is still leaven about; nor may you leave overnight [116]those parts that are to be offered up or [117]to be eaten. You may not leave any part of the festive offering [118]until the third day or any part of [119]the second paschal lamb or [120]the thanksgiving offering until the morning.

It is forbidden to break a bone of [121]the first or [122]the second paschal lamb or [123]to

[124]Lev. 6:10 T
[125]Ex. 12:9 T
[126]Ex. 12:45 T
[127]Ex. 12:48 T
[128]Ex. 12:43 T
[129]Lev. 12:4 T
[130]Lev. 7:19 T
[131]Lev. 19:6-8 T
[132]Lev. 7:18 T
[133]Lev. 22:10 T
[134]Lev. 22:10 T
[135]Lev. 22:10 T
[136]Lev. 22:4 T
[137]Lev. 22:12 T
[138]Lev. 6:16 T
[139]Lev. 6:23 T
[140]Dt. 14:3 T
[141]Dt. 12:17 T
[142]Dt. 12:17 T
[143]Dt. 12:17 T
[144]Dt. 12:17 T
[145]Dt. 12:17 T
[146]Dt. 12:17 T
[147]Dt. 12:17 T
[148]Dt. 12:17 T
[149]Ex. 29:33 T

carry their flesh out of the house where it is being eaten. You must not [124]allow the remains of the meal offering to become leaven. It is also forbidden to eat the paschal lamb [125]raw or sodden or to allow [126]an alien resident, [127]an uncircumcised person or an [128]apostate to eat of it.

A ritually unclean person [129]must not eat of holy things nor may [130]holy things which have become unclean be eaten. Sacrificial meat [131]which is left after the time-limit or [132]which was slaughtered with wrong intentions must not be eaten. The heave offering must not be eaten by [133]an uncircumcised person, or [136]an unclean priest. The daughter of a priest who is married to a non-priest may not [137]eat of holy things. The meal offering of the priest [138]must not be eaten, neither may [139]the flesh of the sin offerings sacrificed within the sanctuary or [140]consecrated animals which have become blemished.

You may not eat the second tithe of [141]corn, [142]wine, or [143]oil or [144]unblemished firstlings outside Jerusalem.

The priests may not eat the sin-offerings or the trespass-offerings outside the Temple courts or [146]the flesh of the burnt-offering at all. The lighter sacrifices [147]may not be eaten before the blood has been sprinkled. A non-priest may not [148]eat of the holiest sacrifices and a priest [149]may not eat the first-fruits outside the Temple courts.

150Dt. 26:14	T	
151Dt. 26:14	T	
152Dt. 26:14	T	
153Lev. 22:15	T	
154Ex. 22:28	T	
155Dt. 23:22	T	
156Ex. 23:15	T	
157Num. 30:3	UM	

One may not eat 150the second tithe while in a state of impurity or 151in mourning; its redemption money 152may not be used for anything other than food and drink.

You must not 153eat untithed produce or 154change the order of separating the various tithes.

Do not 155delay payment of offerings—either freewill or obligatory—and do not 156come to the Temple on the pilgrim festivals without an offering.

Do not 157break your word.

158Lev. 21:7	T	
159Lev. 21:7	T	
160Lev. 21:7	T	
161Lev. 21:14	T	
162Lev. 21:15	T	
163Lev. 10:6	T	
164Lev. 10:6	T	
165Lev. 10:7	T	
166Lev. 21:1	T	
167Lev. 21:11	T	
168Lev. 21:11	T	
169Dt. 18:1	T	
170Dt. 18:1	T	
171Dt. 14:1	T	

Priests

A priest may not marry 158a harlot, 159a woman who has been profaned from the priesthood, or 160a divorcee; the high priest must not 161marry a widow or 162take one as a concubine. Priests may not enter the sanctuary with 163overgrown hair of the head or 164with torn clothing; they must not 165leave the courtyard during the Temple service. An ordinary priest may not render himself 166ritually impure except for those relatives specified, and the high priest should not become impure 167for anybody in 168any way.

The tribe of Levi shall have no part in 169the division of the land of Israel or 170in the spoils of war.

It is forbidden 171to make oneself bald as a sign of mourning for one's dead.

Ref	Verse	Code
[172]	Dt. 14:7	TC / UM
[173]	Lev. 11:11	TC / UM
[174]	Lev. 11:13	TC / UM
[175]	Dt. 14:19	TC / UM
[176]	Lev. 11:41	TC / UM
[177]	Lev. 11:44	TC / UM
[178]	Lev. 11:42	TC / UM
[179]	Lev. 11:43	TC / UM
[180]	Dt. 14:21	UM
[181]	Ex. 22:30	UM
[182]	Dt. 12:23	UM
[183]	Gen. 32:33	J
[184]	Lev. 7:26	UM
[185]	Lev. 7:23	UMT
[186]	Ex. 23:19	UM
[187]	Ex. 34:26	UM
[188]	Ex. 21:28	UM
[189]	Lev. 23:14	T
[190]	Lev. 23:14	T
[191]	Lev. 23:14	T
[192]	Lev. 19:23	T
[193]	Dt. 22:9	T?
[194]	Dt. 32:38	UM
[195]	Lev. 19:26; Dt. 21:20	UM
[196]	Lev. 23:29	J
[197]	Ex. 13:3	J

Dietary Laws

A Jew may not eat [172]cattle, [173]unclean fish, [174]unclean fowl, [175]creeping things that fly, [176]creatures that creep on the ground, [177]reptiles, [178]worms found in fruit or produce or [179]any detestable creature.

An animal that has died naturally [180]is forbidden for consumption as is [181]a torn or mauled animal. One must not eat [182]any limb taken from a living animal. Also prohibited is [183]the sinew of the thigh (gid ha-nashed) as are [184]blood and [185]certain types of fat (helev). It is forbidden [186]to boil lamb in mother's milk or [187]eat of such a mixture. It is also forbidden to eat [188]of an ox condemned to stoning (even should it have been properly slaughtered).

One may not eat [189]bread made of new corn or the new corn itself, either [190]roasted or [191]green, before the omer offering has been brought on the 16th of Nisan. You may not eat [192]orlah or [193]the growth of mixed planting in the vineyard.

Any use of [194]wine libations to idols is prohibited, as are [195]gluttony and drunkenness. One may not eat anything on [196]the Day of Atonement. During Passover it is forbidden to eat [197]leaven (hamex) or [198]anything containing an admixture of such. This is also forbidden [199]after the middle of the 14th of Nisan (the day before Passover). Dur-

[198]Ex. 13:20 J
[199]Dt. 16:3 J
[200]Ex. 13:7 J
[201]Ex. 12:19 J

ing Passover no leaven may be [200]seen or [201]found in your possession.

[202]Num. 6:3 J
[203]Num. 6:3 J
[204]Num. 6:3 J
[205]Num. 6:4 J
[206]Num. 6:4 JT
[207]Num. 6:7 J
[208]Lev. 21:11 JT
[209]Num. 6:5 JT

Nazirites

A Nazirite may not drink [202]wine or any beverage made from grapes; he may not eat [203]fresh grapes, [204]dried grapes, [205]grape seeds or [206]grape peel. He may not render himself [207]ritually impure for his dead nor may he [208]enter a tent in which there is a corpse. He must not [209]shave his hair.

Agriculture

[210]Lev. 23:22 UM
[211]Lev. 19:9 UM
[212]Lev. 19:10 UM
[213]Lev. 19:10 UM
[214]Dt. 24:18 UM
[215]Lev. 19:19 J
[216]Dt. 22:9 J
[217]Lev. 19:19 J
(215-217)—*Symbols of purity*
[218]Dt. 22:10 JUM
[219]Dt. 25:4 UM
[220]Lev. 25:4 J
[221]Lev. 25:4 JUM
(220-228)-*Ancient Israel's law with moral principles of kindness and dependence on God in non-*

It is forbidden [210]to reap the whole of a field without leaving the corners for the poor: it is also forbidden to [211]gather up the ears of corn that fall during reaping or to harvest [212]the misformed clusters of grapes, or [213]the grapes that fall or to [214]return to take a forgotten sheaf.

You must not [215]sow different species of seed together or [216]corn in a vineyard; it is also forbidden to [217]crossbreed different species of animals or [218]work with two different species yoked together. You must not [219]muzzle an animal working in a field to prevent it from eating.

It is forbidden to [220]till the earth, [221]to prune trees, [222]to reap (in the usual manner) produce or [223]fruit which has grown wthout cultivation in the seventh year (shemittah). One may also not [224]till

385

planting year.

[222]Lev. 25:4	JUM	
[223]Lev. 25:5	JUM	
[224]Lev. 25:11	JUM	
[225]Lev. 25:11	JUM	
[226]Lev. 25:11	JUM	
[227]Lev. 25:23	JUM	
[228]Lev. 25:33	JT	
[229]Dt. 12:19	JT	

the earth or prune trees in the Jubilee year, when it is also forbidden to harvest (in the usual manner) [225]produce or [226]fruit that has grown without cultivation.

One may not [227]sell one's landed inheritance in the land of Israel permanently or [228]change the lands of the Levites or [229]leave the Levites without support.

[230]Dt. 15:2	UM	
[231]Dt. 15:9	UM	
[232]Dt. 15:7	UM	
[233]Dt. 15:13	UM	
[234]Ex. 22:24	UM	
[235]Lev. 25:37	UM	
(at real profit)		
[236]Dt. 23:20	UM	
[237]Ex. 22:24	UM	
[238]Lev. 19:13	UM	
[239]Dt. 24:10	UM	
[240]Dt. 24:12	UM	
[241]Dt. 24:17	UM	
[242]Dt. 24:6	UM	
[243]Ex. 20:13	UM	
[244]Lev. 19:11	UM	
[245]Lev. 19:13	UM	
[246]Dt. 19:14	UM	
[247]Lev. 19:13	UM	
[248]Lev. 19:11	UM	

Loans, Business and the Treatment of Slaves

It is forbidden to [230]demand repayment of a loan after the seventh year, you may not, however, [231]refuse to lend to the poor because that year is approaching. Do not [232]deny charity to the poor or [233]send a Hebrew slave away empty-handed when he finishes his period of service. Do not [234]dun your debtor when you know that he cannot pay. It is forbidden to [235]lend to or [236]borrow from another Jew at interest or [237]participate in an agreement involving interest either as a guarantor, witness, or writer of the contract. Do not [238]delay payment of wages.

You may not [239]take a pledge from a debtor by violence, [240]keep a poor man's pledge when he needs it, [241]take any pledge from a widow or [242]from any debtor if he earns his living with it.

Kidnapping [243]a Jew is forbidden.

Do not [244]steal or [245]rob by violence. Do not [246]remove a landmark or [247]defraud.

It is forbidden [248]to deny receipt of a loan or

[249]Lev. 19:11	UM
[250]Lev. 25:14	UM
[251]Lev. 25:17	UM
[252]Ex. 22:20	UM
[253]Ex. 22:20	UM
[254]Dt. 23:16	UM
[255]Dt. 23:17	UM
[256]Ex. 22:21	UM
[257]Lev. 25:39	UM
[258]Lev. 25:42	UM
[259]Lev. 25:43	UM
[260]Lev. 25:53	UM
[261]Ex. 21:8	UM
[262]Ex. 21:10	UM
[263]Dt. 21:14	UM
[264]Dt. 21:14	UM
[265]Ex. 20:17	UM
[266]Dt. 5:18	UM
[267]Dt. 23:26	UM
[268]Dt. 23:25	UM
[269]Dt. 22:3	UM
[270]Ex. 23:5	UM
[271]Lev. 19:35	UM
[272]Dt. 25:13	UM

a deposit or [249]to swear falsely regarding another man's property.

You must not [250]deceive anybody in business. You may not [251]mislead a man even verbally. It is forbidden to harm the stranger among you [252]verbally or [253]do him injury in trade.

You may not [254]return, or [255]otherwise take advantage of, a slave who has fled to the land of Israel from his master, even if his master is a Jew.

Do not [256]afflict the widow or the orphan. You may not [257]misuse or [258]sell a Hebrew slave; do not [259]treat him cruelly or [260]allow a heathen to mistreat him. You must not [261]sell your Hebrew maidservant or, if you marry her, [262]withhold food, clothing, and conjugal rights from her. You must not [263]sell a female captive or [264]treat her as a slave.

Do not [265]covet another man's possessions even if you are willing to pay for them. Even [266]the desire alone is forbidden.

A worker must not [267]cut down standing corn during his work or [268]take more fruit than he can eat.

One must not [269]turn away from a lost article which is to be returned to its owner nor may you [270]refuse to help a man or an animal which is collapsing under its burden.

It is forbidden to [271]defraud with weights and measures or even [272]to possess inaccurate weights.

[273]Lev. 19:15	UM
[274]Ex. 23:8	UM
[275]Lev. 19:15	UM
[276]Dt. 1:17	UM
[277]Lev. 19:15,	UM
rather Ex. 23:3	
[278]Ex. 23:6	UM
[279]Dt. 19:13	UM
[280]Dt. 24:17	UM
[281]Ex. 23:1	UM
[282]Ex. 23:2	UM
[283]Ex. 23:2	UM
[284]Dt. 1:17	UM
[285]Ex. 20:16	UM
[286]Ex. 23:1	UM
[287]Dt. 24:16	UM
[288]Dt. 19:15	UM
[289]Ex. 20:13	UM
[290]Ex. 23:7	UM
[291]Num. 35:30	UM
[292]Num. 35:12	UM
[293]Dt. 25:12	UM
[294]Dt. 22:26	UM
[295]Num. 35:31	UM
[296]Num. 35:32	UM

Justice

A judge must not [273]perpetrate injustice, [274]accept bribes or be [275]partial or [276]afraid. He may [277]not favor the poor or [278]discriminate against the wicked; he should not [279]pity the condemned or [280]pervert the judgment of strangers or orphans.

It is forbidden to [281]hear one litigant without the other being present. A capital case cannot be decided by [282]a majority of one.

A judge should not [283]accept a colleague's opinion unless he is convinced of its correctness; it is forbidden to [284]appoint as a judge someone who is ignorant of the Law.

Do not [285]give false testimony or accept [286]testimony from a wicked person or from [287]relatives of a person involved in the case. It is forbidden to pronounce judgment [288]on the basis of the testimony of one witness.

Do not [289]murder.

You must not convict on [290]circumstantial evidence alone.

A witness [291]must not sit as a judge in capital cases.

You must not [292]execute anybody without due proper trial and conviction.

Do not [293]pity or spare the pursuer.

Punishment is not to be inflicted for [294]an act committed under duress.

Do not accept ransom [295]for a murderer or [296]a manslayer.

[297]Lev. 19:16	UM	
[298]Dt. 22:8	UM	
[299]Lev. 19:14	UM	
[300]Dt. 25:2-3	UM	
[301]Lev. 19:16	UM	
[302]Lev. 19:17	UM	
[303]Lev. 19:17	UM	
[304]Lev. 19:18	UM	
[305]Lev. 19:18	UM	
[306]Dt. 22:6	UM	
[307]Lev. 13:33	UM	
[308]Dt. 24:8	UM	
[309]Dt. 21:7	T	
[310]Ex. 22:17	UM	
(J-ancient)		
[311]Dt. 24:5	UM	
[312]Dt. 17:11	UM	
[313]Dt. 13:1	UM	
[314]Dt. 13:1	UM	
[315]Ex. 22:27	UM	
[316]Ex. 22:27	UM	
[317]Lev. 19:14	UM	
[318]Ex. 21:17	UM	
[319]Ex. 21:15	UM	
[320]Ex. 20:10	J	
[321]Ex. 16:29	J	
[322]Ex. 35:3	J	
[323]Ex. 12:16	J	
[324]Ex. 12:16	J	

Do not [297]hesitate to save another person from danger and do not [298]leave a stumbling block in the way or [299]mislead another person by giving wrong advice.

It is forbidden [300]to administer more than the assigned number of lashes to the guilty.

Do not [301]tell tales or [302]bear hatred in your heart. It is forbidden to [303]shame a Jew, [304]to bear a grudge or [305]to take revenge.

Do not [306]take the dam when you take the young birds.

It is forbidden to [397]shave a leprous scall or [308]remove other signs of that affliction.

It is forbidden [309]to cultivate a valley in which a slain body was found and in which subsequently the ritual of breaking the heifer's neck (eglah arufah) was performed.

Do not [310]suffer a witch to live.

Do not [311]force a bridegroom to perform military service during the first year of his marriage. It is forbidden to [312]rebel against the transmitters of the tradition or to [313]add or [314]detract from the precepts of the law.

Do not curse [315]a judge, [316]a ruler or [317]any Jew.

Do not [318]curse or [319]strike a parent.

It is forbidden to [320]work on the Sabbath or [321]walk further than the permitted limits (eruv). You may not [322]inflict punishment on the Sabbath.

It is forbidden to work on [323]the first or [324]the

[325]Lev. 23:21	J	
[326]Lev. 23:25	J	
[327]Lev. 23:35	J	
[328]Lev. 23:36	J	
[329]Lev. 23:28	J	

seventh day of Passover, on [325]Shavuot, on [326]Rosh Ha-Shanah, on the [327]first and [328]eighth (Shemini Azeret) days of Sukkot and [329]on the Day of Atonement.

[330]Lev. 18:7	UM	
[331]Lev. 18:8	UM	
[332]Lev. 18:9	UM	
[333]Lev. 18:11	UM	
[334]Lev. 18:10	UM	
[335]Lev. 18:20	UM	
[336]Lev. 18:10	UM	
[337]Lev. 18:17	UM	
[338]Lev. 18:17	UM	
[339]Lev. 18:17	UM	
[340]Lev. 18:12	UM	
[341]Lev. 18:13	UM	
[342]Lev. 18:14	UM	
[343]Lev. 18:15	UM	
[344]Lev. 18:16	UM	
[345]Lev. 18:18	UM	
[346]Lev. 18:19	UM	
[347]Lev. 18:20	UM	
[348]Lev. 18:23	UM	
[349]Lev. 18:23	UM	
[350]Lev. 18:22	UM	
[351]Lev. 18:7	UM	
[352]Lev. 18:14	UM	
[353]Lev. 18:6	UM	
[354]Dt. 23:3	UM	
[355]Dt. 23:18	UM	
[356]Dt. 24:4	UM	

Incest and Other Forbidden Relationships.
It is forbidden to enter into an incestuous relationship with one's [330]mother, [331]step-mother, [332]sister, [333]step-sister, [334]son's daughter, [335]daughter's daughter, [336]daughter, [337]any woman and her daughter, [338]any woman and her son's daughter, [339]any woman and her daughter's daughter, [340]father's sister, [341]mother's sister, [342]paternal uncle's wife, [343]daughter-in-law, [344]brother's wife and [345]wife's sister.

It is also forbidden to [346]have sexual relations with a menstruous woman.

Do not [347]commit adultery.

It is forbidden for [348]a man or [349]a woman to have sexual intercourse with an animal.

Homosexuality [350]is forbidden, particularly with [351]one's father or [352]uncle.

It is forbidden to have [353]intimate physical contact (even without actual intercourse) with any of the women with whom intercourse is forbidden.

A mamzer may not [354]marry a Jewess.

Harlotry [355]is forbidden.

A divorcee may not be [356]remarried to her first husband if, in the meanwhile, she had married another.

390

[357]Dt. 25:5	UM	A childless widow may not [357]marry any-
[358]Dt. 22:29	UM	body other than her late husband's
[359]Dt. 22:19	UM	brother.
[360]Dt. 23:2	UM	A man may not [358]divorce a wife whom he
[361]Lev. 22:24	UM	married after having raped her or

[359]after having slandered her.

An eunuch may not [360]marry a Jewess.

Castration [361]is forbidden.

[362]Dt. 17:15	J	**The Monarchy.**
[363]Dt. 17:16	JUM	*(Jewish Ancient—with moral principles)*
[364]Dt. 17:17	UM	You may not [362]elect as king anybody who is
[365]Dt. 17:17	JUM	not of the seed of Israel.

The king must not accumulate an excessive
number of [363]horses, [364]wives, or
[365]wealth.

MAJOR WRITINGS SUPPORTING POSITIONS TAKEN IN THIS BOOK

T HE WHOLE OF THE VIEWPOINT given in this book is a product of my own integrative work. I bear full responsibility for the positions outlined herein. The presentation is in *no way* an exhaustive one and I expect that further study will add to my knowledge and cause the revision of certain positions, but I have confidence in the basic thrust of the book. My position is one gained from study, and I am indebted to many writers, as is evidenced by endnotes. However, I wish here to list major works that support my basic conclusions. The list could be significantly expanded, but only works predominantly in print in America are represented here. Full publication details are listed in the Bibliography. I do not necessarily agree with these works in their entirety.

1. SAMUELE BACCHIOCCHI, *From Saturday to Sunday*

Bacchiocchi is in accord with B. Bagatti's position (see below) and applies his effort to show how the Church severed its Jewish connection and how its practice differed from Messianic Jews of the first century. He emphasizes the switch from Saturday to Sunday worship in the second century as part of this study.

2. B. BAGGATI, *The Church Of the Circumcision*

This unfortunately hard-to-get work (although available in many Catholic university libraries) is a *seminal work*. Bagatti claims that the early movement of followers of Jesus among Jews was far more extensive than most imagine. He also argues that the Jewish Christians were faithful to Torah and that this was in accord with apostolic *example* and teaching as concerns Jewish believers. Bagatti distinguishes the Nazarenes, who fully followed New Testament teaching, and the Ebionites, who did not.

3. MARCUS BARTH, "JEWS AND GENTILES: THE SOCIAL CHARACTER OF JUSTIFICATION IN PAUL"

Barth, the illustrious son of Karl Barth, argues that Paul himself was Torah-loyal. He was not anti-Torah at all, but only against the loss of the sense of open fellowship between Jews and non-Jewish Christians who were to maintain acceptance despite different identities *vis-a-vis* Torah.

4. MARKUS BOCKMUEL, *Jewish Law in Gentile Churches*

This important book by the former Cambridge professor, now at St. Andrews, details the thrust of Paul's position on the continued distinction in Jewish calling and how the law applies differently to Jews and Gentiles. It is very helpful to a Messianic Jewish position. It traces the Pauline position on the potential salvation of Gentiles without circumcision to the Hillel school of the Pharisees.

5. DARRELL L. BOCK AND MITCH GLASER, *To the Jew First: the Case for Jewish Evangelism in Scripture and History*

This amazing collection of essays published in 2008 is very supportive of Messianic Jewish theology. Contributors include esteemed theologians such as Dr. Walter Kaiser, former President of Gordon Conwell, noted Old Testament professor, Dr. Bock himself, and several other high-level thinkers.

6. ALAN COLE, *Epistle of Paul to the Galatians (Tyndale New Testament Commentaries)*

This work is also excellent in these regards. See especially his introduction.

7. JEAN DANIELOU, *The Theology of Jewish Christianity*

It is out of print in America and available in England, also in the magazine *Cross Currents* (1968). Danielou examines the theological concepts of the early Jewish believers and firmly distinguishes the heretical Ebionites from the Nazarenes, whom he emphasizes were true to the New Testament. He also sees the Apostles and the Nazarenes as Torah-loyal and even calls for a wing of the Church which will be liturgically Hebraic. All this from a Catholic cardinal!

8. DAVID DAUBE, *The New Testament and Rabbinic Judaism*

This work outlines the interrelationship very positively. We might note in passing that it is difficult to find *scholars in the area of early Jewish Christianity* who disagree with the above positions since the early sources are so clear in regard to the Jewish loyalty of the Nazarenes.

9. W.D. DAVIES, *Paul and Rabbinic Judaism*

This is a true classic, outlining Paul's debt to and difference from Pharisaical Judaism. Davies argues that Paul was *fully*

Torah-loyal and never gave up his sense of being part of Israel and that Israel was still God's people with a unique calling.

10. GREGORY DIX, *Jew and Greek: A Study in the Primitive Christian Church*

Dix also argues that the Apostolic Church within Jewry saw itself as Torah-loyal and that this was simply part of their calling in Israel.

11. JOHN FISCHER, ED., *THE ENDURING PARADOX*

Many scholars have written supportive essays on Messianic Judaism dealing with a variety of topics and issues.

12. FULLER THEOLOGICAL SEMINARY, STATEMENT ON JEWISH-CHRISTIAN RELATIONS

It includes a section in clear defense of Messianic Jewish Congregations. This is in accord with the School of World Mission at FTS, which argues for the closest identification possible with any culture in reaching them for the Gospel. In line with this, see D. McGaven's *Understanding Church Growth,* sections on Jews (see his index).

13. PHIL GOBLE, *Everything You Need to Grow a Messianic Synagogue*

Goble received his PhD from Fuller and argues passionately for Messianic Judaism.

14. LOUIS GOLDBERG, *God, Torah, and Messiah*

These important essays of Dr. Goldberg, a scholar at Moody Bible Institute, who defended the Messianic Jewish movement for almost forty years, was compiled by Rich Robinson.

15. DOUGLAS HARINK, *Paul Among the Post Liberals*

This important book has a powerful refutation of replacement theology and strongly supports Messianic Jewish conclusions in theology. A must read.

16. RICHARD HARVEY, *Mapping Messianic Jewish Theology, a Constructive Approach*

This important book by British Messianic Jewish scholar Richard Harvey, based on his PhD dissertation, presents the theologies of those who embrace Jewish calling in the New Covenant. It is an important summary and evaluation.

17. JIM HUTCHINS, "THE CASE FOR MESSIANIC JUDAISM"

Hutchins, the former chaplain of Wheaton College, develops the case well and is in accord with most positions taken here.

18. JULES ISAAC, *Jesus and Israel*

The Jewish scholar argues beautifully concerning the positive Jewish identity of Jesus and His teaching to encourage such.

19. ALEX JACOB, THE CASE FOR ENLARGEMENT THEOLOGY

He gives a very fine case for a Messianic Jewish identity and a strong biblical exposition.

20. ELMER JOSEPHSON, *Israel: God's Key to World Redemption*

Josephson argues strongly concerning God's continuing covenant with Israel and her call to Torah. However, Josephson evidences no knowledge of Messianic Judaism, though he says much of positive value about the Law.

21. MARK KINZER, *Post Missionary Messianic Judaism*

In this important book, Messianic Jewish scholar Kinzer makes the case for distinctive Messianic Jewish congregations and its theology. There is very strong exegesis. In this book, on evaluating the last forty years, I do mention some areas of my concern. Also see Kinzer's book *Israel's Messiah and the People of God*, an important Messianic Jewish perspective on many issues by an important Messianic Jewish scholar.

22. RICHARD LONGENECKER'S WORKS

Longenecker is an evangelical scholar who has authored *several excellent books* that deal with issues which concern us. His first book, *Paul Apostle of Liberty*, shows that Paul's philosophy of grace and liberty is not at all inconsistent with his practice of the Law. This book gives an appendix both describing and defending the practice of the first Jewish followers of Yeshua in keeping the Law. His books, *The Christology of Early Jewish Christianity* and *Biblical Exegesis in the Apostolic Period*, also give excellent information for interpreting difficult passages that would relate to Messianic Judaism.

23. THOMAS McCOMISKEY, *The Covenants of Promise*

In this important book on the relationship between the covenants, Professor Dr. McComiskey comes to conclusions that strongly support a Messianic Jewish theology.

24. MARK NANOS, *The Mystery of Romans and The Irony of Galatians*

These books of exposition by a Reform Jewish scholar who takes decidedly Messianic Jewish positions.

25. RAY PRITZ, *Nazarene Jewish Christianity*

In this important book, Pritz demonstrates the theology and perspective of the early Messianic Jewish movement from the first to the fourth centuries and shows continuity with today's Messianic Jewish theology.

26. PETER RICHARDSON, *Israel in the Apostolic Church*

In this important book, some of our central viewpoints on Israel and the Law are espoused—especially in understanding Romans 9–11.

27. RICH ROBINSON, *The Messianic Movement: A Field Guide for Evangelical Christians*

While not important for its theological content, since it leaves out the most important Messianic Jewish thinkers, it nevertheless places Jews for Jesus as aligning with the Messianic Jewish movement. Dr. Robinson is one of the more important scholars in the Jews for Jesus organization.

28. DAVID J. RUDOLPH, *A Jew to the Jews*

This book is based on Dr. Rudolph's PhD dissertation at Cambridge University under Dr. Markus Bockmuel. It is a passionate defense of the distinct calling of Messianic Jewish people with a very strong exposition of First Corinthians 7.

29. HUGH SCHONFELD, *The History of Jewish Christianity*

This work (which is out of print) gives a good summary, as well as a description of the Jewish identity of the early Jewish followers of Jesus. The book does have Ebionite tendencies. Of note is that this book records the tireless efforts of Mark John Levy, the first general secretary to the Hebrew Christian Alliance, who worked for a position similar to our position on the calling of Messianic Jews. Eichorn, in *The Evangelization of the American Jew*, points to Levy as one of the few exceptions to unscrupulous behavior among Jewish Christians and praises Levy's sincerity. Through

Levy's efforts, the Episcopal Church adopted in 1914 a statement which supported Levy's position as well as the establishment of Hebraic congregations.

30. Hans J. Schoeps' Works

Schoep has written several works on the early Jewish Christians. He emphasizes Ebionite history and theology, but does recognize the Torah importance among many early Jewish Christians. The *Jewish-Christian Argument* is one of his few books in print in English.

31. Samuel Schultz, *The Gospel of Moses and Deuteronomy: the Gospel of Love*

As a supporter of Messianic Judaism, these titles already indicate the ground Schultz is breaking.

32. R. Kendall Soulen, *The God of Israel and Christian Theology*

I consider this the most important pro-Messianic Jewish theological perspective written to date from a Christian scholar. Soulen is the Methodist professor of systematic theology at Wesley Theological seminary. His book is a comprehensive theological vision that includes such topics of God's purpose in creation, the eschatological vision, the relationship of Israel and the nations, and Israel and the Church, with very strong implications for Messianic Judaism.

33. David Stern, *Messianic Judaism, Restoring the Jewishness of the Gospel*, and *Jewish New Testament Commentary*

These important books present Messianic Jewish views that are very much in accord with my books.

34. CORRIE TEN BOOM, *In My Father's House*

This book is of note because it describes Corrie's brother, Casper ten Boom, of the famous family. Casper came to Messianic Jewish conclusions in his doctor's thesis in Germany. He concluded that Jewish followers of Jesus were called to maintain their heritage, perhaps in unique congregations. The ten Boom family survivors have been supportive of Messianic Judaism.

35. PETER TOMSON, *Paul and the Jewish Law*

This is an important book detailing the application of law in the writings of Paul and showing very strong distinctions in the calling of Jewish and Gentiles followers of Yeshua. It very strongly supports Messianic Jewish theological conclusions.

36. MICHAEL WYSCHOGROD, IN *Evangelicals and Jews in Conversation* (ED. MARC TANENBAUM, MARVIN WILSON, A. JAMES RUDIN)

Wyschogrod is a Jewish scholar who concludes that Paul was Torah-loyal and expected other Jewish Christians to be Torah-loyal. His issue was not a Jew's call, but forcing Judaism on non-Jewish believers. *Wyschogrod is one of the few Jewish scholars who, without following Yeshua, understands Paul and the Law.* Even his book, which was written to counter Messianic Judaism and Christian missionary efforts among Jews *(Judaism and Hebrew Christianity), fairly* presents Paul and the Law. Wyschogrod argues that the Apostles and Paul still considered themselves part of Israel and practiced Torah, although they understood justification only by grace.

37. JOHN HOWARD YODER, *The Politics of Jesus*

Yoder picks up this theme and argues forcefully that Torah loyalty among Jews was never at issue (see page 220). His most recent collected essays, written shortly before his death, in *The Jewish Christian Schism Revisited*, contains remarkable essays arguing that a Jewish living Jewish Christianity could have survived and could yet again succeed. History is not a fixed logical system.

OTHERS

Already mentioned, the book *Evangelicals and Jews in Conversation,* eds. Marc H. Tanenbaum, Marvin R. Wilson, A. James Rudin (Grand Rapids, MI: Baker, 1978), is a helpful compendium of Jewish and evangelical views. Many articles give a sense of understanding the reaffirmed Jewish calling among the first century Apostles and Jewish believers.

We should also note that the late-nineteenth-century famous scholars, F.J.A. Hort and J.B. Lightfoot came to similar conclusions, especially in writings specifically on Jewish Christianity.

FULLER THEOLOGICAL
SEMINARY NEWS RELEASE

PASADENA, CALIFORNIA—DEAN ARTHUR F. GLASSER and the
School of World Mission faculty of Fuller Theological Seminary have released the following statement:

We of the School of World Mission faculty of Fuller Theological Seminary feel constrained to address ourselves and the Church at large concerning the Jewish people. Particularly so at this time when the third commonwealth of Israel is celebrating its 28th anniversary and when we find ourselves much in prayer that the Jewish presence in the Middle East shall become under God an instrument for reconciliation and peace.

We are profoundly grateful for the heritage given to us by the Jewish people which is so vital for own Christian faith. We believe that God used the Jewish people as the sole repository of the history-centered disclosure of himself to mankind. This revelation began with Abraham and continued to the Jewish writers of the New Testament. Not only were the oracles of God committed to them (Romans 3:2), but it was through this people that God chose to bring Jesus Christ into the world. We believe that he is the only hope of salvation for the Jewish people, and for all mankind. Indeed, we continue to pray that through the mercy and blessing of God, the Jewish people shall turn to the Messiah Jesus and become once again a light to the nations, that his salvation may reach to the end of the earth (Isa. 49:6).

We wish to charge the Church, as a whole, to do more than merely include the Jewish people in their evangelistic outreach. We would encourage an active response to the mandate of Romans 1:16 calling for evangelism "to the Jew first." For this we have the precedent of a great Jewish missionary, the Apostle Paul. Though sent to the Gentile world, he never relinquished his burden for his own kinsmen after the flesh. Wherever he travelled, he first visited the synagogue before presenting Christ to the Gentiles. So it must be in every generation. We must provide a priority opportunity for our Jewish friends to respond to the Messiah. They are our benefactors and it was they who first evangelized us. Furthermore, the Gospel we share with them must be carried to all tribes and peoples and tongues.

We regret exceedingly that Christians have not always shared this Gospel with the Jewish people in a loving and ethical manner. Too often, while interested in Jewish evangelism in general, we have demeaned the dignity of the Jewish person by our unkind stereotyping and our disregard for Jewish sensitivities. How un-Christlike we have been!

Likewise, we have unwittingly encouraged Jewish converts to divest themselves of their Jewish heritage and culture. For this too, we would repent and express our regret that the Western influence on our beliefs has precluded the original Jewish context. Our Church is culturally and spiritually poorer for it.

In our day we are encouraged that thousands of Jewish people are coming to the Messiah. This being so, we cannot but call upon the Christian community to renew its commitment to share lovingly the Gospel of Jesus with the Jewish people. And we heartily encourage Jewish believers in him, including those who call themselves Messianic Jews, Hebrew-Christians, and Jews for Jesus, to retain their Jewish heritage, culture, religious practices and marriage customs within the context of a sound biblical theology expressing Old and New Testament truth. Their freedom in Christ to do this cannot but enrich the Church in our day.

More, we feel it incumbent on Christians in all traditions to reinstate the work of Jewish evangelism in their mission-ary obedience. Jewish-oriented programs should be developed. Appropriate agencies for Jewish evangelism should be formed. And churches everywhere should support those existing insti-tutions which are faithfully and lovingly bearing a Christian witness to the Jewish people.

Pasadena, California, May 12, 1976

WHEN IS RITUAL IDOLATRY?

OVER THE FORTY PLUS YEARS of the Messianic Jewish move-ment, an undercurrent of disagreement concerning the place of Jewish ritual has existed among Messianic Jews. On the mild side, the disagreement is expressed in nonjudgmental terms—"The Spirit of God has led us to include (or exclude) these traditional rituals as part of our life and worship expression." The more radical opinion is sometimes voiced that ritual is idolatry.

Certainly God would never have given rituals if ritual in and of itself was idolatry. The most explicit directions for ritual were given for cleansings, sacrifices, priestly functions, ordinations, and other Temple procedures. The Spirit of God Himself filled the Tabernacle and the later Temple of Solomon, which was the cen-ter of Jewish rituals. Hence, *we can safely and forever conclude that ritual is not idolatry.*

Can ritual, however, become idolatry? Are there dangers in ritual? Are there guidelines for leaders who will, by their leader-ship, be greatly influencing the spiritual life and perspective of their flocks? The answer to all of these questions is "yes."

First of all, it is crucial to define *idolatry* in its broad sense. *Idolatry* is not simply bowing down to a statue. Scripture defines *idolatry* as "worshipping and serving created things rather than the Creator" (see Rom. 1:25).

To worship is to bow down, to give our heart's allegiance. Yet God has said, "You shall love the Lord thy God with all thy heart...." Everything, then, that is loved must be loved *in the Lord*. Hence, idolatry can occur whenever we give an allegiance to something that is not in the Lord. In idolatry, a person derives a meaning or significance from something beyond what it is meant by God to give. These false meanings give a *false basis of self-worth*. External achievements, the pride of position, and even an attachment to family and friends outside of God's order is idolatry. (He that loves father or mother more than Me is not worthy of Me.) The loss of a major idol leads to bitterness, insecurity, and depression. Idolatry is often a projection of self-worship.

In the same way, of course, attachment to ritual and tradition can be idolatry. So can anti-tradition and an idolatrous attachment to spontaneity for its own sake. I have seen so-called free services that were rote and allowed no real moving of the Spirit. We can go through the motions of spontaneous worship without being Spirit-led or empowered! On the other hand, a Jew may be attached to Jewish tradition and ritual or even musical style as an extension of self-worship and the wrong kind of Jewish pride (as opposed to healthy self-esteem).

Let us not forget that there are also Anglican idols and Pentecostal idols! Every group has the potential to spawn its own unique idolatry, a pride expressing self-worship projected into form or anti-form. Ritual can be entered into with a background of fear like unto superstition.

The avoidance of self-worship and idolatry in ritual (and in spontaneous orders of service) is simple and profound. It is the Sh'ma, to love God with our all. *The deeper we enter into the love of God with our all and enter into our position as ascended with the Messiah in the heavenlies* (see Eph. 2:6), *the less we will have of idolatry of any kind. The more we experience of the supernatural love and power of God, the less there is of idolatry.*

Heartless religion is idolatrous self-religion. Preoccupation with form or lack of form will never deliver us, but only pressing into depth with God will deliver. Ritual should be a valuable expression, a tool of teaching, a revealer of God's majesty and grace; or it may be idolatry, a means of avoiding the reality of God, a hiding behind the merely familiar, self-worship, a precluding of the surprise of the Spirit's revelation. Indeed, what it is for one, it may not be for another.

There *are* some ways to lead so as to avoid idolatry. We who are in leadership need to develop a keen sense of the Spirit's leading; leaders should be more keenly aware of the Spirit's prompting. What we are and do will pervade the community. We lead the services, and we model spiritual life. Hence, the Spirit's reality and leading must not be nebulous to us.

Under the New Covenant, we must always be sensitive to the Holy Spirit; He may tell us to do something different or the same. If we assume an order without the Spirit's being free to change our direction, we can fall into rote ritual; this can lead to idolatry at worst or simply be dead habit or laziness. The Holy Spirit may have a reason for telling us to do something quite unusual. Who knows the condition of someone in our midst and how this will impact upon him? Moment-by-moment obedience to the Spirit as a definite presence precludes idolatry. Hence, the chief criterion for a worship leader is not his voice, bearing, diction, etc., but his ability to hear the Spirit in the context of worship. In our congregation, several sensitive men are all free to hear the Spirit in a type of team leadership. When we restrict the Spirit's moving, we have taken a step that brings us closer to idolatry. He may lead us to do the Torah service the same way fifty times, but the fifty-first may be radically different. The fixed elements are not absolutely fixed; the idolatry of those seeking spontaneity for its entertainment value is also precluded by the Spirit, who may lead in repeating some things week to week. We are thus required to perceive new things in the familiar.

How well I recall an elder going to the Ark by a Holy Spirit prompting and taking the scroll out of the Ark during a praise-worship time. At first I was a bit taken aback, but then a sense of God's glory and joy pervaded the service. It was not the usual order, but thank God for this worship leader's chutzpah. Usually we are led to a similar pattern, but not always. Let us not mistake mere human creativity for the Spirit's leading, either. However, one mark of Holy Spirit religion is surprise and newness in which He breaks through and manifests Himself. One mark of His absence is that all things continue always in the same way.

Second, when change *prompted by the Holy Spirit* produces anger, insecurity, and fear, there is idolatry or at least over-attachment and insecurity. We emphasize "prompted by the Spirit" to distinguish it from our own foolishness, though the things of the Spirit may seem foolish to the flesh, the natural man, who receives not the things of the Spirit (see 1 Cor. 2:14)! We must not have ritual as a security blanket or as a source of false identity. Our identity is in Yeshua and the Spirit of the Lord, that we are in the Messiah. The same words may be penned against fleshy spontaneity. Yet the New Covenant age is an age of the Spirit, who can be the leader of our worship and life. Through a genuinely "in tune" spiritual leadership, He will do fresh and sometimes unusual things, demonstrating His presence. It is good to allow for such Holy Spirit leadership and freshness. Furthermore, it is good to have enough change to flush out the idolatry in our midst and to be able to deal with it.

The guard against idolatry can be summarized under the concept of never entering the place where the Spirit may not say "yes" or "no" to our order, either in part or in totality from week to week. It is to enter into the deep things of God. It is to be leaders who know the reality of the Spirit and the Word. In all of this, it is incumbent upon us to educate ourselves and our people so that we may be a people of the Spirit. We must have confidence in our ability to hear Him and the courage to step out in what we hear if tested by the Word. Ritual is as a frame for a picture. The picture is the manifestation of the Lord in power. Messianic Judaism is the means of conveying the power of the Gospel in the most communicative way to the Jewish community. The proper frame enhances this work. Yet, let us not confuse the picture and the frame by improper valuation. God has given a structure of life to preserve our people. Within that structure, the power of God is the essential thing.

ENDNOTES

PREFACE

1. See standard Israeli Dictionary under Messianic Jews in Hebrew (Yihu-dai Mishaheem) in public lecture by Luis Goldberg (Moody Bible Institute forum, 1981).

CHAPTER ONE

1. W.F. Albright, *From the Stone Age to Christianity* (Garden City, NY: Double Day Anchor, 1957). See early chapters on pre-Abrahamic religion in the Near East.

2. Daniel Juster, *The Irrevocable Calling*, second edition (Clarksville, MD: Lederer, 2007), 5-9.

3. Several sources on this are Elmer Josephson Israel, *God's Key to World Redemption* (Hillsburo, KS: Bible Light, 1974), see "circumcision" in Index; and S.I. McMillan, *None of These Diseases* (Westwood, NJ: Fleming H. Revell, 1958).

4. Albright, *From the Stone Age to Christianity*. See material on Exodus and God's name.

5. Dr. Walter Kaiser, former President of Gordon Conwell Seminary in Massachusetts, from my notes in a lecture in 1975 at American Messianic Fellowship in Chicago.

6. See especially Kenneth Kitchen, *Ancient Orient and Old Testament* (Downers Grove, IL: Intervarsity Press, 1966); and *The Reliability of the Old Testament* (Grand Rapids, MI: William B. Eerdmans, 1963); and Meredith Kline, *Treaty of the Great King* (Grand Rapids, MI: William B. Eerdmans, 2003); and *The Structure of Biblical Authority* (Grand Rapids, MI: William B. Eerdmans, 1972).

7. Samuele Bacchiochi, *From Saturday to Sunday* (Rome: The Pontifical Gregorian University Press, 1977). Excellent summary of Adventists views with some solid conclusions and some questionable conclusions.

8. Samuel Schultz, *Deuteronomy, the Gospel of Love* (Chicago: Moody Press, 1973); and *The Gospel of Moses* (New York: Harper and Row, 1974).

9. George Ladd, *New Testament Theology* (Grand Rapids, MI: William B. Eerdmans, 1993), 497ff. Ladd was one of the world's most renowned evangelical New Testament scholars.

10. Juster, *The Irrevocable Calling*, 12-14. *Pirque Avot* in the Talmud notes that the Temple preserved the world.

11. Elmer Josephson, *Israel, God's Key to World Redemption* (Hillsburo, KS: Bible Light, 1974), 219ff. He is one of the few popular Christian writers who comprehend this.

12. Edwin Yamiuchi shows in *E.T.S. Journal* that the usual linguistic identification of Gog, Magog, Meshech, and Tubal to the Soviet Union is suspect.

13. See John Walvoord, *The Millenial Kingdom* (Grand Rapids, MI: Dunham, 1959), who argues cogently for a sacrificial system.

14. On this, see the excellent article by Carl Armerding—"An Evangelical Understanding of Israel" in *Evangelicals and Jews in Conversation*.

15. Markus Bockmuehl, *Jewish Law in Gentile Churches*; also David Rudolph has a Cambridge PhD thesis which

powerfully extends Bockmuel's argument. He has a summary of part of this in his essay "Paul's Rule in the Churches."

16. Charles Ryrie, *Dispensationalism Today* (Chicago: Moody Press, 1979). An excellent summary of a moderate dispensational position.

17. For this see Ian Murray, *The Puritan Hope* (London: Banner of Truth, 1971).

CHAPTER TWO

1. N.T. Wright, *The New Testament and the People of God* (Minneapolis, MN: Fortress, 1992), sections on the Gospels, 373-417. Also, *Jesus and the Victory of God* (Minneapolis, MN: Fortress, 1996).

2. See Richard N. Longenecker, *Biblical Exegesis in the Apostolic Period* (Grand Rapids, MI: Eerdmans, 1975). The whole chapter on Matthew is excellent in this regard.

3. F.F. Bruce, *The New Testament Development of Old Testament Themes* (London: Tyndale, 1968). Emphasizes that John also used a *Moses/Jesus* parallelism in his Gospel. See also Wayne Meeks, *The Prophet King* (New York: E.J. Brill, 1967)—a whole book devoted to this theme.

4. Two writers that are especially good on this section of Matthew and the context of the Kingdom having come are Bishop N.T. Wright, *Jesus and the Victory of God*, and Dallas Willard, *The Divine Conspiracy* (San Francisco: Harper, 1998). The reader should be alerted with regard to N.T. Wright. He is brilliant, but is pervasively replacement in theology.

5. Craig Keener's *A Commentary on the Gospel of Matthew* (Grand Rapids, MI: Eerdmans, 1999) gives an account of the different approaches and interpretations. He represents the consensus.

6. David Instone-Brewer, *Traditions of the Rabbis from the Ear of the New Testament, Prayer and Agriculture, Vol. 1* (Grand Rapids, MI: Eerdmans, 2004), 55.

7. Elmer Josephson, *God's Key to Health and Happiness* (Hillsboro, KS: Bible Light, 1976). On the food lists.

8. This is noted in N.T. Wright, *Jesus and the Victory of God;* Markus Bochmuehl, *Jewish Law in Gentile Churches* (London: T.T. Clark, 2000); and Harvey Faulk, *Jesus the Pharisee* (Eugene: Wipf & Stock, 2003).

9. On these chapters in John, the commentary by Raymond Brown, *The Gospel of John* (Garden City, NY: Doubleday, 1966) is superb and comprehensive.

10. R.N. Longenecker, *Biblical Exegesis in the Apostolic Period* (Grand Rapids, MI: Eerdmans, 1975). Especially see the chapter on Matthew. See also Krister Stendahl, *The School of St. Matthew, and its use of the Old Testament* second ed. (Uppsala: C.W.K. Gleerup, Lund, 1954, 1968).

11. Wright, *The New Testament and the People of God*, 380-381.

12. *Jesus' Promise to the Nations* (in German, 1956), trans. S.H. Hooke (1958) (Minneapolis, MN: Fortress, 1982).

13. R.N. Longenecker, *Biblical Exegesis in the Apostolic Period.* Especially see the chapter on Matthew. See also Krister Stendahl, *The School of St. Matthew.*

14. J.N.D. Anderson—*Christianity, the Witness of History* (London: Tyndale Press, 1969); Pinchas Lapide, *Resurrection, a Jewish Perspective* (Minneapolis, MN: Fortress, 1988)— in which an Orthodox Rabbi argues that the resurrection really happened—and N.T. Wright, *Surprised by Hope* (New York: Harper Collins, 2008).

15. Merrill Tenney, *The Reality of the Resurrection* (New York: Harper and Row, 1963).

16. Meridith Kline, *The Structure of Biblical Authority* (Grand Rapids, MI: Eerdmans, 1972). The whole book solidly supports this thesis.

17. Thomas McComiskey, *Covenants of Promise* (Grand Rapids, MI: Baker, 1985).

18. I. Howard Marshall, *Luke: Historian and Theologian* (Grand Rapids, MI: Zondervan, 1978); and H. Conzelmann, *The Theology of St. Luke* (London, 1960). See also R.L. Harris, *The Inspiration and Canonicity of the Bible* (Grand Rapids, MI: Zondervan, 1976) on Luke.

19. Ibid.

20. Cf. E. Powell Davies, *The First Christian* (Indianapolis, IN: Hackett Publishing, 1957).

21. See R.N. Longenecker, *Biblical Exegesis in the Apostolic Period* on Paul; and the monumental work *Paul and Rabbinic Judaism* by W.D. Davies (New York: Harper Torchbooks, 1948). This is known as the South Galatian theory.

22. James Dunn, The Parting of the Ways (London, SCM, 1991); and N.T. Wright, *The New Testament and the People of God.*

23. Excellently brought out in the *Politics of Jesus* by John Howard Yoder, (Grand Rapids, MI: Eerdmans, 1994), 220. This is now a common view in the new perspective on Paul scholars (Krister Stendahl, James Dunn, N.T Wright, and others), who think the issue in Galatians was not how to attain personal salvation, but inclusion in the fellowship of the people of God. Also see Mark Nanos, *The Irony of Galatians* (Minneapolis, MN: Fortress Press, 2009).

24. See Eusebius, Ecclesiastical history, Ch. 23; and Josephus, *Antiquities* Book 9, Chapter 1.

25. Several books bring this out. Note especially Michael Wyshogrod, "Judaism and Evangelical Christianity," in *Evangelicals and Jews in Conversation*, Eds. Marc H.

Tanenbaum, Marvin R. Wilson, A. James Rudin (Grand Rapids, MI: Baker, 1978), 45-46; H. Schonfeld, *The History of Jewish Christianity* (New York: 1930); and B. Bagatti, *The Church of the Circumcision* (Rome: Pontifical Biblical Institute, 1971).

26. Ibid. Bagatti. See also J. Danielieu, *The Theology of Jewish Christianity* (London: Dartou, Longman and Todd, 1964).

27. On this, see Bochmuehl, *Jewish Law in Gentile Churches;* and David Rudolph, "Paul's Rule in the Churches," who provides us a very complete argument on the implications of this passage. This is a summary of part of his PhD thesis listed in the bibliography.

28. See W.D. Davies, *Paul and Rabbinic Judaism* on this passage references. Also see Longenecker, *Paul the Apostle of Liberty* (Grand Rapids, MI: Eerdmans, 1976), on the same passages. See Acts 22:3; 23:6-7.

29. Longenecker, *Paul the Apostle of Liberty,* Appendix P, 280-281; and W.D. Davies, *Paul and Rabbinic Judaism,* Conclusion.

30. H.L. Ellison, "Paul and the Law," in Ward Gasque and Ralph Martin, eds., *Apostolic History and the Gospel* (London: Paternoster Press, 1970). See also Longenecker, Yoder, and Batatti, quoted above.

31. Opsit. Yoder.

32. W.D. Davies, Conclusion.

CHAPTER THREE

1. Stanely Stowers, *A Rereading of Romans* (New Haven, CT: Yale University Press, 1994).

2. This doctrine is known as corporate solidarity. See H. Wheeler Robinson, *Corporate Personality in Ancient Israel,* revised edition (Edinburgh: T. & T. Clark, 1981).

3. N.T. Wright, *Justification* (Downers Grove, IL: Intervarsity Press, 2009), 109-140. James Dunn, *The Parting of the Ways* (London: SCM, 1991).

4. See Appendix 2 on the 1,050 plus New Testament commands.

5. John Calvin, Institutes of the Christian Religion, Book II, Sec. 7ff.

6. Eric Berne, *Transactional Analysis and Psychotherapy* (Castle, 1961), and Thomas Harris, *I'm Okay—You're Okay* (New York: Harper Perennial, 2004), explicitly bring this out throughout their writings as a psychological confirmation of the teaching on grace.

7. Norman Grubb, *Rees Howells Intercessor,* revised edition (Philadelphia: Christian Literature Crusade, 1986), a great classic on prayer.

8. Markus Bockmuel, *Jewish Law in Gentile Churches* (London: T & T Clark, 2000).

9. See quoted works by W.D. Davies and Charles Caldwell Ryrie in Journal *of Evangelical Theological Society* on "The Israel of God" (Spring, 1978). Also, Carl Armerding, "The Meaning of Israel in Evangelical Thought" in *Evangelicals and Jews in Conversation,* Eds. Marc H. Tanenbaum, Marvin R. Wilson, A. James Rudin (Grand Rapids, MI: Baker, 1978), 128. Also, H. Berkhof, "Israel as a Theological Problem in the Christian Church," *Journal of Ecumenical Studies VI* (Summer 1969), 335.

10. See the fine Article by Armerding on Romans 9–11, as a whole and H.L. Ellison's great book, *The Mystery of Israel* (Grand Rapids, MI: Eerdmans, 1966), a truly fine exposition of Romans 9–11. This is Ryrie's interpretation above. The best explanation of this passage to my knowledge is H.L. Ellison's "Paul and the Law" in Gasque and Martin's *Apostolic History and the Gospel* (London: Paternoster Press, 1970).

11. *New Catachism,* para. 674.

12. N.T. Wright, *The New Testament and the People of God* (Minneapolis, MN: Fortress, 1992) and *Jesus and the Victory of God* (Minneapolis, MN: Fortress, 1996); Stephen Sizer, *Christian Zionism* (Downers Grove, IL, InterVarsity Press, 2004); Gary Burge, *Whose Land, Whose Promise* (Cleveland: Pilgrim, 2003); R. Kendall Soulen, *The God of Israel and Christian Theology* (Minneapolis, MN: Augsburg-Fortress, 1996), and Colin Chapman, *Whose Promised Land* (Tring, Herts, England: Lion Publishing, 1983).

13. Douglas Harink, *Paul Among the Post Liberals* (Grand Rapids, MI: Brazos Press, 2003) for a refutation of the replacement thrust of this interpretation.

14. C.E.B. Cranfield, "A Critical and Exegetical Commentary on the Epistle to the Romans," in *The International Critical Commentary,* vol. 2 (Edinburgh: T & T Clark Limited, 1979); Ellison, *The Mystery of Israel;* and John Murray, *The Epistle to the Romans* (Grand Rapids, MI: Eerdmans, 1997).

CHAPTER FOUR

1. Most *classic* Dispensationalists have taken the non- or anti-Messianic Jewish view.

2. Alan Cole. *The Epistle of Paul to the Galatians: An Introduction and Commentary,* The Tyndale New Testament Commentaries, vol 9 (Grand Rapids, MI: Eerdmans, 1978), Introduction. This is a good commentary on Galatians. Also, Mark Nanos, *The Irony of Galatians* (Minneapolis, MN: Fortress Press, 2009).

3. R. Kendall Soulen, *The God of Israel and Christian Theology* (Minneapolis, MN: Augsburg-Fortress, 1996). This is the ongoing theme of Soulen's book, namely that God desires a variety in creation of mutual blessing. This variety includes the variety of ethnic peoples and Israel and the nations is the first distinction that shows God's intent.

4. John Howard Yoder, *The Politics of Jesus* (Grand Rapids, MI: Eerdmans, 1994), 220.

5. R.A. Cole, The Epistle of Paul to the Galatians.

6. Edward J. Young, *Thy Word is Truth* (Grand Rapids, MI: Eerdmans, 1957), in the section on the Nuzi and Mari tablets and the Patriarchal parallels.

7. Elmer Josephson, *Israel: God's Key to World Redemption* (Hillsburo, KS: Bible Light, 1974) and R.N. Longenecker, *Biblical Exegesis in the Apostolic Period* (Grand Rapids, MI: Eerdmans, 1975) and *Paul: the Apostle of Liberty* (Grand Rapids, MI: Eerdmans, 1976).

8. Introductions in J.W. Bowman, *Layman's Bible Commentaries* (SCM, 1963).

9. Longenecker, *Biblical Exegesis in the Apostolic Period,* chapter on Hebrews; Yigael Yadin, "The Dead Sea Scrolls and the Epistle to the Hebrews," *Aspects of the Dead Sea Scrolls* (Scripture Hierosoly Mitana IV) eds. C. Rabin and Y. Yadin (1958), 36-55. Also, Celsus Spieq quoted in *Longnecker,* 161.

10. See J. Danielou, *The Theology of Jewish Christianity* (London: Dartou, Longman and Todd, 1964) on Essene influence on Jewish Christianity. See also the Zadokite document in T.H. Gaster, *The Dead Sea Scriptures* (Garden City, New York: Doubleday Anchor, 1956).

11. J. Walvoord, *The Millenial Kingdom* (Grand Rapids MI: Dunham, 1959).

12. John Calvin, *Institutes,* Book II, Sec. 7.

13. According to the consensus of scholars on the dating of First Corinthians and Acts 21.

14. The early writings of Mary Douglas argued the first view and the classic commentary by Franz Deleitch the second view see below.

15. See Kiel and Delitzch, *Commentary on Leviticus,* reprint of nineteenth century edition (Peabody, MA: Hendrickson, 1996). Also, E. Josephson, *God's Key to Health and Happiness* (Hillsboro, KS: Bible Light, 1976).

16. The Talmud is very strong on requiring ritual washing and even goes so far as to suggest that failure in this regard can cause one to be precluded from the world to come.

CHAPTER FIVE

1. Ray Pritz, *Nazarene Jewish Christianity* (Jerusalem: Brill and the Magnes Press, Hebrew University, 1988). Also, Josephus, *Antiquities,* and Hegasippus in Eusebius, *Ecclesiastical History.*

2. Justin Martyr, *Dialogue with Trypho the Jew* (130–150), and also, H.J. Schoeps, *Theologie und Geschichte des Juden Christentums* (Tubingen: 1949), the basic book on the Ebionites.

3. Jean Danielou, *The Theology of Jewish Christianity* (London: Dartou, Longman and Todd, 1964), basic book on the Nazarenes.

4. Sources in Josephus, Justin Martyr, Epiphaneius, and Hegasippus, quoted in Danilou, 45-54, and Ray Pritz, *Nazarene Jewish Christianity.*

5. Justin Martyr, *Dialogue with Trypho the Jew* (130–150) in *Anti-Nicene Fathers,* and also Ellison, *The Mystery of Israel* (Grand Rapids, MI: Eerdmans, 1966), 82.

6. Ibid, Ellison.

7. Ibid, See also history recounted in James Parkes, *The Conflict of the Church and the Synagogue* (New York: Atheneum, 1969), Chapter 4.

8. Rosemary Ruether, *Faith and Fratricide* (New York: The Seabury Press, 1974).

9. A. Millagram, *Jewish Worship* (Philadelphia: The Jewish Publication Society of America, 1971), 328.

10. Parkes, *The Conflict of the Church and the Synagogue*, 93.

11. Justin Martyr, *First Apology*, Ch. 31, P.G. VI, 375.

12. The late Louis Goldberg, Chairman of Jewish Studies at Moody, has noted the survival of Messianic Jewish symbols in an Arab community perhaps reminiscent of conversion by force of an ancient Messianic Jewish community.

13. Daniel Boyarin, *Borderlines* (Philadelphia, University of Pennsylvania, 2004).

14. Rosemary Ruether, *Faith and Fratricide*, 123ff.

15. The Hebrew word *echad*, which is used of a compound unity (e.g. in Genesis 2, the man and woman become *one* flesh) was interpreted as *yachid*—an absolute singularity.

16. Rosemary Ruether, *Faith and Fratricide*, Chapter 3 is excellent on this period.

17. Ellison, *The Mystery of Israel*, 82ff.

18. Ibid.

19. Ibid, See note 27.

20. Parkes, *The Conflict of the Church and the Synagogue*, is excellent in cataloguing this legislation. See his Chapter 6 and 7.

21. Both Parkes and Ruether deal with this well. See especially Parkes, *The Conflict of the Church and the Synagogue*, 121-150.

22. Father Flannery, *The Anguish of the Jews* (New York, MacMillan, 1964) is an excellent history.

23. The word for *Judean* and *Jew* is exactly the same in Greek. See M. Ben-hayim, *The American Messianic Jewish Quarterly* (Spring 1979), 20. Countless others have made the same point.

24. Corrie ten Boom, *The Hiding Place*, 25th Anniversary Edition (Grand Rapids, MI: Chosen Books, 1996).

25. Corrie ten Boom, *In My Father's House* (Westwood, NJ: Fleming H. Revell, 1978). Her brother's conclusions are found in his PhD dissertation.

26. See for example, David Max Eichorn, *Evangelizing the American Jew* (Middle Village, New York: Jonathan David Publishers, 1978).

27. Ibid, Eichorn is a Reform Rabbi who notes such people.

28. See Toward Jerusalem Council II: The Story and the History, Dallas, Texas.

29. For the history herein, see Schonfeld, *The History of Jewish Christianity* (New York: 1930), and Louis Goldberg, *Our Jewish Friends* (Loizeaux Brothers, 1983).

30. See Eichorn, *Evangelizing the American Jew*, 186-187.

31. His testimony is in H. Einspruch, *Would I, Would You* (Baltimore: The Lederer Foundation, 1947).

32. Einspruch, *Would I, Would You*, note 6.

33. See the 1909 series of books, *The Fundamentals.*, O. P. see web.

34. See E.J. Carnell, "Fundamentalism," *The Case for Orthodox Theology* (Philadelphia, Westminster Press, 1959), Chapter on Fundamentalism; and Bernard Ramm, *The Evangelical Heritage* (Grand Rapids, MI: Baker Books, 2000).

35. Mitch Glazer, "A Survey of Missions to the Jews," dissertation (Pasadena, CA: Fuller Theological Seminary, 1998).

36. Corrie ten Boom, *In My Father's House*, notes her brother's conviction. Her brother's conclusions are found in his PhD dissertation.

37. D. McGavern, *Understanding Church Growth* (Grand Rapids, MI: Eerdmans, 1970, revised third edition, 1990).

38. Mark Kinzer, *Post-Missionary Messianic Judaism* (Grand Rapids, MI: Brazos Press, 2005).

CHAPTER SIX

1. On these themes, see George Ladd's books, *Jesus and the Kingdom* (London: S.P.E.C., 1966) and *Crucial Questions on the Kingdom of God* (Grand Rapids, MI: Eerdmans, 1952).

2. James Barr, *The Semantics of Biblical Language* (London: Oxford University Press, 1961). Also, A. Berkley Michaelson, *Interpreting the Bible* (Grand Rapids, MI: Eerdmans, 1963); Grant Osborne, *The Hermeneutical Spiral* (Downers Grove, IL: InterVarsity Press, 2006).

3. See J.N.D. Anderson, *The Evidence of the Resurrection* (Downers Grove, IL: InterVarsity Press, 1966); Merrill Tenney, *The Reality of the Resurrection* (New York: Harper and Row, 1963); Pinchas Lapide, *The Resurrection of Jesus, a Jewish Perspective* (Minneapolis, MN: Fortress Press, 1988); N.T. Wright, *Surprised by Hope* (Grand Rapids, MI: Zondervan, 2008). Note: Lapide is very important since he is an Orthodox Jew who does not embrace the divinity of Yeshua or that He is the Messiah of Israel.

4. B.B. Warfield, *The Inspiration and Authority of the Bible* (Philadelphia: Presbyterian and Reformed Publishing Co., 1970). See the article, "It says, Scripture says, God says."

5. See J.P. Free. *Archaeology and Bible History,* Revised by Howard Vos (Grand Rapids, MI: Zondervan, 1992). For an up-to-date compendium, see Walter C. Kaiser, *The NIV Archaeological Study Bible* (Grand Rapids, MI: Zondervan, 2006).

6. Bernard Ramm, *Protestant Christian Evidences* (Chicago: Moody Press, 1953), chapter on "Evidence of Fulfilled Prophecy." Also, Daniel Juster, *The Biblical World View: An Apologetic* (Boston: International Scholars Publications, 1996), 173-218.

7. Meredith Kline, *The Structure of Biblical Authority* (Grand Rapids, MI: Eerdmans, 1972) is a great book on this subject.

8. R. Laird Harris. *The Inspiration and Canonicity of the Bible* (Grand Rapids, MI: Zondervan, 1978).

9. What we are teaching here is more and more supported by scholarship. E.P. Sanders in his classic study, *Paul and Palestinian Judaism* (London: SCM Press, 1977), argues that first-century Judaism was a covenant nomism, namely that one gets into covenant relationship totally by the free grace of God, but one stays within by a walk of obedience. This is similar to Calvinism's view of law and grace. Folks such as N.T. Wright in books referenced before and Kent Yinger, in *The New Persective on Paul* (Eugene, OR: Wipf and Stock, 2011), argue that this was Paul's view as well.

10. This is powerfully argued by Stanley Stowers in *Rereading Romans* (New Haven, CT: Yale University Press, 1997). He argues that Paul is responding to the Greek philosophical idea that studying philosophy and ethics will deliver from bondage to passions and desires leading to dissipation. The Jewish answer to the Greeks was that the study of Torah does this. Paul's answer is that it is only our co-death and resurrection with Yeshua that accomplishes this.

11. For a full presentation of the argument, see Sanders, *No Other Name* (Eugene, OR: Wipf and Stock, 2011).

12. See Elmer Josephson, *Israel: God's Key to World Redemption* (Hillsburo, KS: Bible Light, 1974); Paul Carlson. *Oh Christian, Oh Jew!* (Elgin, IL: David C. Cook, 1974). More recently, the writings of John Hagee have taken a similar position.

13. Whether we interpret the works like the new perspective on Paul as the covenant marks of being within the Jewish community (Circumcision, Sabbath-Feasts, and purity laws) or as good works that earn salvation (the latter though was not first century Jewish theology).

14. H.L. Ellison, *The Mystery of Israel* (Grand Rapids, MI: Eerdmans, 1966).

15. See *Targums* on Isaiah 53, Talmud Sanhedrin 98b.

16. Especially Holy Day Prayers, Al Het, etc.

17. W.D. Davies, *Paul and Rabbinic Judaism* (New York: Harper Torchbooks, 1948).

18. Kenton F. Beeshore, *The Messiah of the Targum, Talmuds and Rabbinical Writers* (Los Angeles: World Bible Society, 1970), on Genesis 3:15.

19. Wayne Meeks, *The Prophet King* (New York: E.J. Brill, 1967).

20. On the idea of Messiah's preexistence and its connection to wisdom and "logos," see Alan Segel, *Two Powers in Heaven* (Leiden, Netherlands: E.J. Brill, 1977), and Daniel Boyarin, *Borderlines* (Philadelphia: University of Pennsylvania Press, 2004).

21. See Sanhedrin in 98B—Sukkah52 of the Talmud for two of several references.

22. Arthur Kac, *The Messianic Hope* (Grand Rapids, MI: Baker, 1975), 76.

23. See Samson H. Levey, *The Messiah: An Aramaic Interpretation* (Cincinnati, OH: Hebrew Union College Press, 1974), 63.

24. F. Kenton Beshore, (*The Messiah of the Targum, Talmuds and Rabbinical Writers* (Los Angeles: World Bible Society, 1970).

25. Ibid. See also R. Moses Abraham Levi, Sanhed, Talmud 97. b, Nachmanidies, and Abarbanel.

26. See J.W. Montgomery, *History and Christianity* (Downers Grove, IL: InterVarsity Press, 1971), and J.N.D. Anderson, *Christianity: the Witness of History* (London: Tyndale Press, 1969).

27. Richard N. Longenecker, in the *Christology of Early Jewish Christianity* (Naperville, IL: Alec R. Allenson, 1970), makes the point that in the New Testament Jewishly-intended writings, Messiahship is central and explicit while divinity is only implied. More recent studies by Richard Bauckham, in *God Crucified* (Grand Rapids, MI: Eerdmans, 1998), and Larry Hurtado, in *One God, One Lord*, second edition, (London: T.T. Clark, 1998), have argued that the first century Jewish context shows that the assertion of the deity of Yeshua is more blatant and pervasive.

28. Orthodox Jewish scholar Daniel Boyarin, in his monumental book *Borderlines*, argues that Wisdom, logos, and the Angel were embraced by the older Judaism of the first century as almost a second person in God. This is argued as well by Margaret Barker in *The Great High Priest* (London: T.T. Clark, 2003). They both argue that Judaism of the Rabbinic period sought to cleanse out these older views. In addition, the first century Jewish leadership could not accept the incarnation of this Wisdom-Logos-Angel figure.

29. Talmuc Sanh. 11a, Baba Bartha 12:a, b. Also, A. Cohen, *Everyman's Talmud* (BN Publishing, 2009), 42-47.

30. See G.E. Wright, *The Old Testament and Theology* (New York: Harper and Row, 1969).

31. *Zohar*, Vol. 1, 288; Vol. 2, 43.

Chapter Seven

1. This is also argued by Arnold Fruchtenbaum, *Hebrew Christianity: Its Theology, History, and Philosophy*, rev. ed. (Oklahoma City, OK: Ariel Ministries, 1995).

2. See A. Koestler, *The Thirteenth Tribe* (New York, 1963), on the possible conversion of the Kzars. Most scholars do not believe there was such a mass conversion such that European Jewry is descended from the Kzars. Indeed, genetic tests today show unity with Sephardic Jews.

3. Samuele Bacchiochi, *From Saturday to Sunday* (Rome: The Pontifical Gregorian University Press, 1977).

4. *Catechism of the Catholic Church.*

5. Richard Siegel, et al., *The Jewish Catalogue* (Jewish Publication Society of America, 1973).

6. That there were four cups of wine in the Seder at the time of Yeshua is somewhat speculative. Luke describes two cups. Also, the bread may have not been the *afikomen*. These traditions may have come after the life of Yeshua and also fit traditions that may have been started by Messianic Jews, especially the three matzohs with the middle one being broken with half hidden and then returned after the meal. The middle one, symbolizing the death of Yeshua and His resurrection, is very common in Messianic Jewish celebration. The important work of David Instone-Brewer credits the four cup tradition as possibly going back to the time of Yeshua and reflected in the Last Supper. See David Instone-Brewer, *Traditions of the Rabbis from the Era of the New Testament: Vol. 1, Prayer and Agriculture* (Grand Rapids, MI: Eerdmans, 2004), 83.

7. See A. Kac, *The Messianic Hope* (Grand Rapids, MI: Baker, 1975), 83-84, 95-97.

8. B.Tal. *Succot.*

9. See instructions in *The Jewish Catalogue.*

10. Franklin Littell, *The Crucifixion of the Jews* (Macon, GA: Mercer University Press, 2000), appendix.

11. Richard Bauckham, *Jesus and the Eyewitnesses: The Gospels as Eyewitness Testimony* (Grand Rapids, MI, Eerdmans, 2008).

12. J. Danielou. *The Theology of Jewish Christianity* (London: Dartou, Longman and Todd, 1964), 339-346.

13. Cyrus Gordon, "Higher Critics and Forbidden Fruit," *Christianity Today* (Nov 23, 1959), 3-6.

14. Ellison, "Paul and the Law" in Gasque and Martin, *Apostolic History and the Gospel* (London: Paternoster Press, 1970).

15. See Donald A. McGavran, *Understanding Church Growth*, rev. and ed., C. Peter Wagner (Grand Rapids, MI: Eerdmans, 1990), sections on Jews.

Chapter Eight

1. Rabbi Jerome Epstein, "A New Compact for Jewish Life," *Washington Jewish Week* (Feb 14, 2002), 1.

Chapter Nine

1. One of the earlier music worship materials from Israel is David and Lisa Loden: *Rejoice*, available from House of David distributors. Since then, many new albums have been produced, not only the classics, in America from Israel's Hope and Lamb, available from Messianic Jewish Publications. However, now some of the best Yeshua-centered content is from Israel.

Chapter Eleven

1. Louis Bouyer, *Eucharist* (Notre Dame, Indiana: University of Notre Dame, 1968), p. 15-135.

2. Daniel C. Juster, *One Law Movements* (Albuquerque, NM: Union of Messianic Jewish Congregations, 2005). The First Fruits of Zion, in Phoenix, was for several years (in many publications) the major organization supporting this view, but they officially broke from this theology in 2009. They now have excellent articles refuting it.

3. The two most important books on this are Batya Wootten, *In Search of Israel* (Shippensburg, PA: Destiny Image, 1988), and Bill Cloud, *Enmity Between the Seeds* (Cleveland, TN: Voice of Evangelism, 2004).

A SELECTED BIBLIOGRAPHY

1. Albright, William Foxwell. *From the Stone Age to Christianity*. Garden City, NY: Double Day Anchor, 1957.

2. Anderson, J.N.D. *Christianity the Witness of History*. London: Tyndale Press, 1969.

3. Armerding, Carl. "An Evangelical Understanding of Israel." *Evangelicals and Jews in Conversation*. eds. Marc H. Tanenbaum, Marvin R. Wilson, A. James Rudin. Grand Rapids, MI: Baker, 1978.

4. Bacchiocchi, Samuele. *From Sabbath to Sunday*. Rome: The Pontifical Gregorian University Press, 1977.

5. Bagatti, B. *The Church from the Circumcision*. Rome: Pontifical Biblical Institute, 1971.

6. Barr, James. *The Semantics of Biblical Language*. London: Oxford University Press, 1961.

7. Barth, Marcus. "Jews and Gentiles: The Social Character of Justification in Paul." *Journal of Ecumenical Studies*, Spring 1968.

8. Bauckham, Richard. *Jesus and the Eyewitnesses: The Gospels as Eyewitness Testimony*. Grand Rapids, MI: Eerdmans, 2008.

9. Bockmuel, Markus, *Jewish Law in Gentile Churches*. London: T & T Clark, 2000.

10. Bock, Darrell L. and Mitch Glazer. *To the Jew First*. Grand Rapids, MI: Kregel, 2008.

11. Bowman, John W. *The Layman's Bible Commentary: Hebrews, James, I & II Peter*. Richmond, VA: John Knox Press, 1959.

12. Boyarin, Daniel, *Borderlines*. Philadelphia: University of Pennsylvania Press, 2004.

13. Brown, Raymond. *The Gospel of John*. Garden City, NY: Doubleday and Company, Inc., 1966.

14. Bruce, F.F. *The New Testament Development of Old Testament Themes*. London, 1968.

15. Calvin, John. *Institutes of the Christian Religion*. trans. Ford Lewis Battles, Philadelphia: The Westminster Press, 1960.

16. Cole, R. Allen. *The Tyndale New Testament Commentaries, Vol 9: The Epistle of Paul to the Galatians*. Grand Rapids, MI: Eerdmans, 1978.

17. Conzelmann, Hans. *The Theology of St. Luke*. London, 1960.

18. Danielou, Jean. *The Theology of Jewish Christianity*. London: Dartou, Longman and Todd, 1964.

19. Daube, David. *The New Testament and Rabbinic Judaism*. London: Athlone, 1965.

20. Davies, W.D. *Paul and Rabbinic Judaism*. New York: Harper Torchbooks, 1948.

21. Dix, Dom Gregory. *Jew and Greek: A Study in the Primitive Christian Church* (Dacre Press, 1953).

22. Dunn, James. *The Parting of the Ways*. London: SCM, 1991.

23. Eichorn, David Max. *Evangelizing the American Jew*. Middle Village, NY: Jonathan David Publishers, 1978.

24. Einspruch, Henry. *Would I, Would You?* Baltimore, MD: The Lederer Foundation, 1947.

25. Ellison, H.L. *The Mystery of Israel.* Grand Rapids, MI: Eerdmans, 1966.

26. Fischer, John, ed. *The Enduring Paradox.* Clarksville, MD: 2000.

27. Flannery, Father Edward. *The Anguish of the Jews.* New York, MacMillan, 1964.

28. Free, Joseph P. *Archaeology and Bible History.* rev. Howard Vos. Grand Rapids, MI: Zondervan, 1992.

29. Gasque, W. and Ralph Martin, eds. *Apostolic History and the Gospel.* London: Paternoster Press, 1970.

30. Gaster, T.H. *The Dead Sea Scriptures.* Garden City, NY: Doubleday Anchor, 1956.

31. Goble, Phil. *Everything You Need to Grow a Messianic Synagogue.* Pasadena, CA: William Carey Library Pub., 1982.

32. Goldberg, Louis. *God, Torah, and Messiah.* San Francisco: Purple Pomegranate, 2009.

33. Harink, Douglas. *Paul Among the Post Liberals.* Grand Rapids, MI: Brazos Press, 2003.

34. Harris, R. Laird. *The Inspiration and Canonicity of the Bible.* Grand Rapids, MI: Zondervan, 1976.

35. Harvey, Richard. *Mapping Messianic Jewish Theology: a Constructive Approach.* Carlisle: Paternoster, 2009.

36. Hutchins, Jim. "The Case for Messianic Judaism." Ph.D. thesis at Fuller Theological Seminary.

37. Isaac, Jules. *Jesus and Israel.* Holt, Rinehart and Winston, 1971.

38. Jacob, Alex. *The Case for Enlargement Theology.* Saffron, Waldon, England: Glory to God, 2010.

39. Josephson, Elmer. *Israel: God's Key to World Redemption.* Hillsburo, KS: Bible Light, 1974.

40. -----. *God's Key to Health and Happiness.* Hillsboro, KS: Bible Light, 1976.

41. Josephus. *Antiquities of the Jews.* trans. Whiston. Grand Rapids, MI: Kregel Publications, 1960.

42. Juster, Daniel. *Jewishness and Jesus.* Downers Grove, IL: InterVarsity Press, 1977.

43. Kac, Arthur. *The Messianic Hope.* Grand Rapids, MI: Baker, 1975.

44. Kaiser, Walter. *The Old Testament in Contemporary Preaching.* Grand Rapids, MI: Baker, 1973.

45. Kinzer, Mark, *Post-Missionary Messianic Judaism.* Grand Rapids, MI: Brazos Press, 2005.

46. -----. *Israel's Messiah and the People of God.* Lutterworth Press, 2012.

47. Kitchen, Kenneth. *Ancient Orient and Old Testament.* Downers Grove, IL: InterVarsity Press, 1966.

48. Kline, Meredith. *Treaty of the Great King.* Grand Rapids, MI: Eerdmans, 1963.

49. -----. *The Structure of Biblical Authority.* Grand Rapids, MI: Eerdmans, 1972.

50. Koestler, Arthur. *The Thirteenth Tribe.* New York, 1963.

51. Ladd, George. *Crucial Questions and the Kingdom of God.* Grand Rapids, MI: Eerdmans, 1952.

52. -----. *Jesus and the Kingdom.* London: S.P.E.C., 1966.

53. -----. *A New Testament Theology.* Grand Rapids, MI: Eerdmans, 1975.

54. Lapide, Pinchas. *The Resurrection, a Jewish Perspective.* Minneapolis, MN: Fortress, 1988.

55. Levey, Samson H. *The Messiah: An Aramaic Interpretation.* Cincinnati, OH: Hebrew Union College Press, 1974.

56. Littell, Franklin. *The Crucifixion of the Jews.* Macon, GA: Mercer University Press, 2000.

57. Longenecker, Richard N. *Biblical Exegesis in the Apostolic Period.* Grand Rapids, MI: Eerdmans, 1975.

58. -----. *The Christology of Early Jewish Christianity.* Naperville, IL: Alec R. Allenson, 1970.

59. -----. *Paul: The Apostle of Liberty.* Grand Rapids, MI: Eerdmans, 1976.

60. Marshall, I.H., *Luke: Historian and Theologian.* Grand Rapids, MI: Zondervan, 1978.

61. McComiskey, Thomas. *Covenants of Promise.* Grand Rapids, MI: Baker, 1985.

62. McMillan, S.I. *None of These Diseases.* Westwood, NJ: Fleming H. Revell, 1958.

63. Meeks, Wayne. *The Prophet King.* New York: E.J. Brill, 1967.

64. Michaelson, A. Berkeley. *Interpreting the Bible.* Grand Rapids, MI: Eerdmans, 1963.

65. Millagram, A. *Jewish Worship.* Philadelphia: The Jewish Publication Society of America, 1971.

66. Nanos, Mark. *The Mystery of Romans.* Minneapolis, MN: Fortress, 2002.

67. -----. *The Irony of Galatians.* Minneapolis, MN: Fortress Press, 2009.

68. Parkes, James. *The Conflict of the Church and the Synagogue.* New York: Atheneum, 1969.

69. Pritz, Ray. *Nazarene Jewish Christianity.* Leiden, Netherlands, and Jerusalem: Brill and the Magnus Press of Hebrew University, 1988.

70. Ramm, Bernard. *Protestant Christian Evidences.* Chicago: Moody Press, 1953.

71. Richardson, Peter. *Israel in the Apostolic Church.* Boston: Cambridge University Press, 2005.

72. Robinson, Rich. *The Messianic Movement: A Field Guide for Evangelical Christians.* San Francisco: Purple Pomegranate, 2005.

73. Rudolph, David J. *A Jew to the Jews.* Tubingin, Germany: Mohr Siebeck, 2011.

74. Ruether, Rosemary R. *Faith and Fratricide.* New York: The Seabury Press, 1974.

75. Ryrie, Charles C. *Dispensationalism Today.* Chicago: Moody Press, 1979.

76. Schonfeld, Hugh. *The History of Jewish Christianity.* New York, 1930.

77. Schoeps, Hans J. *Theologie und Geschichte des Juden Christentums.* Tubingen, 1949.

78. Schultz, Samuel. *Deuteronomy: The Gospel of Love.* Chicago: Moody Press, 1973.

79. -----. *The Gospel of Moses.* New York: Harper and Row, 1974.

80. Segal, Alan F. *Two Powers in Heaven.* Leiden, Netherlands: E.J. Brill, 1977.

81. Siegel, Richard, et al. *The Jewish Catalogue.* Jewish Publication Society of America, 1973.

82. Soulen, R. Kendall. *The God of Israel and Christian Theology.* Minneapolis, MN: Augsburg-Fortress, 1996.

83. Stendhal, Krister. *The School of St. Matthew.* Uppsala: C.W.K. Gleerup, Lund, 1954; 2nd ed., 1968.

84. Stern, David. *Messianic Judaism.* Baltimore, MD: Lederer Messianic Publications, 2007.

85. -----. *Restoring the Jewishness of the Gospel.* Clarksville, MD: Messianic Jewish Resources International, 2010.

86. -----. *Jewish New Testament Commentary.* Clarksville, MD: Messianic Jewish Resources International, 1992.

87. Tomson, Peter J. *Paul and the Jewish Law.* New York: E.J. Brill, 1991.

88. ten Boom, Corrie. *In My Father's House.* Westwood, NJ: Fleming H. Revell, 1978.

89. Tenney, Merril. *The Reality of the Resurrection.* New York: Harper and Row, 1963.

90. Walvoord, John. *The Millennial Kingdom.* Grand Rapids, MI: Dunham, 1959.

91. Warfield, Benjamin B. *The Inspiration and Authority of the Bible.* Philadelphia: Presbyterian and Reformed Publishing Co., 1970.

92. Wilson, Mark, Marc Tanenbaum, Janis Rudin. *Evangelicals and Jews in Conversation.* Grand Rapids, MI: Eerdmans, 1978.

93. Wright, G.E. *The Old Testament and Theology.* New York: Harper and Row, 1969.

94. Wright, N.T. *Surprised by Hope.* New York: Harper Collins, 2008.

95. Yamauchi, Edwin. "Meshech, Tubal, and Company: A Review Article." *Journal of the Evangelical Theological Society,* 19.3, Summer 1976.

96. Yoder, John Howard. *The Politics of Jesus.* Grand Rapids, MI: Eerdmans, 1994.

97. Young, E.J. *Thy Word is Truth.* Grand Rapids, MI: Eerdmans, 1957.

ABOUT DANIEL JUSTER

Dr. Daniel Juster is the director of Tikkun Ministries and the senior pastor of Beth Messiah Congregation. He hungered for more knowledge of the Messiah, of his own Jewish roots, and of the role of the Church in Israel's salvation. His search led him through five Bible colleges, four degrees, and nearly three decades of intensive study.

LD101	Israel, the Church and the Last Days	$9.99
LD1025	From Iraq to Armageddon	$7.99
LD103	Revelation: The Passover Key	$6.99
MJ201	Jewish Roots	$14.99
MJ202	Growing to Maturity	$9.00
MJ203	Jewishness and Jesus	$1.00
AM304	The Apple of His Eye	$7.99
AM305	Covenant Relationships	$14.99
AM306	Dynamics of Spiritual Deception	$5.99
AM307	Due Process	$8.99

Name _____ Phone _____

Address _____

All items available to ministries and bookstores, in quantities of 5 or more, at 40% discount.

Please fill out the complete information for each book order: item number; cost of the book; number of item you would like to order; amount of each item; the amount enclosed.

ITEM	COST/BOOK	NO. ORDERED	AMOUNT
		Subtotal	
	Maryland residents add 5% Sales Tax (or send tax exempt certificate for our files)		
		15% P 6k H ($2.00 minimum)	
		TOTAL ENCLOSED	

Mail all orders with checks payable to:

TIKKUN MINISTRIES
P.O. Box 2997
GAITHERSBURG, MD 20886

IN THE RIGHT HANDS, THIS BOOK WILL CHANGE LIVES!

Most of the people who need this message will not be looking for this book. To change their lives, you need to put a copy of this book in their hands.

> *But others (seeds) fell into good ground, and brought forth fruit, some a hundred-fold, some sixty-fold, some thirty-fold* (Matthew 13:8).

Our ministry is constantly seeking methods to find the good ground, the people who need this anointed message to change their lives. Will you help us reach these people?

> *Remember this—a farmer who plants only a few seeds will get a small crop. But the one who plants generously will get a generous crop* (2 Corinthians 9:6).

EXTEND THIS MINISTRY BY SOWING
3 BOOKS, 5 BOOKS, 10 BOOKS, OR MORE TODAY,
AND BECOME A LIFE CHANGER!

Thank you,

Don Nori Sr., Founder
Destiny Image
Since 1982